The Science of Violent Behavior Development and Prevention

T0372733

This book describes the lives of twelve people born in Europe and North America during the Second World War. They became leading scholars on the development and prevention of violent human behavior. From the first to the last page, the book introduces contrasting life stories and shows how the paths of these scholars crossed, allowing them to create a relatively unified body of knowledge regarding how human violence develops and how it might be prevented. The authors describe the similarities and differences in their family backgrounds, university training, theories, and collaborations – not to mention how they differ in research methods and scientific conclusions, and their influence on the research published today. These comparisons celebrate the diversity of their experiences as well as their achievements. Knowing their stories, you can stand on the shoulders of these giants to look to the future of this subject and potentially contribute to its next steps.

Richard E. Tremblay is Emeritus Professor of Pediatrics and Psychology at Université de Montréal, Canada. He received the Stockholm Prize in Criminology, the American Society of Criminology's Sellin-Glueck Award, the Academy of Experimental Criminology's Joan McCord Prize, and the award for lifetime contributions to research on aggression from the International Society for Research on Aggression.

The Science of Violent Behavior Development and Prevention

Contributions of the Second World War Generation

Edited by

Richard E. Tremblay

Université de Montréal

CAMBRIDGE
UNIVERSITY PRESS

Shaftesbury Road, Cambridge CB2 8EA, United Kingdom

One Liberty Plaza, 20th Floor, New York, NY 10006, USA

477 Williamstown Road, Port Melbourne, VIC 3207, Australia

314–321, 3rd Floor, Plot 3, Splendor Forum, Jasola District Centre, New Delhi – 110025, India

103 Penang Road, #05–06/07, Visioncrest Commercial, Singapore 238467

Cambridge University Press is part of Cambridge University Press & Assessment, a department of the University of Cambridge.

We share the University's mission to contribute to society through the pursuit of education, learning and research at the highest international levels of excellence.

www.cambridge.org
Information on this title: www.cambridge.org/9781108819893

DOI: 10.1017/9781108877138

© Cambridge University Press & Assessment 2021

First published 2021
First paperback edition 2022

A catalogue record for this publication is available from the British Library

Library of Congress Cataloging-in-Publication data
Names: Tremblay, Richard Ernest, editor.
Title: The science of violent behavior development and prevention :
    contributions of the second world war generation / edited by
    Richard E. Tremblay, Université de Montréal.
Description: New York, NY : Cambridge University Press, 2021. |
    Includes bibliographical references and index.
Identifiers: LCCN 2020037947 (print) | LCCN 2020037948 (ebook) |
    ISBN 9781108834810 (hardback) | ISBN 9781108819893 (paperback) |
    ISBN 9781108877138 (epub)
Subjects: LCSH: Violence–Prevention. | Violence–Psychological aspects. |
    Violence–Treatment. | Criminology.
Classification: LCC HM1116 .S373 2021 (print) | LCC HM1116 (ebook) |
    DDC 303.6–dc23
LC record available at https://lccn.loc.gov/2020037947
LC ebook record available at https://lccn.loc.gov/2020037948

ISBN   978-1-108-83481-0   Hardback
ISBN   978-1-108-81989-3   Paperback

Contents

Preface

The publication of this book was planned for the 75th anniversary of the end of the Second World War II. The **first** aim of the book is to describe the research of 12 scientists, born during World War II, who made important contributions to the advancement of knowledge on the development and prevention of violent behavior, defined as *the use of physical force against others*. The **second** aim is to describe the life-course development of these 12 scientists through autobiographies. The **third** aim is to place their scientific contributions within the past 2,500 years of the philosophical and scientific history of knowledge on violence and its prevention. The **fourth** aim is to understand their scientific contributions within the social and technological changes of the past 75 years, which brought together individuals who were born in countries that were on opposite sides during World War II (Canada, Finland, Germany, Great Britain, Italy, the Netherlands, and the United States) and who have managed, over the last 50 years, to collectively advance knowledge on the development and prevention of violent behavior. The **fifth** aim is to present the points of view of younger investigators concerning the scientific contributions of the World War II babies and the research agenda for the next few decades.

Thus, there are four important historical perspectives to this book: **First, world history** from the 1939–1945 war to the major social, technological, financial, and scientific changes that unfolded over the following 75 years; **second,** the **history of research on violent behavior,** to which the book's authors eventually made numerous key contributions; **third,** the **personal and professional history of the World War II babies,** who became highly productive scientists; and, **fourth,** the **life course development of the children** the authors followed with their longitudinal and experimental studies.

The authors describe the circumstances of their births between 1939 and 1945, the education they received, the studies they designed, and the collaborations they created to understand and prevent the development of human violence. The book provides an excellent description of the present state of knowledge regarding the development and prevention of violent behavior, from early childhood onward. **It also gives a unique inside view on the development of the scientists, the development of scientific collaborations, the development of the science of behavior development, and the development of experimental preventive interventions**.

The book clearly highlights the slow but effective creation of an interdisciplinary bio-psycho-social approach to understanding human development and preventing the development of violent behavior. From this perspective, it should be required reading for students in criminology, education, law, pediatrics, psychiatry, psychology, public health, and social work.

There is no doubt that two classic philosophers, Thomas Hobbes and Artistotle, would have recommended this book. First, it attempts to understand and prevent what Hobbes described as the original state of humanity: **'war of all against all'**. Second, the common method used by the investigators follows Aristotle's main conclusion concerning scientific investigations: 'He who considers things in their first growth and origin, ... will obtain the clearest view of them'.

Why Is This Book Original?

First, it is written by scientists who were born when their countries were involved in World War II and who created ongoing longitudinal and experimental studies in order to understand the development and prevention of violent behavior.

Second, the authors describe the advances in their research domain in line with their own scientific careers, starting from early childhood education through elementary, secondary, and university education. These descriptions allow the reader to understand the development of the theories, methods, and findings based on the autobiographies of the main contributors. Interestingly, these stories show that the lives and work of successful scientists are largely dependent on serendipity.

Third, because the authors of the different chapters worked on related topics, and often collaborated, the reader will be able to understand how the networking of scientists from different countries contributed to the development of an interdisciplinary science of violent behavior development and prevention.

Why Should This Book Be Read?

1. For the pleasure of reading biographies of successful humans.
2. To understand the developmental trajectories of high-achieving scientists born in Europe and North America during the Second World War.

3. To understand the development of international cooperation among scientists over the past 50 years.
4. To understand how younger scientists perceive the contributions of the World War II babies.
5. To understand the development of the science of violent behavior prevention from antiquity to the 21st century.

How Should This Book Be Read?

1. **Like a novel** from the first to the last page. The reader will discover 12 main actors. Although each has his or her own very different story, their paths eventually crossed, and they produced a network of scientists who created a relatively unified body of knowledge concerning human development and the prevention of behavior problems.
2. **Like a textbook,** where you focus on specific questions. For example, what are the similarities and differences in the scientists' family backgrounds? In their university training? In their theories? In their collaborations? In their research methods? In their conclusions? What influence do they have on research published today? How will this field of research evolve over the next 30 years?

1 Introduction: A Young Science with a Long History

Richard E. Tremblay

> We must address the roots of violence. Only then will we transform the past century's legacy from a crushing burden into a cautionary lesson.
>
> Nelson Mandela[1]

1.1 From Rags to Riches: 1939–2019

The babies born in Europe and North America between 1939 and 1945 (World War II babies) did not come into the world of humans at the best of times. Their parents were living in what could then be considered the most civilized cultures ever. However, these highly civilized cultures were creating the worst carnage ever. Between 70 and 85 million humans[2,3] were killed during World War II, including 6 million Jewish people in extermination camps, through mass shootings, and in gas chambers.

The parents and grandparents of World War II babies suffered from this Second World War before they had recovered from the numerous negative impacts of World War II. They most certainly could not foresee that their World War II babies would have the exceptional good fortune of growing up, with their own children and grandchildren, in a world that would manage to maintain the longest relative peace yet achieved among the major countries involved in World War II. From that perspective, the World War II babies born in Europe and North America can probably be considered the luckiest humans who have ever lived … until the Covid-19 pandemic!

A demographic anomaly appears to be one of the most important causes of their good fortune. Indeed, the World War II babies were born

---

[1] Forward in Krug, E. G., Dahlberg, L. L., Mercy, J. A., Zwi, A. B., & Lozano, R. (Eds.) (2002), *World report on violence and health*. Geneva, Switzerland: World Health Organisation.
[2] Wikipedia. (n.d.-a). The Holocaust. Retrieved November 21, 2019, from https://en.wikipedia.org/wiki/The_Holocaust
[3] Wikipedia. (n.d.-b). World War II casualties. Retrieved November 21, 2019, from https://en.wikipedia.org/wiki/World_War_II_casualties

just ahead of a major increase in their countries' birth rates during the 20 years that followed the end of World War II (Jones, 1980; Owram, 1997; Statistics Canada, 2011). Labeled the 'baby boom', this demographic phenomenon is generally considered to have started immediately after the end of World War II and lasted until the mid-1960s. Being born just ahead of the baby boom, the World War II babies surfed on the crest of an exceptionally large wave of births occurring at the same time as remarkable progress in wealth, education, health care, and technology, which was labeled 'The Golden Age of Capitalism' (Schor & Marglin, 2011).

A good example of the underlying mechanism by which the World War II babies hugely benefited from the baby boom relates to the profession of the 11 authors of this book: university professor.

In the late 1960s, universities had to hire an increasing number of new faculty to provide higher education to the large wave of baby boomers who were starting to knock at their doors. For example, official statistics for the age distribution of faculty in Canadian universities show that, for the 1970 academic year, they had the largest proportion (20%) of faculty who were less than 31 years old. The babies born between 1939 and 1945 were now between 25 and 31 years old, and were being offered faculty positions at the end of their PhD studies, and even sooner.

The window of opportunity for being appointed to a faculty position at a relatively young age was short. By 1980, the proportion of faculty who were not yet 31 years old in Canada had declined to 5%, and by 1990 they had essentially disappeared.

Unprecedented opportunities for the World War II babies went much beyond getting a faculty position at a relatively young age. Because the amount of research funding for university faculty was increasing, and new research funding agencies were created, the competition to receive funding for research was probably at its lowest ever. For example, the British Economic and Social Research Council was created in 1965, while its equivalent in Canada (the Social Sciences and Humanities Research Council) was created in 1977.

With an early faculty position and relatively easy funding opportunities for their research, the World War II babies also benefited from the sustained economic growth in North America and Europe that followed the end of World War II.

Economic growth was also associated with growth in technology. The World War II babies benefited from the fastest growth in technology the planet had ever seen. For example, during his early childhood (1944–1950), the author of this introduction had an uncle who was a 'milkman' and delivered milk bottles with a horse-drawn carriage to his parents' house, only 1 km from the center of Canada's capital. Less than 10 years

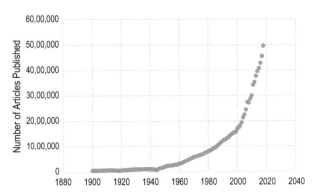

Figure 1 Number of scientific articles published between 1900
and 2018
(Compiled by Vincent Larivière, University of Montreal,
September 11, 2019)

later, astronauts were circling the globe in spacecraft, and it took only
10 more years for astronauts to walk and drive on the moon!

The globalization of trade, space research, and holidays was also
accompanied by the globalization of human development research. The
World War II babies from Europe and North America who studied
human development were the first to easily visit each other regularly,
meet at international conferences, write research proposals and scientific
papers together, get funding from different countries, and exchange
students from all over the planet.

The acceleration of scientific productivity can be seen in Figure 1.1,
which illustrates the number of scientific articles published since the
beginning of the 20th century. Note the substantial increase in the
number of scientific papers published after the 1940s, which was
followed by a more extraordinary increase since the start of the second
millennium. It is hard to imagine a steeper curve than the acceleration in
scientific publications over the past 20 years, when the World War II
babies were in their prime (Larivière, Gingras, Sugimoto, & Tsou, 2015).

1.2   Research on the Development and Prevention of Violent Behavior: 384 B.C.–A.D. 2019

To help the reader understand the scientific contributions of the World
War II babies to research on the development and prevention of violent
behavior, **defined as the use of physical strength that causes physical harm (physical aggression),** it is useful to briefly summarize the
long history of this research area.

1.2.1   *The Philosophers' Perspectives: 500 B.C.–A.D. 1762*

The tendency to use physically violent behavior among humans was most probably at the center of the first human reflections on human behavior and its development. In the Bible we read that the author (Cain) of the first murder was the son of the first woman (Eve), who incited the first man (Adam) to sin.

The intellectual debate on the origins of human violent behavior also has a long history. In his book *On Politics*, Aristotle (384–322 B.C.) proposed a basic methodological step to understand the origins of any phenomenon: 'He who considers things in their first growth and origin, will observe the clearest view of them' (Aristotle, 1943, Book 1, ch. 2). The authors of the present book are among the 'modern' investigators who adopted Aristotle's advice to study the early origins of the phenomena they wished to understand. In particular, they initiated numerous longitudinal studies of children in order to understand the early development of violent behavior.

Aristotle, like others who observed the development of children from early childhood, concluded: 'anger and will and desire are implanted in a child from their very birth, but reason and understanding develop as they grow older' (Aristotle, 1943, Book 7, ch. 15, p. 405).

He added: 'It is by our actions in the face of danger and by training ourselves to fear or courage that we become either cowardly or courageous. It is much the same with our appetites and angry passions ... So, the difference between one and another training in habits in our childhood is not a light matter, but important, or rather, all-important' (Aristotle, 1943, *Nicomachean Ethics*, Book II, ch. 1, pp. 101, 102).

Three centuries later in Rome, Seneca (4 B.C.–A.D. 65) wrote one of the best descriptions of human anger and its relation to violent behavior:

> You have demanded of me, Novatus, that I should write how anger may be soothed, and it appears to me that you are right in feeling especial fear of this passion, which is above all others hideous and wild: for the others have some alloy of peace and quiet, but this consists wholly in action and the impulse of grief, raging with an utterly inhuman lust for arms, blood and tortures, careless of itself provided it hurts another ... and greedy for revenge even when it drags the avenger to ruin. (Seneca, 1900, p. 48)

Fast forward across three more centuries and we find Saint Augustine (365–430) writing in his *Confessions* how he conceived the idea of 'original sin'. In his effort to discover when he had started to sin, he realized that he could not remember his early childhood well enough to identify at what age he had committed his first sins. He decided to observe babies and toddlers with the hypothesis that they did what he had done when he was their age. He reports in Book 1 of his *Confessions*:

Who remindeth me of the sins of my infancy? doth not each little infant, in whom I see what of myself I remember not? What then was my sin? was it then good, even for a while, to cry for what, if given, would hurt? ... to do its best to strike and hurt, because commands were not obeyed ... ? The weakness then of infant limbs, not its will, is its innocence. Myself have seen and known even a baby envious; it could not speak, yet it turned pale and looked bitterly on its foster-brother. Who knows not this? (Saint Augustine, A.D. 401, Book I, para. 11)

To understand one of the basic sources of misunderstanding among experts of the development of violent behavior throughout history, it is important here to reflect on Saint Augustine's point when he writes: 'The weakness then of infant limbs, not its will, is its innocence'.

Saint Augustine tells us that we tend to view young children as unable to be violent (physically hurt others) because they do not have the physical strength to hurt us. When we investigate the origins of violent behavior by observing the behavior of young children, we need to ask ourselves, if this child were suddenly 6 feet tall and continued to behave in the way he is presently behaving, would we label the behavior violent?

The Greek and Roman philosophers' tradition of observing early childhood development in order to understand human development was continued by Erasmus of Rotterdam in his 1529 book *On Education*. Following Saint-Augustine's insight, he writes:

We should be especially careful with our children during their first years. For at this stage their behavior is guided by instinct more than by reason, so that they are inclined equally to good and evil – more to the latter perhaps – and it is always easier to forget good habits than to unlearn bad ones.

This truth was already known to pagan philosophers and caused them great perplexity, but their speculations were unable to penetrate **the real cause**, and it was left to Christian theology to teach the truth that since Adam, the first man of the human race, **a disposition to evil** has been deeply ingrained in us.

While this is indisputably man's condition, however, we cannot deny that the greater portion of this evil stems from corrupting relationships and misguided education, especially as they affect our early and most impressionable years. (Erasmus, 1985, p. 321)

We can see that Erasmus was following a 2,000-year-old philosophical tradition, beginning with Aristotle, of associating humans' aggressive behavior with 'biological' inheritance (labeled 'original sin' by Saint Augustine). However, Erasmus also highlights the 'greater' effects of the environment during early childhood development.

A century later, a British philosopher who fled to France (1640–1651) during the English Civil War, Thomas Hobbes, modernized the same basic idea in his classic book *On the Citizen*:

Unless you give infants everything they want, they cry and get angry, they even beat their own parents ... Thus an evil man is rather like a sturdy boy, or a man of childish mind, and evil is simply want of reason at an age when it normally accrues to men by nature governed by discipline and experience of harm ... It is evident therefore that all men (since all men are born infants) are born unfit for society; and very many (perhaps the majority) remain so throughout their lives, because of mental illness, or lack of training (*disciplina*) ... Therefore, man is made fit for society not by nature but by training. (Hobbes, 1642/1998, p. 11)

The challenge to 2,000 years of relative agreement on the biological and environmental mechanisms leading to aggressive, violent, antisocial behavior came one hundred years after Hobbes from a citizen of the Republic of Geneva, where Calvin (1509–1564) imposed a stern reformation which outlawed entertainment, including music!

Jean-Jacques Rousseau published his classic book *Émile, or On Education* in 1762. It was immediately burned by the Geneva authorities, but the book became the new bible for an 'age of reason' that was turning to a 'romantic' perception of human behavior. The first phrase of the book is a good summary of the philosophical and social revolution Rousseau apparently intended: 'God makes all things good; man meddles with them and they become evil' (Rousseau, 1762/1957, p. 5).

This condemnation of civil societies had profound impacts on the social sciences from their 'creation' in the 19th century to the present day. For example, exactly 201 years after Rousseau, the most frequently cited psychologist at this point in time, according to Google Scholar, Albert Bandura, appears to have simply rewritten Rousseau's phrase in Emile – 'There is no original sin in the human heart; the how and why of the entrance of every vice can be traced' (p. 56) – when he wrote: 'People are not born with preformed repertoires of aggressive behaviors; they must learn them in one way or another' (1973, p. 61).

Rousseau was the first who dared to say, with elegance, what most of us like to think: Humans were happier when they lived in a paradise where they could benefit from the fruits of the earth without having to share them with others and obey social rules. Societies are corrupt, and they corrupt our children. The idea of the good savage who lives alone in harmony with nature is still a dream shared by many 'modern' humans.

1.2.2   *The Beginning of the Scientific Approach: 19th Century*

The use of the scientific approach to understand social behavior and society started during the 19th century. The groundbreaking research done by Adolfe Quetelet and Charles Darwin is a good illustration of the advancement of knowledge on the development of aggressive and violent behavior. Similarly, the work of British social reformer Mary Carpenter is a good example of the systematic preventive efforts that started during the 19th century.

1.2.2.1 Adolfe Quetelet: The Introduction of Statistics to Understand Human Development Like Rousseau, Adolphe Quetelet was born in the 18th century. However, these two men lived in very different worlds. Rousseau was born at the beginning of the century (1712), while Quetelet was born only 4 years before its end (1796). We have seen that there were no important differences in the methods used by Aristotle, Saint Augustine, Erasmus, Hobbs, and Rousseau to explain human development and violent behavior. They relied on their life experiences, their logic, and what others had written based on their experience and logic.

A quantum leap was made with the work of Adolfe Quetelet. Trained in mathematics and astronomy, Quetelet relied on systematic and quantifiable observations. Born in Belgium (Ghent), he apparently was attracted to drawing and poetry during his childhood. However, he eventually studied mathematics and astronomy. One of his major contributions to astronomy was the creation of the Brussels Observatory.

Surprisingly, Quetelet was also interested in human development. In fact, the word 'interested' is an understatement. In his determination to study humans' physical, cognitive, and moral development, as well as the effectiveness of medical interventions, he made major contributions to the development of statistics.

Before his 40th birthday, he had published an extensive study of human behavior titled *On Man and the Development of his Faculties, or An Essay on Social Physics* (Quetelet, 1835). He writes, in the Preface, that the book is a summary of all his work on statistics. In the first part he summarizes the statistical facts. In the second part he outlines his theory on the average man and on the organization of the social system. The scope of his statistical studies is difficult to imagine, even in our digital world. He studied factors involved in population-wide fertility, causes of death, population growth, the role of political and religious institutions, physical growth and strength development, physiological development, intellectual development, and moral development, including criminal behavior.

The physical growth studies he did were based on physical measures that had been made on soldiers to provide them with well-fitting clothes. This study led him to create the Body Mass Index, which we still use today to assess body fat. The work he did to understand the development of moral behavior led him to identify one of the most often replicated findings in modern criminology: the age–crime curve. Using data on the age of prisoners in France between 1826 and 1829, he measured the association between age and criminal convictions. For physical aggressions he showed that the frequency increased from 16 years of age to 25–30 years and then decreased. This observation was very frequently replicated in the 20th century (Farrington, 1986).

Quetelet's work on moral development also led him to study differences between males and females. For example, he calculated the ratio of males and females who were accused of homicide between 1826 and 1829 in France. He found that there were 947 men and 111 women, a ratio of 11.72 women per 100 men (Quetelet, 1831). If we compare this ratio to the female–male ratio for homicides in the United States in 2018, we observe a similar, but magnified, difference: 7.14 (10,306 men and 1,443 women) (Statista, 2019).

It has been suggested that this female–male difference concerning the use of physical aggression is due to women's weaker physical strength, rather than their superior morality (Archer, 2009). However, Quetelet's interpretation was somewhat more nuanced. He concluded that, besides physical strength, there were two other differences between men and women that explained the sex difference in homicides. The first related to the moral domain: Women have a stronger tendency to feel shame and modesty. The second, sex difference, was related to opportunities to commit crimes: Women are more dependent and more 'home-based'.

The recent scientific debate on female–male differences in aggression opposed two different theoretical perspectives, which, to a certain extent, relate to Quetelet's explanations 200 years ago. The first, a Darwinian perspective, concludes that female–male differences originate from an evolutionary selection of females for qualities related to investment in their offspring, while males were selected for their ability to physically compete with other males (Archer, 2009). The second perspective on female–male differences in aggression focuses on females' and males' social roles. It is suggested that these differences are based on the way children are socialized by their parents and their social environment. Girls are socialized to stay at home and care for children, while boys are socialized to work in the community, where there are more risks of conflict (Eagly & Steffen, 1986). Thus, the debate is not on female–male differences in social roles but on the determinants of these social roles: children learning from their environment to behave according to their sex (Eagly & Steffen, 1986) versus genetic mechanisms accumulated during evolution which determine neurobiological differences that are reinforced by social learning in the family and the wider environment (Archer, 2009).

1.2.2.2   Charles Darwin: Human Development and Evolution of Life on Earth Charles Darwin was born 13 years after Quetelet (1809). In his autobiography, Darwin writes that his physician father wanted him and his older brother to become physicians as well (Darwin, 1876/1983). After two years of medicine at Edinburgh University, Darwin decided that he would not be a physician. However, he followed another of his father's admonitions and went to Cambridge University to become a clergyman. He established a strong relationship with the Reverend John Stevens Henslow, a professor of botany and mineralogy, whom his brother had described as 'a man who knew every branch of science' (Darwin, 1876/1983, p. 36). Through Henslow, Darwin was offered the chance to be a 'naturalist' without pay on a ship that would sail around the world for 5 years. He accepted, against the advice of his father, and went on to collect all the geological information he could in order to understand the history of our planet, while also collecting all the varieties of plants and animals he could in order to study the origins of differences among animals. This huge investment led him to the idea of the evolution of life on earth (Darwin, 1859).

The scope of Darwin's interests can be seen by comparing his book on the role of worms in agriculture (Darwin, 1881) with his book on the expression of emotions in animals and humans (Darwin, 1872). Darwin compared the development of basic emotions in animals and humans as a means of understanding the evolution of human behavior from animal behavior.

With this evolutionary perspective in mind, Darwin described his first child's emotional behavior from birth onward.[4] He specifically noted his son's angry reactions and aggressive behavior. For example, Darwin wrote:

from his eighth day and for some time afterwards, I often observed that the first sign of a screaming-fit, when it could be observed coming on gradually, was a little frown, owing to the contraction of the corrugators of the brows; the capillaries of the naked head and face becoming at the same time reddened with blood. As soon as the screaming-fit actually began, all the muscles round the eyes were strongly contracted, and the mouth widely opened ... ; so that at this early period the features assumed the same form as at a more advanced age. (pp. 151–152)

Darwin's notes describe the development of anger and aggression during early childhood (Darwin, 1888):

> Doddy at 11 months: *'During the last week has got several times in passion with his playthings, especially when the right one has not been given him. When in a passion he beats & pushes away the offending object.'*

---

[4] William Erasmus (Doddy) became a successful banker

Doddy at 13 months: *'Has for some time often gone into passions for smallest offences – for instance with Anne the nurse for trying to take piece of cake from his lips with her fingers, when he wished her to take it with her mouth – out of his mouth – he tried to slap her face, went scarlet, screamed & shook his head. How has he learned that slapping gives pain – like the just-born crocodile from egg, learns to snap with its weak jaws, i.e., instinctively.'*

Doddy at 27 months: *'Doddy is a great adept at throwing things & when choleric he will hurl books or sticks at Emma (mother). About a month since, he was running to give Anny a push with a little candlestick, when I called sharply to him & he wheeled around & instantly sent the candlestick whirling over my head – He then stood resolute in the middle of the room as if ready to oppose the whole world – peremptorily refused to kiss Anny, but in short time, when I said "Doddy wont throw a candlestick at Papa's head" & he said "no wont kiss Papa" – I shall be curious to observe whether our little girls take so kindly to throwing things when so very young. If they do not, I shall believe it is hereditary in male sex, in the same manner as the S. American colts naturally amble from their parents without having been trained.'*

'Doddy was generous enough to give Anny the last mouthful of his gingerbread & today he again put his last crumb on the sofa for Anny to run to & then cried in rather a vainglorious tone "Ok kind Doddy, kind Doddy"'.

'Doddy used bit of a stick as lever to break doll.' (pp. 418–423)

Although many 19th-century investigators of animal and human behavior explicitly stated that understanding a given behavior required the description of that behavior's development from conception onward (Cairns, 1983), not all scientists agreed. One of the fiercest debates concerning the origins of species in the 1820s, described at the time by Goethe as a volcanic eruption, was sparked by the decision of a French naturalist, Etienne Geoffroy Saint-Hilaire, to start comparing the development of animal fetuses rather than continue to compare only the anatomy of adult animals (Appel, 1987). Some 30 years later, Charles Darwin cited the work done by Saint-Hilaire and others on the differences in the development of fetuses as one of the best to support his theory of evolution (Darwin, 1859, p. 409).

1.2.2.3 Mary Carpenter: The Prevention of Delinquency through Educational Reform Mary Carpenter was born two years before Darwin (1807). Her father was a Unitarian minister and teacher who directed his own school.

Mary was 22 years old when she opened a school for girls, with her mother and sister. In 1846 she created a school for poor children, and 4 years later she created a reformatory school for boys, followed by a reformatory school for girls.

In 1851 she published a book: *Reformatory Schools for the Children of the Perishing and Dangerous Classes and for Juvenile Offenders* (Carpenter, 1851). The book explained the principles of the Reformatory Schools and described a variety of other schools for at-risk children: Evening Hagged Schools, Free Day Schools, Industrial Feeding Schools, Gaols and Penal Reformatory Schools. She focused on the different schools' principles and potentially positive as well as negative effects. Interestingly, Mary Carpenter was the first woman to publish a paper in the *Journal of the Royal Statistical Society*. The 1857 paper was titled 'On the Importance of Statistics to the Reformatory Movement, with Returns from Female Reformatories and Remarks on Them' (Carpenter, 1857).

The importance given to social statistics on delinquency at the time was clearly related to the idea that families and neighborhoods were the main environmental causes of serious delinquent behavior. This is beautifully illustrated in colorful maps of London made during the last two decades of the 19th century. They were created by a well-off owner of steamship lines. Influenced by the strong belief that social facts needed to be systematically observed and quantified, Charles Booth decided to use his wealth to do a survey of poverty in London (Mary Morgan and the London School of Economics, 2019). He paid a squad of observers over more than 15 years to map the wealth and poverty of London, street by street. The rating scale they used to describe the levels of poverty for each London Street went from a 'wealthy' street to a 'chronic want' street on to the lowest-class street, which was labeled 'vicious, semi-criminal'.

1.2.3   Research during the First Half of the 20th Century

1.2.3.1   Research on Juvenile Delinquency The educational and scientific preoccupation with juvenile delinquency, which started in the middle of the 19th century, continued throughout the 20th century. A good example of the chronic nature of the juvenile violence problem, even in the wealthiest and most technologically advanced nation at the end of the 20th century, was the creation of a panel of experts by the U.S. National Research Council and the Institute of Medicine to propose a means of preventing 'The dramatic rise in juvenile violence, particularly homicides, which began in the mid- to late 1980s and peaked in the early 1990s' (National Research Council and Institute of Medicine, 2001, p. 1).

The work of William Healy, a physician, is a good example of the scientific approach to the treatment of juvenile delinquency initiated at the beginning of the 20th century. In 1909, Healy was asked by reformers in the city of Chicago to become the head of a residential institution for juvenile delinquents. In 1915, he published a detailed psychological, social, and medical description of the boys he was trying to help (Healy, 1915). He eventually went to Boston to work with the Judge Baker Clinic (Healy & Bronner, 1936). Healy's work had a wide influence, including on Cyril Burt (1925), a British pioneer in the scientific study of delinquency.

The best early 20th-century examples of the modern scientific method applied to understanding the development and prevention of antisocial behavior include the longitudinal studies of Sheldon and Eleanore Glueck and the Cambridge–Somerville Study, a randomized preventive experiment (McCord, 1978; Welsh, Dill, & Zane, 2019).

These two very long-term studies of delinquency development and prevention can be traced back to a medical doctor who, in hindsight, was at the right place at the right time. Dr. Richard C. Cabot (Welsh, Zane, & Rocque, 2017) was born in a wealthy family and introduced social work at Boston's Massachusetts General Hospital by paying social workers from his own financial resources. He held chairs in both clinical medicine and social ethics at Harvard University. One of his cousins (Francis Pickering Cabot) was Judge of the Boston juvenile court and presided over the creation of the Judge Baker Clinic, where Healy and Bronner were hired to study juvenile delinquency.

In one of his ethics courses at Harvard, Richard C. Cabot apparently convinced a law student, Sheldon Glueck, to study the long-term outcome of interventions with juvenile delinquents. The results (Glueck & Glueck, 1930) showed that interventions with juvenile delinquents were clearly not having the positive impacts they were meant to have (Glueck & Glueck, 1930).

In a discussion of the results from the Glueck and Glueck study (Glueck & Glueck, 1930), Richard C. Cabot concluded, 'What piece of social work … is able to declare (with good grounds for its belief) that it has not failed in 88 percent of its endeavors?' (McCord in McCord & Tremblay, 1992, p. 198). From this clear evidence that court-based interventions with juvenile delinquents did not help as they were meant to, Richard C. Cabot concluded that if the treatment of juvenile delinquents did not work, a mentoring intervention which started before adolescence might prevent the juvenile delinquency that leads to criminal careers. This led him to plan the first randomized clinical trial during elementary school to prevent delinquency during adolescence.

According to Gordon W. Allport (1951), Cabot had planned a preventive intervention with a counselor that started early and lasted 10 years. In fact, the experiment, which included 650 boys between 5 and 13 years of age (mean: 10.5 years), lasted a mean of 5.5 years, but in some cases the relationship with the counselor was maintained informally after the official end of the experiment (Powers & Witmer, 1951, p.322). The study was designed to avoid stigmatization of the boys involved. To that end, half of the 650 boys in the experiment had behavior problems, while the other half did not. Each boy in the sample was matched to another boy on characteristics, such as family background, intelligence, and behavior. Within each pair, one boy was randomly selected for the preventive intervention, which involved home visits and activities with the counselor, who was meant to be a role model. Some of the boys also attended summer camps (Welsh, Dill, et al., 2019).

Richard C. Cabot died before the end of the experiment but left funds to evaluate the long-term impacts of the preventive intervention. The first evaluation, 3 years after the end of the intervention (1948), did not identify any significant impacts (Powers & Witmer, 1951). The second and third evaluations were done during the second half of the 20th century and will be described in the following section.

In 1940, Sheldon and Eleanore Glueck initiated another important long-term study of delinquent development with 500 juvenile delinquents (age 10–17 years) matched to 500 non-delinquents. This study, published in 1950 (Glueck & Glueck, 1950), also had a strong influence on the science of deviant behavior development over the next half century and beyond because two young criminologists eventually decided to find and interview the boys who had taken part in the study (Sampson & Laub, 2005).

1.2.3.2 Research on the Development of Aggressive Behavior Systematic research on the development of human aggression also started to appear in the first half of the 20th century and, surprisingly, followed Aristotle's advice to study very young children. The research was done in the 1920s and 1930s, funded in part by the Rockefeller Foundation through their financial support for nursery schools in universities (Banham Bridges, 1931). The creation of nursery schools was part of the Child Study and the Mental Health Movements initiated in the early 20th century in North America (Beers, 1929; Bertolote, 2008). Katharine Banham-Bridges did some of the best pioneering work on physical aggression during early childhood within the McGill University nursery in Montreal (Canada).

Born in England, Katharine Banham received a BA degree from Manchester University. She went on to do graduate work at Cambridge

14   *Richard E. Tremblay*

University, where they were not giving official degrees to women! She was nonetheless hired to teach psychology at the University of Toronto in Canada and eventually moved to McGill University in Montreal, where her husband J. W. Bridges had been appointed to the psychology department. The couple did research in a residential home for juvenile delinquents, and Katharine Banham was appointed to do research in the McGill University nursery school. Her results were published in the newly created and now famous journal *Child Development*. She also published a book that became a classic: *The Social and Emotional Development of the Pre-School Child* (Banham Bridges, 1931).

The book describes the creation of an instrument to assess the social and emotional development of children from 2 to 5 years of age. The instrument is based on behavioral observations she did in the nursery school over a 3-year period. The behaviors were classified with reference to anger and fear. These behaviors included hitting, punching, pushing, pulling, fighting for toys or a specific space, destroying other's work, harassing others, biting and spitting, teasing, pressing services on others against their will, and telling untruths to impress others.

Similar research was done at the same time by Florence L. Goodenough within the University of Minnesota Child Development Institute, created in 1925. Goodenough gave the first undergraduate and graduate courses in that now-famous institute which created *Child Development*. To investigate the development of anger in preschool children (Goodenough, 1931), she asked mothers who had some college training and a child between 7 and 94 months to note every time they had an anger outburst over a 1-month period. The spread in age created a cross-sectional study, similar to the study done by Quetelet a century earlier on the age of prisoners, which led him to identify the classic age–crime curve. The results showed that the developmental trajectory pattern for anger outbursts was similar to the developmental trajectories of crim- inal behavior observed by Quetelet (1831). The lowest frequency of anger outbursts was for children below 1 year of age. The peak in frequency of anger outbursts was between 13 and 23 months. From 23 months to 94 months the frequency of anger outbursts substantially decreased. It is important to remember that both the Quetelet study with prisoners and the Goodenough study with preschool children were cross-sectional studies rather than longitudinal studies, where the same individuals are followed over long periods of time.

The first large-scale national longitudinal study of children from birth onward started 1 year after the end of World War II, apparently as an afterthought (Butler & Golding, 1986b). At the end of World War II, the British College of Obstetricians and Gynecologists decided to gather information on the birth conditions of a representative sample of newborn children (N = 5,362). Known as the National Survey of Health and Development, data was collected at age 2 years to verify the health status of the babies. This evaluation of the 1946 national sample of births was repeated regularly with a home visit in 2015 (see Jean Golding, Chapter 3).

One of the best summaries of research on the development and prevention of aggressive and delinquent behavior before 1950 can be found in the first report published by the World Health Organisation, which was created in 1948. The report was an attempt to provide guidance to the delinquency problems that resulted from the social chaos created by World War II. The author was a Swiss child psychiatrist, Lucien Bovet (1951). From his analysis of the scientific and clinical literature at the time, as well as his extensive tour of research institutions in the United States and Europe, he concluded that effective prevention of juvenile delinquency needed to be based on a vast mental health campaign. He specifically pointed to the importance of taking an intergenerational perspective by helping girls with behavior problems. He wrote: 'Treatment of the non-delinquent little girl or teen-age girl might perhaps have been the most efficacious prophylaxis for the delinquency which a few years later will break out in her sons' (Bovet, 1951, p. 46).

1.2.4   Research between 1950 and 1970

The World War II babies started their research careers in the 1970s. There was no clear break in the type of research on the development of aggression which was done up to 1950 and during the following 20 years. But the research between 1950 and 1970 most certainly had a strong influence on their training and their initial research[5].

1.2.4.1   Longitudinal Studies and Experimental Preventive Interventions

First, the creation of longitudinal studies from birth, which was initiated in Great Britain by the National Survey of Health and Development (Butler & Golding, 1986a), led to comparative longitudinal studies of birth cohorts from different countries. One of these was initiated in 1955 by the International Center for Children, which had its base in Paris. The longitudinal study included birth samples from Brussels, London, Paris,

---

[5] For those who would like a detailed view of the state of knowledge on aggressive behavior by 1975, see de Wit, J. E., & Hartup, W. W. (1974). *Determinants and origins of aggressive behavior*. The Hague, Netherlands: Mouton.

Stockholm, and Zurich. One area of interest was the development of temper tantrums. Analyses of the Brussels sample replicated, with longitudinal data, the results of the cross-sectional study that Goodenough did in Minneapolis during the late 1920s. The frequency of temper tantrums increased from 9 to 18 months of age, and then substantially decreased until the children reached 72 months (Sand, 1966). As will be discussed later (see Richard Tremblay, Chapter 10), similar developmental patterns were observed for physical aggressions in studies with children of the same age but in the 1980s and 1990s (Tremblay et al., 1999).

In 1956, Joan McCord started working on the second evaluation of the Cambridge–Somerville Youth Study (CSYS) with her husband William McCord. He had recently finished his PhD at Harvard University with Sheldon Glueck. For more than twenty years, Joan McCord did the exceptionally long and hard work that led to a surprising conclusion: The 5-year intensive preventive intervention with elementary school boys at risk of delinquency increased the likelihood of alcoholism and early death (McCord, 1978). Using the CSYS, Joan McCord also published numerous articles on the potential 'causes' of delinquency, once she realized that the control group of the randomized control trial could be used to study the childhood factors associated with delinquency and alcoholism during adolescence and adulthood (Sayre-McCord, 2007; Tremblay, Welsh, & Sayre-McCord, 2019).

The groundbreaking Cambridge–Somerville experiment and its exceptionally long-term follow-up by Joan McCord, clearly demonstrated that experimental work with very long-term follow-ups could be done in the psycho-social domain. Three other important lessons for research on the prevention of behavior problems were learned from the Cambridge–Somerville experiment. First, preventive interventions that start during elementary school may not be early enough. Second, and counter-intuitively, interventions during elementary school may be early enough to worsen the problem for some children, if we do not respond adequately to their needs.

The third lesson was learned in the past year. Brandon Welsh and colleagues published results from the last assessment of the study, 72 years after the end of the intervention in 1945! The comparison between the treated and untreated boys showed that there were no significant differences between the experimental and control groups for age at death (446 had died and 42 were still alive [Welsh, Zane, Zimmerman, & Yohros, 2019]). Thus, the results from three assessments over 70 years show that a long-term preventive intervention for children can have, in sequence, neutral, negative, and again neutral effects. The story does not end with the death of the original cohort of children. Planning is under way by Welsh and his colleagues to study the lives of the children of the boys in the CSYS to evaluate whether the intervention had long-term impacts on the second generation (Welsh, Dill, et al., 2019).

The St. Louis Child Guidance clinic study is another long-term study that had a large impact after its publication by Lee Robins (1966). She retrospectively studied 300 children, comparing those who were treated two decades earlier in a child guidance clinic to 100 who lived in similar socio-economic conditions. She reported that 44% of the boys who had been treated for antisocial behavior committed major crimes during adulthood, compared to 3% of the boys who were not treated. Another interesting finding of that study, which was replicated in later studies, was the long-term negative impact of being sent to juvenile court (e.g., Gatti, Tremblay, & Vitaro, 2009; Petitclerc, Gatti, Vitaro, & Tremblay, 2013).

The oldest study conducted by one of the World War II babies (see David Farrington, Chapter 6) started in 1960 after Dr. C. L. E. H. Sharp, the Schools' Medical Officer at Bedford, England, suggested to the Institute of Criminology at Cambridge University (England) that they 'sponsor a long-term study of normal young children with the ultimate object of identifying the characteristics of the minority who become delinquent in later years' (West, 1969, p. x). The study was planned and directed by D. J. West (1969), a Fellow of Darwin College at Cambridge University. It started in 1962 with boys who were in their second grade of elementary school in the Greater London area. The boys have been followed under the direction of David Farrington since 1982.

1.2.4.2   The Gene–Environment Debate One of the most important intellectual debates concerning the developmental origins of aggression among humans reached a peak between 1966 and 1973. It centered on the nature versus nurture origins of aggression. In his book *On Aggression* (1966), the ethologist and future Nobel Prize winner Konrad Lorenz followed Darwin's logic of evolution and used his observations of animal behavior to conclude that humans, like all other animals, inherit an 'aggressive instinct' that could lead to the destruction of humanity.

Lorenz had only studied animal behavior and was generalizing his systematic observations of animal behavior to human behavior. However, from the 1960s onward, an impressive number of child development specialists used the ethological approach to study preschoolers' behavior, including physical aggression. To a certain extent, they were continuing the tradition of direct observations of children's behavior in their natural environment that Banham Bridges (1931) had pioneered in the late 1920s (see pages x, x).

For example, in North America, Francis Floyd Strayer did his PhD on social interactions among macaques and went on to do systematic observational studies of the role of aggressive behavior among preschool children during their everyday social interactions (Strayer & Strayer, 1976). In Great Britain, Robert Hinde (1974), a Cambridge University ornithologist and primatologist, who mentored the work of Jane Goodhall (2017) with chimpanzees, also initiated a longitudinal study of preschool children using ethological methods of data collection.

Following Rousseau, Albert Bandura, a social psychologist, promoted a very different perspective in a 1973 book titled *Aggression: A Social Learning Perspective* (Bandura, 1973).[6] The main evidence Bandura presented for the social learning of aggression was based on observations of children in a laboratory situation. Children were shown to spontaneously imitate an adult hitting a large inflated doll (Bobo doll). As noted earlier, Bandura concluded from these observations that: 'People are not born with preformed repertories of aggressive behaviors; they must learn them in one way or another' (Bandura, 1973, p. 61).

Support for that social learning perspective came from studies of the effects of television on children's behavior. Between the 1950s and the 1960s, television became available to all children, and numerous studies based on social learning theory were driven by the hypothesis that children were learning to aggress from the violence they saw on television (Eron, Huesmann, Lefkowitz, & Walder, 1972; Eron, Walder, Toigo, & Lefkowitz, 1963; Huesmann, Lagerspetz, & Eron, 1984).

Some investigators eventually decided to study both environmental and genetic effects on the development of children by doing longitudinal studies with monozygotic and dizygotic twins. For example, David C. Rowe was one of the first (with his supervisor Robert Plomin) to use twin studies to study genetic and environmental determinants of aggressive behavior (Rowe & Osgood, 1984). The number of these twin studies has substantially increased during the past 30 years, and the results indicate that the frequency of physical aggressions and indirect aggressions is associated with both genetic and environmental factors; however, genetic effects are surprisingly strong from early childhood onward (Dionne, Tremblay, Boivin, Laplante, & Pérusse, 2003; Lacourse et al., 2014; Rhee & Waldman, 2002; Tackett, Waldman, & Lahey, 2009).

The discovery of genetic mechanisms after World War II was one of the major scientific breakthroughs concerning the nature of living organisms.

---

[6] Bandura is the most frequently cited psychologist ever, according to Google Scholar

Crick and Watson (1953) published their discovery of the structure of DNA when the World War II babies were between 8 and 13 years of age. Their work, and the work of many others afterward, enabled the systematic study of intergenerational inheritance mechanisms that had been observed since humans realized that children looked and behaved similarly to their parents.

Advances in molecular genetics led to the precise measurement of genes and their cumulative impacts for different physical and mental health problems, including aggression (e.g., Hamshere et al., 2013; Maher, 2015), as well as to the measurement of the impact of the environment on gene expression (DNA methylation). A study of maternal behavior with rats showed that maternal licking of the rat pups after birth had important long-term impacts on brain development, behavior, and longevity (Weaver et al., 2004). This study led to numerous investigations of epigenetic effects in humans. Recent studies by the World War II babies and their students showed associations between chronic aggression in childhood and DNA methylation during adulthood (Provençal et al., 2013; Wang et al., 2012) as well as associations between DNA methylation at birth and later behavior problems (Cecil, Walton, Pingault, et al., 2018). These studies are now being led by the former students of the World War II babies, who use the longitudinal and experimental studies that the World War II babies initiated or have continued since the 1970s (e.g., Cecil, Walton, Jaffee, et al., 2018; Cecil, Walton, Pingault, et al., 2018).

With the acceleration of research on genetics and environmental effects which impact gene expression (epigenetics) and brain development, we can expect that the old gene–environment debate will remain, but at a very different scientific level compared to the Lorenz–Bandura debate of the 1960s and 1970s. Companies are already offering couples the ability to select their embryos (Regalado, 2019) based on genome-wide association studies (Hamshere et al., 2013). As we have seen for assisted reproduction, couples who have the financial means will be the first to use embryo-selection technology. However, if effective, it should be offered to those who are most in need. Use of genetic profiling to select embryos, combined with educational support to at-risk parents from pregnancy onward, could be a powerful prevention strategy for numerous intergenerational problems, including the prevention of cognitive and behavior problems which are associated with violent behavior (Barker et al., 2007).

1.2.5   *World War II Babies Come of Age: 30 Longitudinal and
          Experimental Studies with 80,000 Children*

The World War II babies who studied the development and prevention of violent behavior were far from facing a blank slate. They inherited a very long tradition of investigations into the moral behavior of humans. From the writers of the Bible, as well as from the writings of the Greek and Roman philosophers, they learned that the gene–environment debate concerning violent behavior had long been a central issue. From philosophers of the Enlightenment and from 19th-century scientists, they learned that empirical work is needed, not only to address the old philosophical questions but also to find effective means of preventing children from engaging in serious antisocial and violent behavior. From early 20th-century scientists, they learned the importance of systematic longitudinal studies and large samples to understand the developmental trajectories of violent behavior. From that very rich intellectual period, they also found an excellent model of experimental preventive interventions to sort out effective from ineffective and iatrogenic preventive interventions.

Who could have predicted, in 1945, that the babies born in Britain, Germany, Canada, Italy, the United States, and the Netherlands, during the worst human carnage ever, would have such good fortune? Not only did they inherit a long philosophical and scientific heritage but they also had exceptional financial and technological resources with which to collaborate on large-scale longitudinal and experimental studies of violent behavior development and prevention.

The 12 World War II babies who contributed to this book were involved in at least 30 longitudinal studies with more than 80,000 children. Six of these studies included experimental preventive interventions. Four studies started during the pregnancy of more than 37,000 women, five studies started soon after the birth of close to 24,000 children, five studies started when approximately 8,000 children were between 3 and 6 years of age, 12 studies started during the elementary school years of approximately 8,000 elementary school children, and four studies started during adolescence, with a total of approximately 4,000 children.

The World War II babies describe their own developmental trajectories from pre-conception in the following 11 chapters. They also describe their main research on the development and prevention of violent behavior from the 1970s to 2019. The sequence of chapters follows the birthdates of the authors, from 1939 to 1945. Interestingly, the three oldest authors are three of the four World War II baby girls who contributed to this book. This sex difference was not planned but helps to highlight major differences in the careers of the World War II baby girls and boys. From the sex differences we have been observing in the past three decades for graduate students involved in research on human development, we can expect that women will make up the majority of authors of the book written in 30 years by violence researchers born after 1970!

In the last chapter, violence investigators who were born between 1948 and 1977 describe the lessons they learned from reading about the lives and career trajectories of the World War II babies. They give their perspectives on the legacy of the research done by the World War II babies and on the research that will be needed during the next half century. They also suggest priorities of research on the development and prevention of violent behavior for the next half-century. Finally, they suggest changes that are needed in training the next generation of researchers on the development and prevention of violent behavior.

References

Allport, G. W. (1951). Foreword. In E. Powers & H. Witmer (Eds.), *An experiment in the prevention of delinquency: The Cambridge-Somerville Youth Study*. New York, NY: Columbia University Press.

Appel, T. A. (1987). *The Cuvier-Geoffroy debate: French biology in the decades before Darwin*. New York, NY: Oxford University Press.

Archer, J. (2009). Does sexual selection explain human sex differences in aggression? *Behavioral and Brain Sciences, 32*(3–4), 249–266.

Aristotle. (1943). *On man in the universe*. New York, NY: Classics Club, Walter J. Black.

Bandura, A. (1973). *Aggression: A social learning analysis*. New York, NY: Holt.

Banham Bridges, K. M. (1931). *Social and emotional development of the pre-school child*. London, England: Kegan Paul, Trench, Trukner.

Barker, E. D., Séguin, J. R., White, H. R., Bates, M. E., Lacourse, E., Carbonneau, R., & Tremblay, R. E. (2007). Developmental trajectories of male physical violence and theft: Relations to neurocognitive performance. *Archives of General Psychiatry, 64*(5), 592–599.

Beers, C. W. (1929). *A mind that found itself*. New York, NY: Doubleday, Draw. (Original work published 1908)

Bertolote, J. (2008). The roots of the concept of mental health. *World Psychiatry, 7*(2), 113–116.

Bovet, L. (1951). *Psychiatric aspects of juvenile delinquency: A study prepared on behalf of the World Health Organization as a contribution to the United Nations Programme for the Prevention of Crime and Treatment of Offenders*. Geneva, Switzerland: World Health Organization.

Burt, C. (1925). *The young delinquent*. New York, NY: Appleton.

Butler, N. R., & Golding, J. (1986a). *From Birth to Five: A Study of the Health and Behaviour of Britain's 5 Year Olds*. Oxford, England: Pergamon Press.

Butler, N. R., & Golding, J. (1986b). Introduction. In N. R. Butler & J. Golding, (Eds.), *From birth to five* (pp. 1–11). Oxford, England: Pergamon Press.

Cairns, R. B. (1983). The emergence of developmental psychology. In P. H. Mussen (Ed.), *Handbook of child psychology* (Vol. 1, pp. 41–102). Toronto, Ontario, Canada: John Wiley.

Carpenter, M. (1857). On the importance of statistics to the reformatory movement, with returns from female reformatories, and remarks on them. *Journal of
the Statistical Society of London, 20*(1), 33–40.

Carpenter, M. (1968). *Reformatory schools for the children of the perishing and
dangerous classes and for juvenile offenders.* London, England: Woburn Press.
(Original work published 1851)

Cecil, C. A. M., Walton, E., Jaffee, S. R., O'Connor, T., Maughan, B., Relton,
C. L., … Ouellet-Morin, I. (2018). Neonatal DNA methylation and early-
onset conduct problems: A genome-wide, prospective study. *Development and
Psychopathology, 30*(2), 383–397.

Cecil, C. A. M., Walton, E., Pingault, J. B., Provencal, N., Pappa, I., Vitaro,
F., … McCrory, E. J. (2018). DRD4 methylation as a potential biomarker for
physical aggression: An epigenome-wide, cross-tissue investigation. *American
Journal of Medical Genetics Part B: Neuropsychiatric Genetics, 177*(8), 746–764.

Darwin, C. (1872). *The Expression of the emotions in man and animals.* London,
England: John Murray.

Darwin, C. (1881). *The formation of vegetable mould through the action of worms:
With observations on their habits.* London, England: John Murray.

Darwin, C. (1888). *The correspondence of Charles Darwin. Vol. 4: 1847-1850.*
Cambridge, England: Cambridge University Press.

Darwin, C. (1965). *The expression of the emotions in man and animals* (3rd ed.). In
P. Ekman (Ed.). London, England: Harper Collins. (Original work published
1872)

Darwin, C. (1983). *Autobiography.* Oxford, England: Oxford University Press.
(Original work published 1876)

Darwin, C. (1987). *On the origin of species.* Brooklyn, NY: Gryphon. (Original
work published 1859)

Dionne, G., Tremblay, R. E., Boivin, M., Laplante, D., & Pérusse, D. (2003).
Physical aggression and expressive vocabulary in 19 month-old twins.
Developmental Psychology, 39(2), 261–273.

Eagly, A. H., & Steffen, V. J. (1986). Gender and aggressive-behavior – A meta-
analytic review of the social psychological literature. *Psychological Bulletin, 100*
(3), 309–330.

Erasmus, D. (1985). *Collected works of Erasmus. Literary and educational writings*
(Vol. 4, p. 321). Toronto, Ontario, Canada: University of Toronto Press.

Eron, L. D., Huesmann, L. R., Lefkowitz, M. M., & Walder, L. O. (1972). Does
television violence cause aggression? *American Psychologist, 27*(4), 253–263.

Eron, L. D., Walder, L. O., Toigo, R., & Lefkowitz, M. M. (1963). Social class,
parental punishment for aggression, and child aggression. *Child Development,
34*(4), 849–867. doi:10.1111/j.1467-8624.1963.tb05159.x

Farrington, D. P. (1986). Age and crime. In M. Tonry & N. Morris (Eds.), *Crime
and justice: An annual review of research* (Vol. 7, pp. 189–250). Chicago, IL:
University of Chicago Press.

Gatti, U., Tremblay, R. E., & Vitaro, F. (2009). Iatrogenic effect of juvenile
justice. *Journal of Child Psychology and Psychiatry, 50*(8), 991–998.

Glueck, S., & Glueck, E. (1950). *Unraveling juvenile delinquency.* Cambridge,
England: Cambridge University Press.

Glueck, S., & Glueck, E. T. (1930). *500 criminal careers*. New York, NY: Knopf.

Goodall, J. (2017). Remembering my mentor: Robert Hinde. Retrieved from https://news.janegoodall.org/2017/01/20/remembering-my-mentor-robert-hinde/

Goodenough, F. L. (1931). *Anger in young children*. Westport, CT: Greenwood Press.

Hamshere, M. L., Langley, K., Martin, J., Agha, S. S., Stergiakouli, E., Anney, R. J., … Neale, B. M. (2013). High loading of polygenic risk for ADHD in children with comorbid aggression. *American Journal of Psychiatry*, *170*(8), 909–916.

Healy, W. (1915). *The individual delinquent: A text-book of diagnosis and prognosis for all concerned in understanding offenders* . Boston, MA: Little, Brown.

Healy, W., & Bronner, A. F. (1936). *New light on delinquency and its treatment*. London, England: Yale University Press.

Hinde, R. A. (1974). *The biological basis of human social behaviour*. New York, NY: McGraw-Hill.

Hobbes, T. (1998). *On the Citizen*. New York, NY: Cambridge University Press. (Original work published 1642)

Huesmann, L. R., Lagerspetz, K., & Eron, L. D. (1984). Intervening variables in the TV violence–aggression relation: Evidence from two countries. *Developmental Psychology*, *20*(5), 746–775. doi:10.1037//0012-1649.20.5.746

Jones, L. Y. (1980). *Great expectations, America and the baby boom generation*. New York, NY: BookSurge.

Lacourse, E., Boivin, M., Brendgen, M., Petitclerc, A., Girard, A., Vitaro, F., … Tremblay, R. E. (2014). A longitudinal twin study of physical aggression in early childhood: Evidence for a developmentally dynamic genome. *Psychological Medicine*, *44*(12), 2617–2627.

Larivière, V., Gingras, Y., Sugimoto, C. R., & Tsou, A. (2015). Team size matters: Collaboration and scientific impact since 1900. *Journal of the Association for Information Science and Technology*, *66*(7), 1323–1332.

Lorenz, K. (1966). *On aggression*. New York, NY: Harcourt, Brace, and World.

Maher, B. S. (2015). Polygenic scores in epidemiology: Risk prediction, etiology, and clinical utility. *Current Epidemiology Reports*, *2*(4), 239–244.

Mary Morgan and the London School of Economics. (2019). *Charles Booth's London poverty maps*. London, England: Thames & Hudson.

McCord, J. (1978). A thirty-year follow-up of treatment effects. *American Psychologist*, *33*(3), 284–289.

McCord, J., & Tremblay, R. E. (Eds.). (1992). *Preventing antisocial behavior from birth through adolescence: Experimental approaches*. New York, NY: Guilford Press.

National Research Council and Institute of Medicine. (2001). *Juvenile crime, juvenile justice*. In J. McCord, C. S. Widom, & N. A. Crowell (Eds.), *Panel on juvenile crime: Prevention, treatment, and control*. Washington, DC: National Academy Press.

Owram, D. (1997). *Born at the right time: A history of the baby-boom generation*. Toronto, Ontario, Canada: University of Toronto Press.

Petitclerc, A., Gatti, U., Vitaro, F., & Tremblay, R. E. (2013). Effects of juvenile court exposure on crime in young adulthood. *Journal of Child Psychology and Psychiatry*, *54*(3), 291–297.

Powers, E., & Witmer, H. (1951). *An experiment in the prevention of delinquency: The Cambridge-Somerville Youth Study*. New York, NY: Columbia University Press.

Provençal, N., Suderman, M. J., Caramaschi, D., Wang, D. S., Hallett, M., Vitaro, F., … Szyf, M. (2013). Differential DNA methylation regions in cytokine and transcription factor genomic loci associate with childhood physical aggression. *PLoS ONE, 8*(8), 1–19 (e71691).

Quetelet, A. (1831). *Research on the propensity for crime at different ages*. Bruxelles, Belgium: M. Hayez.

Quetelet, A. (1835). *Essay on social physics: Man and the development of his faculties*. New York, NY: Franklin.

Regalado, A. (2019). The world's first Gattaca baby tests are finally here. Retrieved from https://www.technologyreview.com/s/614690/polygenic-score-ivf-embryo-dna-tests-genomic-prediction-gattaca/

Rhee, S. H., & Waldman, I. D. (2002). Genetic and environmental influences on antisocial behavior: A meta-analysis of twin and adoption studies. *Psychological Bulletin, 128*(3), 490–529.

Robins, L. N. (1966). *Deviant children grown up: A sociological and psychiatric study of sociopathic personality*. Baltimore: William and Wilkins.

Rousseau, J.-J. (1957). *Émile, or On Education*. London, England: J. M. Dent. (Original work published 1762)

Rowe, D. C., & Osgood, D. W. (1984). Heredity and sociological theories of delinquency: A reconsideration. *American Sociological Review, 49*(4), 526–540.

Saint Augustine. (A.D. 401). *The Confessions of Saint Augustine*. Retrieved from www.gutenberg.org/files/3296/3296-h/3296-h.htm#link2H_4_0001

Sampson, R. J., & Laub, J. H. (2005). A life-course view of the development of crime. *The Annals of the American Academy of Political and Social Science, 602*(1), 12–45.

Sand, E. A. (1966). *Contribution à l'étude du développement de l'enfant. Aspects médico-sociaux et psychologiques*. Bruxelles, Belgique: Éditions de l'Institut de sociologie de l'Université libre de Bruxelles.

Sayre-McCord, G. (2007). *Crime and family: Selected essays of Joan McCord*. Philadelphia, PA: Temple University Press.

Schor, J., & Marglin, S. A. (2011). *The golden age of capitalism: Reinterpreting the postwar experience*. New York, NY: Oxford University Press.

Seneca, L. A. (1900). *Of Anger (Book I)*. Retrieved from https://en.wikisource.org/wiki/Of_Anger/Book_I

Statista. (2019). Murder in the U.S.: Number of offenders by gender 2018. Retrieved from https://www.statista.com/statistics/251886/murder-offenders-in-the-us-by-gender/

Statistics Canada. (2011). *Generations in Canada*. Ottawa, Ontario, Canada: Statistics Canada.

Strayer, F. F., & Strayer, J. (1976). An ethological analysis of social agonism and dominance relations among preschool children. *Child Development, 47*, 980–988.

Tackett, J. L., Waldman, I. D., & Lahey, B. B. (2009). Etiology and measurement of relational aggression: A multi-informant behavior genetic investigation. *Journal of Abnormal Psychology, 118*(4), 722.

Tremblay, R. E., Japel, C., Pérusse, D., McDuff, P., Boivin, M., Zoccolillo, M., & Montplaisir, J. (1999). The search for the age of 'onset' of physical aggression: Rousseau and Bandura revisited. *Criminal Behavior and Mental Health*, 9(1), 8–23.

Tremblay, R. E., Welsh, B. C., & Sayre-McCord, G. (2019). Crime and the life-course, prevention, experiments, and truth seeking: Joan McCord's pioneering contributions to criminology. *Annual Review of Criminology*, 2, 1–20.

Wang, D., Szyf, M., Benkelfat, C., Provençal, N., Caramaschi, D., Côté, S. M., … Booij, L. (2012). Peripheral SLC6A4 DNA methylation is associated with in vivo measures of human brain serotonin synthesis and childhood physical aggression. *PLoS ONE*, 7(6), 1–8 (e39501). doi:10.1371/journal.pone.0039501

Watson, J. D., & Crick, F. H. (1953). *The structure of DNA*. Paper presented at the Cold Spring Harbor symposia on quantitative biology.

Weaver, I. C. G., Cervoni, N., Champagne, F. A., D'Alessio, A. C., Sharma, S., Seckl, J. R., … Meaney, M. J. (2004). Epigenetic programming by maternal behavior. *Nature Neuroscience*, 7(8), 847–854. doi:10.1038/nn1276

Welsh, B. C., Dill, N. E., & Zane, S. N. (2019). The first delinquency prevention experiment: A socio-historical review of the origins of the Cambridge–Somerville Youth Study's research design. *Journal of Experimental Criminology*, 15(3), 441–451.

Welsh, B. C., Zane, S. N., & Rocque, M. (2017). Delinquency prevention for individual change: Richard Clarke Cabot and the making of the Cambridge–Somerville Youth Study. *Journal of Criminal Justice*, 52, 79–89.

Welsh, B. C., Zane, S. N., Zimmerman, G. M., & Yohros, A. (2019). Association of a crime prevention program for boys with mortality 72 years after the intervention: Follow-up of a randomized clinical trial. *JAMA Netw Open*, 2(3), e190782.

West, D. J. (1969). *Present conduct and future delinquency*. London, England: Heinemann.

2 From Birth in a British Orphanage to Assessments of American Indians' Development

Elizabeth Jane Costello

Jane Costello was born February 2, 1939, in Birmingham, England. She received her PhD in social psychology from the University of London School of Economics in 1981. Her first faculty appointment was in 1988 at Duke University (United States) where she is now Professor Emerita of Psychiatry and Behavioral Sciences, and former Director of the Center for Developmental Epidemiology. She participated in two U.S. National Academy of Medicine panels on aggressive and violent behavior. In 2000 she received, with Adrian Angold, the American Academy of Child and Adolescent Psychiatry's Ruane Prize for Psychiatric Research. In 2003 she was awarded the Koch Prize for Epidemiology and Statistics by the American Public Health Association, and in 2017 she received the Harvard Award in Psychiatric Epidemiology and Biostatistics.

Jane Costello began her academic career as an epidemiologist, with the goal of integrating many areas of expertise. Epidemiology evolved into developmental epidemiology as she began to incorporate ideas and methods from the developmental sciences into the basic framework of the distribution of disease in time and space (Costello & Maughan, 2015).

Her interest in aggressive behavior was aroused in her first studies of access to care for children with psychiatric illnesses (Costello et al., 1988). A cost analysis of a random sample of children showed that the average annual cost for the care of children between 9 and 16 years with a diagnosis of conduct disorder was many times higher than that of care for children with other diagnoses (Costello, Sung, Worthman, & Angold, 2007). The main reason for the high cost of caring for aggressive children was the cost of incarceration and the high likelihood that these children would spend time locked up. But incarcerating children follows from adult decision making as much as from the behavior of the children themselves.

This revived her interest in decision analysis, the topic of her doctoral dissertation. With Adrian Angold she initiated a United States–Great Britain study at the Pittsburgh University Medical Center and at the University of London Institute of Psychiatry. The aim was to describe how diagnoses were made in the two medical care systems. They observed that the behavior of the experts involved in the case conferences that were studied (psychiatrists, psychologists, social workers, etc.) directly contravened the basic principles of decision making: They made up their minds on the basis of irrelevant criteria that confirmed–disconfirmed, their hypotheses (Simon, 1983).

The next step was to compare clinical decision making with diagnosis made on the basis of structured interviews designed to instantiate the highest standard of diagnostic practice: the *Diagnostic and Statistical Manual* of the American Psychiatric Association (American Psychiatric Association, 1994). This required writing and testing a diagnostic interview that put the criteria of the *DSM* into interview format; developing age-appropriate versions of the interview for young children, older children, adolescents, and adults; and testing all these versions for reliability and validity. It took at least 5 years to write the interviews; create the data entry programs and scoring codes; and then raise the funds to train interviewers, recruit test samples, test and retest the interviews, revise them, and publish the results.

One aim of all this work was to pursue etiologic questions on the role of puberty in the development of psychiatric illnesses, such as conduct disorder and depression, using the Great Smoky Mountains Study (GSMS), which has been funded by the National Institute of Mental Health (NIMH) for 25 years (Costello, Compton, Keeler, & Angold, 2003). The study was conducted in an 11-county area of western North Carolina in the United States. Colleagues from many disciplines were involved in this long-term developmental study. With a team of graduate students, they analyzed blood samples for testosterone and other markers of pubertal development. Results showed that testosterone only predicted conduct disorder in the presence of already existing conduct problems. In the absence of conduct problems, testosterone predicted 'leadership' qualities (Rowe, Maughan, Worthman, Costello, & Angold, 2004).

One important aspect of the GSMS was the opportunity to compare the development of American Indian and non-Indian participants in response to a 'natural experiment'. The study began to collect data in 1993, and in 1996 the American Indian families first received a portion of the profits of a newly opened casino. Jane Costello and her colleagues compared the impact of this 'natural experiment' on children's behavioral problems from the 4 years before and the 4 years after the distribution of the money began. Results showed that it had no effect on the children of the well-off members of the American Indian community, but it had a marked effect on children from poor families (Costello et al., 2003). The participants have now been followed into their 30s, and results show a lasting effect that points to a critical period of exposure early in the teenage years (Copeland, Brotman, & Costello, 2015). These results seem to indicate a bio-psycho-social phenomenon, which also has considerable economic and social effects (Suleiman & Dahl, 2017).

In the past decade the idea of a 'Universal Basic Income' (UBI) as a way of preventing several social ills, including criminality, has become a serious proposal currently being tested in several countries and states. The GSMS is one of very few studies to meet the basic requirements of a natural experiment, with no exclusion criteria except race. Economists are currently working on the effects on social costs. The work of Jane Costello and her colleagues has also pointed to a close interplay between environmental stressors and biological development in the origins of criminality.

Jane Costello has been on the epidemiology review committee of NIMH for more than 20 years. She was also on the editorial board of the *Journal of Child Psychology and Psychiatry* for 8 years. She is a member of several other review panels, and in 2019 she received an award for the best political science paper from the Midwest Political Science Association.

2.1   Parents

Reading the history books, you might think that, as a young child during World War II, I grew up in fear and want, but life was not like that at all. With a loving family and lots of exciting activities, we never felt insecurity or anxiety. Nor, thanks to my father's work, did the 300 severely deprived children among whom I grew up feel deprivation or insecurity either. Thinking about what I remember from that time gives me some sort of insight into what turned my career toward psychiatric epidemiology – the study of patterns of mental illness in time and place. As you will see, I made some mistakes on my career path, but something (was it the long walks with my father?) eventually nudged me back to a concern for children.

My parents were children during World War I. Although far from well off, they were upwardly mobile; they and their siblings were the first of their families to go to university. My father received a Master's degree in Education and taught at a teachers' training college. He was a sincere

Christian all his life, a Methodist in his parents' footsteps, and he became a lay preacher – a layperson accredited by the Methodist Church to lead worship and preach. All through his working life, he spent 40 weekends of the year traveling and preaching.

My mother spent her first 10 years in Glasgow, Scotland, and left for England determined never to return: She had suffered too much physical punishment (the 'taws' or leather strap) at school. She went on a scholarship to a distinguished girls' high school in London and received a college scholarship to University College, London, on condition that afterward she train as a teacher. She must have been one of the worst teachers of her cohort: She was much too lively minded and distractible for classroom teaching. She was not at all religious, though highly moral and argumentative, especially on ethical topics. Both of my parents were left-wingers from the moment they began to take an interest in politics and remained firm Labour Party supporters all their lives.

My parents met in 1931 and became engaged a year later, but they could not get married until my father got a job that could support them both (in those days, married women did not hold paying jobs). My mother took the opportunity, however, to abandon teaching and start training to be a nurse, which she greatly enjoyed. In 1936 my father became the governor of a residential care home for children, or what was in those days called an 'orphanage', and my parents could then marry; in those days his job was without question taken to involve her full participation.

2.2   The National Children's Home and Orphanage

In 1869 the Rev. Dr. Thomas Bowman Stephenson founded a home for orphan boys (the Boy's Home), which grew rapidly, becoming the *National Children's Home and Orphanage* (now *Action for Children*), with over 4,000 boys and girls housed in some 40 homes around the United Kingdom. The Princess Alice Orphanage, where I grew up just outside Birmingham, was built between 1882 and 1906 to accommodate up to 300 children, originally orphan boys, but later both sexes as well as children who had been abandoned or for various reasons did not have a stable home. It consisted of several small group homes built around a green, with a school, farm, and chapel, and later a hospital, community hall, swimming bath, and workshops. Groups of 10 or 12 children were cared for by two 'Sisters' ordained by the Methodist Church. Each group, of both sexes and mixed in age, was referred to as a 'family'.

The National Children's Home also supported several homes for children with special needs: babies, children with tuberculosis, and children with a range of physical and mental handicaps. As approaches to caring for these children advanced, they were more and more integrated into regular families. The same was true of the 'orphans'; over the years the National Children's Home devoted itself increasingly to supporting children in their own homes where possible, and to fostering and adoption. It still runs some group homes, but on a much smaller scale than it did in the 1930s.

2.3   Approved Schools

Several of the Children's Homes later became 'Approved Schools' for delinquent boys and girls. The first were founded in 1857 to solve problems of juvenile vagrancy. The Approved School Rules of 1933 allowed magistrates to remand disorderly children to residential institutions in the United Kingdom, usually for committing offences but sometimes because they were deemed to be beyond parental control. Most Approved Schools were run by voluntary bodies and cared for remanded children with an emphasis on preventing crime. The National Children's Home ran several Approved Schools at various times, and, although Princess Alice Orphanage – where I lived – was not one, my father later became responsible for several aspects of them, and I became familiar with them through him.

2.4   The War

My parents had three children before and during the early war years: I was born in February 1939, my middle sister in September 1941, and my youngest sister in October 1942. (They also took on a fourth daughter, in 1952; a half-Indian orphan who lived with us until she married. She was very bright, and a terrific actress in our family dramas, but quite a handful.)

Well before September 1939, it was clear that another war was coming. My father, too old for front-line fighting, enlisted in the Air Force before war was declared and was drafted into security and intelligence work. He had fascinating stories about inspecting troops of Home Guards armed only with pitchforks and first aid posts with only one set of equipment, which the staff hurried from tent to tent while he and his colleagues chatted between inspections.

Early in 1942 he was sent to South Africa, with the job of helping to prevent spying by the South African pro-Boer *'Afrikaner Broederbond'* – a secret Calvinist organization in South Africa dedicated to the advancement of Afrikaner interests and racial segregation – and the

Ossewabrandwag – the 'ox-wagon sentinels' – founded in 1938 with similar goals. Both were strongly pro-German. My knowledge of his activities during the war is based entirely on his (very discreet) letters and on conversations with him later in childhood, as he committed none of his experiences to writing. He told me that he needed to recruit observers, and the best source was from the Black South Africans, but because most of them, at that time, were not taught to read or write, he invented non-verbal 'intelligence tests' that identified the brightest minds – for example, picking out the King from a newspaper group photograph. These youths would report to him on rumors going around that might be linked to people passing information to Germany on allied shipping around the Cape or to planned shipments of industrial diamonds to Axis countries. It all sounded terribly exciting, and perhaps it was. One story involved a car chase up the whole of Africa that ended in Cairo, running the smuggler down with a sock full of industrial diamonds under his mattress. But, judging from his letters home, my father seemed to have had plenty of time for playing golf.

As for us, the children, the idea that Britain could or would lose the war never entered our minds. We would try to imagine what a banana looked like, or cornflakes, and became expert at identifying our own and enemy planes by the sound of their engines, but not for one moment did we think about invasion or a German victory.

Meanwhile, at home, my *mother* was worrying about what would happen if Germany did invade. The Children's Home where we lived was built just off the main road from Coventry to Birmingham, both major armaments producers and bombing targets, and in later years my mother described standing beside the road trying to decide what she would do if German tanks came rolling up it, as seemed more than likely in 1940 and 1941. She was clear that her job was to protect the children in the orphanage at all costs, despite ugly rumors about what was happening to orphans in Germany. Fortunately, the invasion never happened, and she never had to decide, although we endured months and years of heavy bombers using the road at full moon to guide planes on their bombing route between the two cities; the sound of a heavy twin-engine plane still gives me goosebumps. A couple of bombs landed unnervingly close but only killed the milkman's horse. Meanwhile the children ran a brisk black market in bits of shrapnel.

2.5   Orphanage Life

Although my sisters and I lived with our mother in our own home, we spent most of our time playing with the other children in the orphanage, attending the same kindergarten and primary school, and often sharing their meals. Princess Alice Orphanage was originally set up with a grant from a wealthy businessman 'for the destitute children of Christian parents'. It soon widened its remit to included abused and neglected children of both sexes, as well as children of unmarried mothers and broken and dysfunctional families, and during the war to victims of bombing and evacuation. Most children were White, but as the **London docks** were increasingly bombed, we received more children of color, including a family who lived in our house for several months. This must have been a trial to them, as my younger sister, missing her daddy, used to slip into their bedroom in the morning, pull off the bedclothes, and shout 'There he is! There's the daddy!'

We shared the other orphanage children's beliefs ('The Germans eat little children' or 'Those men [the home guard with blackened faces exercising in the grove in front of our house] are really Germans') and folk stories ('If you curl up in bed you will wake up crippled'), as well as a healthy respect for the housemothers, who would rap our elbows with a wooden spoon if we put them on the table during meals. This treatment was applied impartially to me and my sisters if we were eating with one of the families. I do not remember any particularly badly behaved boys or girls, but then I was perhaps too young to have noticed them. On the contrary, my sisters and I were looked after affectionately by 'the girls', as we referred to them collectively, especially by the older girls who often missed their own families. We saw less of the boys, but I don't remember anyone bullying us, and one or two of the boys became close friends.

My mother meanwhile kept up people's spirits by organizing concerts and plays. It was one of the trials of my mother's life that she was expected to take on a couple of 16-year-old girls to 'train' to become domestic servants. Since she had grown up without servants, she had only the haziest idea of how to do this and tended to leave too much to their initiative. I can remember one girl's habit of bursting into the living room when my mother had guests and saying, 'Those people aren't staying to tea, are they?'

2.6   Rationing

Over two-thirds of Britain's food was imported at the outbreak of war, but the government, prepared by the previous war, had already printed ration books for everyone: different colors for children, pregnant women, and people on special diets. By January 1940 bacon, butter, and sugar were rationed. Meat, tea, jam, biscuits, breakfast cereals, cheese, eggs, lard, milk, and canned and dried fruit were rationed soon after, as well as clothing, gas, and even furniture. Almost all foods apart from vegetables and bread were rationed by August 1942, and some forms of rationing continued until July 1954. In a psychologically brilliant move to confer an illusion of control, some items were distributed on 'points'; for your points you could choose between, say, a can of fruit and a bar of chocolate.

Rationing was hard for single people and families, but we were protected from the most severe limitations because the Children's Home had its own farm, which provided milk, butter, eggs, vegetables, and some meat. Also, kind people frequently brought gifts or shared food parcels from abroad. Clothes, too, were less of a problem for us because the tradition of handing-down was well developed in the Children's Home. Then once the American troops arrived they adopted the Children's Home and used to sweep us off in their terrifying backless trucks for food, games, and movies at their camp, returning us emotionally exhausted, each with a sock full of sweets (we kept the sweets, but the socks were collared and redistributed by the Governor).

2.7   Delinquency

Delinquent behavior was probably common, but I have to say I don't remember it. There certainly was bullying, as one boy records in his memoirs:

It was quite easy for an older member of the group to make you cry. Sister was not present for every minute of the day. This gave plenty of opportunity for older members of the family to pick their moment if they decided to have some fun. It need not always be physical; words could be equally harmful and threats about what could be done to me were enough to make me cry.

One bit of bullying I do remember was inflicted by girls: one day in the woods, I came upon two of them, offended by a young boy's imperfect bladder control, trying to screw a lemonade bottle top onto his penis.

2.8   Punishment

The climate of discipline and punishment nowadays is very different from what it was when my father was responsible for Princess Alice Orphanage. Children could be, and were, hit with a wooden spoon or slipper by a Sister, or sent to the Governor for more severe physical punishment with a cane. However, evidence from a punishment book of the 1960s records rather modest degrees of physical punishment: one stroke was the norm.

My first personal experience of physical punishment occurred when I was five, and had just started school. I did not go out at break, as we were supposed to, and was smacked on my hand with a ruler. It certainly taught me an important lesson: never, ever, get found out.

The Sisters tended to be firm, but alongside the wooden spoon was a lot of common sense. The following is from an anonymous Sister who worked in one of the Approved Schools for delinquent boys:

Boys come to us from all kinds of homes, in fact, some of them have had no homes at all, and no training other than that they have got in the streets, while others have had the advantage of Christian training at home, but with one and all, the first thing is to try and gain their affections. Let a boy once feel that you care for him, that you are sorry when he is naughty and has to be punished, and on the other hand how pleased you are to see him try to do right. It is not every woman who is fitted for the work of training boys. A woman, really to get on well with boys, must be firm, though not over strict, tender, patient, conscientious, faithful in the discharge of her own duties, have a good amount of self-control and be a good disciplinarian. In the training of boys, you should keep before you what their previous surroundings have been, and at first be as lenient as possible that they may not find it irksome to try to do right. Don't show up every small fault before the other boys, but in a quiet way show him when he is alone how a thing should be done; for to be laughed at by the other boys for doing a thing awkwardly will make it very hard for some boys to do it well. Some natures feel far more keenly being exposed before the other boys than they would any severe punishment ...

Of course, housework does not come natural to boys, but with patience and care they can be taught to do it to equal any girl. Give a boy a room to scrub on his first entering the Home, he knows nothing about it, and probably has never seen a room scrubbed; to teach him you must be sure you understand how to do it yourself, and then take the brush and scrub a piece, you will do more in that way than by talking for an hour. In the same way with polishing a grate, do a part of it yourself while he stands by, and let him see the result. A sister in the Children's Home should not mind putting her hand to anything the children have to do.

2.9   Postwar Years

In 1946 my father came home from Africa, and we moved to London, where he became part of the administrative group running the Children's Homes, with special responsibility for education and staff training. I no longer lived in day-to-day contact with the children, but we frequently had them staying with us. My father's assumption that my mother was part of the team, and would cooperate unquestioningly with his plans, was borne out. We used to get the ones who were going on to university or medical school for a bit of middle-class polishing. My sisters and I were so merciless to these poor nervous youths that we probably put back their development by several years.

Soon after the war, the Children's Home sent a group of staff to rescue homeless children from the streets of Germany and from displaced persons' camps in Denmark. They brought back about 100 boys, of whom two were lodged temporarily with my family. This was the first time I had seen truly wild children. Manni and Jonni fought constantly over everything – food, toys, clothes – until anyone tried to separate them. Then they would cling to each other, bare their teeth, and attack. It was my first experience of how extreme circumstances can bring out the raw elements of survival in children.

In fact, the Children's Home had some problems with these children at first. When put in groups so that they could speak German to each other, the boys ganged up in almost militaristic formation and would speak to no one else. Separated, they became passionately 'English' and refused to speak to the German-speaking adults that the Children's Home brought in to encourage them to remember their language and culture. Interestingly, the story is that when they grew up most of them returned to Germany and forged impressive business careers.

The period from 1946 to 1950 was a tough one for Britain – tougher in many ways for the general public than the wartime period had been. Rationing got fiercer, and there was a shortage of the most basic materials for clothing or fixing one's house. At the height of the coal shortages during the icy winter of 1946–1947, trains delivering coal were frozen onto the railway lines. My mother and all my sisters were in bed with flu, and my father and I had to wheel the family perambulator down to the train station to get it filled with coal to keep us from freezing.

Education was another problem, as bombing had left many areas of London seriously bereft of schools as well as homes. Many children were moved from the decimated dockland areas in a program we all knew as 'slum clearance' and were crammed into suburban neighborhoods like the one I lived in. The only school willing to take my sisters and me had 45 children in a class. Life in the playground was rough, and at first I was mocked by the bigger kids for my 'posh' accent. But I survived and made friends, although looking back I am not sure how I managed it. For my last two years I was fortunate to move into the class of an absolutely outstanding teacher, Miss B., a tough little Anglo-Catholic lady of a certain age. Miss B. had no difficulty at all keeping potentially trouble-some boys under control; she managed a class of obstreperous kids using collective methods. We were divided into groups that won and lost points as a group for good and bad behavior, so that there was terrific pressure from your team to behave well and work hard. For a reward, Miss B. would read to us at the end of the day, choosing books that appealed to boys as well as girls. She introduced us to authors like H. Rider

Haggard (*King Solomon's Mines*) and Anthony Hope (*The Prisoner of Zenda*), as well as Louisa May Alcott *(Little Women)*. She produced plays with us and took me to my first London Shakespeare production (*Hamlet*). She used to tease anxious student teachers who came into her classroom to practice teaching. For example, she would draw cartoons on the blackboard while the poor teacher was facing the class, or have us pass an alarm clock under our desks around the classroom. No, troublesome little boys didn't bother Miss B.

2.10   Meritocracy

The post-war years saw the flowering of the meritocratic system propounded by William Beveridge, R. A. Butler, and others as a solution to the class-ridden and financially insecure structure of prewar British society. William Beveridge, an economist, pushed through Parliament a package of reforms that still undergirds the 'Welfare State': the Family Allowances Act (1945), the National Insurance (Industrial Injuries) Acts of 1946 and 1948, the National Insurance Acts of 1946 and 1949, the National Health Service Act (1946), the Pensions (Increase) Act (1947), and the Rent Control Act of 1949. In 1941 Butler became president of the board of education in Winston Churchill's wartime coalition and oversaw the Education Act that introduced universal free secondary education for the first time in the United Kingdom. This was critical to my future, as my parents had high expectations but a very low income.

Bypassing the local state grammar schools, they entered me for a competitive examination to a 'direct grant' grammar school, a type of selective secondary school in England and Wales that existed between 1945 and 1976, with fees paid by a combination of the Local Education Authority and private pupils. A scholarship to one of these, which I won in 1951, paid for my secondary education. Local Education Authority support saw me through university as well, and later also paid for a second undergraduate degree and a PhD, so that my education cost me nothing. This made it possible for my parents to find 30 pounds a term (about 60 dollars) for me to have fun with. Although this degree of public responsibility for educational costs has been greatly curtailed in recent years, it has left a basic level of support that counts for a lot in equalizing opportunities. On the whole, social changes planned during the war continue to have effects that have lasted surprisingly well. Some, such as the National Health Service, have survived for over 60 years and continue to provide a safety net that affects everyone's life by removing some of the fear and uncertainty associated with accidents, illness, and old age.

2.11 College Education

I enjoyed my high school years and did well enough for my teachers to encourage me to take the entrance examination for Oxford. We were, I think, much more easily directed into lines of study and careers than are children these days. The state-run exams, Ordinary level (age 16) and Advanced level (age 18), governed our decisions, and we tended to go off to study what we did best in at school. In my case this was Classics (classical Greek and Latin), and when I went to Oxford in 1958 I obediently studied classical languages and later classical Arabic as well. This was all a serious mistake on my part, from which it took me several years to recover.

2.12 Marriage and Motherhood

I had become engaged in my first year at college, which saved me from much of the hassle of being a female at a university where males outnumbered females by 10 to 1. I got married 2 weeks after I graduated and became pregnant 2 weeks later. I had three babies in 4 years before we figured out how to make birth control work. So, the first few years of marriage were committed to bringing up children – in fact we adopted a fourth child, intermediate in age to the other three. Lack of nursery schools in England – they were all closed after the war ended – was a serious problem to mothers of young children at that time. Psychoanalysis was in full swing, and we were warned that handing our young children over to others for even an hour would ruin their lives. In revolt against this dogma we began what quickly became the Preschool Movement, with 100,000 kids enrolled around the country. I started a preschool group in a friend's basement and taught it for 3 years until my youngest started Primary School. This experience taught me that I wanted to learn more about both individual behavior and its social context, and social psychology seemed to fit. In fact, I was grateful to the vagaries of life for showing me that my real interest lay not with books but with people.

2.13 Social Psychology

I applied and was admitted to the social psychology department at the London School of Economics and Political Science (LSE). At the LSE I got to know Daniel Kahneman (Princeton University) and Amos Tversky (Stanford University), as well as Tom Cook from Northwestern University, while they were on sabbatical in my department. It was Tom who pointed out that the ideas I was struggling with for my dissertation had a name: decision analysis. *Prescriptive decision making* addresses how optimal decisions can be made by a fully rational person with full information, while *descriptive decision making* explains how people actually make decisions in the real world. This was a career changer for me. For the first time I realized that social psychology, hitherto in my mind a 'descriptive' study of what people *had done* in the past, could become a predictive study of what they *would do* in the future and was therefore, to use Karl Popper's term, falsifiable. It was the work of Kahneman and Tversky, together with that of Herb Simon from Pittsburgh, a later mentor, that showed experimentally and decisively that humans are on the whole poor and biased decision makers who tend to use very limited information to make choices (Simon, 1983).

I wrote a doctoral dissertation on how people collect and combine information (mistakenly in most cases) to make decisions, and the effect of current and past psychiatric disorders on their decisions. Later I used this approach to examine how psychiatrists and other professionals collect information about children when making diagnoses. Using tape-recorded case conference data, my colleagues and I found that specialists tend over and over to follow what Kahneman and Tversky called the confirmation bias, asking questions that elicit information confirming what they already believe, rather than testing the falsifiability of their beliefs (Tversky & Kahneman, 1974). This is an example of a fundamental attribution error or cognitive bias that leads us to overemphasize personality-based explanations for behaviors observed in others, while underemphasizing the role and power of situational influences on the same behavior. The tendency to attribute childhood deviancy to individual bad behavior is, I believe, one of the reasons why we have made relatively little progress in reducing delinquency. But I'll come to that later.

2.14   Becoming a Psychiatric Epidemiologist

In 1975 I moved with my husband and children to the United States. After postdoctoral training in psychiatric epidemiology in Pittsburgh, I took over running the psychiatric epidemiology training program there, got my first National Institutes of Health (NIH) grant, and published my first papers. I had already developed an interest in psychiatric disorders, and I attended all the lectures that I could.

In 1987 I moved to Duke University and eventually ran a program of research with a focus on the development of psychiatric disorders, including conduct disorder. Incidentally, I have benefited enormously from the meritocratic system of competitive grant funding in the United States. This has paid for nearly all my research over more than 30 years.

2.15   Great Smoky Mountains Study (GSMS)

The focus of my research until I retired in 2018 has been how psychiatric disorders develop across childhood and adulthood, with a special interest in how biological, social, and environmental factors affect the development of psychiatric disorders, including the various aspects of delinquency. I shall focus here on one study: the 25-year GSMS, which was first funded by NIMH and the National Institute on Drug Abuse (NIDA) in 1993.

The GSMS (named after the area in the Appalachian Mountains of North Carolina where it takes place) includes over 1,400 children aged 9, 11, or 13 when the study began. They were recruited by randomly selecting names from school registers in 11 mainly rural counties. Because we wanted to understand more about the American Indians in the area, these were oversampled and comprise a quarter of the sample. Each participant is interviewed at home; a parent is interviewed separately until the participant is 16. Over the years, some 12,000 interviews have been collected.

Of over 300 published papers only a small sample can be discussed here. We concentrate on the relationships among childhood and adult crime and delinquency, the effects of bullying and being bullied, and the impact of additional income on misbehavior.

2.16   Delinquency and Crime: Childhood to Adolescence

Between ages 9 and 13, 14.4% of children were positive in at least one interview for conduct disorder and/or oppositional/defiant disorder (Rowe, Maughan, Pickles, Costello, & Angold, 2002). In young adulthood (21–30) the majority of cases of antisocial personality disorder, including substance abuse disorder, had at least one psychiatric diagnosis in childhood or adolescence. Early conduct disorder predicted later antisocial personality disorder and/or substance use disorder, but early oppositional disorder, without conduct disorder, only predicted adult anxiety disorders.

2.17   Predictors of Delinquency and Crime in Adulthood

We examined the impact of childhood disorders on seriously negative adult outcomes by age 30, including severe psychiatric symptoms and harmful life events such as unemployment, incarceration, and suicidality (Copeland et al., 2015). Six out of 10 of those who met criteria for a common childhood psychiatric disorder reported an adverse outcome, compared with only about one in five individuals without any history of childhood psychiatric diagnoses. Participants with a childhood disorder had six times higher odds of at least one adverse adult outcome compared with those with no history of psychiatric problems and nine times higher odds of two or more such indicators. These associations persisted after statistically controlling for childhood psychosocial hardships and adult psychiatric problems. Risk, however, was not limited to those with a *DSM* diagnosis: Participants with sub-threshold psychiatric problems had three times higher odds of adult adverse outcomes and five times higher odds of two or more outcomes, and here, too, risk persisted after controlling for adult psychopathology. Of those who had died by age 30, the majority had a history of antisocial behaviors of one sort or another.

2.18   Findings Relevant to Bullying in Childhood and Adulthood

Another line of research has examined the short-term and long-term effects of bullying, a fairly common childhood behavior (Copeland, Wolke, Angold, & Costello, 2013). Over a third of participants were bullied in childhood, and more than a quarter reported being bullied at multiple assessments, showing that this is not a short-term problem for children. Although deviant in childhood, bullies, but not their victims, were at risk for antisocial personality disorder in adulthood, but not for other disorders, while their victims were at increased risk for a wide range of problems, including depression, anxiety, and suicidal behavior. These effects were maintained even after accounting for pre-existing psychiatric problems or family hardships. This strongly suggests that the effects of victimization by peers on long-term adverse psychiatric outcomes are not simply the result of other childhood factors.

2.19   The Impact of Universal Basic Income (UBI) on Crime and Delinquency

After the study had been running for 4 years, the Eastern Band of Cherokee Indians (EBCI), in a move that we had not anticipated when the study started, introduced what is nowadays called a UBI supplement. Using proceeds from a greatly expanded gambling casino, they have distributed a portion of the profits as a cash income supplement (the 'per-cap') to each individual member of the Tribe, irrespective of age, sex, employment status, or history of crime. Moneys for children are held in trust until they are 18 if they graduate from high school, otherwise until 21. The amount varies with the casino's profits, but has generally been around $4,000–$6,000 a year. The people living in the counties surrounding the Qualla Boundary, the home of the ECBI, of course, receive nothing. We have been able to compare results from before the casino opened to afterward, both cross-sectionally (American Indians vs. Whites) and longitudinally (pre- vs. post-UBI) (Costello et al., 2003).

2.20   Effects of UBI on Crime in Adolescence

Analyses for ages 16–21 showed that children from families that received casino payments were 22% less likely to have been arrested at ages 16–17 than their untreated counterparts. At ages 18–21, the additional household income had no direct effect on criminal arrests, possibly because direct parental control diminished after age 18 (Akee et al., 2018). Therefore, the diversion in criminal behavior and arrests appears to be directly related to the child's minor status. The reduction in these criminal arrests was restricted to male criminal activity; there was very little female criminal activity in general.

2.21   Effects of UBI on Drug Abuse and Adult Crime

At age 21 significantly fewer Indians than non-Indians had a psychiatric disorder (Akee, Copeland, Keeler, Angold, & Costello, 2010), particularly alcohol and cannabis abuse or dependence, or both. In the youngest age-cohort of Indian youth, who had the longest exposure to the family income, planned comparisons showed that fewer of the youngest Indian age-cohort had any psychiatric disorder than the Indian middle cohort or the youngest non-Indian cohort. At age 30 the youngest Indian cohort had less than half the number of psychiatric disorders as the youngest non-Indian cohort, especially anxiety and depression. They reported less substance abuse overall, and fewer legal problems. On the other hand, they were more likely to be dependent on cocaine and other illicit drugs, and drug offences were the main reason for incarceration.

Although the focus of the study was psychiatric disorders, data on education and crime was collected, and the study shows that, so far, the cohort with the longest exposure to the per-cap while living at home has still maintained lower rates of drug abuse as adults. They have also maintained higher levels of education as adults and committed fewer minor criminal offenses than the rest. This has been particularly marked for those whose families lived below the federal poverty line before the per-cap but rose above it once they began receiving the extra money. It is worth noting that, unlike some other income interventions, the income supplement has not been accompanied by any restrictions on how it is spent, or who receives it; for instance, those who have been convicted of a crime or incarcerated still continue to receive it.

This work attracted the attention of Congress, and the U.S. Committee on Indian Affairs (John Hoeven, Chair) asked me to testify on the impact of the income supplement on children's behavior.

2.22   Students and Colleagues

While in Pittsburgh I ran the psychiatric epidemiology program and got the grant renewed. Craig Edelbrock, PhD, now Dean and Professor at the University of Alabama, was a wonderful early mentor. Students and colleagues whom I particularly remember from those days are David Brent, MD, now Academic Chief of Child and Adolescent Psychiatry and Professor of Psychiatry, Pediatrics and Epidemiology, at the University of Pittsburgh School of Medicine; Mina Dulcan, MD, now Head of Child Psychiatry at Northwestern Memorial Hospital; and Susan Janiszewski, PhD, a gifted data analyst. Collectively we published several papers together (e.g., Costello & Edelbrock, 1985; Costello & Janiszewski, 1990; Dulcan et al., 1990).

At Duke, I have mentored many graduate students, postdocs, and MDs, several of whom have contributed to work on conduct disorder and delinquency. Chief among them is my colleague Bill Copeland, now a professor at the University of Vermont, who has worked with me on the GSMS and has several other publications on bad behavior, including important work on bullying (Copeland et al., 2013). Another group that has been very important is led by Randy Akee from Harvard and Emilia Simeonova from Johns Hopkins, economists who have expanded our work on UBI (Akee et al., 2010; Akee, Copeland, Costello, & Simeonova, 2018;). For more than a decade I ran a NIDA-funded genetics center with Lindon Eaves and colleagues to genotype the GSMS participants and explore gene–environment interactions (Aberg et al., 2013), and I still collaborate with them. Finally, among several overseas colleagues on delinquency, I cherish Barbara Maughan and Richard Rowe.

2.23   The Next Generation

I am retired and have passed the next generation on to others. I hope that one of their achievements will be to untangle the gene–environment question and figure out how to apply their findings to preventing conduct problems and delinquency.

2.24 Conclusions

I changed careers midstream and have never regretted it. However, the world I grew up in has changed drastically. Since the war years, in the world of childcare there has been an increasing emphasis on adoption, foster homes, and small group homes in regular houses rather than purpose-built 'Children's Homes'. Children tend to stay in residential care for much shorter periods, and they may move around quite often as different solutions are sought.

Although rates of serious juvenile crime have fallen to a new low, a recent review in the United Kingdom found that half of children in youth custody came from foster or residential care (Guardian, 2017). A very careful analysis of Swedish data (Lindquist & Santavirta, 2014) shows that the association between foster care placements and adult criminal behavior is roughly 25% higher than their never-placed counterparts among boys aged 13–18 at first placement. This is a striking contrast to the associations found for girls who were placed at ages 13–18, and for those of younger children, which were not significantly different from those of never-placed children. Including preplacement juvenile delinquency shrank the negative association but did not qualitatively change the results. Other countries (van Krieken, 1992) also report harmful effects on adult crime of out-of-home care, but their studies are less well controlled than the Swedish study. Lack of care for young adults leaving foster care has been blamed for much homelessness (Dworsky, Napolitano, & Courtney, 2013) and young adult crime (Yang, McCuish, & Corrado, 2017).

In general, out-of-home care seems to be deleterious, which makes me wonder why I noticed so little bad behavior as a small child. One reason may be that the children I met were quite young: In those days they mostly left school and got a job at 16 at the latest. Linked to this, children tended to arrive at a Children's Home quite young and to stay until they left home to take a job. This relative stability conflicts with the current belief in the importance of getting children back to their parents as soon as possible. Also, the children whom I mixed with were very closely supervised by the Sisters and other staff, and time was quite closely apportioned, so that there was relatively little opportunity to misbehave. Of course, 75 years is a long time ago, and I undoubtedly enjoy a very selective memory.

A second set of reasons harks back to my work on decision analysis. In the case conferences that we recorded, learning that the patient was a boy in his early teens nearly always led to the assumption that his was a case of conduct disorder. No one asked any 'disconfirming' questions, not even to rule out comorbidities. In a smaller earlier study that I did in Pittsburgh, where we compared children receiving treatment with a random population sample, there was a group of boys with *only* anxiety disorders, but not one of them was receiving any treatment, despite quite severe symptoms. This suggests to me that a treatment system that makes fewer assumptions and does more open-minded diagnostic work could serve children better. In epidemiologic thinking, the first stage in getting rid of a disease is to control it by whatever means available at the time, often by incarceration or hospitalization. The second stage is to develop treatments for the disease, and the third stage is to prevent it by medical or social interventions and to protect society by eliminating exposure. Psychiatric disease, especially delinquency, has lagged shockingly behind other disorders, and the urgent challenge for the future is to address the second and third stages.

This brief review of a lifetime's experience suggests that life in the orphanage protected me and many unfortunate children from some of the uncertainties and exposure to fear that we might otherwise have experienced, even during a world war, and gave us a safe and friendly place to grow up.

References

Aberg, K. A., Xie, L. Y., Nerella, S., Copeland, W. E., Costello, E. J., & van den Oord, E. J. C. G. (2013). High quality methylome-wide investigations through next-generation sequencing of DNA from a single archived dry blood spot. *Epigenetics*, *8*(5), 542–547.

Akee, R., Copeland, W. E., Costello, E. J., & Simeonova, E. (2018). How does household income affect child personality traits and behaviors? *American Economic Review*, *108*(3), 775–827.

Akee, R., Copeland, W. E., Keeler, G., Angold, A., & Costello, E. J. (2010). Parents' incomes and children's outcomes: A quasi-experiment using transfer payments from casino profits. *American Economic Journal: Applied Economics*, *2*(1), 86–115.

American Psychiatric Association. (1994). *Diagnostic and statistical manual of mental disorders* (4th ed.). Washington, DC: American Psychiatric Association.

Copeland, W. E., Brotman, M. A., & Costello, E. J. (2015). Normative irritability in youth: Developmental findings from the Great Smoky Mountains Study. *Journal of the American Academy of Child & Adolescent Psychiatry*, *54*(8), 635–642.

Copeland, W. E., Wolke, D., Angold, A., & Costello, E. J. (2013). Adult psychiatric outcomes of bullying and being bullied by peers in childhood and adolescence. *JAMA Psychiatry*, *70*(4), 419–426.

Costello, E. J., Burns, B. J., Costello, A. J., Edelbrock, C., Dulcan, M., & Brent, D. (1988). Service utilization and psychiatric diagnosis in pediatric primary care: The role of the gatekeeper. *Pediatrics, 82*(3), 435–441.

Costello, E. J., Compton, S. N., Keeler, G., & Angold, A. (2003). Relationships between poverty and psychopathology: A natural experiment. *Journal of the American Medical Association, 290*(15), 2023–2029.

Costello, E. J., & Edelbrock, C. S. (1985). Detection of psychiatric disorders in pediatric primary care: A preliminary report. *Journal of the American Academy of Child Psychiatry, 24*(6), 771–774.

Costello, E. J., & Janiszewski, S. (1990). Who gets treated? Factors associated with referral in children with psychiatric disorders. *Acta Psychiatrica Scandinavica, 81*(6), 523–529.

Costello, E. J., & Maughan, B. (2015). Annual research review: Optimal outcomes of child and adolescent mental illness. *Journal of Child Psychology and Psychiatry, 56*(3), 324–341.

Costello, E. J., Sung, M., Worthman, C., & Angold, A. (2007). Pubertal maturation and the development of alcohol use and abuse. *Drug and Alcohol Dependence, 88*, S50–S59.

Dulcan, M. K., Costello, E. J., Costello, A. J., Edelbrock, C. S., Brent, D., & Janiszewski, S. (1990). The pediatrician as gatekeeper to mental health care for children: Do parents' concerns open the gate? *Journal of the American Academy of Child & Adolescent Psychiatry, 29*(3), 453–458.

Dworsky, A., Napolitano, L., & Courtney, M. (2013). Homelessness during the transition from foster care to adulthood. *American Journal of Public Health, 103* (S2), S318–S323.

Guardian. (2017). Half of children in youth custody have been in care system. Retrieved from https://www.theguardian.com/society/2016/may/23/children-in-care-crime-custody-review-prison-reform-trust

Lindquist, M. J., & Santavirta, T. (2014). Does placing children in foster care increase their adult criminality? *Labour Economics, 31*, 72–83.

Rowe, R., Maughan, B., Pickles, A., Costello, E. J., & Angold, A. (2002). The relationship between DSM-IV oppositional defiant disorder and conduct disorder: Findings from the Great Smoky Mountains Study. *Journal of Child Psychology and Psychiatry, 43*(3), 365–373.

Rowe, R., Maughan, B., Worthman, C. M., Costello, E. J., & Angold, A. (2004). Testosterone, antisocial behavior, and social dominance in boys: Pubertal development and biosocial interaction. *Biological Psychiatry, 55*(5), 546–552.

Simon, H. A. (1983). *Reason in human affairs*. Stanford, CA: Stanford University Press.

Suleiman, A. B., & Dahl, R. E. (2017). Leveraging neuroscience to inform adolescent health: The need for an innovative transdisciplinary developmental science of adolescence. *Journal of Adolescent Health, 60*(3), 240–248.

Tversky, A., & Kahneman, D. (1974). Judgment under uncertainty: Heuristics and biases. *Science, 185*(4157), 1124–1131.

van Krieken, R. (1992). *Children and the State: Social Control and the Formation of Australian Child Welfare*. Sydney, Australia: Allen & Unwin.

Yang, J., McCuish, E. C., & Corrado, R. R. (2017). Foster care beyond placement: Offending outcomes in emerging adulthood. *Journal of Criminal Justice, 53*, 46–54.

3   From Rationing, Illness, and Stress to the Creation of a Major Longitudinal Birth Cohort

Jean Golding

Jean Golding was born in Hayle, England, September 20, 1939. She received her PhD in Human Genetics and Biometry from University College London in 1979. Her first faculty appointment (1972) was in Clinical Epidemiology at the University of Oxford, England. She received honorary degrees from the University of Bristol (2013) and University College London (2017). Among many prestigious awards and recognitions, she is a Fellow of the Academy of Medical Sciences (2002) and was awarded the Order of the British Empire by Queen Elizabeth II in 2012. The University of Bristol named their newly formed Institute of Data Science the Jean Golding Institute in 2018, and, during the celebration of the 70th anniversary of the UK's National Health Service, she was named one of seven 'Research Legends'.

Jean Golding is best known for having planned and directed the Avon Longitudinal Study of Parents and Children (ALSPAC), also known as 'Children of the 90s'. The overall aim of this longitudinal study, initiated with 14,500 pregnant women, was to determine the ways in which different aspects of the environment are associated with child health and development, and how these factors may be influenced by genetics (Golding, Pembrey, & Jones, 2001). It was intended, from its inception, that the children of the cohort would be followed into adulthood, with a design that incorporated assessing factors that led to criminality. The study has resulted in a highly detailed dataset concerning children born in the Avon area in 1991–1992, their parents, and, as time has gone on, their own children.

Jean Golding started planning longitudinal studies of birth cohorts in 1978, when the UK Department of Health created the National Perinatal Epidemiology Unit. She was asked to join, with the aim of designing a new British National Birth Cohort to follow on from those that had taken place in 1946, 1958, and 1970 – each of which had involved 1 week of births across the whole country. She had discovered her epidemiological abilities in 1966 when she joined a research group to analyze the data from the 1958 British National Perinatal Mortality Survey (BPMS).

In 1985 she was a member of a group tasked by the World Health Organisation (WHO) to develop plans for an international European birth cohort study. She became the director of this international study, which included ALSPAC, now used by researchers across the world to study numerous issues related to child development. As of 2019, over 2,000 peer-reviewed papers based on ALSPAC have been published on every aspect of children's development, from the prenatal period to adulthood.

The Avon Longitudinal Study of Parents and Children has been used to do numerous international comparisons. For example, a comparison of children's development in a high-income country (ALSPAC in Britain) was made with a low–middle-income country (Pelotas in Brazil). As expected, the prevalence of children's conduct problems, hyperactivity, and violent crime were more prevalent in Brazil than in Britain, but Britain had more nonviolent crimes. Interestingly, conduct problems and hyperactivity predicted nonviolent and violent crime similarly in both countries. Two other results from these birth cohorts are important for orienting preventive interventions. The associations between behavior problems during childhood and criminality were partly explained by perinatal health factors and childhood family environments. Furthermore, and importantly, sex differences in prevalence rates were larger where behaviors were less common: larger for conduct problems, hyperactivity, and violent crime in Britain, and larger for nonviolent crime in Brazil. Thus, conduct problems and hyperactivity were similar precursors of crime and violence across very different living conditions.

One of the important decisions made by Golding and her colleague Marcus Pembrey was to take blood samples at birth to study genetic determinants. However, they could not have anticipated that 20 years later the blood samples would be used for another purpose than simply describing inherited genetic coding. The Avon Longitudinal Study of Parents and Children may now be the longitudinal child development study that has produced the largest number of epigenetic studies (DNA methylation) associated with behavior problems. For example, Cecil et al. (2014) published the first long-term prospective analysis indicating that maternal psychopathology assessed during pregnancy may have a long-term impact (birth to age 13 years) on their children's genetic expression of the oxytocin receptor, which is associated with higher callous–unemotional traits at 13 years of age, a behavior problem linked to violent behavior.

In 2006 Golding retired officially (65 being the standard retirement age at that time in the UK) from her position at the head of ALSPAC, but she continued as Editor-in-Chief of the journal *Paediatric and Perinatal Epidemiology*. In 2006 she was commissioned jointly by the National Institutes of Health (NIH) and the WHO to write a detailed description of how to mount a longitudinal birth cohort, which was published in 2009 and widely distributed by the WHO, with the aim of encouraging low- and middle-income countries as well as industrialized countries to carry out such studies (Golding, Birmingham, & Jones, 2009).

Golding has continued to carry out research on the ALSPAC resource long into 'retirement' and is the principal investigator on a number of funded grants. Currently she is concentrating on three major threads: (1) assessing the (possibly causal) associations of prenatal exposures such as paracetamol (acetaminophen), mercury, and diet with cognitive and behavioral outcomes of the developing child, particularly in regard to hyperactivity and conduct disorders (Golding et al., 2016; Hibbeln et al., 2007); (2) researching, with the psychologist Stephen Nowicki at Emory University, the personality characteristic 'locus of control' of ALSPAC parents and children, and how this characteristic appears to influence abilities and behaviors (Golding, Gregory, Ellis, Iles-Caven, & Nowicki, 2017; Nowicki, Iles-Caven, Gregory, Ellis, & Golding, 2017); (3) and studying, with Marcus Pembrey, various trans- and intergenerational nongenetic influences to determine whether exposures of grandparents and great-grandparents influence outcomes of their grandchildren and great-grandchildren, including behavior (see Golding, Northstone, Gregory, Miller, & Pembrey, 2014).

Over the years she has often been asked to advise on aspects of study design, including for the American National Children's Study and the European Union study on pesticides, which resulted in her suggestions for creating a new independent scientific institute particularly to consolidate information from cohort studies (which would include concentration on criminality, among other outcomes) to determine the safety of pesticide products (Golding, 2018).

3.1   The War Years

It was September 29, 1939, and there was a census in Britain. This was just 3 weeks after the start of World War II and my first experience of a survey – I was just 7 days old. As became the norm for me, I was not where I was expected to be at the time, as my mother and I were still in the small house run by a midwife for the birth of those babies who were not delivered at home. I had already become a statistical outlier, having been delivered by the breech (the normal rate for term deliveries is 3–4%). My propensity to be an outlier then became more extreme as I developed pyloric stenosis (prevalence of about five per 10,000 births). This disorder, which was often fatal at the time, is defined by a thickening of the pylorus muscle, which stops milk from leaving the stomach, and results in projectile vomiting. The failure of the milk to be absorbed results in dehydration and malnutrition. To state the obvious – I survived, but I think it was a close-run thing. The whole episode at the start of the war must have been exceedingly difficult for my parents.

My father was then aged 29, having been born in 1910. His own mother had died during his first year of life, at which point his two elder siblings went to live with their grandmother. This he did not know until his early 20s; he had been brought up by his stepmother as though she were his biological mother. His father came from a long line of builders' laborers, who gradually set up their own building business in Hayle in the County of Cornwall (a county with a dramatic wild coast and beautiful beaches). Under my paternal grandfather's direction, this organization became increasingly successful – until the point where, unfortunately, he was declared bankrupt. He appears to have then built up a new business as a haberdasher (and is reported to have been made bankrupt again); he died shortly thereafter when my father was aged 13. This left his step-mother and a younger half-brother with no source of support (there is no evidence that his older siblings helped, as both had married by this time), so my father left school as soon as he was 14 (the law was such in the UK at the time that children had to stay in full-time education until that age) and took a clerical job. This was based in the small dockyard at Hayle, where petroleum (gas) was imported and distributed around the county.

My mother's background was quite different. She was Canadian, born to British parents. Her father had gone to Canada at the age of 17, attended agricultural college there, and, after a period of apprenticeship, took advantage of the advertisements of 'free' land. (Under this Canadian government policy 160 acres cost only $10, but the homesteader had to build a house, often of log or sod, and cultivate a specified area within 3 years). He carved out two square miles of land, which he developed into a wheat farm in the Province of Saskatchewan. When the farm was prospering he bought and developed a farm on Vancouver Island on the west coast of the country (wheat farming was such that he traveled to the prairies for planting and the harvest, but left a manager there for the rest of the year). Alas, they had a run of poor harvests in the early 1930s, and the family (parents and six children) moved back to the prairies and sold the farm on the Island. My mother was then in her teens and really missed the coast and beaches on which she had spent many happy years. She had many contacts in Britain, and in 1937 she visited her mother's relatives in Hayle, where she met my father. She accepted his proposal of marriage after she had gone back to Canada. She returned to Britain, and they married in November 1938. A rough calculation indicates that I must have been conceived almost immediately.

The family continued to be based in Hayle for the duration of the war. This town, with a population of about 4,000 in the 1930s, had, in the past, been known for its industry – with an iron foundry at the western end and a copper smelter at the eastern end. In spite of Hayle's being relatively small, there was considerable rivalry (and some bitterness) between the two ends of the town: The population living in the eastern end (known as Copperhouse) where my father was brought up were largely Wesleyan Methodist, with strict codes of abstinence in regard to alcohol and frivolity. Sundays were strictly observed with sober behavior, such as reading or going for a walk – definitely not having fun or playing games. My father had been brought up attending Chapel for three services each Sunday. The Methodist population believed that those living at the foundry end of the town (where my mother's relatives lived) were rather stuck-up – whether or not that was true, they tended to belong to the Church of England and to have a more liberal attitude toward alcohol, and their children were allowed to play games on a Sunday. These differences, relatively small to us now, did result in deep social antagonisms, rivalries between the two industries, and even occasional fights.

In retrospect, I suspect my mother's pregnancy must have been accompanied by increasing stress, as the threat from Hitler's Germany and talk of war increased. My mother was isolated from her close family, who were all in Canada. However, this was an era when letter writing was at its peak, and my mother received letters from her mother at frequent intervals (letters I still possess). My father was in what was referred to as a reserved occupation – one deemed to be of national importance to the running of the country. As well as teachers and doctors, these occupations included builders, coal mining, and dockyard work. My father was still a clerk based in the small port of Hayle, where small (by today's standards) tankers brought in petroleum (gas) and unloaded it into huge tanks. From there it was distributed around the county. During the war my father had to spend every alternate night guarding and sleeping beside these tanks, with the knowledge that a direct hit would be fatal. I never found out whether the fact that he did not join the armed forces resulted in prejudice from the rest of the small town in which we lived, but I imagine this was not unlikely.

There were other sources of stress. Throughout his fatherhood he was always very careful with money, which was illustrated, for example, when my parents cut short their honeymoon in London as they had run out of money! Although it was deemed okay to have a mortgage to buy a house, borrowing money for any other purpose was frowned upon (credit cards had not been invented). More importantly, as far as I was concerned, was his reluctance to give his children any pocket money. I don't think this tightness with money had a major effect on my mother, as her parents had never had much money themselves. I grew up with the understanding that money was not very important, provided one didn't get into debt.

Added stress for my mother during the war concerned three of her younger brothers (the fourth was too young to serve) – each of whom joined the Canadian Air Force as soon as they could; they spent some of their service based in, and flying sorties from, Britain; my mother acted as a conduit between these young men and her parents in Canada. They would spend leave with us in Cornwall whenever they could. Alas, the elder of these, a spitfire pilot, crashed and was killed in 1942; then the next oldest was shot down and captured by the Italians in North Africa, and transferred to prison in Italy; when the Italians capitulated, he escaped before the Germans took over the prison camp and hid in the mountains before eventually being captured by the Germans. As far as the family was concerned he was missing presumed dead, and was not heard of until after the end of the war (he had had a very traumatic time, which he did not talk about until long afterward). The third brother Peter crashed in Burma in 1945.

By the time my mother was expecting the first of my two brothers in 1942, I added to the general trauma when I was hit with two separate bouts of extra-pulmonary TB, each of which involved hospitalization of several months, the first at age 2 and the second at 3. Hospitalized children at that time were looked after in adult wards; mothers were only allowed to visit once a week at most (because it upset the children!). Thus, although I was not exposed to traditional measures of violence, in retrospect I was traumatized and was very unsure of myself as a young child. Long afterward (even into my 20s) I could see the aftereffects, as I would break out in a cold sweat if I came across the smell of the disinfectant used on the ward or the smell of a particular meal of minced meat specifically given to young children during their hospital stays.

Having noted these stressors, many of which had long-term effects on me, I cannot claim that the war itself had an impact on my psyche. I was vaguely aware of what was going on in the rest of Britain and Europe, but my only experiences that I can remember were of heavy Allied bombers flying over, long lines of battleships making their way across the horizon far out at sea (I think heading toward the D-Day landings), and a glow in the night sky, which I remember being told was the city of Plymouth burning (however, this seems very unlikely as I would have only been 18 months old and Plymouth was 56 miles away; it may have been the town of Penzance, which was only eight miles away and was bombed by the Luftwaffe on several occasions when I was about three).

For those who were not actively fighting, the war resulted in a particular camaraderie resulting in mutual help and concern. One example of this in the small town where we lived, and where everyone knew one another, concerned a telegram that the postman was supposed to deliver to my mother – he knew that this contained news of the death of one of her brothers. Instead of delivering it directly to her, he went to my father's workplace and gave him the telegram to take home and break the news to my mother and support her.

One of the major consequences of the outbreak of war concerned the need for food rationing. The consequence was that food was very restricted – for example, beginning in 1940, an adult was allowed one egg per week, 2 oz of cheese, but 8 oz of sugar. The restriction on eggs and meat lasted until the mid-1950s. However, there was no restriction on fish: This was probably because fish was very difficult to get, since the fishermen and many of their boats had been commandeered for other purposes. In larger towns and cities, fish and chip shops were allowed to flourish – but these were not available in Hayle. For vegetables, the members of the population who had gardens were encouraged to dig up lawns and flower beds and grow as many vegetables as possible. My parents did so with both the garden of their bungalow and that of my father's widowed sister. The overwhelming attitude to shortages in Britain during the war and after was one of stoicism. There were very few toys on sale, but we were quite happy using what was available – whether this was building towers with saucepans, cutting newspapers into shapes, or making patterns with sand.

3.2   The Postwar Years

It was only after the war was over that we ever saw such apparent luxuries as a banana or an orange. Nevertheless, food rationing remained in operation until September 1953 (for butter, bacon, and sugar) and July 1954 (for meat, jam, tea, biscuits, eggs, cheese, breakfast cereals, lard, milk, and canned and dried fruit). Clothes rationing had been initiated in 1941 (and lasted until 1949) so that there would be enough material to make uniforms for the armed forces as well as those in protected occupations, including miners, nurses, factory workers, and land girls (the young women who worked on the farms while the male farm workers were away). This lack of ability to go and buy clothes or material to make them was irritating and resulted in many alterations and reworkings of clothes that had been used for some time – or by others. There were two consequences – (1) I learnt skills in sewing and dressmaking; and (2) my mother received clothes parcels from her sister in Canada with clothes that her nieces, who were two to three years older than me, had outgrown. We had been brought up through the war with the slogan 'Make do and mend'. This was something that I have found hard to disregard – often to the irritation of my staff and children!

In 1950, as the result of a good wheat harvest the previous year, my maternal grandparents invited us to go and visit them in Canada for the summer, and importantly, paid for the tickets. My father had to stay behind and work, but, with my mother and my two younger brothers, we took a liner from Liverpool to Montreal. I remember our amazement as we came across a mixture of interesting and tasty foods and had our first ice creams made with real cream. Later in the holiday I recall watching the pained face of my mother as she saw her sister make an angel cake – this involved taking the whites of 12 eggs, but the horrifying thing for her was that the yolks were all thrown away (in Britain eggs were still rationed!).

When I was seven my father's job took the family to the city of Plymouth. This city had suffered badly during the war – the two main shopping centers and nearly every civic building had been destroyed, along with 26 schools, eight cinemas, and 41 churches. In total, 3,754 houses were destroyed, with a further 18,398 seriously damaged. I recall this as being a happy time, although by today's standards we would be classified as poor – we did not have a car or a television, and holidays were spent with relatives in Hayle. There were two major ways in which we spent our free time – (1) we were avid readers and would borrow three or four books a week from the local public library; and (2) we spent free time outdoors, playing in the fields that bordered our house, or going on long walks in the local countryside. These would be full of encouragement from my mother to spot and name different birds, butterflies, and wildflowers. I attended the local primary school; when I was age 11 the English education system divided children according to a measure of their academic abilities (known as 'the 11-plus'), based roughly on an IQ test, a system that still operates in Plymouth. This selected me to attend one of the academically focused grammar schools in Plymouth – my father decided which one on the basis of the quality of their sports reputation, as it was the one area in which he felt he was knowledgeable, having played rugby and cricket for Cornwall. Thus, I entered a single-sex secondary school that included girls from all except the upper social echelons, and made friends with many from different walks of life.

I really enjoyed this school, but after 3 years, when I was 13, my father's job took him further north, to the city of Chester. Again, my father examined the sports reputations of the different secondary schools – this time it was the girls' school that was predominantly populated by the upper social echelons that satisfied his criteria! This I found an incredibly difficult transition – my perception was that these girls had grown up with totally different attitudes and behaviors than the down-to-earth approaches that I had found in Plymouth. In retrospect I found this very stressful – and within a month this was illustrated with a severe headache and high temperature, heralding the development of polio and, once again, several months in hospital while I tried to learn how to walk with a very weak left leg. Eventually after 3 months in hospital and much physiotherapy I started walking again (first with a full-length leg calliper and later with a pronounced limp but no calliper). I returned to school after a year and gradually caught up with most of the subjects. I passed the appropriate national exams at age 15–16. At this stage in England, one entered the sixth form and the number of subjects was restricted to three or four. I took chemistry, physics, and pure and applied mathematics, in spite of the fact that my real passion was zoology. This decision had been made on the basis that there would be too much fieldwork and laboratory work for my rather frail state (nowadays with so many clever devices available this would not have been so much of an issue).

This series of events shaped my background and interests. I was an observer. The various hospital admissions had been in public hospitals, where I was surrounded by people from all walks of life (nurses, cleaners, and doctors from around the world, as well as other patients) and with different beliefs and attitudes. I realize now that this enabled me to have an understanding of the various attitudes and habits of all members of the population whom I later studied in the longitudinal survey that I designed; in particular it enabled me to develop questionnaires to investigate the ways in which these differences may have impacted the health and development of the study children. But this was all in the future and not part of my aims at that time.

During my adolescent years, in my spare time, I would read books on the psychological behaviors of birds and animals, in particular those by Niko Tinbergen and Conrad Lorenz. This introduced me to the world of detailed observational sciences, including psychology. My other major interest was chemistry, which I also found fascinating. However, because of my disability I was advised that taking such scientific subjects at university would be too physically taxing, and I was persuaded to aim to read mathematics. Although none of my first- or second-degree relatives had been to university, I had never doubted that that was what I should do – and, in spite of my headmistress's prediction that there was no chance that I would get into a good university, I managed to be offered a place at Oxford (which was, and is, one of the most prestigious universities in the UK). There was general mystification as to how I had pulled this off – but many years later I learnt of the probable explanation. As part of the system for choice of students, a series of interviews was arranged. One of these was with Lady Ogilvie, the head of St Anne's College in Oxford. I didn't know this at the time, but she had a reputation for picking students whom others would not think of admitting – we were known by the rest of the College staff as Lady O's 'funnies'. However, I had got there, I really had the most marvelous 3 years. One of the advantages of the Oxford college system is that there was a complete mixing of students from all disciplines – I spent most of my time with undergraduates reading for arts rather than science degrees, including with my future first husband, Alan Fedrick, who was studying modern languages and specializing in medieval French – not exactly a valuable background for the career I ended with but valuable in expanding my horizons. At that stage most young men were expected to spend 2 years in the armed forces after leaving school and, when relevant, before starting at university. Women had no such stipulation – consequently the male undergraduates were about two years older than the female ones. At Oxford they also outnumbered us about 10 to one, especially in mathematics and the sciences.

Oxford University, like Cambridge University at that time, structured its learning largely around self-instruction and exploration of concepts. Lectures were optional, but hour-long tutorials on a one-on-one or one-on-two basis were mandatory and considered the most valuable feature. The honors mathematics degree that I was enrolled in was a 3-year course encompassing many different features of mathematics, some of which were optional. Statistics was one of the optional subjects; I went to the first lecture, which was very clearly delivered – enough to persuade me it was not for me. When the lecturer stated that an equation was approximately equal to another, I rejected the concept. Little did I know that I would spend my academic life working with statistics! At this point I considered myself a 'pure' mathematician.

The other point at which I made a rather stupid decision concerned the possibility of changing courses. There was a rather attractive course known as PPP (psychology, philosophy, and physiology). I was really tempted to change to this (and that would have been really useful) – but I did not do so for one reason: I was sure that I was not able to write essays in a format that would be good enough for the tutorial system whereby one had to write an essay prior to the tutorial and then read it to the tutor, who would discuss it with you critically. I therefore stuck to the maths course, but I spent much spare time going to talks on various topics. Oxford attracted many famous intellects, and I remember presentations from Father Trevor Huddleston on his struggle against apartheid in South Africa, W. H. Auden on his poetry, and J. R. R. Tolkien on linguistics, to name but a few. At the beginning of the second year Alan and I realized that if we were to get useful jobs in the future, we would have to show that we had been successfully involved in extracurricular activities at Oxford. By then it was too late to join a society and work one's way up to a prominent position, so we decided to start our own society. We looked at all the many thriving societies and discovered that there was no astronomical society. I knew very little about the subject, Alan knew slightly more – but we got a group of interested students together and created a program with, on the one hand, famous astronomers coming to speak to us and, on the other hand, experts in various art fields, including the illustration of the heavens by the grand masters and the depiction of astronomy in literature. Although I don't think the fact that we did this ever meant that we obtained any advantage in the job market, the whole experience of organizing a society and meeting various famous luminaries gave me a good background for the future when I would need to talk to and persuade many eminent scientists and politicians in different fields of the value of longitudinal studies.

All of this was immensely enjoyable. I had been doing the minimum amount of work (an Oxford maths degree just required one to pass two sets of exams – at the end of the first year and the end of the third year). Thus, the second year was totally free of tests, apart from having to produce worked examples (not essays) for the tutorials. It was as the third year progressed that the pressure of impending exams became apparent – and at this point I developed glandular fever and was hospitalized for a week and then sent home for bed rest until the major fatigue diminished somewhat. This took about three months; by this time, it had been agreed that I should give in and retake the last year of the course. I made another stupid decision – I was beginning to feel better and thought I should try to go back. This I did for a couple of weeks, but I really was not well – very fatigued and still feverish. I therefore went to my general practitioner in Oxford, who must have thought I was just trying to get out of the exams – he told me I needed 'moral fiber' and that he would not sign the appropriate certificate. The exams were a nightmare, as I went in and out of a fever. Amazingly I did pass, but only just! Thus, I obtained a BA, which, according to the Oxford University system, automatically became an MA a few years later.

It was 1961 and there was then the question as to what to do with my life. There was a careers advisory service in Oxford, but almost all young women were told that there were just two possibilities – teaching in a secondary school or taking a typing course and becoming a secretary. I opted for teaching. In a very short period of time I had taught mathematics at a girls' grammar school for a year, married, had two children in quick succession, and divorced my husband. It was the 1960s – I was then in London and with two small children to support. I obtained a variety of tasks, paid by the hour, that I could undertake at home – when by chance I answered an advertisement from a research group headed by Drs. Eva Alberman and Neville Butler, pediatricians with an expertise in epidemiology. They were analyzing data from the 1958 British Perinatal Mortality Survey (BPMS) and needed someone numerate to assist. This was a national survey that was designed to investigate reasons for the relatively static perinatal mortality rate in Britain. It involved a detailed study of over 7,000 stillbirths and neonatal deaths occurring in a 3-month period (March–May 1958), with a control sample of all births in Britain in 1 week of March 1958 (n ~ 17,000).

This was the chance turning point to what became my career. I became fascinated by the associations with the causes of mortality that were unfolding. I wanted to find out why such differences existed in health and disease, not just across different areas of Britain, but between different social groups and environments. Eva was a wonderful teacher. She explained patiently all the various intricacies of physiology and medicine. I studied congenital malformations and learnt about embryology and teratology; I studied the non-malformed deaths and learnt about fetal growth, nutrition, and physiology; I learnt about the intricacies of obstetrics and neonatology and how various practices might protect the fetus and newborn (at this stage the 1 week of births was a control sample and not yet of interest in its own right). I spent 2 years with the group – the aim of which was to put together a series of chapters for the book *Perinatal Problems*.

By now, I was absolutely hooked on the epidemiological method and the intriguing associations it could uncover. In spite of having no formal education in the area, I obtained a 3-year fellowship and registered for a PhD at University College London in the Department of Human Genetics and Biometry under the gentle direction of the biomathematician Professor C. A. B. Smith. Here I had the advantage of learning the statistical techniques required to analyze problems of genetic linkage. My fellowship was to study the etiology of neural tube defects, particularly of the malformation anencephalus. This invariably lethal condition had an intriguing geographical and social pattern, being more likely to be found in the Celtic fringes of the British Isles (Cornwall, Wales, Scotland, and Ireland), and in the more deprived social classes. These patterns led me into a detailed study of the ways in which the diet of the mother might affect the fetus, the different aspects of the water supply (the defects were more likely to occur in soft-water areas), and occupational exposures, especially those involving trace metals.

After my fellowship I needed to find a job – and was focused on trying to obtain one in the epidemiology field. The early 1970s was a time when women were still very much the underdogs. Prejudice against women was rife, even though it may not have been openly acknowledged. For example, when I was interviewed by a famous statistician during this time, he told me that 'all things being equal' he would employ a man rather than a woman. I became determined to make things as unequal as possible, and, although lacking the support of a steady income, I carried on writing papers and improving my CV, obtaining some part-time income from tutoring children on a one-on-one basis, proofreading, and indexing books.

I had almost exhausted my savings after 6 months, when I became extremely fortunate in obtaining employment at the Unit of Clinical Epidemiology, Department of the Regius Professor of Medicine at the University of Oxford, under the direction of Sir Richard Doll. There I continued to work with Neville Butler on the BPMS as well as on the Oxford Record Linkage Study. The latter was a project funded by the UK Government's Department of Health, which had the task of linking together the data on all hospital admissions to individual residents in the counties of Oxfordshire and Berkshire. The aim of this research project was to determine whether certain disorders occurred together more often than would be expected by chance, and thence to identify clues to the etiologies of each. Although this was an ambitious project, it proved difficult for two reasons: (1) Individuals in the UK do not have a unique identifier that is universally recorded in the way that, for example, residents of the Scandinavian countries do; consequently linkage involved the matching of identifying information, such as names and dates of birth as recorded on the hospital records, with all the problems of mistyping, use of pet instead of official names, changes of surname particularly of women, but also of children as their mother changed partner; and (2) the study counties were almost in the center of England, with much inward and outward mobility, and no coherent method of knowing dates on which individuals had migrated across the county borders.

Consequently, without an accurate denominator, it was impossible to calculate with any degree of accuracy how many individuals would be expected to have any two disorders. Although I was able to analyze and publish the data for a number of studies on unexpected linkages, most of the publications from this database were perforce concerned with straightforward epidemiological studies looking at the cross-sectional distribution of medical conditions in regard to social, demographic, and environmental features. I mostly concentrated on obstetric, neonatal, and childhood conditions.

Although the data were less than perfect, I had the advantage of being in a thriving epidemiology department, with many different areas of interest from cancer to coronary heart disease. As well as Professor Sir Richard Doll, the members of the department who made the most intellectual impact on me were the cancer specialists Malcolm Pike, Leo Kinlen, and Julian Peto. Importantly I had also made links with obstetricians and pediatricians in Oxford. One of my most memorable contacts was Dr. Meg Ounsted. She was in her fifties and had only recently started her research career. As often happened at that time, although she had obtained her medical qualifications, she had married and had four children within 5 years and while bringing them up had been employed in what was considered a dull job in the blood transfusion service. Only when her children were of a sufficient maturity did she start her research career. She was way ahead of her time in considering both the genetic and environmental components as being important to development, and carried out a carefully designed longitudinal study enrolling infants who were small-for-dates, large-for-dates, and a control sample. She first studied the etiological factors associated with different growth patterns and then followed-up the children to assess their long-term outcomes. She was one of the two female academics in Oxford that I looked up to. The other was Dr. Alice Stewart, who had set up an important case control study of childhood cancer and had had the foresight to consider events during pregnancy as well as those nearer the time at which the first symptoms appeared. It was Alice who first identified abdominal x-rays during pregnancy as being important, particularly in the etiology of leukemia. I learnt two things from her: (1) the importance of studying events and environment during pregnancy, even if one was looking at outcomes that were only revealed years later; and (2) the very real prejudice that there was against women in academia. In consequence of her understandable bitterness (and the obvious pain) that she suffered as a result, I decided that that was a path that I should avoid as much as possible by developing a thick skin and keeping my head down. This was a strategy that saw me through various traumas in later years.

I had intermittently carried on with my PhD thesis when I moved to Oxford as I kept thinking of different research questions and continued adding chapters until, in 1979 after 13 years (another outlier!), my tolerant supervisor, Cedric Smith, said that he could not think of any further excuses to give to the University of London to extend its date of submission further – so my thesis was finally submitted, and the degree awarded.

I was still enjoying analyzing the BPMS data with Neville Butler, who was then based in Bristol, when I was approached in 1978 by Iain Chalmers, an obstetrician who had recently completed a course on epidemiology at the London School of Hygiene and Tropical Medicine. He had been asked to set up a National Perinatal Epidemiology Unit in Oxford. He asked me to join him with the remit of designing a new national birth cohort. I took this on with great enthusiasm. There had been three previous British national cohort studies – in 1946 (to determine the ways in which births and care of the newborn occurred, and the costs to the family), in 1958 (the control sample of the BPMS), and in 1970 (designed to assess neonatal health). All were built on surveys of births occurring in 1 week in spring. None had been designed as a longitudinal study – even when planning the 1970 birth survey this was not considered in spite of the fact that the previous cohorts had been showing valuable results.

To design a new cohort study was a very exciting opportunity – I had been particularly influenced by Neville Butler to look at the individual as a whole, including psychological as well as physical influences and consequences. I spent very rewarding months picking the brains of experts in various fields, holding workshops, and reading the latest journals in a huge variety of disciplines from toxicology to physiology, psychology to pathology, epidemiology to anthropology. Although I ended with a coherent plan for a birth survey to take place, this was not funded (for a variety of reasons – mostly political). At the time this was humiliating and traumatic – but it turned out to be an advantage in the long run. The key things I had learnt from the exercise were that: (1) starting a cohort study at birth would not be ideal scientifically – starting as early in pregnancy as possible would be far better; (2) many environmental exposures were undetectable unless one obtained and analyzed biological samples; (3) planning a longitudinal study with financing for a prolonged period of time would be counterproductive – planning for the future was important but to estimate costs for 20 years would antagonize many; and (4) collecting information across the range from psychology to physiology was very important.

In 1980 I moved to the city of Bristol to work further with Neville Butler, whom many have described as a 'flawed genius'. I was fortunate enough to be able to learn a lot from him. At the time he had a small team analyzing data collected from what had become the 1970 birth cohort. This I joined and spent many happy hours assessing factors that were associated with childhood health conditions and behaviors. The 1980s turned out to be quite varied but generally very important in regard to introducing me to various aspects of the technicalities of running large studies. Not only was I involved in the planning of a future sweep of the 1970 birth cohort, but I was also fortunate to be approached by the pediatricians Dr. Chryssa Tzoumaka-Bakoula from Athens, Greece, and Dr. Deanna Ashley from the Ministry of Health in Jamaica in regard to advising on surveys in their countries. In Greece, I helped design a national birth survey, studying all births in the country over a 1-month period in 1983. Once the data were available, one of the pediatricians involved in the data collection, Vasso Lekea-Karanika, came to Bristol to analyze the data under my supervision, for which she was awarded a PhD in 1993.

The Jamaican study was a more ambitious affair. Dr. Deanna Ashley, a Jamaican pediatrician, had recently been appointed to the Ministry of Health. She had the remit of reorganizing the island's health services and wanted some advice on how to determine which individual pregnancies were most at risk in Jamaica, to enable appropriate screening and monitoring to be introduced. She funded me to go out to Jamaica to learn about the country and decide how to approach the question. I flew out expecting to stay three or four days, but I ended up staying a couple of weeks, during which time (with Deanna's help) I designed a study (based largely on the BPMS), wrote the grant proposal, and designed the questionnaires to be used – and fell in love with the island and its people. Fortunately, the study was funded by the Canadian International Development Research Centre (IDRC), and in what seemed a very short space of time we were in the field. Deanna had engaged Affette McCaw-Binns, a very resourceful (and forceful) head of the data collection for the 2-month birth survey on the island (the control sample); in parallel there was a detailed study of the stillbirths and neonatal deaths on the island – for which I had persuaded Dr. Jean Keeling, a pediatric histopathologist with whom I had worked on sudden infant deaths in Oxford, to come to Jamaica and encourage the adult pathologists on the island to take a scientific interest in perinatal deaths. Due, I think, to the enthusiasm and energy of the Jamaicans at all levels, but especially of the leaders, the study was an amazing success, with an estimated 94% of total births included in the study. We had no prior knowledge as to how many perinatal deaths would be expected, but the reality was far greater than anticipated, giving a rate of 40 per 1,000 total births. The results highlighted the importance of two major causes of death: those occurring during or shortly after labor to an otherwise normal fetus/baby (intrapartum deaths), and those concerning perinatal and maternal deaths associated with maternal pre-eclampsia. As well as Dr. Keeling advising on the causes of death, I was very fortunate to engage the eminent Regius Professor of Obstetrics from Aberdeen Ian McGillivray, who had retired to live in Bristol, to visit the island and advise on obstetric matters.

There were several important consequences of this study: (1) having identified intrapartum causes of death as of major importance, changes were made to the delivery of obstetric care, with proven benefits in reduction in the death rate; (2) recognition of the dangers of maternal pre-eclampsia led to changes in the identification and treatment of affected pregnancies by the Jamaican health service; (3) Professor McGillivray undertook a study to enquire of women (or their relatives) what had happened prior to an eclamptic fit, from which a program to empower women to recognize symptoms of impending eclampsia and demand treatment was developed; (4) success in increasing the knowledge and ability on the island in regard to investigation of perinatal deaths; and (5) in order to develop epidemiological understanding and techniques further, two of the Jamaicans who had been involved in the data collection, Affette McCaw-Binns and Maureen Samms-Vaughan, came to Bristol University to work on the analysis of the data over two to three years. Both obtained PhDs and produced a number of important publications from this before returning to Jamaica to academic posts. They each subsequently achieved full professorships, as did one of the pathologists.

Thus, the Jamaican study was a major morale booster for me in regard to the amount achieved, the quality of the data, and the contacts made, but there were several downsides. One of the aims of the study had been to follow-up the children who had been born in the 2-month birth survey. We had assumed that the funders would see how valuable it would be to follow these children up, but our powers of persuasion failed. Consequently, although we were able to show how valuable the study had been in regard to prevention of mortality, we were unable to extend those findings to the follow-up of the children during the important early years of life. This would have been particularly valuable in regard to the study of the Jamaican boys, who have so much difficulty in controlling their behavior in adolescence and young adulthood. I also found it hard to grasp the fact that, although the study was excellent in regard to quality and breadth of the data, and many of the findings had been published in international journals, the results are not widely quoted; it seems that because the study took place in Jamaica there was an assumption that the results were not relevant to other parts of the world.

Meanwhile, back in Europe other influences were nudging me into finally succeeding in developing a longitudinal study. The Jamaican birth survey had taken place in 1986. In 1985 I had been contacted by Marsden G. Wagner, the perinatal epidemiologist at the European branch of the WHO based in Copenhagen. He asked me to attend a meeting of representatives from a number of European countries with the aim of designing a cross-European study. The weeklong meeting was held in Moscow. Its aim was to design a study to address the question of how to assess what the health problems were among Europe's children, whether they were similar in each country, and how to improve the situation. By the end of the week I had persuaded my colleagues that birth cohorts (starting in pregnancy) were the way to go, and we had started the design of the European Study of Pregnancy and Childhood (ELSPAC).

This was 1985, and there was much to do. The study design was to collect data in similar ways, using identical questions to study the pregnant mother, her partner, and ultimately the child until age 7. The questions were to be administered to the parents by means of postal questionnaires; this caused controversy, as most of the group generally felt that it should be medics who completed the questionnaires, not the study participants. The WHO asked me to carry out a pilot study to address the feasibility and comparability of using self-completion questionnaires in three different countries: England, Greece, and the USSR. In consequence three of us received a small amount of funding to address this question – Thalia Dragonas, a social psychologist based in Athens who subsequently had a successful academic career in educational psychology and is currently a Member of Parliament in Greece; Rimma Ignatyeva, pediatric information expert from the All-Union Semasko Institute for Research on Social Hygiene and Public Health, Ministry of Health of the USSR; and myself. We tested two types of questionnaire – one enquired about details of medical circumstances that could be checked later against medical records, and the others comprised the feasibility and acceptability of psychological questions concerning attitudes, moods, and feelings. The results vindicated my conviction that parents (and, later, their offspring) could be trusted to provide accurate information if they were allowed to do so anonymously. Thus, for such a study to be successful, trust in the teams collecting the data was crucial.

Having then developed a study design with the aim of being broad enough to consider many features of health, behavior, and development in the early years, all Departments of Health in Europe were contacted by the WHO, recommending that they join the study. Their letter did, however, make it clear that funding for the studies would have to be provided by the countries themselves. In spite of this, there were a number of countries that volunteered to take part, but once piloting started several dropped out for various reasons: The major ones concerned (1) the difficulty of having access to all pregnant women in areas where there was private practice, and (2) problems when the political circumstances changed radically – this was particularly true for countries that had been in the Soviet Bloc (we were planning the study just as the Berlin Wall was coming down and Russia's hold over the countries of Eastern Europe was weakening). Nevertheless, a number of countries started the study: Russia, Czechoslovakia (which later split into the Czech Republic and Slovakia), Ukraine, Greece, Spain, and the Isle of Man and Avon in the British Isles. The four ex-Soviet bloc countries found that a major disadvantage was the need to find their own funding for research, whereas prior to 1991 their governments had been the funding source; nevertheless the Czech Republic managed to continue under the direction of Dr. Lubomir Kukla; Ukraine managed to link with the University of Illinois at Chicago (with the help of Dr. Susan Monaghan) and the National Institutes of Environmental Health Sciences (NIEHS) (Dr. Ruth E. Little); Dr. Ignatyeva continued to collect data for 2 years, but her son, Dr. Vadim Kagramanov (a pediatrician) obtained an opportunity to go and work in the United States, and she moved with him, and the Russian cohort was abandoned. One of my major problems in trying to organize the collaboration between the countries that remained in the study concerned the difficulty at that time of obtaining funds to run the organization. Nevertheless, the directors of the studies that remained in ELSPAC for the initial years (Czech Republic, Ukraine, Russia, the Isle of Man and Avon) met regularly every year for an intense week during which we would design the subsequent sweeps of the study and go through the new questionnaires line by line (the meetings were largely funded in the early years by the WHO). Although exhausting, this was very valuable, as we were able to come to appreciate the different attitudes, environments, and priorities from the backgrounds of the participating countries.

One of the rules for joining ELSPAC was that the basic core structure of data collection should be followed but that each center could build onto this without restriction, provided the basic ethics were followed. The Avon study, which came to be known as ALSPAC, took this structure to extremes. Building on what I had developed when designing the aborted 1982 national cohort, as well as the other cohorts I had worked on, formed the basis of many of the additions. An advantage of the link I had made with Dr. Dragonas in Greece was that I was invited to speak at a conference in Athens in 1989. I gave a talk on some results from the

1970 birth cohort, after which one of the other speakers asked me if there was any chance that blood for genetic testing could be obtained from that cohort. I thought not, but that the study I was planning would be ideal for this. This was the first time I met Marcus Pembrey, and it was the start of a long and scientifically productive collaboration. It was this chance meeting that changed the aims of ALSPAC from a study of the environment on health and development to a study of the environment and its possible interactions with genetics on health and development.

The geographic area that formed the basis of the study was the county of Avon, which comprised the city of Bristol and the surrounding rural areas, small towns, and larger urban areas. I knew that it had comparatively little outward migration. I was fortunate that in the latter half of the 1980s colleagues from Oxford were appointed as Heads of the Departments of Child Health (David Baum) and Obstetrics and Gynaecology (Gordon Stirrat). Both were enthusiastic and very supportive of the study, which became known locally as 'Children of the Nineties', but academically as ALSPAC (the Avon Longitudinal Study of Parents and Children).

Although this study has become famous and fulfilled all my hopes, it did not start that way. The major funders who now contribute to the core funding were very negative when first approached. The Wellcome Trust, although they were supporting me personally at the time through a Wellcome Senior Lectureship, declared that the UK Government should fund the core data collection. The UK Medical Research Council (MRC) stated that, although it would be interested in funding focused sub-projects, it would not contribute to the core funding. The consequence was that for the first 10 years of the cohort, funding of the core had to be derived from a 'cobbling together' of funds that had been raised for specific projects. It was difficult to persuade a funder of a specific project to contribute toward the core costs of the study as well as pay for the actual cost for the component part. It took a considerable amount of optimism for my staff to keep going at a time when the likelihood of any one grant being successful was about 25%. However, the morale of many is what kept the study going – the local media (TV, radio, and newspapers) were very enthusiastic, and that resulted in equal enthusiasm from the parents we were enrolling. It also resulted in excellent individuals offering their services – not so much career researchers but people (mostly women) from various backgrounds who had heard what we were aiming to do and offered to help. They formed the basis of the study team who had personal contact with the study parents.

Interestingly, the media and the general public had no problem with understanding that our aim was broad – we had said that there was so much that we did not know as to what influenced the mental and physical health of our children that we wished to look at all possibilities from the food we ate, the air we breathed, our medications, features of the household and neighborhoods, and our genetics. In contrast the scientific community in general thought this was crazy – like the MRC, they advised that I should take a narrow focus. This is where my background experience of keeping my head down and battling on came into play once more. The study was proving a great success in regard to the response rate and the quality of the data. It was recognized as innovative at the time for its approach to ethical issues; for its starting in pregnancy; for including fathers from the outset; for collecting biological samples (including the whole placenta); and for obtaining permission at the very beginning for generic genetic analyses. Unfortunately, it was also innovative in spending more money than it was raising! Fortunately, it was allowed by the University of Bristol to continue with an accumulating debt. I had been able to persuade the university that the study was a valuable asset. I was fortunate in that the Vice-Chancellor at the time, Sir John Kingman, was a mathematician with an interest in genetics who, together with Ian Crawford, the Finance Director, and Professor Brian Pickering, the Deputy Vice-Chancellor, had agreed to the unusual strategy of allowing us to go into debt, to keep the study running (and paying it back via overhead income on grants awarded). The Finance Director was convinced that the study would prove a valuable investment for the university. This it was in terms of the science that resulted, and the local public engagement with the university, but that was only acknowledged much much later.

Meanwhile, my academic route had benefited from the support of the Wellcome Trust. Having awarded me a senior lectureship, they insisted that the university should take over my funding after 5 years; thus I became a bona fide member of academia. Shortly thereafter (in 1991) I was promoted to a full professorship. At this stage there were only four female full professors in the whole of the university, compared with 131 male professors! It was still a struggle to convince my male colleagues that women could achieve. Consequently, I thought I should try and increase my degrees by submitting to the University of Bristol for a DSc, a degree that is awarded on the basis of published work. This I was awarded in 1994.

From the time that I first moved to the University of Bristol, I had been based within clinical departments, with the bonus of being able to keep abreast of the clinical problems and challenges that arose. I was geographically apart from colleagues in the epidemiology department, many of whom were very skeptical of my approach. Consequently when Sir John took up a prestigious post as the Director of the Isaac Newton Institute at the University of Cambridge in 2001, the new Vice Chancellor of Bristol University was approached by senior members of the epidemiology department claiming that the ALSPAC study should be put in their hands, as they had a far better view as to how it should be organized. I had stupidly waited for him to settle in before approaching him. I was aware that planning should be under way for a successor to the directorship of the study, but he said that he wished to carry out a review of ALSPAC first.

The review only got under way in 2004. I was not privy to how it was conducted but only became aware of the results when I heard that the feeling in the university was that it should be mothballed until the study children reached the age at which they would be having heart attacks! I was 'gobsmacked'. After many years of incredibly hard work by my whole team, and fantastic input from all the participants, the study was beginning to be widely admired, particularly by our American collaborators in the NIH (especially Drs. Ruth Little of NIEHS and Joseph Hibbeln of the National Institute on Alcohol Abuse and Addiction [NIAAA], who worked with us on the effects of maternal alcohol and diet, respectively, on the developing fetal brain) and the Centers for Disease Control (CDC) (particularly Dr. Carol Rubin, with whom we worked on the measurement of puberty in the cohort). In 2003–2004, we were planning the data collection on the study offspring, who were approaching late adolescence with all its accompanying personality, mood, and behavior problems. For example, we had contacted David Farrington to discuss the data that we should collect in order to assess the antecedents of criminality.

The group trying to mothball the study was made up of experts in the epidemiology of physical disorders and did not seem to understand the importance of mental health in adolescence and young adulthood. Fortunately, by 2000 we had achieved core funding from both the Wellcome Trust and the MRC – both organizations were angry and offended at the assumption that they had funded a poor project. They were able to insist that the study continue, albeit with a new director. I had always known that I would have to hand over the study in 2005 (unlike America, in most UK organizations there were strict rules on the age of retirement, which, at that time, had to be at 65). I will not go into the difficulties at this time – it was humiliating to be informed that the study could have been designed far better by others; it certainly warranted another period of finding that thick skin and keeping my head down!

3.3   The Post-Retirement Years

I had been very much influenced by Professor Ian McGillivray as to how to behave on retirement. When he was appointed as Regius Professor in Aberdeen, his famous predecessor (Sir Dugald Baird) had continued to attend his departmental meetings and been very difficult to cope with. I had (and have) therefore largely stayed away from any forum where I might be considered to be interfering and have kept a low profile – even though sometimes it has been difficult not to say 'I wouldn't do it that way'!

Fortunately, I did not need to keep my head down for long. I was approached by Drs. Danuta Krotoski from the National Institute of Child Health and Human Development (NICHD) and Jennie Pronczuk of the WHO to develop a guide to undertaking birth cohort studies, to be written so that it could be used by both the developing and developed world. This was a wonderful way to fill my time after giving up the directorship of ALSPAC. Provided with some funds for expenses I enrolled two colleagues who had worked with me on ALSPAC (Richard Jones and Karen Birmingham) to help develop such a guide, which was peer reviewed by very distinguished scientists prior to being published. It was then widely distributed by the WHO.

From that time on I was privileged to be allowed to continue to apply for funds for staff to analyze and publish data from the ALSPAC cohort. Among the topics that I have been investigating relevant to this book have been the environmental factors associated with adverse child behaviors, especially those related to hyperactivity and conduct disorder. Such studies have allowed me to continue productive collaborations such as those with (1) Dr. Joseph Hibbeln from the NIH in regard to associations with maternal prenatal mercury exposures and the protective effect of fish intake and (2) Professor Stephen Nowicki of Emory University on the protective effects of parental internal locus of control. Both collaborations are ongoing as we try to develop interventions based on our results.

The most exciting of ongoing collaborations, however, is with Marcus Pembrey. He has been at the forefront of the studies of intergenerational and transgenerational associations of environmental exposures on later generations. Starting with collaborations with a Swedish group headed by Professor Lars Ovov Bygren, he next analyzed data from the 1958 British birth cohort, and we have been working with ALSPAC data on such associations since 2013. We have, for example, shown associations between the grandmother smoking in pregnancy and various outcomes in the grandchild, independent of whether or not the mother smokes. We now have a grant from the John Templeton Foundation to obtain further information, with the aim of determining possible effects lasting for three or more generations and assessing whether such antecedents are discernible using biomarkers such as DNA methylation.

3.4 A Postscript

Writing this chapter has been taxing in trying to determine which features in my background influenced my progression through academia. How is it that after failing in many respects throughout my first 60 years, I am now getting so many messages of appreciation? Looking back, the hardships were largely associated with (1) being female and (2) not being medically qualified while working in a largely medical field. I don't think I am being paranoid in thinking that both were definite drawbacks (not intellectually, as I made sure that I knew as much as either men or medics working in epidemiology). On the plus side, I do not think my physical disability – even after 2004 when I needed to use an electronic wheelchair (the post-polio syndrome having caught up with me) – resulted in any sense of inequality. Fortunately, I have (almost) always been able to laugh at myself and see the funny side of things.

In retrospect, I was lucky – my scientific achievements developed in response to a number of illnesses, stresses, and chance occurrences, and I am humbled by the success I have had. I am especially fortunate in that I now have the privilege of having raised funds to employ a strong research team to continue to work with me on the ALSPAC data that has been collected. I am still excited by the epidemiological method and hope to continue to push forward the science with my academic colleagues by continuing to push back the boundaries for many years to come.

Acknowledgments

I have an enormous number of people to thank who have not appeared in this chapter. My legacy is the ALSPAC study, which has proved such a very rich resource because of (1) the strange series of events that resulted in my being nudged into this exciting enterprise; (2) all the people, paid and unpaid, who worked with me and encouraged me to make it happen; (3) my friends, family, and colleagues who have supported me at various times; and, most of all, (4) the 14,000 families that have had faith in the study, have contributed to it, have shared their abilities and disabilities, and are rightly proud of how their contributions to research have helped expand knowledge and improve aspects of health and development worldwide.

References

Cecil, C. A. M., Lysenko, L. J., Jaffee, S. R., Pingault, J. B., Smith, R. G., Relton, C. L., ... Barker, E. D. (2014). Environmental risk, oxytocin receptor gene (OXTR) methylation and youth callous–unemotional traits: A 13-year longitudinal study, *Molecular Psychiatry, 19*(10), 1071–1077.

Golding, J. (2018). Long-term strategy for the creation of a dedicated independent institute to develop methodologies for the assessment of pesticides and herbicides – A personal view. *SAPEA, Science Advice for Policy by European Academies. Improving authorisation processes for plant protection products in Europe: A scientific perspective on the assessment of potential risks to human health.* (pp. 88–111). Berlin, Germany: SAPEA.

Golding, J., Birmingham, K., & Jones, R. W. (2009). A guide to undertaking a birth cohort study: Purposes, pitfalls and practicalities. *Paediatric and Perinatal Epidemiology, 23*(s1), 1–236.

Golding, J., Gregory, S., Ellis, G., Iles-Caven, Y., & Nowicki, S. (2017). Maternal internal locus of control is associated with offspring IQ at eight years mediated by parenting attitudes, SES and perinatal lifestyle exposures: A longitudinal birth cohort study investigating possible mechanisms. *Frontiers in Psychology, 1429* (10.3389).

Golding, J., Gregory, S., Emond, A., Iles-Caven, Y., Hibbeln, J., & Taylor, C. (2016). Prenatal mercury exposure and offspring behaviour in childhood and adolescence, *Neurotoxicology, 57*, 87–94.

Golding, J., Northstone, K., Gregory, S., Miller, L., & Pembrey, M. (2014). The anthropometry of children and adolescents may be influenced by the prenatal smoking habits of their grandmothers: A longitudinal cohort study, *American Journal of Human Biology, 26*(6), 731–739.

Golding, J., Pembrey, M., & Jones, R. (2001). ALSPAC – The Avon Longitudinal Study of Parents and Children. I. Study methodology. *Paediatric and Perinatal Epidemiology, 15*(1), 74–87.

Hibbeln, J., Davis, J. M., Steer, C., Emmett, P., Rogers, I., Williams, C., & Golding, J. (2007). Maternal seafood consumption in pregnancy and neurodevelopmental outcomes in childhood (ALSPAC study): An observational cohort study. *The Lancet, 369*(9561), 578–585.

Nowicki, S., Iles-Caven, Y., Gregory, S., Ellis, G., & Golding, J. (2017). The impact of prenatal parental locus of control on children's psychological outcomes in infancy and early childhood: A prospective 5 year study. *Frontiers in Psychology, 8*, 546.

4 From Country Girl in Southern Finland to Longitudinal Research into Alternatives to Aggression and Violence

Lea Pulkkinen

Lea Pulkkinen was born October 29, 1939, near Heinola in Finland. She received her PhD in psychology from the University of Jyväskylä (Finland) in 1969. Her first faculty appointment (1970) after her PhD was at Jyväskylä University, where she became Emeritus Professor in 2004. In 1994 she became a member of the Finnish Academy of Science and Letters. She was President of the International Society for the Study of Behavioral Development (ISSBD) between 1991 and 1996. In 2001 she was awarded the Finnish Science Prize by the Finnish Ministry of Education and Culture.

Lea Pulkkinen is best known for creating the ongoing Jyväskylä Longitudinal Study of Personality and Social Development (JLSPSD). Initiated during her PhD, with 8-year-old children (N = 369, 52% males), she aimed to test the hypothesis that the human brain allows for more variation in behavior than the simple 'fight or flight' response observed in animal studies of aggression. She further hypothesized that humans' capacity for cognitive control over emotional behavior was the key factor involved in controlling aggressive behavior. These hypotheses led her to devise an impulse-control model to depict behavioral alternatives, which she tested with teacher and peer ratings of aggressive and nonaggressive behaviors.

Forty years later, the JLSPSD revealed the long-term significance of self-regulation for socio-emotional behavior. In the impulse-control model that she devised in 1967, the idea of cognitive control of emotional behavior was novel. Cognitive control was used in the study to explain individual differences in aggressive and nonaggressive behaviors from childhood to middle age. Her aims were to understand the development of both aggressive and nonaggressive behavior, to prevent aggressive and violent behavior, and to promote a more peaceful society. Results from the study showed that aggressive behavior during childhood tends to be associated with other types of under-controlled behavior during

71

adulthood. On the other hand, 'constructive' behavior in childhood tends to lead to positive social relations, mental health, and successful integration in the work force. The development of what she termed 'styles of life' is a cumulative process associated with parenting, living conditions, and genetic factors. In her efforts to apply her research results to the education of children, she highlighted the importance of child-centered parenting and of a school environment enriched by the arts and other interesting activities.

When teacher-rated aggression at age 8 was used to predict long-term unemployment during adulthood, results showed that it predicted school maladjustment at age 14, which was both directly and indirectly related to long-term unemployment via problem drinking and lack of occupational alternatives at age 27. Furthermore, child-centered parenting and prosocial tendencies of aggressive 8-year-old children significantly lowered the probability of long-term unemployment during adulthood (Kokko & Pulkkinen, 2000).

The results of the JLSPSD were compared with similar longitudinal studies in other countries. For example, a comparison of the JLSPSD boys at ages 6, 8, and 10 years with boys of the same age, but born 20 years earlier and living in Canada (Pulkkinen & Tremblay, 1992), found eight comparable behavior clusters and highlighted the importance of subcategorizing aggressive-hyperactive boys into three categories: (1) bully, (2) uncontrolled, and (3) multi problem. International comparisons were also made with samples of children from Sweden (Kokko, Bergman, & Pulkkinen, 2003; Pulkkinen, Virtanen, Klinteberg, & Magnusson, 2000) and from other countries (Duncan et al., 2012; Kokko et al., 2014).

While publishing more than 550 scientific papers, Lea Pulkkinen also filled important academic, administrative, and social functions. She became Dean of the Faculty of Social Sciences at the University of Jyväskylä, and she chaired the Finnish Center of Excellence for Research on Human Development.

Lea Pulkkinen received numerous other distinctions during her long career: the Publisher's Prize for the book *Kotikasvatuksen psykologia* [*The Psychology of Rearing Children*] in 1978; the 1983 'Woman of the Year in Finland' awarded by the Finnish Branch of the International Federation of Business and Professional Women; membership in the Academia Europaea in 1989; the 1992 Scientific Communication Award by the Association of the Newsletter Editors of Finnish Universities; the 1992 'Professor of the Year' award from the Finnish Union of Professors; membership in the Finnish Academy of Science and Letters in 1994; Academy Professor, awarded by the Academy of Finland in 1996; State

Honorary Member of the Delta Kappa Gamma Society International in 1992; the 2003 Aristotle Prize, awarded by the European Federation of Psychologists Association; the 2004 Elsa Enäjärvi-Haavio Award (awarded by the Family Federation of Finland, Helsinki); the 2005 Award for Distinguished Scientific Contributions to Child Development (awarded by the Society for Research in Child Development [SRCD], Atlanta, United States); the 2006 Award for Distinguished Work for the Application of Behavioral Development Theory and Research (awarded by the ISSBD, Melbourne, Australia); the 2009 Doctor Honoris Causa in Education at the University of Joensuu/East Finland; the 2010 Advanced Researcher Prize for Successful Research Career (awarded by Psykonet and the Finnish Psychological Association); the 2011 State Award for Life-Time Work on the Dissemination of Scientific Knowledge (awarded by the Finnish Ministry of Education and Culture); the 2013 Paul Harris Fellow (awarded by the Rotary Foundation, Rotary International); the 2016 ISSBD Fellow in Recognition of Outstanding Contributions to the Field of Lifespan Human Development; Distinctions from the President of the Republic of Finland; the 1982 *Suomen Leijonan I luokan ritarimerkki* [The First Category Decoration of the Order of the Lion in Finland]; the 1989 *Sotilasansiomitalli* [Military Service Medal]; the 2001 *Valtion virka-ansiomerkki* [Civil Service Medal of the State]; and in 2002 the Knight Commander's Cross of the Order of the Lion in Finland.

4.1   A Healthy Daughter Was Born

My parents were married in 1938 in the shadow of sorrow because my mother's father had drowned on the eve of their wedding day while fishing on a nearby lake. After a year of marriage, the war separated them. The outbreak of the Second World War in September 1939, with the German invasion of Poland closely followed by the Soviet occupation of the east of that country, put Finland in an increasingly dangerous position. Full mobilization of the Finnish army in the form of the training of reserves began on October 14. My father was among these men. I was born on October 29, 1939, my parents' first child, and my father heard on the radio that 'a healthy daughter was born' to him. On November 30, the Soviet Union's invasion of Finland started the so-called winter war. My father and his two brothers fought against the Soviet Union. Fighting ended on March 13, 1940. It was followed by the Armistice (or Interim Peace), which lasted until June 1941, and by the Continuation War, which, in turn, lasted until September 1944.

My first two sisters were born in 1941 and 1943, while my third sister was born after the war, in 1947. My mother tried to protect us from the horrors of the war. Due to her wise approach to parenting, my basic trust in people and life developed well, in spite of the war. I only remember my mother crying once. I went to look for her at night and found her weeping while writing a letter to my father. She told me that she was worried about him. I remember that the windows had to be covered so that light from the house could not be seen from the planes. I also remember seeing the smoke from the bombing of the town 20 km away and the anxiety it caused us. I was forbidden to run from the house to the cowshed if planes were flying overhead.

The war with the Soviet Union ended in September 1944. The small Finnish army was able to defend the country against the planned Soviet invasion and thus maintained the independence Finland had enjoyed since it became an independent republic in 1917. Finland had been part of the Kingdom of Sweden for centuries, but, as a consequence of a war between Sweden and Russia, it became an autonomous Grand Duchy in the Russian Empire from 1809 to 1917. The Finnish language does not belong to the Indo-European languages, as Swedish and Russian do, but rather to the family of non-Indo-European languages, and hence Finland has its own cultural heritage. For the defense of its independence during the 1939–1945 war, Finland (with a population of around 4 million people) lost around 271,000 men, 57% of its army (475,000 were mobilized in 1941 [Screen, 2014]), while the Soviet Union lost 700,000–800,000 men. The terms of the peace treaty were tough for Finland, including the loss of land in the southeast and the northeast, the lease of a site near Helsinki (for a Soviet army base) for 50 years, and huge war reparations that Finland finished paying in full in 1952. Around 340,000 railway wagonloads were needed to deliver all the war reparations.

I was almost five years old when my father returned from the war. He was not physically wounded, but the war had affected him negatively, as it did many other men in various ways. His problems were manifested in the heavy periodic use of alcohol that later motivated my study on drinking behavior. My mother said that the man who returned from the war was not the same man whom she had married. My father died of a heart attack in 1961 at the age of 47 years, on the day he was supposed to visit the hospital to see my newborn baby and me. My mother lived as a widow with some bitter memories until the age of 90. After her death, I had a dream in which my daddy was lying on a sofa with his head on my mom's lap, and they looked happy together. It was a good feeling: They had found each other again. For me, he was a dear daddy, who loved me and set high expectations for me.

My parents had attended the same primary school. My father (1914–1961) went to secondary school and then returned home and took part in the business at his home farm. After returning from the war, he expanded his business into manufacturing building elements. My parents met in 1937, when my father went to repair the roof of a farmer's house and set his eyes upon the farmer's daughter. My mother (1915–2005) completed her elementary studies in a school run by the church, moving from one farm to another. She only went to the municipal school when she was 10 years old because it was far away, some 7 km through a forest. Her parents had chosen this school because it was better than the local school. She had to stay at someone else's house during the week and was very homesick. She loved learning – I remember that she knew her textbooks by heart – and she had an excellent memory until the day she died. She would have liked to attend teacher-training college, but her parents sent her to a school of domestic science. After this she went back home to work on the farm. My mother's ancestors had owned a large mansion since the 1640s.

My father's family moved from the West Coast of Finland to southern Finland. I find similarities between my paternal grandfather's and my own characteristics in terms of energy and mental entrepreneurship, typical of people on the West Coast, whereas my mothers' southern Finnish characteristics laid a basis for my tenacious work in science. My grandfather (1890–1940) had suffered, like many other children in West Finland at that time, from not having a father around, because at that time many farmers immigrated to Canada or the United States to look for a better life. In his early teens, my grandfather went to work in a town, and he was only 19 when he got married to a Finnish-Swedish farmer's daughter (1887–1960). They had 16 children (no twins; two died in childhood) between 1910 and 1930. The couple first set up a shop and then bought a farm. My grandfather became involved in business, including international trade and real estate. It turned out, however, that the emerging economic recession of the 1920s made it difficult to sell an estate in southern Finland. He and his two partners in the company decided that one of them had to settle at and run the estate, but which one of them would it be? They drew lots three times, and every time my grandfather selected the winning lot. When my grandmother also drew the winning lot in the spouses' game, the decision was clear: My grandparents had to move. Religion strengthened their belief that this was a call that they had to follow.

It was a cold winter's day in January 1922 when the family, with its servants, was packed into a freight train. When the train stopped, the animals were fed and the cows were milked. The last 60 km of the journey they traveled in frosty conditions in 30 horse-drawn sleighs collected from local farmhouses. Upon arrival at the mansion, they found it to be in poor condition, and only one room had been warmed. The history of the estate goes back to 1649; the estate had changed hands several times.

My grandfather started to work. He became interested in forestry and established a sawmill, improved the cultivation of the fields and established a flourmill, and worked to improve the condition of the cattle and establish a dairy. The estate was made a training farm for animal husbandry and gardening. The river that ran through their land enabled them to produce their own electricity. He himself was a skilled blacksmith and shared his skills with farm laborers. My grandfather was invited to various positions of trust, such as church and municipal councils, and juryman. On Sundays, my grandparents ran a Sunday school for children. They were active forces for the establishment of an orphanage. Furthermore, the mansion was one of the places where around 400,000 people evacuated from East Finland, Karelia, were to be resettled. In the winter of 1940, 60 people were taken care of for months on the estate.

My home was located 3 km from my grandparents' estate. It was a small farm separated from the estate (all 14 children had inherited a plot of land). The estate provided my mother and her children with material and psychological security during the war. We also took Karelian evacuees into our home, and they gave me love and care when my mother had to take care of the younger children, the cattle, and the cultivation of the land.

4.2   How Did I Manage to Do What I Did?

A longitudinal study is inevitably intertwined with world events, such as an economic recession, which affects the participants; with the history of science, which brings up new theoretical ideas and methods to be considered; with the professional and personal history of the scientist conducting the study; and with technological advancements. Computing capacities and the methods of handling study data have hugely evolved over the almost half-century in which the study I created has taken place: from manual computing to punch cards on to very effective laptops. Each decade of my life has contributed to my development, each in its own way, and has informed and strengthened me in my mission to promote a good childhood for future generations on a scientific basis.

4.2.1   Country Time in the 1940s

I was eager to go to school, and for years my favorite game was to play school with and for other children. I remember an older woman who used to say when she watched my school arrangements, 'I wonder what kind of teacher Lea is going to become'. The school starting age in Finland is 7 years, but I often joined the neighborhood children during the year before I turned seven. I went to school voluntarily because the teacher of the combined first and second grade had given me permission to do so. The distance from my home to the school was almost 4 km, which I walked or skied in winter. When I actually started school, the teacher moved me into the second grade after a couple of weeks. The grades from 3 to 6 were also combined, and I enjoyed listening to the lessons taught to the classes above mine. I have a special memory from a school radio program, which motivated my later research work. The program was about a noble Finnish lady, Mathilda Wrede (1864–1928), who had started to work voluntarily with prisoners. She was convinced that prisoners were normal people who had lived in unfortunate conditions and needed understanding and care. Another motivating event for my future was my teacher's request to me to present at the school's spring festival a *kronikka* [a chronicle, a poem] that she had written about pupils leaving the school after finishing the sixth grade. I did not understand what *kronikka* meant, but I accepted the request with pleasure. Similar situations occurred many times in my life. I accepted tasks that others invited me to take on, without understanding exactly what they involved.

Life in the countryside was financially modest, but I did not lack anything. My life was rich, from observing the activities of the adults around me and caring for the animals that I loved. My mother was skilled in everything she did. I have vivid memories of how to make potato flour, syrup, soap, sausages, and fruit and berry conserves; how to milk a cow by hand and feed the animals; and how to grow linen and shear sheep and spin thread from the linen and the wool for clothes making. I also enjoyed gatherings with relatives where we sang together and played fun games in which the adults also participated. My father had a motorbike and a car, and we took trips together. On Sunday, we often went to church, and sometimes I performed a special singing program with my sisters. Alternatively, we went to the Sunday school run by my grandmother in a different home each Sunday. The journey to Sunday school was sometimes a long one, but my parents trusted me to go there by horse-driven sleigh. The nice horse accepted the small driver.

My great pleasure was to stay with my paternal grandmother and observe the multiple activities that took place on the estate. Christmas festivals and the many weddings held there were particular highlights. The early death of my grandfather left my grandmother alone with a huge household. It is a miracle how my grandmother managed to cope with all sorts of tasks without the help of her six sons, who were serving in the Continuation War (1941–1944). All her sons returned home alive, but my mother's brother died. My maternal grandmother and my godparents were all very supportive of me, particularly, when my mother was ill or when she traveled to see my father somewhere near the battlefields.

The pupils who attended my country school rarely went on to study at secondary school because to do so they had to move to a town called Heinola. The distance was only 22 km, but the public transport was poor at that time, and, therefore, it was not possible to attend secondary school and live at home. My teacher, however, encouraged my parents to allow me to take the secondary school entrance examination when I had finished the fifth grade, and I passed it. I was then 10 years old. I did not know much about studying. I was 7 years old when I became aware of the fact that other languages existed. My younger sister had been in hospital, and she had heard people speaking words that sounded like nonsense to her. Obviously, they spoke Swedish, the second official language in Finland spoken by about 5% of the population. There were no Swedish-speaking Finns in our area. It is so different today with television, the Internet, and the ease of traveling abroad.

4.2.2   Secondary School in the 1950s

My first memories from the large secondary school are associated with the feeling of loneliness. I did not know anybody. I stayed at my aunt's place. She was often away and did not feed me properly. I was hungry. My parents had arranged piano lessons for me with a Russian woman. She was worried about my situation and asked the parents of another one of her students, who was a classmate of mine, whether they could have me stay at their place. They agreed. I packed my things onto my bed, and my classmate (who was also 11 years old) and I carried the bed with its load to her home, a few blocks from my aunt's place. Once there, I called my mother and told her that I had moved. She was upset and never fully understood why I had made this move, particularly, because my aunt never admitted to her nor apologized for any neglect. When I began the second grade of secondary school, my family moved to Heinola because of my father's business, and the country home was sold at auction.

The secondary school consisted of eight grades, five in the lower secondary school and three in the higher secondary school, which led on to a matriculation exam. Most students left the school after the fifth grade, but it was clear to me that I wanted to continue my studies. At school, I enjoyed mathematics but criticized the teacher for her poor teaching. I made notes about how I would teach if I were a teacher. My most positive memories are of the teacher who taught us Finnish language and literature in the higher secondary school. She encouraged us to use our imagination while writing essays. She also directed a Shakespeare play, *Much Ado about Nothing*, in which I played the main role of Hero. She also asked us to prepare a presentation about a Finnish author of our choice. I chose Aaro Hellaakoski (1893–1952), who was a scientist, a teacher, and a poet. His life and poems deeply influenced the development of my self-awareness. My scientific work on human development was perhaps anticipated by a game that I played in my teens, imagining the kind of children the adults I knew had been in the past and the kind of adults the children I knew were going to become in the future.

I finished higher secondary school in 1958 by coming first in my class, but as no one in my family had been to university, it was difficult for me to plan my academic studies. From childhood onward, I had only been aware of what I did not want to become: a stay-at-home mother and a farmer. My father wanted me to become a medical doctor, but I was not interested in biology. I worked in his office during the summer, and one day he came and asked me whether I had applied for university. When I said I hadn't, his reply was, 'Be aware that you cannot stay and continue your work here!' I had to think, what should I do? I did not want to study in Helsinki, but I had heard that a new university was being established in Oulu in North Finland. It turned out, however, that students would only be admitted to this new university a year later. I was advised to phone Jyväskylä, where the Pedagogical Institute was being expanded by the inclusion of a new Liberal Arts Faculty, and my call was put through to the rector (president) of the institute. When he asked me what I would like to study, I asked what could I study there? My reply was to list the three subjects in the same order that the rector had listed them. At the end of the telephone call, he encouraged me to submit an application.

4.2.3   University Studies in the 1960s

In 1958, I was admitted to the Pedagogical Institute of Jyväskylä (which became a university in 1965) to study Finnish language, literature, and psychology. I was happy about having been offered a place at the university, but my father was not, because he thought that I was becoming a schoolteacher, and this was not good enough, from his point of view. When I changed my major to psychology a year later, he said that he had never seen any job advertisements for psychologists. This was true, because the profession was still young. I did not, however, study psychology in order to become a psychologist. I studied psychology because I was interested in the subject, and I was particularly inspired by Professor of Psychology Martti Takala. As my father died in 1961 at a young age, he did not live to see that I always had interesting work, which continuously boosted my social standing.

The 1960s began with my marriage to my psychometrics teacher, which meant the change of my surname from Marttunen to Pitkänen. Through my husband, I became part of the community of researchers at the Department of Psychology. This was very important to me. I enjoyed the intellectual company of my husband and the other researchers – something that I had never experienced before. My first daughter was born in 1961. I demonstrated my objection to becoming a stay-at-home mum by not preparing any meals until the last weeks of my pregnancy, when I was too big to go to restaurants. At the end of my maternity leave, we hired a woman to work in our tiny studio, and, at the age of 21, I was a married woman who had to supervise somebody to take care of the housework and the baby. My husband had said that my studies and work were fine with him as long as I took responsibility for the tasks that 'belonged to women'. He never did any domestic chores. However, when her first grade teacher asked our daughter, 'What do your parents do?', she answered that her mom was preparing a doctoral dissertation and that her daddy was washing the clothes! She did not know what her daddy was doing, but she had heard that, after her birth, her father had gone to a shop and bought a primitive washing machine when I had asked him to wash the baby's clothes. We had wonderful girls who stayed with us for years, and I am deeply grateful to them for making my work outside the home possible.

My younger daughter was born in 1964. I enjoyed the children and became interested in their development and in an important issue: whether parents can protect their children from negative influences, such as the substance use that was increasing at the time. At present, my younger daughter (Pitkänen, 2006) is an adjunct professor whose doctoral dissertation on alcohol consumption was partly based on the longitudinal study that I conducted. When she was 11 years old, she said that she was going to become an associate professor to continue her mom's work: 'Who else but me would do it?' My eldest daughter (Merita Petäjä) dreamed of becoming a teacher trainer. These days she, a psychologist by training, is in that position as a project manager at a university and as

Director of Theatre for Business in which she uses drama methods in her consulting work to mirror and improve organizational life.

From my first weeks at university onward, I worked at the university library. In my third year, Professor Takala invited me to work as his research assistant and, later, as a teaching assistant. His research work concerned children's motivational characteristics as defined by Murray: the need for achievement, affiliation, and aggression. I was puzzled by the inconsistent findings of different measures. I started to develop my own hypothesis about the multidimensionality of motivational characteristics. I chose aggression, because it was more easily observable than affiliation or achievement, and because the phenomenon of aggression puzzled me. I constructed a model that included the intensity dimension and qualitative dimensions for defensive (reactive) versus offensive (proactive) aggression, and direct versus indirect aggression (see Pulkkinen, 2014; Pulkkinen, 2017). I tested the model with kindergarten teachers' observations of 6-year-old boys and found that the model was relevant. The results were included in the first part of my doctoral dissertation (Pitkanen, 1969).

The study revealed that only a few children were frequently aggressive. I became interested in how to describe children who were not aggressive in order to understand how to encourage positive behavior (Pulkkinen, 2017). Nonaggressive behavior in children was not a theme that was being studied in the literature; the boom in studying prosocial behavior did not begin until the late 1970s. As a result of an intensive period of thinking based on the available literature on frustration and coping processes, in 1967 I had the novel idea that the human brain allows for more variation in behavior than just the 'fight or flight' response known from animal studies of aggression. I speculated that it is the human being's capacity for cognitive control over his or her emotional behavior that makes him or her capable of deciding between alternative behaviors. I devised an impulse-control model to depict behavioral alternatives and tested it in 1968 with 8-year-old children (N = 369, 52% males) by gathering teacher and peer ratings of aggressive and nonaggressive behaviors. For this method, I harmonized some aggression items with those used by Walder, Abelson, Eron, Banta, and Laulicht (1961), which made it possible to carry out comparative studies between these two longitudinal studies on aggression 40 years later (Kokko et al., 2014).

The results at age 8 supported the impulse-control model. They were published in the second part of my dissertation (Pitkanen, 1969). This cross-sectional study was the starting point for the Jyväskylä Longitudinal Study of Personality and Social Development (JYLS), although it was only in the discussion section of my dissertation that I foresaw that,

'A longitudinal study would make it possible to examine the stability of the individual patterns of behavior' (Pitkanen, 1969, p. 190).

The participants in the study were born in 1959. They were native Finns, children of people who had survived the war: The average birth year of their fathers was 1929 and that of their mothers was 1932. When the participants were growing up, Finland was slowly recovering from the war. The sample was formed by drawing 12 school classes randomly from the schools of a town with a population around 60,000 located in Central Finland. It is both a university and an industrial town. All pupils in these classes were studied using peer and teacher ratings (see Pulkkinen, 2017, pp. 24–25), as accepted by school authorities; gaining parental consent was not required in 1968, and thus it did not cause any sample bias. The sample represented the social structure of the Finnish population in the 1960s. When the participants were 42 and 50 years old, the distributions of several demographic variables among them were compared with those in the age cohort born in 1959 (N ~ 75,000) as obtained from Statistics Finland, and they were found highly similar. At age 50, the retention rate from the initial sample was 73% for males and females, and the participation rate from the eligible sample was 84% (Pulkkinen, 2017, pp. 16–21).

At the time of my PhD, doctoral dissertations in my field were generally in Finnish, but I wanted to publish my dissertation in English in order to make it internationally available. I had only taken a short course in English, and, therefore, I needed the help of a student translator. During the translation process, I worked very hard on the draft translations, as I needed to provide the translator with adequate terminology. As a result, I developed heart failure caused by serious burnout. My 5-year-old daughter came to my bedside and said, 'Mom, go on tapping' (for her, the tapping sound of the typewriter meant that all was well).

4.2.4   *The Search for a Position in the 1970s*

At the beginning of the 1970s, I was aware that I had to go abroad to learn English. I applied for a British Council scholarship to study at Sussex University and was awarded the scholarship for the 1972–1973 academic year. The funds that I received were not enough to support the whole family, and since I could not leave my children behind, I hired a young woman who spoke some English to look after the children, packed her and my own children into a Volvo, and started to drive toward England. We encountered many problems, but we managed well. My children attended a local school, and I was happy to have Professor Marie Jahoda, my first female academic teacher, as the supervisor of my postdoctoral studies. Through her project on the Ugandan Asians that Idi Amin had expelled to England, I learned to understand the difficulties of non-Europeans in settling down in England, as well as a new semi-structured interview technique and a form of data processing, both of which I later employed in the longitudinal study.

I had to pay a heavy toll for my rich experiences during my postdoctoral year. In early spring, my husband wrote to me to say that he wanted a divorce. The return home was hard. In 1975, I married Paavo Pulkkinen, Associate Professor of Finnish Language at Jyväskylä. He was a widower with one son, and thus we had three adolescent children in the house. He played the violin, and I sang in a choir; music was our shared and beloved hobby. We lived happily together until his death in 2018, by which time we had 12 grandchildren (b. 1983–2004) and three great-grandchildren together. My husband was a great support to me in many ways during my busy years, not least through his cooking and editing of my Finnish texts.

I was an associate professor in education before going to Sussex but came back to an appointment as an associate professor in psychology. My first tasks included supervising the Master's theses of six students. To trace the children I had studied in 1968 for my doctoral dissertation when they were 8 years old, I received a small grant from the Academy of Finland. However, it did not even cover the cost of materials, such as the tapes on which to record the interviews. Unique personal identification numbers were not yet available, and therefore, we traced the sample by using school records and other sources. The participants were found to be located in 78 classes (they were originally in 12 classes) in several municipalities. We worked with great enthusiasm. Teacher and peer ratings were collected for 96% of the initial sample (369 children), but the interviews with the participants and one of their parents had to be limited to a selected group from the initial sample (see Pulkkinen, 2017). With another group of Master's degree students, we eventually conducted semi-structured interviews with this selected sample again when they were 20 years old (in 1979–1980), aiming to understand the young people's lifestyles and growing independence from their parents. I also organized the collection of criminal records for the whole initial sample.

In 1977 I published a book, *Kotikasvatuksen psykologia* [*The Psychology of Rearing Children*], in which I described the results that revealed the continuity in children's socio-emotional behavior from 8 to 14 years of age, both in terms of aggression and different types of nonaggressive behaviors, as well as factors affecting the development of self-regulation, particularly child-centered parenting. The book explains how parents can organize their behavior from the perspective of the child, by providing a context in which the child can feel the parents' warmth and acceptance, sustained involvement, and interest in his or her activities, opinions, and need for comfort and guidance. I applied the research results to daycare settings and prepared with students a program to improve children's self-regulation and to strengthen constructive behavior.

In 1979, I was invited by Finland's government to sit as an expert member on a parliamentary committee whose task was to define educational objectives for daycare. I was successful in convincing the committee that the task of daycare is to support the parents in child rearing. Moreover, daycare settings with a homely atmosphere, good quality relationships between the caretaker and the child, and opportunities for children's activities have a strong impact on children's development in all areas: physical, social, emotional, intellectual, aesthetic, and ethical (Committee Report 1980; Pulkkinen, 1989). The Parliament amended daycare legislation accordingly in 1983, and the importance of peace education in daycare was included in the legislation. These daycare objectives and guidelines remained in force until 2015.

Scientific conferences opened doors for me to international contacts. I attended many conferences of the International Society for the Study of Aggression (ISRA) from its first conference in 1974 onward, became its council member, and volunteered in assuming responsibility for the scientific program of the Sixth International Meetings of ISRA in Turku, Finland, in 1984. In 1976, I was pleased to be invited by Adam Fraczek to Warsaw to a meeting of researchers working on the theme of aggression, among them Norma Feshbach and Seymour Feshbach. There I gave a presentation in a symposium chaired by Professor Paul Mussen from Berkeley. He invited me to visit him in 1977. This was very important for me. I enjoyed the American research atmosphere that encouraged innovations, and I came to know Jeanne Bloch and Jack Block, with whom I shared many ideas (see Pulkkinen, 2017, pp. 59–61). I became friends with Paul Mussen and his wife, and later stayed with them at their home on a number of occasions. In their home, I met Nancy Eisenberg, Paul's former student and then Professor at Arizona State University. In 1992, I took over her professorship for half a year. Paul encouraged my applied interests and became an important mentor.

A meeting with Professor Urie Bronfenbrenner at a conference likewise led to us visiting one another. He also encouraged my applied interests and ecologically valid research. In a research seminar held in his backyard on a Sunday morning in 1984, I met his bright student Avshalom Caspi, with whom I later produced a book based on an international conference that I organized in Finland (Pulkkinen & Caspi, 2002). When I saw how enthusiastic Urie was about his new personal computer, I thought, 'I will also learn to use one of these'. I bought an Apple IIC that soon became my most important domestic appliance!

4.2.5 Breaking through the Glass Ceiling in the 1980s

At the 1979 Biennial Meeting of the ISSBD (Lund), Professor Paul Baltes chaired my symposium. He invited me to write an article based on the JYLS, in which I described the role of self-control in individual differences in aggression and nonaggression (Pulkkinen, 1982). He also pulled me into the activities of the ISSBD, with the result that in 1989 I organized the 10th Biennial Meeting of the ISSBD in Jyväskylä, Finland, which included around 800 foreign participants.

In 1982, a conference was organized by Dan Olweus in Norway, where I gave a presentation on impulse control (Pulkkinen, 1986) and was able to make new acquaintances, including Robert Hinde. I shared with him an interest in peace education (Pulkkinen, 1989) and aggression (Hinde & Pulkkinen, 2001). Robert became Master of the St John's College in Cambridge and invited me to visit the university as an overseas visitor in 1999. In the beginning of the 1980s, I analyzed the criminal registers of the study participants (Pulkkinen, 1983), and I was pleased to receive an invitation to attend a European Science Foundation workshop on psychosocial risks in development held in the UK (Pulkkinen, 1988). There, for the second time, I met David Farrington, with whom I shared an interest in delinquent development. This led years later to my visiting the Criminological Institute at Cambridge, which was directed by Friedrich Lösel at the time, and to David and I co-editing a special section for the journal *Aggressive Behavior* on lifespan longitudinal studies of aggressive and criminal behavior.

In 1982 I was invited to attend a prestigious National Civil Defense Course (for 4 weeks) organized by the Finnish Ministry of Defense. I had become interested in peace education, against the backdrop of the threatening Cold War atmosphere of the time, which included the possibility of nuclear war, and I criticized official defense policies for being too militaristic and not highlighting the importance of peaceful cooperation. My proposal – that the female perspective on defense politics should receive serious consideration – led to the formation of a group of influential women to work on this matter. Our 1986 report outlined new ways of thinking that were later incorporated into official documents. I ran a project, funded by the National Board for Social Welfare, in which we developed material for peace education in daycare.

When I received the commendation of the 1983 Woman of the Year in Finland, I promoted peace education. I felt that I had to speak up about constructive behavior as an alternative to aggression and violence. Additional activities in the applied field included the establishment of an NGO for strengthening the significance of childrearing and working to establish a multidisciplinary family research center at the University of Jyväskylä.

I was successful in receiving grants for the continuation of the JYLS in 1986 when the participants were 27 years of age. Once again, I worked with Master's students to collect data from the whole initial sample (retention rate for males was 90% and for females 85%). The participants' addresses were obtained through the Population Register Centre. We used semi-structured interviews for the study of the transition into adulthood and personal lifestyles.

I came up against the glass ceiling in 1982 when a deputy professor was needed to replace Martti Takala, Professor of Psychology, who had been elected President of the University. The female Minister of Education appointed me, because several parties had appealed to the Ministry of Education in opposition to the proposal made by the mostly male faculty for appointing a male candidate. I was aware that there would also be stiff competition for Takala's professorship at his retirement in 1989 and thus felt the need to increase my credentials for this post. I had, however, very little time for research. In addition to my scientific work and organizing the ISSBD Biennial Meetings in Jyväskylä in 1989, I was in the 1980s the head of the department, and for two years I was Dean of the Faculty of Social Sciences. Thus, it was a day of joy, three days before my 50th birthday, when all of the external reviewers ranked me first. The President of Finland appointed me Full Professor of Psychology in February 1990. I was the successor to my dear and respected mentor Martti Takala, who 30 years earlier had revealed to me, a country girl without an academic background, the treasures of psychology and science.

4.2.6   *Prime Time in the 1990s*

The 1990s had much to offer me. I received the honorable position of President of the ISSBD from 1991 to 1996. It meant participating in many committees, meetings, and workshops across all continents. I was particularly interested in and impressed by our workshop series in Africa. My closest collaborator during that time was Rainer Silbereisen.

The Academy of Finland appointed me Academy Professor from 1996 to 2001, and, in 1997, our research unit was appointed the National

Center of Excellence for Research on Human Development and Its Risk Factors. I was the chair of the center for nine years, and Sir Michael Rutter from the UK was the chair of the advisory board. With the funds available from the Academy of Finland, we continued the JYLS in 1996 by collecting data with the then 36-year-old participants on many areas of psychological and social functioning. The retention rate was 85%. We used internationally known inventories and conducted more structured personal interviews than we had done previously because coding semi-structured interviews had turned out to be too time-consuming. I integrated the concept of emotion regulation, which had become a hot topic in the literature, into the impulse-control model (see Pulkkinen, 2014, 2017). On the funds for Academy Professor, I was also able to establish a laboratory to study the self-regulation of the offspring of the longitudinal participants.

At the same time, I became involved in another longitudinal study when Richard J. Rose, Professor of Psychology and Medical Genetics at Indiana University, Bloomington, approached me and invited me to participate in a twin study, FinnTwin 12, with expertise in the study of children. This collaboration has continued to the present day and has expanded internationally (e.g., Bartels et al., 2018). The twin study increased my understanding of genetic and environmental factors in the development of aggressive and nonaggressive behaviors (Pulkkinen, Kaprio, & Rose, 2006).

In the 1990s, in order to find time for writing without being interrupted by the flow of various invitations to meetings and requests to give speeches, I worked abroad for various periods of time: in Berkeley; at Arizona State University; at the University of North Carolina, Chapel Hill; and at Cambridge University. In 1992, the Finnish Union of University Professors elected me Professor of the Year. In my speech of thanks, I proposed increased cooperation between universities and the creation of the National Faculty of Psychology covering all six universities that offered training in psychology. Even with all six universities put together, our resources were less than in one American university. This idea later developed into the form of a university network Psykonet, within which we still collaborate on many levels. I was the chair of the Psykonet for 2 years.

Furthermore, my efforts to establish the Family Research Unit at the University of Jyväskylä led to its founding in 1990; however, the university did not provide resources for it. I directed the board and activities of the unit until 1995 as part of the remit of the Department of Psychology. The new female president of the university was supportive of our family research activities and provided us her backing. In 1996,

Eeva Ahtisaari, the spouse of the President of Finland, invited me to the president's residence with a request to speak to a small group of guests about a family matter that concerned me. I spoke about children's lonely afternoons. A reason for these is the half-day school tradition in which the school week for 7- to 9-year-old children is only about 20 hours long, while both parents work 37–40 hours per week (Pulkkinen, 2012). Mrs. Ahtisaari offered me her help, and we made this problem visible in many ways. I was very pleased that Mrs. Ahtisaari attended my 60th birthday party in 1999.

Other activities included serving as a member of the Board of Governors for Statistics in Finland from 1996 to 2002 and on the Task Force on the National Strategy for the Centers of Excellence Policy, where, in 1997, I floated the idea of the Psykocenter (similar to Biocenters established at other universities). This idea was received very positively in Jyväskylä, and, within three years, new premises were built to house the Psykocenter and Info-Tech-Center, which we combined under the name 'Agora Center', with the mission to promote human-centered technology.

4.2.7   'Retirement' in the 2000s

The Agora Center that we created offered an excellent multidisciplinary context and infrastructure for research. The Center of Excellence, including also a longitudinal study on dyslexia conducted by Heikki Lyytinen, Professor of Neuropsychology, was relocated to the Agora Center. The national Center of Excellence Policy brought generous and long-standing funding for our research projects from the Academy of Finland and resources from the University of Jyväskylä. New data were collected with the longitudinal participants of our study when they were 42 years old (in 2001) with a retention rate of 77%. We repeated the measures used at age 36 as much as possible and added medical exam-inations. The data was saved in the Finnish Social Science Data Archives. Excellent doctoral dissertations were completed.

The confirmation of longitudinal research findings in other countries is necessary in order to understand what is universal in the results. International collaboration involved comparative studies on aggression with Canadian (Pulkkinen & Tremblay, 1992), Swedish (Kokko et al., 2003; Pulkkinen et al., 2000), U.S. (Dubow, Huesmann, Boxer, Pulkkinen, & Kokko, 2006), and multiple datasets (Duncan et al., 2012; Kokko et al., 2014). From 2003 to 2013, Dr. Katja Kokko and I were members of the Center for Analysis of Pathways from Childhood to Adulthood (CAPCA) coordinated by Michigan

University, United States, which focused on comparative analyses of longitudinal datasets.

I received prestigious invitations to act as a member of the Science and Technology Policy Council of Finland, chaired by the Prime Minister (2002–2005), and as a member of the Board of Governors for the Finnish Academy of Science and Letters (2003–2008). I also took on international tasks, such as assuming membership on the International Advisory Panel of New Opportunities for Research Funding Agency Cooperation in Europe (NORFACE), 2004–2009, and sitting on the Expert Panel for Psychology in charge of the project of the European Reference Index for Humanities, from 2007 to 2010 (serving as the chair for the last 2 years).

A group of Finnish Parliament members invited me to develop a program to improve schoolchildren's social skills and reduce aggression. I designed a pilot of a school day, which integrates learning as well as extracurricular activities. I directed the project for 3 years (2002–2005). The Minister of Education chaired the project board, and the Speaker of the Parliament was its patron. The results confirmed the benefits of the integrated school day in reducing children's anxiety when loneliness was reduced, and, particularly, the value of the arts in improving social skills and skills for work (such as concentration). The project led to amendments to school legislation in 2004, mandating municipalities to provide morning and afternoon activities for first- and second-grade children (Pulkkinen, 2012).

When I turned 65 years in 2004, the prevailing law forced me to retire (a more flexible law was passed in 2005, but I was born 2 months and 2 days too early to benefit from this). I was however, allowed to work at the university after my pension. I continued with my research work, with supervising doctoral students, and other activities. When the JYLS participants turned 50 years old, it was time for a new round of data collection. I applied for funding, and the Academy of Finland awarded it for 2009–2012. In 2013, I transferred the role of Principal Investigator to Dr. Katja Kokko, who had participated in the JYLS since 1995, first as a Master's and doctoral student and later as a colleague. She is now Research Director at the Gerontology Research Centre of the University of Jyväskylä. To my delight, she will be collecting new data from the JYLS participants as they turn 60 in 2019–2020.

4.2.8   Integration in the 2010s

It had been in my mind for years to write an English book about the JYLS, and the new decade brought more room for it. The aim of my book (Pulkkinen, 2017) was to outline a broader picture of human development than the detailed analyses for specific research questions published in articles for scientific journals. Metaphorically expressed, the process of writing the synthesis of the articles was like assembling a huge jigsaw puzzle without seeing the completed picture in advance. The picture included many details, among which the impulse-control model was the most relevant one for me.

The results revealed four paths from childhood to adult styles of life, which differed in behavior and emotion regulation as depicted schematically in Figure 1. The development of styles of life is a cumulative process associated with parenting, living conditions, and genetic factors. The paths are based on personality characteristics, educational attainments, work success, human relationships, health behavior, and adjustment into society. Impulsive, self-focused behavior in childhood increases the likelihood of aggression that tends to be linked with other types of *under-controlled* behavior, which is predictive of further problems in social adjustment. At the other end of the dimension for behavior regulation is norm-focused, compliant behavior. If it is consistent and strict, it may lead to the style of life termed *over-controlled*. In the dimension of emotion regulation, children's constructive behavior – including active coping with a problem, positive thinking, and consideration of others – leads to the *resilient* style of life and successful adulthood in work and human relationships leading to mental well-being. Low emotion regulation, in turn, may lead to anxiety and helplessness in handling situations, and the style of life termed *brittle*.

Human beings are capable of reflecting on their own behavior and emotions and can be agents of their own lives. Children's development can be promoted by encouraging their unique individuality and agency, guiding their adaptation to a complex society, and enriching their experiences with culture. In my applied work, I have highlighted the role of child-centered parenting and school environments enriched by the arts and other extracurricular activities to promote children's positive development.

In 2009, I was invited to serve on the Advisory Board of the Family Platform funded by the European Union's Seventh Framework Programme. I was very pleased to join the board, due to my interest and engagement in family research. There I met like-minded people, with the result that in 2012 I joined the Alliance for Childhood European Network Group (based in Brussels). Its mission is to improve the quality of childhood in Europe. I became a member of the Council and one of the editors of books that were based on a series of speeches on the quality of childhood delivered in the European Parliament house (www.allianceforchildhood.eu). In Finland, I was instrumental in the establishment of the Haukkala Foundation, which supports children's welfare (www.haukkalansaatio.com/English). In addition, the Ministry of Social Affairs and Health invited me to serve as the co-chair of the scientific committee of a governmental project to improve social services for children and families. These activities satisfied my interests in the applied field. To me, the ultimate goal of research work is to increase understanding of life and advance well-being in society. I was proud when I saw in a magazine a characterization for me: Speaker for Children.

In 2014, I moved to Helsinki, but my scientific and applied work continued. I was and still am deeply sorry that in 2017 the new president of the university dissolved the Agora Center, which had been highly successful in its multidisciplinary work. The problem – as far as I have understood - was that administratively it did not fit into the classic structure of the university. In my mind, it represented a new way of thinking and working in networks of researchers across disciplines. My name remained, however, in the former location of the Agora Center, where meetings are held in the Lea Pulkkinen Hall!

4.3   The Lessons Learned for a More Peaceful World

The concept of 'peaceful world' includes different levels, such as the lack of war between nations; the lack of violence between groups; and the lack of violence between individuals. Individual aggressiveness can be observed in violence between groups and individuals, but it rarely plays a part in international wars, as noted by Hinde and Pulkkinen (2001). War is an institution in itself. It may induce revenge, or at times aggressiveness might be encouraged, but, generally, aggressive killing is not allowed. War is a military-industrial-scientific complex, a nested set of institutions, where the career ambitions of individuals are driven by the arms industry, scientific recognition, and heroic behavior. Nevertheless, I have found it important to work at the individual level, because non-aggressive individuals have the ability to create a culture of peace and cultivate a will for peace. According to the UNESCO recommendation of 1974, member states should strengthen the contribution of education to international understanding and cooperation, to the establishment of social justice, and toward the eradication of prejudices against other groups and nations (Hinde & Pulkkinen, 2001). Developments in Europe, through the establishment of the European Union, have been promising for the creation of a more peaceful world. Finland has been a member since 1995, but it does not belong to NATO.

My personal research work on increasing understanding of both aggressive and nonaggressive behaviors was motivated by my childhood during the Second World War and thereafter in the independent but partly ruined country that struggled to pay enormous war reparations to its attacker. All energy had to be mobilized for the rebuilding of Finland. It also became part of my nature to work hard and to do my best in whatever I took on. My energy resources have been vast, as were those of my grandfather, who worked hard and effectively for his estate and community before the war. I also recognize that my mother's wise parenting has helped me grow through various developmental processes toward generativity that reflects a willingness to care about people and the things that one has produced. Supportive parenting and the socially active behavior of the child are prerequisites of generativity in our JYLS sample. Generativity correlates in adulthood with people-oriented behavior, career management, and psychological and social well-being, and with being a parent, which is also true for my life and me. Having children of the same age as the study participants motivated me to begin and continue the longitudinal study. Becoming a grandparent has given me wonderful opportunities to observe the development of individual differences in children.

What are the results of my work that might contribute to building a more peaceful world? First, an increase in the understanding of aggression, which I would not define as an individual's need or a personality trait but as a vulnerability trait that causes risks to social and personal adjustment. My studies on aggression over five decades resulted in 28 insights into aggression (Pulkkinen, 2018), including, for instance, differentiating between self-defensive reactive aggression and proactive aggression without provocation. In my understanding, aggression is primarily a self-defensive reaction whose regulation can be learnt. In unfortunate living conditions (and also for neurological reasons), this learning process may remain underdeveloped, or external conditions may become overwhelming, which may cause the excessive use of aggression for self-defense. Aggression may also be used proactively if it is found to be effective in gaining power over other people or in producing suffering in others that may satisfy an emotionally unbalanced mind. Proactive aggression is a high risk for criminal behavior among those whose level of childhood aggression is above the 75th percentile. Continuity of aggression from childhood to adulthood exists if aggression is high both in childhood and in adolescence. Knowing this, I deem it important that ways are found to reduce aggressive behavior during the school years and to encourage constructive behavior.

I am thankful to my students and colleagues for their productive teamwork, and to the University of Jyväskylä for providing us with excellent working conditions. I am also thankful to Finnish society for funding this work. My mission to work for a better world for future generations was based on a call that I received in the 1970s and that has given me much strength.

References

Bartels, M., Hendriks, A., Mauri, M., Krapohl. E., Whipp, A., Bolhuis, K., ... Boomsma, D. I. (2018). Childhood aggression and the co-occurrence of behavioural and emotional problems: Results across ages 3–16 years from multiple raters in six cohorts in the EU-ACTION project. *European Child & Adolescent Psychiatry*, 27(9), 1105–1121.

Committee Report (1980). *Educational objectives in day care (in Finnish)*. Helsinki, Finland: Government Printing Centre.

Dubow, E. F., Huesmann, L. R., Boxer, P., Pulkkinen, L., & Kokko, K. (2006). Middle childhood and adolescent contextual and personal predictors of adult educational and occupational outcomes: A mediational model in two countries. *Developmental Psychology*, 42(5), 937–949.

Duncan, G. J., Bergman, L., Duckworth, K., Kokko, K., Lyyra, A.-L., Metzger, M., ... Simonton, S. (2012). The role of child skills and behaviors in the intergenerational transmission of inequality: A cross-national study. In J. Ermisch, M. Jäntti, & T. Smeeding (Eds.), *From parents to children: The intergenerational transmission of advantage* (pp. 207–234). New York, NY: Russell Sage.

Hinde, R., & Pulkkinen, L. (2001). Human aggressiveness and war. *Pugwash: Occasional Papers*, 2, 5–37.

Kokko, K., Bergman, L. R., & Pulkkinen, L. (2003). Child personality characteristics and selection into long-term unemployment in Finnish and Swedish longitudinal samples. *International Journal of Behavioral Development*, 27(2), 134–144.

Kokko, K., & Pulkkinen, L. (2000). Aggression in childhood and long-term unemployment in adulthood: A cycle of maladaptation and some protective factors. *Developmental Psychology*, 36(4), 463–472.

Kokko, K., Simonton, S., Dubow, E., Lansford, J. E., Olson, S. L., Huesmann, L. R., ... Dodge, K. A. (2014). Country, sex, and parent occupational status: Moderators of the continuity of aggression from childhood to adulthood. *Aggressive Behavior*, 40(6), 552–567.

Pitkanen, L. (1969). *A descriptive model of aggression and nonaggression with applications to children's behaviour*. Jyväskylä Studies in Education, Psychology and Social Research, No. 19. Jyväskylä: University of Jyväskylä.

Pitkänen, T. (2006). *Alcohol drinking behavior and its developmental antecedents*. Jyväskylä, Finland: Jyväskylä University Printing House.

Pulkkinen, L. (1982). Self-control and continuity from childhood to late adolescence. In P. B. Baltes & O. G. Brim (Eds.), *Life-span development and behavior* (Vol. 4, pp. 63–105). New York, NY: Academic Press.

Pulkkinen, L. (1983). The search for alternatives to aggression. In A. P. Goldstein & M. Segall (Eds.), *Aggression in global perspective* (pp. 104–144). New York, NY: Pergamon Press.

Pulkkinen, L. (1986). The role of impulse control in the development of antisocial and prosocial behavior. In D. Olweus, J. Block, & M. Radke-Yarrow (Eds.), *Development of antisocial and prosocial behavior* (Vol. 2, pp. 149–175). New York, NY: Academic Press.

Pulkkinen, L. (1988). Delinquent development: Theoretical and empirical considerations. In M. Rutter (Ed.), *The power of longitudinal data: Studies of risk and protective factors for psychosocial disorders* (pp. 184–199). Cambridge, England: Cambridge University Press.

Pulkkinen, L. (1989). Progress in education for peace in Finland. In R. Hinde & D. A. Parry (Eds.), *Education for peace. Nottingham: Spokesman* (pp. 88–101). Nottingham, England: Russell.

Pulkkinen, L. (2012). The integrated school day – improving the educational offering of schools in Finland. In C. Clouder, B. Heys, M. Matthes, & P. Sullivan (Eds.), *Improving the quality of childhood in Europe 2012* (Vol. 3, pp. 40–67). Brighton, England: ECSWE.

Pulkkinen, L. (2014). Self-control at the heart of successful development. In R. M. Lerner, A. C. Petersen, R. K. Silbereisen, & J. Brooks-Gunn (Eds.), *The developmental science of adolescence: History through autobiography* (pp. 373–385). New York, NY: Psychology Press Taylor & Francis.

Pulkkinen, L. (2017). *Human development from middle childhood to middle adulthood: Growing up to be middle-aged.* London, England: Routledge.

Pulkkinen, L. (2018). Longitudinal study of personality and social development: Insights about aggression after five decades. In A. T. Vazsonyi, D. J. Flannery, & M. DeLisi (Eds.), *The Cambridge Handbook of Violent Behavior and Aggression* (2nd ed.). Cambridge, England: Cambridge University Press.

Pulkkinen, L., & Caspi, A. (2002). *Paths to successful development: Personality in the life course.* Cambridge, England: Cambridge University Press.

Pulkkinen, L., Kaprio, J., & Rose, R. J. (2006). *Socioemotional development and health from adolescence to adulthood.* New York, NY: Cambridge University Press.

Pulkkinen, L., & Tremblay, R. E. (1992). Patterns of boys' social adjustment in two cultures and at different ages: A longitudinal perspective. *International Journal of Behavioural Development, 15*(4), 527–553.

Pulkkinen, L., Virtanen, T., Klinteberg, B. A., & Magnusson, D. (2000). Child behaviour and adult personality: Comparisons between criminality groups in Finland and Sweden. *Criminal Behaviour and Mental Health, 10*(3), 155–169.

Screen, J. E. O. (2014). *Mannerheim: The Finnish years.* London, England: C. Hurst.

Walder, L. O., Abelson, R. P., Eron, L. D., Banta, T. J., & Laulicht, J. H. (1961). Development of a peer-rating measure of aggression. *Psychological Reports, 9*(3), 497–556.

5 From the Occupied Netherlands to the Pittsburgh Longitudinal Studies

Magda Stouthamer-Loeber and Rolf Loeber

Magda Stouthamer-Loeber was born September 21, 1942, in Zandvoort, the Netherlands. Rolf Loeber was born June 5, 1942, in Hilversum, the Netherlands. Magda Stouthamer-Loeber and Rolf Loeber worked and lived together throughout their careers. They both received their PhDs from Queens University (Canada), in 1972 for Rolf and in 1979 for Magda. Their first faculty appointments were at the University of Pittsburgh in 1984. Rolf Loeber eventually became Distinguished University Professor of Psychiatry, Professor of Psychology, and Professor of Epidemiology at the University of Pittsburgh. He was also Professor of Juvenile Delinquency and Social Development at the Free University in Amsterdam, the Netherlands, between 1997 and 2002. Magda Stouthamer-Loeber was Associate Professor of Psychiatry and Psychology at Pittsburgh University until her retirement in 2011. Rolf Loeber received numerous prestigious awards during his career, including the Distinguished Contribution Award of the American Psychological Association (2003), the Lifetime Achievement Award of the American Society of Criminology Division of Developmental and Life-Course Criminology (2013), and the Outstanding Contributions Award (1998) from the Office of Juvenile Justice and Delinquency Prevention (OJJDP) for the book *Serious and Violent Juvenile Offenders: Risk Factors and Successful Interventions*.

After receiving their PhDs, the Loebers were invited by Gerald Patterson to join the Oregon Social Learning Center in Eugene, Oregon, where they became responsible for the pilot work that led to the Oregon Youth Study. During this period, Rolf Loeber published seminal papers on the stability of antisocial behavior and the first meta-analysis of predictors of delinquency (Loeber & Dishion, 1983).

The Loebers had major impacts on the science of violent behavior development and on the translation of this scientific knowledge into improved public policy. First, they pioneered the articulation and expansion of developmental and life-course criminology. Starting in the early 1980s they clarified the formulation of key concepts and published almost 300 empirical papers that provided longitudinal evidence of the onset, persistence, and desistance of offending from late childhood through early adulthood.

Second, realizing that new developmental data was necessary to advance knowledge, the Loebers initiated and maintained two landmark longitudinal studies in the United States, which started in childhood and continued with regular assessments into early adulthood. The first, the Pittsburgh Youth Study (PYS), consisted of three age groups of 1,517 boys, originally in grades 1, 4, and 7 in public schools, who were followed for more than 20 years. The second was the Pittsburgh Girls Study, in which a random sample of four age groups of 2,451 girls (ages 5, 6, 7, and 8) were followed into their 20s. The Pittsburgh Girls Study was the first major large-scale study in the United States on the development of female delinquency between childhood and early adulthood (Loeber, Jennings, Ahonen, Piquero, & Farrington, 2017).

The Loebers were the first to have the data to study which youths are at highest risk to commit homicide or become a victim of homicide. They showed that the processes leading to homicide were often in place during late childhood (Farrington, Loeber, & Berg, 2012; Loeber & Farrington, 2011).

Rolf Loeber was also the first to empirically demonstrate the escalation processes, from minor problem behavior to serious forms of offending, which unfold in systematic ways along three distinct developmental pathways of overt, covert antisocial/delinquent behavior, and authority conflict. Knowledge of these pathways has been a key component of the formulation of interventions, which were evaluated by means of a randomized controlled trial (Loeber et al., 1993).

With their longitudinal study of girls, the Loebers found that girls differed from boys not only in terms of types of delinquency but also in how cumulative risk factors affect girls differently than boys, with more of the girls as compared to the boys being at high risk in the tail end of the distribution (Loeber et al., 2017).

Rolf Loeber and his colleagues also advanced knowledge on factors influencing the age–crime curve. They found that the factors significantly varied according to the neighborhood in which offenders lived. They also found that youths who were cognitively impulsive or had low IQ tended to have higher and wider age–crime curves (Lynam et al., 2000).

Magda Loeber was responsible for designing data collection procedures, which led to high participation rates and thus set the standard for the field. In addition, data collection, cleaning, and documentation methods were given high priority so that data analysis was done on the best possible set of data (Stouthamer-Loeber & Van Kammen, 1995).

Rolf Loeber was dedicated to knowledge transfer and to improving delinquency and justice communication channels between Europe and North America. He was the only criminologist who oversaw three successive U.S. study groups on important life-course and developmental criminological topics (serious and violent juvenile offenders; child delinquents; and the transition from juvenile delinquency to adult crime) and three similar study groups in Europe.

Rolf Loeber authored 14 criminology books, several of which are widely used in the teaching of graduate-level students. He published nearly 300 peer-reviewed papers in criminology, psychiatry, epidemiology, and psychology, and over 150 chapters. Although he died in 2017, Rolf Loeber is still among the most cited authors in criminology and child development. With more than 79,000 citations at the end of 2019 (according to Google Scholar), he ranks second after David Farrington for citations on 'juvenile delinquency' and fourth for citations on 'child development'.

In addition, the Loebers extensively published on Ireland: six books on literature, colonialism, and architecture, and more than 60 papers on colonial power and conflict, warfare, colonial settlement studies, literature, historical geography, and architecture (Loeber, Campbell, Hurley, Montague, & Rowley, 2014; Loeber, Stouthamer-Loeber, & Burnham, 2006).

Funding agencies recognized the innovation and quality of the Loebers' research. Without interruption from 1978 to 2017, they received major research grants, totaling $66,773,200 in order to advance knowledge about brain functioning and delinquency. Before his death, Rolf Loeber played an important role in launching a new longitudinal delinquency study on approximately 3,000 10- to 11-year-olds (the Adolescent Brain Cognitive Development [ABCD] Study in the United States) to assess brain functioning from ages 9–10 and 19–20.

The Loebers practiced what they often publicly said; namely, that 'open science' is a prerequisite for advancing knowledge, which includes making data and documentation available to scholars and students. They successfully encouraged European and North American scholars to analyze and write papers using data from the longitudinal studies and have arranged for the depositing of the PYS data at the National Archive for Criminal Justice Data in Michigan. Further, they shared their expertise in the starting up of longitudinal studies in the Netherlands, Belgium, England, Norway, and Switzerland.

The Loebers' research also greatly influenced criminal justice policy in the United States and the Netherlands. Rolf Loeber's last European study group led directly to the Dutch government passing a law on special treatment for young adult offenders. Persons up to age 23 can now be processed under the jurisdiction of the juvenile justice system. The U.S. Assistant Attorney General also expressed interest in special courts for young adult offenders aged 18–24.

Rolf Loeber was a Member of the Royal Dutch Academy of Sciences; an Honorary Member of the Royal Irish Academy; Fellow of the American Society of Criminology (2000); Fellow of the American Psychological Association (1998); and Life Fellow of Clare Hall, University of Cambridge (1998). He was also an Advisor to the World Health Organisation's Second World Report on Violence and Health (2011–2012); a member of the International Advisory Board to the Brain and Cognition Council, Dutch Science Foundation (2010–2016); Co-Chair of the Dutch Study Group on the Transitions from Juvenile Delinquency to Adult Crime (2010–2012); Co-Chair of the Dutch Study Group on Very Young Offenders (2008–2010); Co-Chair of the U.S. National Institute of Justice Study Group on Transitions from Juvenile Delinquency to Adult Crime (2008–2011); Co-Chair of the U.S. OJJDP Study Group on Very Young Offenders (1998–2000); Co-Chair of the U.S. OJJDP Study Group on Serious and Violent Juvenile Offenders (1995–1997); Vice-Chair of the Division of Developmental and Life-Course Criminology, American Society of Criminology (2013–2016); Institute Fellow of the Institute of Criminology, University of Cambridge (2004–2017); Senior Fellow of the Netherlands Institute for the Study of Crime and Law Enforcement (2008–2017); and a recipient of the Justice for Children Award, OJJDP (2000).

Two books were published honoring Rolf Loeber (2019, 2020). The first, containing his collected articles on Irish architecture, was prepared by some of his Irish friends. The second contains photographs Rolf took over the past 10 years.

5.1   Introduction

It is an interesting and daunting task to write one's life history and that of one's partner, particularly if the partner can't speak for himself anymore. Since Rolf died at the end of 2017, I will have to write his part of the story as well. I am sure it will be different from the story Rolf would have told, but I will try to be as careful as possible to reflect what I think he might have written. Since I know more about my own youth than Rolf's, the description of my youth will be longer than that of Rolf's.

Life is very exciting and I do not know many people who have a plan early on and stick to it. For me, life has been a series of serendipitous opportunities, which I could take or forgo. Every fork in the road provided new choices later on. In other words, for the longest time, Rolf and I did not have a life plan. However, once you start a longitudinal study, commitment and structure is required. I am sure that the path longitudinal researchers take to the point of starting a longitudinal study is varied, but once a longitudinal study has started, I think for most of us the curiosity of 'what is next' takes over. It is like a good book that you cannot put down, and the eventual termination of a project may be painful.

I will try to pinpoint early events and characteristics that may have contributed to the eventual longitudinal studies, but as I mentioned in the previous paragraph, serendipity played a large role.

5.2   Our Early Lives

Rolf and I were both born in the Netherlands in 1942, during the war. Holland was invaded by the Germans on May 10, 1940. Holland surrendered on May 15 after the Germans had thoroughly bombed Rotterdam and Middelburg and threatened to do the same with Utrecht. The 5 years that followed saw the removal of many Jews and other Dutch to concentration camps and work camps: Eventually 140,000 Jews were transported and only 30,000 survived. Another 107,000 non-Jewish citizens died; some 18,000 died from starvation during the last winter of the war when Germany cut off all food and oil to the Netherlands. There were also 30,000 casualties from the Japanese invasion of Indonesia, at that time a Dutch colony. None of these casualties included any relatives of ours. Nevertheless these events dominated our early years in terms of anxiety on our parents' part and shortages of every kind, particularly of food and amenities that make life a little easier. It took a number of years after the war before, for instance, oranges and bananas were available, and clothing and shoes were for a long time hand-me-downs or home-made. Since this was the situation after the war for most people, it did not feel like deprivation. We were all in the same boat! It was probably more difficult for our parents to figure out how to provide for us than it was for us children.

5.3   Rolf

Rolf's parents lived in Hilversum, a well-to-do part of Holland, and moved in a circle of well-off families. Rolf was born on the June 5, 1942, the third of what would eventually become four children. His parents did not fare as well financially as the previous generation had. Rolf's grandfathers had been successful businessmen, but Rolf's father did not have the knack for, and the interest in, the family business of making and selling paper. He took early retirement, and his father-in-law added financial support for many years. Rolf's parents did not have a happy marriage, and, while Rolf's father traveled a lot, he was not always faithful. He was actually a pretty egocentric man who grew up without siblings, and in his later life he did not pay much attention to his wife or his children. He was a good writer and artist, though, and he spent his retirement years researching the history of papermaking. Rolf's mother, like many mothers at that time, did not have a job at any time in her life. She had one brother and two sisters to whom she was close. She was kind and caring with her children.

Living in this well-to-do area meant you had to keep up with the Joneses in the form of field hockey lessons and a sailing club membership. During his childhood, Rolf had a lazy eye and had to use an eye patch for quite a while. It did not quite cure the problem, and as a result Rolf could not see well in two dimensions. This made his field hockey career unsuccessful. He was also not a star student, but, unlike his three siblings, he finished high school by working on his own in the summers on the subjects he was weak in. He also worked with his neighbor, who was a contractor. Rolf made architectural drawings. For a while he thought of becoming an architect but decided he was not creative enough.

After high school he went to a business school. Business was not Rolf's passion, but, since the whole family was in business, the choice was approved by his family. Rolf did not enjoy it and was absent as much as possible. After he was asked to leave the school, though, Rolf decided to finish his BA in business just to show he could do it. In order to get his degree he had to write a thesis about a business abroad. He went to Kent to write up a paper mill. However, this was a family business and, although Rolf was allowed to see how paper was made, he did not get access to the business side of the mill. This meant he did not have anything to write a thesis on. While in Kent he stayed in a home for patients with multiple sclerosis, and he decided to write a thesis on the time perspective of these patients. I can't quite understand why the business school accepted this, but this creative move got him his BA in business.

While in business school he had decided to study psychology, but he first had to fulfill his conscription duty in the Dutch army. He was enrolled in officer training, but after a month he was demoted to private because he did not show the proper zeal in leading soldiers into battle. The rest of his time in the service he spent painting trucks, and when there were no more trucks to be painted he became manager of the bar for the pilots on the base. This consisted of making coffee and reading psychology books in preparation for going to university. He was allowed to leave the service early in order to start his studies in September.

At university he never had high grades, but he was very organized and efficient. His system was to read the material for an exam, and, while reading, he would write down questions. Then he would go through the questions and strike off those he could answer until he was able to answer all the questions. In this way he did all his exams in no time. After we met he tried to teach me his method, but I was far too uncertain that I would continue to remember all the answers after just one time, so I stuck to my more plodding way of preparing for exams.

While Rolf was working for his BA in psychology, he earned money by translating English short stories into Dutch for an upscale women's magazine. The work apparently paid very well. A publisher then asked Rolf to make an anthology of Irish short stories in translation, which he did. Rolf needed to write an introduction, but he had never been to Ireland. So he went and fell in love with the landscape and architecture (mainly in ruins). The anthology was published in 1967, around the time we met.

5.4   Magda

I was born in Zandvoort, on September 21, 1942, the third of what eventually would be seven children. My father was a police sergeant. He had been trained as a carpenter, but there were no carpentry jobs during the depression. My mother had been trained as a cook. They met in Middelburg, a town in the south of Holland, where my mother lived and my father was a conscript in the army. He found a job as a military policeman and later transferred to the ordinary police force. This allowed my parents to marry and move to Zandvoort in the north of Holland. My mother's parents were farm laborers, and my mother had no siblings. My father's father was a harbor laborer, and my father had two elder sisters.

Zandvoort is on the North Sea coast, but during the war the Germans had built a concrete wall in the dunes, mined the beach, and torn down all the houses on the seafront to repel the British if they would try a landing. Near our house were installations for shooting off missiles to England. They made a terrible racket, and some misfires landed close by. Most people in our neighborhood had been evacuated. We lived there because my father was a police sergeant. I have never fully known what it was like for him to serve under the Germans. I know that the police often sabotaged German requests, such as rounding up all radios. They would first go to the Nazi sympathizers and take away their radios before looking for other ones. Small acts of insurrection!

I do not remember much of the war except that I had been instructed to duck and shelter against a wall if there was a noise in the sky. My two older brothers would sometimes bring wood home for the stove, which was illegal. They threatened me that we all would be killed if the visiting game warden found out. There was a shortage of food, especially in the winter of 1944. However it was apparently not at a starvation level for us because my brothers, from a safe distance from the house, would yell to my mother, asking what there was for dinner, and when my mother answered 'sugar beet pulp loaf', their answer was 'we are not coming'. My father would go into the countryside to visit farmers and see if he could get some food in exchange for valuables, such as jewelry. These trips by bicycle could never be very far because you had to be home by curfew. I remember that soon after the war ended, Swedish Red Cross planes flew over and dropped food. I ran home to be safe from this danger in the sky, but my father took me on his arm and said 'wave'. I still remember my confusion.

It took a long time after the war for life to become normal again, but as a child you do not know any better. I do remember, though, my first dress made from a new piece of fabric and my first new shoes. We did not have many toys, but my father's workshop was not locked and one of the joys of my childhood was to hammer nails in the wooden fence posts of the garden. Soon after the war I was given a Chinese doll with a porcelain head, and porcelain hands and feet. Unfortunately it had a very short life because my father stepped on it and broke its head. For a long time I kept the hands and feet, but they were of no use without the head.

My parents were amazing! They loved each other and they loved us. My parents never told any of us that we were special, smart, or beautiful, but we knew instinctively that they were there for us and that they loved us. There were eventually seven children, and my mother cooked, knitted, sewed, and canned. She could also be overbearing and was clearly in control of the household. My father had for a while an extra job in a plant nursery, and usually he took Monday off to help my mother with the washing (without a washing machine or dryer). There was also no refrigerator, so food had to be prepared fresh every day. I was there when all this happened, but now I can hardly imagine how they did it. My parents were religious, and after dinner my father would read from the Bible. To make sure we paid attention, he would suddenly stop, and we all had to recite the last sentence. To this day I can still recite the last sentence I have heard. Even though I lost my faith in my early teens, I am glad that I had a strong moral upbringing. My parents also taught us that a job was not worth doing unless you did it to the best of your abilities, whatever your abilities were. Most important was that you were a decent person, and I think my parents succeeded in bringing up seven decent persons.

My school years were marked by my mother moving me from one school to another. I am not quite sure why, but I was never longer than 2 years in one school. It is not a good recipe for making long-term friendships, but I liked my own company and I had my own large family at home. My older brothers allowed me at times, probably under pressure from my mother, to share their adventures. These involved pulling up snares that poachers had set in the dunes. They did this at the request of the local landlord; however my brothers always waited until there was a rabbit in the snare. We grew up on rabbit meat. I learned early on to skin and clean rabbits and chickens and ducks, maybe not very useful while living in a city, but it is good to know that one has some survival skills. My brothers also took me on more dangerous adventures, finding unspent bullets left over from the war and hammering them flat. It is a miracle that we did not get hurt. I imagine many kids in postwar zones do the same: playing in bomb craters and finding war spoils.

In addition I had my mother's little babies to help look after. The youngest was 14 years younger than I. There must have been times that I did not want to look after my little siblings, but I have conveniently forgotten that and remember the joy of caring for them, and the wonder in their eyes when telling them stories. I remember with less pleasure the endless number of chores that I had to help my mother with. With seven children, the house was often chaotic.

Another joy in my childhood involved animals. My mother was the person in the neighborhood whom you would go to for dropping off animals in need. So we had little rabbits (eventually eaten), birds fallen out of nests, birds with broken wings, and so on. We had tame crows, magpies, and blue jays, cats and a dog. And every spring our neighbor had young goats. Our dog also helped the household by digging up rabbits in the dunes and bringing them home. I still love animals, and I still love wild rabbit meat, too.

My mother was not somebody to be disobeyed. I remember when I was 14 and summer was approaching, my mother told me to go and find a summer job. She put me outside and locked the door. When it was clear to me that she meant business, I went out and found a job in a bed-and-breakfast place. The process of going to ask for a job was agony, since I was quite shy. My mother had other terrible jobs for me, such as collecting subscription money for the church magazine, or selling eggs or skinned rabbits to neighbors. Awful! But my mother would not take no for an answer. I guess what I learned from this is that there is no use postponing unpleasant jobs. You might as well bite the bullet and be done with it.

My parents knew their place in society, and that meant not having too high expectations for their children. We all went to a high school that did not prepare you for university (MULO, extended lower education). However, my brother, who was three years older than I, was very smart, and the principal encouraged my parents to let him go on to a high school that would allow him to go to university (HBS, higher civic school). My parents thought it was a little presumptuous but allowed it. Since the Dutch government gave bursaries for students with good grades and with parents who could not afford to pay for university, my brother went on to university and eventually got a PhD in chemistry. To illustrate how extraordinary this was for the son of a police sergeant, the mayor of our town and the local landlord came to the public defense of my brother to witness this.

What my brother had done made it possible for me to take the same path. I loved learning and was very happy to have a chance to go on. The choice of psychology was more or less by elimination. I did not want to study languages because I did not want to be a teacher; another choice would have been sociology, but that sounded even more vague than psychology. So, I went to Leiden in 1960; it was the first time I lived by myself. On the one hand I was happy to escape home and my mother's bossiness; on the other I missed my family and the ready-made companionship. I was ready to look after my own finances and was able to live within my means. Since Holland is so small, most students can go home every weekend. However, I often stayed in Leiden to train myself to be at ease by myself. Since I was a shy person, I thought counting on myself was a better bet than developing many friendships. I think this early training helps me now that Rolf has died. I did make a few life-long friends, though.

I went to Amsterdam to do my MA in clinical psychology in 1965. There I was taught Rogerian therapy, at which I was very bad. I am a problem solver and apparently not a good listener. It is just as well that I did not pursue a career in a therapeutic field. I enjoyed Amsterdam more than Leiden because it was not just a university town. In Leiden the students felt they were very special, whereas in Amsterdam you were just another person – more anonymous, I guess.

As a student I traveled a fair amount. I spent two summers traveling in the United States. At that time you could get a 3-month Greyhound bus ticket for $99. The trip back and forth was in an old Liberty ship from World War II. I also hitchhiked, unbeknownst to my parents, throughout

Europe to Italy and in Spain with a friend and had a wonderful time expanding my horizons beyond the borders of my small country. None of these trips had a particular purpose beyond curiosity and the adventure of it all.

5.5   Adventures

I have called this section 'Adventures' because that's what my life has been since I met Rolf in June 1967. I could also have called it 'A Love Affair' because that is what it has also been for 50 years, but that sounds kind of mushy for a serious chapter. It is not that Rolf and I always agreed or never irritated or even hurt each other, but basically we had a strong bond that withstood whatever ups and downs came our way. When I met Rolf I was finishing my MA. He had just finished his BA.

Soon after we met we moved in together under the motto 'Why waste time if you find someone good?' After a few weeks we knew that most likely we would stay together, and we were married within a year. The immediate, practical reason was that I was tired of sneaking into the flat (through the bicycle cellar) where Rolf had his room. After I finished my MA, and while waiting for Rolf to finish his, I had a job at the Criminological Institute. I wrote some papers about personality tests for delinquents and made literature summaries of criminal psychology. It was not a strenuous job and did not make me grow. My strongest memory of this time was of playing tennis every Friday morning and of feeling as if I were accomplishing nothing, which is not good for one's self-esteem. Rolf's MA work concerned behavior therapy.

We did not really have clear plans about our future, so when, in 1968, we met a Dutch psychiatrist who was the head of a state mental hospital in Bolivar, Tennessee, and he offered us jobs, we, together with two friends, signed up. We were planning to go there after Rolf finished his MA (1969). Before we went to the states we took a car trip to India with other friends. We still had some Dutch money, and we had visions of earning big fat dollars later on, so what better time to go on a crazy trip! Our parents did not think it was such a great idea, but we were young and naïve. All the countries that are a bit dicey to travel to now – Turkey, Iran, Afghanistan, Pakistan, and Kashmir – were maybe not the safest places to be but were at least travelable then. It was an amazing trip, and it taught us that as 'poor' Dutch students we were very fortunate compared with many people we saw along the way.

When we returned there was a letter from the State of Tennessee that our jobs had been cut due to a general budget reduction. Of course we were disappointed, not because we were not going to Tennessee, but because our next adventure was cancelled. Determined to go some-where, anywhere, we wrote to various people and in no time had job offers from the Kingston Psychiatric Hospital in Ontario, Canada. Applying for a work permit at that time was easy, and we left for Kingston on November 18, 1969. The Dutch government paid for our trip and some freight, and gave us 'landing money'. I guess this was a holdover from the time just after the war when people were encouraged to emigrate. It was strange that after the government had paid for our education, they were happy to see us go. I still get a little pension from the generous Dutch government.

One thing about living in Holland that we only realized after we had left was that we had grown up in an atmosphere where there was little or no competition. In school we were never graded on a curve. Of course, you knew who was smart and who was rather dumb, but it was never stressed. With regard to going to university, you had to pass your high school exam and the university had to accept you. (This is not the case anymore, which may be related to the fact that, as the war babies, we preceded the baby boomers, who had to compete much more to enter university and find jobs because there were many more of them). However, in our time you did not have to be the smartest or compete against other students. Our schools did not have sports teams, and when we had to play field hockey for gym, nobody cared who won. I often was a goalie and stood around leaning on my stick until the action came close my goal, and then I just stepped aside, so that I would not be hit by a hard object. Nobody blamed me; we were just running around! That was exercise enough. I only realized with gratitude, after having moved to North America, how free of stress our upbringing had been. That, apart from my family, has been the biggest gift Holland has given me. Maybe I should add to this what they would call in the United States 'a socialist outlook on politics'. This applies particularly to the United States and not so much to Canada.

We had a small, furnished apartment in the middle of Kingston, overlooking the market square. The day after we arrived, we bought our first car and started working the next week. Rolf was in the long-term schizophrenia ward, and I had a position in the short-term admission ward. Our jobs were mainly doing psychological evaluations. Neither job was strenuous; we had regular hours and no work on the weekends. The pace was leisurely. Rolf decided to apply for graduate school and was admitted at Queens University for the fall of 1970. He had planned ahead of time what his dissertation was going to be on (therapist behavior as influenced by the client), and he finished in 2 years, while still working part-time. While he was doing this, he was also researching and writing on Irish architectural history. He was successful in obtaining grants from the Canada Council for his Irish research. I remember my consternation when Rolf told me that he was applying for a grant. I pointed out to him that he had no training, no background in architectural history, but Rolf calmly said that he might as well try. In the meantime he was also writing psychology papers. I guess all these activities were possible because we did not have any children (by choice) and no television, and because Rolf was an amazing person who knew how to organize and entertain himself.

The same day that Rolf defended his thesis we flew to Ireland for a year-long stay. Rolf was to coordinate a group of architectural history scholars for the writing of an architectural dictionary. People were assigned periods to cover. Rolf's period was the 17th century. We had a flat in an old country house – Castletown House, outside Dublin – owned by Desmond Guinness, who let us stay there and who also organized a grant for Rolf that covered part of our living expenses. The view outside our windows was amazing, with the Wicklow Mountains in the background. The flat was very cold, but one got used to it after a while. We traveled around the country looking at old buildings and building sites. Rolf worked in various libraries and archives, and I sometimes helped him with his research. I also took courses in art history at Trinity College. We met many scholars in architectural history, Irish history, archaeology, and geography. These people have been our friends for 50 years. One of the reasons for these friendships was that Rolf was always very generous in sharing findings from his research, and, since he was an amateur, he was not in competition with anyone for jobs or honors.

After a year we had to start earning a living again. We had looked at job offerings in Holland, but our hearts were not in it. Eventually we went back to Kingston, Ontario, where Rolf got his old job back, and I worked part-time as a behavior therapist. Not a good fit! Later I found a position as a psychometrist at the Frontenac County Board of Education to support teachers and principals when they encountered problems with students. The territory I had to cover was very large, and I entertained myself while driving by designing in my head efficient houses. In the end we bought an 1850s limestone farmhouse, which we renovated. We did not know much about plumbing, electrical wiring, carpentry, reroofing, and putting in insulation in the roof and the walls. You learn as you go along. We also made a whole new set of friends who were all restoring old houses. We helped each other and exchanged tips. We also had dinner parties that lasted until the sun came up. We became Canadian citizens because we felt we would live there forever.

I decided to get my PhD as well, since I realized that if we stayed in Canada it would be useful. I was not impressed by the psychology department of Queens University, but getting my PhD was just a means to an end, so that did not matter. I dare say that the faculty was probably also not impressed by my lack of zeal to learn from them. I refused to do several internships on the ground that I had supervised graduate students in my job at the mental hospital and at the board of education. My dissertation was on classroom observation, more specifically, the unit on which the reliability of the system should be measured. Generally, the reliability of a coding system is measured by individual units. My thesis was that it should be measured according to whether coders could agree on a behavior and its response. While I was developing this idea, Rolf, interested in my work, decided to visit Jerry Patterson in Eugene, Oregon, and Jerry invited Rolf to come for the summer. We drove to Oregon and lived in an unfurnished apartment with makeshift furniture. By that time I was writing up the results of the first-grade classroom observations that were made by the community college students I had trained. We had a great time, and I learned from Jerry how exciting psychology can be. I will always be thankful for that.

Jerry invited Rolf to come and work with him. This was exciting, particularly because Kingston did not have much to offer. So, the evening I finished my PhD in June 1979, we had a party on a boat on the St. Lawrence River and the next day we set out for Oregon. We had acquired U.S. work permits. We were slightly worried because during the summer we spent in Eugene we had noticed that it was not the most stable place with regard to personnel relations, but we had some savings and no children, and we felt we could always somehow land on our feet. We were right to worry because there was no job for me, and a week after we arrived someone else came to Eugene with the promise of a job – but there was no job. Eventually I was put on the payroll.

We had barely settled in when Jerry told us that he and Marion Forgatch, his partner, were going to Stanford on a year's sabbatical and that Rolf was in charge of a study in preparation for a longitudinal study on antisocial behavior and delinquency. I was designated to work under Rolf. There were several worrisome aspects to this plan. First, Rolf and I had never had a course in developmental psychology. Second, even though I had worked at a criminological institute in Amsterdam, neither one of use had ever had a course in criminology. Third, we did not know anything about making interview questions or running a study with two interview waves. Fourth, even though Rolf and I got on well together, we had never worked together. It seemed to us that this might either be a wonderful experience or lead to the end of our relationship. We accepted the challenge and started to learn at a furious tempo about all the things we needed to know to do this job. This was how we started on our careers in developmental criminology. Circumstances, not choice, led us down that path.

We had to work very hard to get somewhat up to speed. Everything was new: consent forms, contacting schools for their cooperation, making questionnaires, hiring staff, keeping track of the budget. Rolf was often in touch with Jerry, and John Reid and Patty Chamberlain were often of help, although none of them had ever set up a large study.

We were in awe of visitors, like Delbert Elliott, who seemed to have such a grasp of the literature while we were just bumbling along. Del mentioned something that was reassuring: He said that he never had done a study that did not have a flaw. This took the pressure down a notch. Our goal had been to do everything perfectly. Knowing that even under the best of circumstances there are things that you regret placed our goals in a better perspective.

We did a credible job with the preparatory study. The next step was to write a proposal for the actual longitudinal study. Writing proposals was not entirely a new activity, but now the stakes were higher, and we learned a lot. In the meantime Rolf was reading as much as he could to get up to speed on the literature. We stayed in Eugene for 5 years and mostly had a wonderful time. It was certainly a fruitful time. We published on skill deficits of male delinquents, a review paper on family factors related to delinquency, early predictors of delinquency, and on a multistage assessment procedure of identifying youth at risk for delinquency (Dishion, Loeber, Stouthamer-Loeber, & Patterson, 1984; Loeber & Dishion, 1983; Loeber, Dishion, & Patterson, 1984). In the end we had learned what we could, and the autocratic structure of the place became stifling. We handed in our resignations and expected to need a year to find other jobs. We had planned to do some Irish research in the meantime and were looking forward to that. However, before we left Eugene we were offered jobs for both of us at the psychiatry department of the University of Pittsburgh.

5.6   Pittsburgh

We had not applied for jobs at the University of Pittsburgh. Craig Edelbrock had suggested to the director of the psychiatry department, Dr. Detre, and to his second in command, Dr. Kupfer, that we might have the potential to bring in grant money. The psychiatry department did not advertise for jobs but tried to find people whom they thought had promise. After all, most medical schools are business enterprises. I had to giggle at the opulence of the place. We had been advised to come up with big plans, so we proposed a large longitudinal study. We were hired to work together and were offered a 3-year contract to see if the perceived promise could be fulfilled.

We got offices, a secretary, research assistants, and some research money. We started our jobs there in April 1984. We wrote some smaller proposals. My first proposal was on lying in young children, and Rolf wrote a proposal for developing a screening instrument for youth at risk for delinquency. However, our largest proposal was for a longitudinal study on the development of antisocial behavior and delinquency. David Farrington, whom we had met when he visited the Oregon Social Learning Center, was our co-investigator and for many years our collaborator. We shared many ideas about how to set up and run a longitudinal study, and about its goals. The study would consist of contacting about 850 boys in grades 1, 4, and 7 each. After screening we would follow-up about 500 boys in each grade, half of whom were at high risk for delinquency and half randomly selected from the remainder. Data would be collected regularly from the boys, their main caretakers, and teachers. Eventually criminal records and data from Child Welfare were collected as well. We applied to the proposal what we had learned in Eugene and submitted it to the National Institute of Mental Health (NIMH). Even though it received a good score, it was never funded because the agency was already funding Gerry Patterson's study.

We received funding for our smaller studies but also responded to a request for proposals for a longitudinal study on delinquency from the OJJDP for the bigger study (the PYS) with David Farrington. We were successful, together with Terry Thornberry and David Huizinga. When we applied, we did not know that the three studies had to collaborate, but we did it fairly cheerfully to make sure that each other's protocols were covered. After a while the people at OJJDP called Rolf, Terry, and David 'the three amigos'. The initial grant was for 5 years.

We also succeeded in getting money for a longitudinal study with a clinical sample. We did this project together with Ben Lahey, and the data collection was done in Pittsburgh and Georgia. We met Ben at a conference in Houston (1984), where we decided to write a proposal. Ben also spent some time in Pittsburgh before he moved to Chicago with Kate Keenan, who had worked with us. We also worked on the lying grant and the screening grant, so we were busy. Our vacations and evenings we spent on Irish historical matters.

5.7   Settling Down

Starting all these studies meant our wandering days were over. There was at least the commitment for the period of the grants, but longitudinal studies require a next grant and a next. After the lying grant was finished (Stouthamer-Loeber, 1986), I did not start another independent project because working with Rolf was far more satisfying than running a project on my own. So we pooled both our skills and energy to run the PYS as best we could (Loeber, Farrington, Stouthamer-Loeber, & Van Kammen, 1998; Loeber, Farrington, Stouthamer-Loeber, & White, 2008). We were a good team; our skills and inclinations were different and complemented each other. Rolf was the person who made most of the outside contacts, read more criminology papers, wrote more papers, and was creative in finding money and flushing out ideas. I was the how-to and planning person who looked after the budget, staffing, data collection, and data quality. We considered our operation a mom-and-pop store where any success was achieved by both of us. Rolf was good at pitching ideas in Washington; I was good at making the funders trust us to do the best possible job. Meanwhile, we had a good time. Our evenings were for Irish literature and architectural history, and we discussed problems and plans in a coffee shop before we would go to the gym for an hour in the morning. Life was harmonious – a lot of work but not a great deal of stress. The department left us alone to run our business.

When we needed to reapply for the next 5 years, the three studies were under the impression that OJJDP would continue to fund us. To our surprise, we were told at an American Society of Criminology meeting in Baltimore that there would be no next grant. This was unfortunate timing; it would have been better to have known a few months earlier so that we could have written proposals to other agencies. On the way back from Baltimore, we stopped at a gas station, and Rolf made various phone calls to other agencies and to people who might be of help. Eventually we received money from the Pew Foundation to prevent having a gap in data collection and later on a grant from NIMH. Actually, OJJDP continued to give us grants for many years but for data analyses only.

We continued to follow-up the youngest and oldest samples into their 30s. The intervals varied from 6 months initially to 1 year and eventually a longer period. The middle sample was followed-up until it overlapped in age with the oldest sample and once more 12 years later. Criminal records were collected until the last assessment. The samples were half Caucasian and half African American. Eventually, with grants from OJJDP, we prepared the data and the constructs to be lodged in the National Archive of Criminal Justice data at the University of Michigan. This required another round of careful data cleaning and making sure the construct files were uniform and well documented. Dustin

Pardini – originally a postdoctoral student and now a professor at the University of Arizona in Phoenix – and I were involved, but particularly Rebecca Stallings, who was even pickier than I and did a terrific job. The data are now publicly available for qualified researchers.

I was less involved in the Developmental Trends Study. Participants were 177 outpatients who were first assessed at 7–12 years of age. Seventy percent were white and 30% were African American; 75% were boys. They were followed-up till ages 18 –19. The goal was to predict antisocial personality disorder from childhood symptoms (Lahey, Loeber, Burke, & Applegate, 2005). The study was very successful and achieved its goals, showing the relationships between early symptoms of CD and ADHD, and later problem behaviors. Stephanie Green and Jeffrey Burke played an important role in this study.

We had always felt that the PYS was a good start but that girls needed to be studied as well. Since the base rate of delinquent behavior in girls is lower, such research would require a large sample and, therefore, needed to have a study of its own. We started the Pittsburgh Girls Study in 2000, with a census of a large part of the city to find girls of the appropriate age, oversampling in less advantaged neighborhoods. We culled over 200,000 households, which was an enormous job, but at least we knew where our girls came from. Our sample consisted of 2,450 girls spread out over four cohorts (ages 5, 6, 7, and 8). The study is still ongoing, and the older girls are in their 20s. However, now that Rolf and I are not involved with this study anymore, the focus has changed from antisocial behavior and delinquency to the offspring of the sample, depression, and personality disorder, reflecting the interests of the current investigators: Allison Hipwell, Stephanie Stepp, and Kate Keenan.

Delinquency has been studied in the girls study up to age 19 (Loeber et al., 2017). The prevalence of self-reported delinquency was lower than it is for boys. The prevalence of violence showed a typical age–crime curve, whereas drug dealing showed a steady increase over time. Frequency increased with age. Most of the delinquent careers were short, but an early onset predicted a longer duration. Just as with boys, a small number of delinquents were responsible for a large number of delinquent acts. One in 10 of the delinquents committed more than 10 acts. The caveat is that in this study, data were used till age 19, and for at least a number of participants their delinquent careers would continue while others might have started committing offenses later.

I retired in 2011, and Rolf was meant to follow me soon. However, he was having too much fun to give it up. At one time he did retire but was immediately rehired. I guess he still had grant-getting power. He was involved in the large study on the effects of early marijuana use – Adolescent Brain and Cognition Development (ABCD). This is a longitudinal study of 11,000 subjects. Pittsburgh is one of its data collection sites. MRIs will be done at regular intervals. This study is now underway. Rolf noticed that the main study did not have many questions about delinquency, so he applied for a grant for a longitudinal sub-study to collect information on delinquency in five sites. He was awarded this grant a month before he died. Duncan Clark and Lia Ahonen are conducting this study now.

5.8   Other Activities

5.8.1   Sub-Studies

Since we realized that our expertise was limited and that the opportunities for expansion of our studies were great, we always were happy to entertain sub-studies. Rolf and I have been involved in 17 sub-studies, and I am sure that the girls study has added more. We worked with Terrie Moffitt, Avshalom Caspi, Adrian Raine, a team of geneticists, Jane Costello, Helene White, and many more (see Angold et al., 1996; Costello, Loeber, & Stouthamer-Loeber, 1991; Gatzke-Kopp, Raine, Loeber, Stouthamer-Loeber, & Steinhauer, 2002; Loeber, Farrington, Stouthamer-Loeber, Moffitt, & Caspi, 1998; Loeber et al., 2001; Lynam et al., 2000; Messer et al., 1995; White, Tice, Loeber, & Stouthamer-Loeber, 2002; White, Xie, Thompson, Loeber, & Stouthamer-Loeber, 2001).

5.8.2   Appointment in Amsterdam

From 1997 until 2012 Rolf also had an appointment at the Free University in Amsterdam, the Netherlands, where he gave seminars and lectures, and supervised theses. This led to 13 Dutch students spending time in Pittsburgh and using the various datasets for their theses. These students were terrific; they applied for their own grants, organized their own accommodations, and did not need any mothering, even though some of their mothers asked me to look after them. Some of them now have academic positions, and others work in clinical settings.

5.8.3   Supervision

Apart from the Dutch students, we supervised 31 additional theses and had 17 postdoctoral students. We learned from them, and they could benefit from our datasets. Their unique questions and views enriched the output of our studies. Since the datasets were so large, there was more than enough room for people to pursue their own ideas, and we encouraged their use of the data.

5.8.4   Publications

We were involved in the writing of over 400 papers, book chapters, and books. This was mainly Rolf's or Rolf-instigated work. I was easily distracted by practical problems and management tasks. One of the very interesting papers that Rolf wrote concerned the prediction of homicide and homicide victims (Loeber & Farrington, 2011; Loeber et al., 2005). We had not expected that there would be enough subjects to analyze and write about. He also wrote an empirical paper (further elaborated in a book) about the escalation over time from minor problem behaviors to serious delinquency, showing that this was not a random process (Loeber et al., 1993, 2008). Knowledge of these pathways is a key component of the formulation of intervention programs. Further, Rolf studied the age–crime curve and factors that influenced the start as well as the duration of the curve (Loeber et al., 2012). Rolf and Lia Ahonen worked on some papers to show that the majority of violent acts are not perpetrated by diagnosed mentally ill people, contrary to popular opinion (Ahonen, Loeber, & Brent, 2019).

I wrote a small book about data collection and management (Stouthamer-Loeber & Van Kammen, 1995). It was published in 1995, but I still get royalty checks, so there must be a need for practical information. In this electronic age, an update would be great, but that is for someone else to do. I also wrote on the influence of positive behavior on the outcome of delinquency.

5.9   Research Specifically Related to Violence

In 1998 we wrote an article about the development of juvenile aggression and violence (Loeber & Stouthamer-Loeber, 1998). This paper laid out some misconceptions about the development of violence in males. The paper shows that there is a substantial amount of research showing that desistance from physical aggression continues from childhood through adolescence and also that violence can start at different ages. The paper features the pathway model illustrating development from less serious to more serious behavior. As of 2012 the study had 2.6% homicide offenders, 2.6% homicide victims, and 20.2% individuals who had been wounded or killed by a gunshot. One in five of the participants reported carrying a gun sometime before turning 18. Ninety-two percent of the homicide offenders were African American, as were 95% of the homicide victims. One possible explanation for this is that the African American boys were more exposed to risk factors. Drug use often played a role in the life of persisters as well as desisters in violence. The paper also cites evidence of a large array of predictors as well as protective factors playing a role in the development of violence.

5.9.1   Study Groups

Rolf organized six study groups, two of which were parallel groups in the Netherlands. The U.S. groups were led by Rolf and David Farrington. The topics included very young offenders, gangs, violent and serious offending, and the continuity between youth and adult crime. For each of these topics, panels of experts were formed whose mandate was to think ahead, outside the box, and more widely than they had before. Each panel would convene a few times. I attended two meetings, and my impression was that there was a collegial atmosphere, even while people were pushed to 'take the next step'. These panels resulted in books (Loeber & Farrington, 2011, 1998, 2001; Loeber et al., 2008) – some written by the editors; others written with different authors for each chapter. The Dutch book on the continuity between youth and adult crime directly influenced the Dutch justice system by putting in an intermediate category between juvenile and adult crime for dealing with perpetrators.

An additional task that Rolf took on was to be a member of a committee to select the winner of the Spinoza Prize in Holland, which was awarded each year by the Dutch Academy of Sciences, as an equivalent to the Nobel Prize but only for Dutch citizens. The topics ranged over all academic subjects, and Rolf really enjoyed reading about areas entirely different from his own. He was sorry that the committee membership was only for 4 years.

5.9.2   Consultancy

Over the years Rolf has been a consultant for many government agencies, university departments, granting agencies, and research projects in the United States, Canada, and Europe (the Netherlands, Belgium, England, Sweden, and Norway). Through this means, he influenced government policy, research projects, and intervention projects. Another way of influencing the field was by reviewing manuscripts for journals.

My consultancy work was mainly restricted to consulting on research design, data collection, and management, although I did also review proposals for grants and manuscripts for publication.

These consulting and reviewing activities took up a fair amount of time, but we felt obliged to share our knowledge, as other people had shared theirs with us.

5.9.3   Honors/Memberships

Rolf received various honors from the American Psychological Association, American Society of Criminology, OJJDP, and the Dutch Institute for the Study of Crime and Law Enforcement, and membership in the Royal Dutch Society of Sciences. Rolf and Magda were listed as two of the most cited psychologists/criminologists over many years.

5.10   In Retrospect

Longitudinal studies are large operations and require more than one investigator and a large staff. What stands out for me is the happy and harmonious time Rolf and I spent trying to do the best work possible. That may not be the most important message for others, but it helps to have a positive relationship with one's colleagues and to trust that you have each other's backs and are working toward the same goal. I guess our noncompetitive upbringing in Holland made collaboration a natural thing. Rolf's creativity and the hard work on both our parts made it possible to do what we have done. There is still a lot of work to do for the next generations of longitudinal researchers, particularly in the area of the development of positive behaviors that can counteract or ameliorate the development of problem behaviors. In our studies we could have done a better job of that. Mostly, positive behaviors were framed as the absence of negative behaviors.

As the participants grow older, white-collar crime starts to play a role. Since most of the study had been focused on overt antisocial behaviors, we were not as well prepared for that as we were to follow-up gangs or murders. The study of covert antisocial behaviors is very important, though, and may shed light on some nefarious practices of business people and elected officials.

Another issue is how to collect and store data. We started out with interview booklets until we had a whole warehouse full of them. Then we switched to interviews where the interviewer put in the answers electronically. I do think that face-to-face interviewing is still the best in terms of participant cooperation as well as the validity of the data. There may be reasons for researchers to use telephone interviews or give participants laptops or have them send in paper questionnaires, but the identity of the participant cannot be verified by these methods. In addition, the participation rate is most likely lower. We trained our interviewers to be the ambassadors of the study in order to make sure that subjects wanted to participate again, and we kept in contact with them between interviews. A study is only as good as the participation rate and the quality of the data.

Over time we started to use social media to find subjects. I have not kept up with all the developments in this area, but it is a great source for reconnecting with hard-to-find participants.

One final thought. As a longitudinal researcher you will always regret not having included certain areas in the study. One's thinking changes and society also changes over the length of the study. It is inevitable that one feels one should have done a better job. However, one cannot foresee all the issues that will become important over the time of the study. So it is for future researchers to focus on the issues of their day. That is why it is important to start new longitudinal studies at regular intervals.

5.11   Irish Work

Throughout our careers we kept our evenings and vacations free for research on Irish matters. This provided a wonderful counterbalance to our work. Even more than our ordinary work, it was worry free. We were amateurs and only had to please ourselves. Because of our amateur status we were also not a threat to academic scholars; we were not in competition with anyone and freely shared our findings. The fun was being part of a scholarly community of Irish researchers. Since our focus changed over the years from architectural history, to colonial history, to literature, to archeology, and so on, we made new friends all the time, and our trips to Ireland were full of meetings with old and new friends, in between library- and fieldwork. Rolf was a member of the Kildare Street and University Club, which allowed us to stay in the center of Dublin. It was also the place where we gave a very large dinner party to thank our Irish friends for their generosity and hospitality for over 50 years. Rolf was very prolific and so was I to a lesser extent. Together we published six books, one of which was an edited volume. The topics ranged from a biographical dictionary of Irish architects (1600–1720), to the geography and practice of the English colonization of Ireland (1534–1609), to a guide to Irish fiction (1650–1900), to architecture from 1600–2000. In addition, over 60 articles or chapters were published. Rolf was honored by memberships in the Royal Irish Academy, Royal Institute of Architects, and the Royal Society of Antiquaries. The time periods covered in these publications ranged from the late Middle Ages to 2000. It was wonderful to undertake research in unknown areas and learn about a whole new field.

Among the most influential books we wrote is *A Guide to Irish Fiction*, written together with Anne Mullin Burnham (Loeber et al., 2006). It is a compilation of all novels published in Ireland or about Ireland. The goal was to increase the known canon of Irish literature. We wrote it from the perspective of social history. If a book had been written and published, we included it, regardless of merit as seen through contemporary eyes. We had a great time compiling this work. Rolf, in his travels, would find and buy unknown books, and I would read them and make short summaries. I read about 1,000 books for this project. Rolf wrote a great introduction, summarizing the themes in the book, based on empirical data from the large spreadsheet we had made. We were sorry that the project ended, but now it is a standard work for libraries, book dealers, Irish literature students, and collectors. Sometimes one can find in a book dealer's catalogue the remark 'not in Loeber'. It does not happen often because we were pretty thorough, but if it is a book that we had missed, the price goes up.

The other important book of which Rolf was the main editor was on Irish architecture, written for the Royal Irish Academy (Loeber et al., 2014). It had about 200 contributors. Rolf wrote many of the entries, but one of his tasks was to keep 200 people happy and producing the essays that they had promised to write. They selected Rolf to be the main editor because they had faith that he would be able to deliver the product. It is a beautiful book, published by Yale University Press.

Rolf was preparing a new book on the history of Irish demesnes and gardens. It meant that on our last trips in Ireland, instead of looking at the architecture, we would turn our back to the house and ruin, and study the landscape. The project was not far enough advanced for anyone to take it over, so it will never come to fruition. More important, however, is that Rolf immensely enjoyed working on it.

I still have an Irish project going, a transcription of the diary of a Quaker woman – not a diary of herself, but of her village. It covers the years 1760–1826. When I am done with it, it will be published by the Irish Manuscript Commission. It is bittersweet, actually heart-wrenching, to return to Ireland, but it is also heartwarming to see our many friends.

5.12   Photography

I want to briefly mention another aspect of Rolf's life that gave him great pleasure – photography. He had a small Leica that he could carry in his pocket and use to photograph whatever he saw that was unusual. Lots of his pictures had to do with reflections and unusual shapes. The person who printed the pictures for him, Tom Undereiner, became a good friend, and together they would look at a new crop of pictures and decide which should be printed, whether full or cropped, and at what size. Rolf had an unusual eye, and he enjoyed roaming around in nature to see what would catch his fancy. A professional photographer who liked Rolf's pictures once asked him how many shots he took for each picture. Rolf looked a little confused and said 'one'. After this encounter he tried to take more than one picture, but it did not suit him, and he returned to the one-shot picture. I have a huge number of Rolf's photographs, and I am thankful to him for showing us beauty in unusual places and opening our eyes to see the world differently.

5.13 Conclusion

In the end, what counts is a life well spent. For some people that means leaving a legacy, for others it means learning how to do a difficult hobby or task, yet for others it is to be happy. For Rolf, all these things counted, but their importance was in the reverse order from the previous sentence. Leaving a legacy was the least important for him. For me, happiness and doing a job to the best of my abilities were the most important. Nevertheless our work has had some impact, and it is for future generations to build on it and address questions that we have left unanswered, and there are many of those. I wish them happy hunting, but, above all, a satisfied life. I also wish them a wide view of the possibilities in life. A university degree gives you the tools and confidence that can be applied to new, related, or unrelated fields, which makes the journey through life really exciting.

References

Ahonen, L., Loeber, R., & Brent, D. A. (2019). The association between serious mental health problems and violence: Some common assumptions and misconceptions. *Trauma, Violence, & Abuse, 20*(5), 613–625.

Angold, A., Erkanli, A., Loeber, R., Costello, E. J., Van Kammen, W. B., & Stouthamer-Loeber, M. (1996). Disappearing depression in a population sample of boys. *Journal of Emotional and Behavioral Disorders, 4*(2), 95–104.

Costello, E. J., Loeber, R., & Stouthamer-Loeber, M. (1991). Pervasive and situational hyperactivity – confounding effect of informant: A research note. *Journal of Child Psychology and Psychiatry, 32*(2), 367–376.

Dishion, T. J., Loeber, R., Stouthamer-Loeber, M., & Patterson, G. R. (1984). Skill deficits and male adolescent delinquency. *Journal of Abnormal Child Psychology, 12*(1), 37–53.

Farrington, D. P., Loeber, R., & Berg, M. T. (2012). Young men who kill: A prospective longitudinal examination from childhood. *Homicide Studies*, *16*(2), 99–128.

Gatzke-Kopp, L. M., Raine, A., Loeber, R., Stouthamer-Loeber, M., & Steinhauer, S. R. (2002). Serious delinquent behavior, sensation seeking, and electrodermal arousal. *Journal of Abnormal Child Psychology*, *30*(5), 477–486.

Lahey, B. B., Loeber, R., Burke, J. D., & Applegate, B. (2005). Predicting future antisocial personality disorder in males from a clinical assessment in childhood. *Journal of Consulting and Clinical Psychology*, *73*(3), 389–399.

Loeber, R. (2019). *Irish houses and castles, 1400–1740*. (K. Whelan & M. Stout, Eds.). Dublin, Ireland: Four Courts Press.

    (2020). *Rolf Loeber, photographs 2007–2017*. Berkeley, CA: Edition One. (privately printed)

Loeber, R., Campbell, H., Hurley, L., Montague, J., & Rowley, E. (Eds.). (2014). *Architecture, 1600–2000*. New Haven, CT: Yale University Press.

Loeber, R., & Dishion, T. J. (1983). Early predictors of male delinquency: A review. *Psychological Bulletin*, *94*, 68–99.

Loeber, R., Dishion, T. J., & Patterson, G. R. (1984). Multiple gating: A multistage assessment procedure for identifying youths at risk for delinquency. *Journal of Research in Crime and Delinquency*, *21*(1), 7–32.

Loeber, R., & Farrington, D. P. (2011). *Young homicide offenders and victims: Risk factors, prediction, and prevention from childhood*. New York, NY: Springer.

Loeber, R., & Farrington, D. P. (Eds.). (1998). *Serious and violent juvenile offenders: Risk factors and successful interventions*. Thousand Oaks, CA: Sage.

    (Eds.). (2001). *Child delinquents: Development, interventions and service needs*. Thousand Oaks, CA: Sage.

Loeber, R., Farrington, D. P., Stouthamer-Loeber, M., Moffitt, T., & Caspi, A. (1998). The development of male offending: Key findings from the first decade of the Pittsburgh Youth Study. *Studies on Crime and Crime Prevention*, *7*(2), 141–171.

Loeber, R., Farrington, D. P., Stouthamer-Loeber, M., Moffitt, T. E., Caspi, A., & Lynam, D. R. (2001). Male mental health problems, psychopathy, and personality traits: Key findings from the first 14 years of the Pittsburgh Youth Study. *Clinical Child and Family Psychology Review*, *4*(4), 273–297.

Loeber, R., Farrington, D. P., Stouthamer-Loeber, M., & Van Kammen, W. B. (Eds.). (1998). *Antisocial behavior and mental health problems: Explanatory factors in childhood and adolescence*. Mahwah, NJ: Lawrence Erlbaum.

Loeber, R., Farrington, D. P., Stouthamer-Loeber, M., & White, H. R. (2008). *Violence and serious theft: Development and prediction from childhood to adulthood*. New York, NY: Routledge.

Loeber, R., Jennings, W. G., Ahonen, L., Piquero, A. R., & Farrington, D. P. (2017). *Female delinquency from childhood to young adulthood: Recent results from the Pittsburgh Girls Study*. Cham, Switzerland: Springer.

Loeber, R., Menting, B., Lynam, D. R., Moffitt, T. E., Stouthamer-Loeber, M., Stallings, R., ... Pardini, D. (2012). Findings from the Pittsburgh Youth Study: Cognitive impulsivity and intelligence as predictors of the age–crime curve. *Journal of the American Academy of Child and Adolescent Psychiatry*, *51*(11), 1136–1149.

Loeber, R., Pardini, D., Homish, D. L., Wei, E. H., Crawford, A. M., Farrington, D. P., ... Rosenfeld, R. (2005). The prediction of violence and homicide in young men. *Journal of Consulting and Clinical Psychology*, *73*(6), 1074–1088.

Loeber, R., & Stouthamer-Loeber, M. (1998). Juvenile aggression at home and at school: A new perspective. In D. S. Elliott & B. A. Hamburg (Eds.), *Violence in American schools* (pp. 94–126). New York, NY: Cambridge University Press.

Loeber, R., Stouthamer-Loeber, M., & Burnham, A. M. (2006). *A guide to Irish fiction, 1650–1900*. Dublin, Ireland: Four Courts Press.

Loeber, R., Wung, P., Keenan, K., Giroux, B., Stouthamer-Loeber, M., Van Kammen, W. B., & Maughan, B. (1993). Developmental pathways in disruptive child behavior. *Development and Psychopathology*, *5*, 103–133.

Lynam, D. R., Caspi, A., Moffit, T. E., Wikström, P.-O., Loeber, R., & Novak, S. (2000). The interaction between impulsivity and neighborhood context on offending: The effects of impulsivity are stronger in poorer neighborhoods. *Journal of Abnormal Psychology*, *109*(4), 563–574.

Messer, S. C., Angold, A., Loeber, R., Costello, E. J., Van Kammen, W. B., & Stouthamer-Loeber, M. (1995). Development of a short questionnaire for use in epidemiological studies of depression in children and adolescents: Factor composition and structure across development. *International Journal of Methods in Psychiatric Research*, *5*, 251–262.

Stouthamer-Loeber, M. (1986). Lying as a problem behavior in children: A review. *Clinical Psychology Review*, *6*, 267–289.

Stouthamer-Loeber, M., & Van Kammen, W. B. (1995). *Data collection and management: A practical guide*. Newbury Park, CA: Sage.

White, H. R., Tice, P. C., Loeber, R., & Stouthamer-Loeber, M. (2002). Illegal acts committed by adolescents under the influence of alcohol and drugs. *Journal of Research in Crime and Delinquency*, *39*(2), 131–152.

White, H. R., Xie, M., Thompson, W. D., Loeber, R., & Stouthamer-Loeber, M. (2001). Psychopathology as a predictor of adolescent drug use trajectories. *Psychology of Addictive Behaviors*, *15*(3), 210–218.

6   From Boy to Man

From Delinquent Development to Old Age Crime

David P. Farrington

David P. Farrington was born in Ormskirk, England, on March 7, 1944. He received his PhD in psychology from the University of Cambridge (England) in 1969. His first faculty appointment (1974) was in Criminology at the University of Cambridge, where he is now Emeritus Professor of Psychological Criminology. Among numerous prestigious awards, he has received the 2013 Stockholm Prize in Criminology, the 2018 John Paul Scott Award for lifetime contributions to research on aggression from the International Society for Research on Aggression (ISRA), and the Joan McCord Prize from the Academy of Experimental Criminology in 2005.

David Farrington is probably best known for his work on the Cambridge Study in Delinquent Development (CSDD), which is a prospective longitudinal survey of 411 London males. These males have been followed-up from age 8 to age 61 in records and in repeated personal interviews, primarily to investigate the development of offending and antisocial behavior from childhood to adulthood. In addition, their parents and teachers were interviewed when the boys were aged 8–15, and more recently their children have been interviewed to investigate the intergenerational transmission of social problems.

The CSDD appears to be the most famous, most cited, and longest lasting British criminological research project. It was initiated by Donald West in 1961. David Farrington began to work on the study in 1969 and took over as Director in 1982. There have been over 280 publications from the CSDD. The CSDD has advanced knowledge about the development of offending and antisocial behavior (including drug and alcohol use) from childhood to adulthood and about the relationship between offending and other life problems, such as in accommodation, relationships, and employment. It has also advanced knowledge about risk factors for offending, especially those measured in childhood, such as impulsiveness, low school achievement, poor parental supervision, and disrupted families. It has also advanced knowledge about the effects of life events, such as getting married, becoming separated, and becoming unemployed, on the course of development of offending. It has also advanced knowledge about the intergenerational transmission of anti-social behavior.

There have been many studies of aggression and violence in the CSDD, and these have been reviewed recently in 'The Development of Violence from Age 8 to 61' (Farrington, 2019b), which focused on the development and continuity of violence over time, and on early risk factors. There have been numerous CSDD publications on risk factors for aggression, violence, bullying, and intimate partner violence. A fruitful collaboration with Leonard Berkowitz produced an article comparing individual and group fights at age 18 (Farrington, Berkowitz, & West, 1982). This article was based on unstructured tape-recorded accounts of physical fights, and it showed that individual and group fights were very different.

Based on results from the CSDD about risk factors and on evidence from his reviews of the effectiveness of interventions, David Farrington has consistently advocated for early intervention targeting risk factors in order to reduce offending. For example, poor parenting can be targeted using early home visiting programs and parent management training; impulsiveness can be targeted in child skills training; and low achievement can be targeted in preschool intellectual enrichment programs. These ideas now seem quite widely accepted in the UK, but they were rather new and unfashionable when they were put forward over 30 years ago (e.g., Farrington, 1986). At that time, the UK Home Office mainly focused on situational or physical crime prevention and on criminal justice measures of retribution and deterrence.

As an example of David Farrington's influence on public policy, he was asked to advise Prime Minister Tony Blair about the Action Plan on Social Exclusion, which proposed risk-focused prevention, including evidence-based programs such as nurse home visiting, parent training, multi-systemic therapy, and treatment foster care. The Prime Minister acknowledged Farrington's influence and published his paper on 'Childhood Risk Factors and Risk-Focussed Prevention' (Farrington, 2007) on his website.

David Farrington's research has also had some influence in other countries. He was a co-principal investigator of the Pittsburgh Youth Study (PYS) for 20 years from 1986, and he collaborated with Professor Rolf Loeber in chairing four study groups, funded by the U.S. Office of Juvenile Justice and Delinquency Prevention (OJJDP), the U.S. Centers for Disease Control (CDC), and the U.S. National Institute of Justice (NIJ). Along with Rolf Loeber, he was awarded the OJJDP Outstanding Contributions Award in 1998 for the book *Serious and Violent Juvenile*

Offenders: Risk Factors and Successful Interventions (Loeber & Farrington, 1998).

David Farrington has collaborated in many different longitudinal studies. For example, he studied early predictors of childhood aggression in Mauritius (Raine, Reynolds, Venables, Mednick, & Farrington, 1998), and compared self-reported and official delinquency careers in the Seattle Social Development Project (Farrington, Jolliffe, Hawkins, & Catalano, 2003). He was also Vice-Chair of the U.S. National Academy of Sciences panel on violence and co-directed a NATO Advanced Study Institute on *Biosocial Bases of Violence* (Raine, Farrington, Brennan, & Mednick, 1997).

David Farrington was President of the American Society of Criminology (ASC) in 1998–1999 (the first and only person from outside North America to be elected to this office), and has also been President of the European Association of Psychology and Law, President of the British Society of Criminology, and President of the Academy of Experimental Criminology. He is the first and only person to receive the four major awards of the ASC: the Edwin Sutherland Award in 2002 for outstanding contributions to criminology, the Sellin-Glueck Award in 1984 for international contributions to criminology, the August Vollmer Award in 2014 for outstanding contributions to the prevention of delinquency, and the Herbert Bloch Award in 2018 for outstanding service contributions to criminology.

David Farrington has published more than 1,000 journal articles, book chapters, books, and monographs on criminological and psychological topics. According to GoogleScholar, in July 2020, his publications were the most frequently cited in the field of juvenile delinquency, with 105,622 citations and an h-index of 167.

6.1   The Early Years

I was born in Ormskirk, Lancashire, in the north of England, during the war. My mother used to tell a story about when I was born in hospital. Apparently, the nurses commented that I was intelligent, because I was the only one of the babies in the ward to pay attention when the planes were going overhead! I don't remember much about the war, but I do remember the rationing and ration books that we had after the war. I was the youngest of four children, and we were a poor family living in old rented accommodations with no bathroom and an outside toilet. My mother used to exchange our coupons with a richer single lady who lived nearby. We gave her our clothes coupons, and she gave us her food coupons in exchange. Of course, I remember very well the happy day when the rationing of sweets ended in 1953!

Like most other children in Ormskirk, I went to the local state primary school, and I remember very well the announcement of King George's death in 1952. The primary school was rigorously streamed, with A, B, C, and D classes, and about 40 children in each class. Luckily, I was a clever child, and I was always in the A stream. I recall that where you sat in class each week depended on your performance in the test on the previous Friday, and fortunately I was usually top of the class. At that time, at age 11 about 20% of state school children went to grammar schools (depending on passing the 11-plus examination), while the remaining 80% went to secondary modern schools. I recall a teacher telling me that it would be a miracle if I failed the 11-plus examination. Luckily, I passed!

Ormskirk Grammar School was also rigorously streamed into A, B, C, and D classes, and again I was always in the A stream. My best subjects at school were mathematics and chemistry, and I was fortunate enough to win a State Scholarship for my school examination performance at age 18 in mathematics, physics, and chemistry. At that time, these scholarships were given to the top 2,400 children in each age cohort (out of a total of about 670,000), of whom about 800 went to Cambridge University, 700 went to Oxford University, 400 went to London University, and 500 went elsewhere. Luckily, I got into Cambridge University after taking its entrance examinations. I started off doing mathematics, physics, and chemistry, but eventually graduated in psychology, a subject which had fascinated me from an early age.

When I was 16, I had our local library order many of Freud's books, and I read them avidly: *Psychopathology of Everyday Life, The Interpretation of Dreams* (of course, I kept a notepad next to my bed and tried to write down my dreams when I woke up!), *The Ego and the Id, Totem and Taboo, Civilization and Its Discontents, The Future of an Illusion* (see Wollheim, 1981). Public libraries were great! I was also inspired by Eysenck's books: *Uses and Abuses of Psychology* (Eysenck, 1953) and *Sense and Nonsense in Psychology* (Eysenck, 1956). However, Cambridge University focused very much on experimental psychology and the scientific method, and so I was soon taught that these idols had feet of clay!

6.2   Cambridge University

The greatest influence on my undergraduate career was a Lecturer in Psychology called Alan Watson. He supervised me in psychology and very conscientiously went through all my essays line by line. In super-visions, he would constantly say, 'How does this follow from that?' and 'What do you mean by this?' He would challenge me to write more clearly and to be more explicit about what I wanted to say. Under his tutelage, my writing style and clarity improved enormously. Cambridge was great for me as an undergraduate because I felt that its stimulating environment greatly expanded my intellectual abilities.

After graduating in psychology in 1966, I applied to do a PhD degree in Cambridge and, fortunately, was accepted. Alan Watson agreed to supervise my PhD, which tried to test different theories of human learning, focusing on the ability of Cambridge undergraduates to learn three-digit numbers. I had a very good memory for numbers myself and had always been good at mental arithmetic. The model of the Cambridge PhD was very much one of master and apprentice, and again I learned a great deal from Alan Watson about conducting and writing up experiments, reviewing the literature, and so on.

My PhD thesis described 12 experiments that I carried out with Cambridge undergraduates. My meetings with Alan Watson were very stimulating because we would take stock of the results obtained in the last experiment, talk about the loose ends and new questions raised, and then plan the next experiment to address these new hypotheses. Actually, it was very reminiscent of the logical deductive methods I had used in chemistry, for example, in trying to discover what an unknown substance was. It was very much the model of an experimental science. Nowadays, this work would fall within cognitive psychology.

Unfortunately, Alan Watson was very busy. He was a very clever man indeed, but he was Acting Head of the Psychological Laboratory in the mornings and Senior Tutor (Chief Executive Officer) of Fitzwilliam College in the afternoons and evenings. Consequently, our meetings were often in the Psychological Laboratory at 7:00 a.m. or in Fitzwilliam College at midnight. He read most of my drafts (and much else) in the middle of the night. Since he spent most of his time in teaching and administration, he rarely published anything, and the one thing he did not do was teach me how to publish. Consequently, although my PhD thesis was accepted with no changes (a rare event) in 1969, I never published any of my 12 experiments in journals, which I should have done.

6.3   Over to Criminology

As I was coming to the end of my PhD in 1969, I was becoming disillusioned with experimental psychology. Much of it seemed rather irrelevant to real life, and I wanted to do something more socially relevant. At that time, I was interested in sociology and believed that it might have something to offer. Consequently, when I saw an advertisement in the Psychological Laboratory for someone to work as a Research Officer on a longitudinal study of delinquency, based in Cambridge, I applied for it, and was offered the job by Donald West in 1969. It suited me to stay in Cambridge, and I knew enough about longitudinal studies to know that they were unusual and interesting.

I knew nothing about criminology at the time. However, Donald West appointed me because of my statistical and computing skills. When I started my PhD in 1966, Alan Watson had encouraged me to learn Fortran programming, and so I knew how to analyze data using the computer, which was a fairly new thing at the time. The only other thing I did for my PhD thesis that has ever come in useful was to learn all about ROC curves (as applied to human learning and memory), which were also quite new at the time. ROC curves are now extremely important in criminology in quantifying the strength of the relationship between a prediction score and a dichotomous outcome such as conviction or reconviction (see, e.g., Farrington, Jolliffe, & Johnstone, 2008).

Criminology was an alien environment. In 1969–1970, British criminology was dominated by sociologists, who were stridently anti-empirical and anti-scientific. They talked in impenetrable jargon (described as 'gobbledegook' by a *Cambridge News* journalist in 1969) and were very critical of Donald's longitudinal study, which they regarded as an atavistic throwback to the work of the then-hated Gluecks (who were later revived by Sampson & Laub, 1993). However, I enjoyed working with Donald on this survey and thought that it was really fascinating. Donald was a very careful researcher. Like many psychiatrists, his first question was, 'What is the evidence for that?', and I very much liked this. I think Donald's previous career as a parapsychology researcher had made him unusually careful. Whereas many criminologists accepted positive results rather uncritically, any positive results in psychical research were strongly challenged, which meant that it was important to be very careful and to think of and try to test possible alternative explanations of all findings.

I worked on soft money for 5 years, until I managed to get a permanent post in Cambridge in 1974. I really enjoyed the research, but the financial uncertainties were troubling. Happily, I was appointed to a university teaching post in 1974, but unhappily I then became Director of the MPhil Course in Criminology from 1975 to 1978. During this period, I shouldered a heavy burden of university teaching and administration and also did a lot of college teaching. None of this was conducive to publishing journal articles.

6.4   The Cambridge Study in Delinquent Development (CSDD)

In the first few years of my career, I worked mainly on the CSDD, which is a prospective longitudinal survey (now from age 8 to age 61) of the development of offending and antisocial behavior in 411 London males mostly born in 1953. The CSDD began in 1961, and for the first 20 years it was directed by Donald West. As mentioned, I started working on it in 1969, and took over as Director in 1982. The CSDD has been funded primarily by the Home Office and secondly by the Department of Health. Results of the Study have been described in seven books (Farrington, Piquero, & Jennings, 2013; Piquero, Farrington, & Blumstein, 2007; West, 1969, 1982; West & Farrington, 1973, 1977; Zara & Farrington, 2016), in seven summary reports (Farrington, 1995, 2003a, 2019a; Farrington et al., 2006; Farrington, Coid, & West, 2009; Farrington & West, 1981, 1990), and in a total of over 280 publications (listed on my Cambridge Institute of Criminology website).

The original aim of the CSDD was to describe the development of delinquent and criminal behavior in inner-city males, to investigate to what extent this could be predicted in advance, and to explain why juvenile delinquency began, why it did or did not continue into adult crime, and why adult crime often ended as men reached their 20s. The main focus was on continuity or discontinuity in behavioral development, on the effects of life events on development, and on predicting future behavior. The CSDD was not designed to test any one particular theory about delinquency but to test many different hypotheses about the causes and correlates of offending, and many different mechanisms and processes linking risk factors and antisocial behavior. However, I did propose a developmental theory (Farrington, 2005, 2020) that has been empirically tested (Farrington & McGee, 2017, 2019); see Farrington and Ttofi (2018) and McGee and Farrington (2019) for reviews of developmental theories of offending.

6.5   Early Results of the CSDD

The boys were tested in their schools by CSDD psychologists at ages 8, 10, and 14, and their parents (usually the mothers) were interviewed about once a year by CSDD psychiatric social workers from when the boys were eight until when they were 15. When I joined the CSDD in 1969, the interviews at age 16 were under way, and the psychiatric social workers were coming to the end of their interviews with the parents. I was in charge of computerizing all the data, I carried out all the analyses that led to the book *Who Becomes Delinquent?* (West & Farrington, 1973), and I was very much involved in devising the interview at age 18, which was carried out in 1971–1973.

Unfortunately, the then Director of the Institute of Criminology, Sir Leon Radzinowicz, wanted all Cambridge research published in books in the *Cambridge Studies in Criminology* that he edited, and so he discouraged junior staff from publishing articles. Nevertheless, I published three articles in 1971–1973 on predictors of self-reported violence at age 14 compared with convictions at ages 10–14 (Farrington & West, 1971); on school effects on delinquency (Farrington, 1972) that showed that the different delinquency rates of the secondary schools were largely driven by their different intakes of boys from the primary schools at age 11; and on self-reported delinquency (Farrington, 1973) that focused on psychometric properties such as test-retest stability, concurrent validity, and (unusually) predictive validity. Large family size, low nonverbal IQ, and high daring were among the strongest predictors of self-reported violence at age 14.

The main thrust of *Who Becomes Delinquent?* (West & Farrington, 1973) was to investigate which childhood risk factors measured at ages 8–10 predicted juvenile convictions. The most important predictors included troublesome behavior (rated by peers and teachers), convicted parents (based on records), low nonverbal IQ (90 or less, based on the Progressive Matrices test), low family income, large family size (five or more children in the family), and poor parental child-rearing behavior (cold or rejecting parental attitude and harsh or erratic parental discipline) – all rated by the psychiatric social workers based on interviews with parents. One chapter focused on aggression, as measured by self-reports, teacher ratings, and aggressive attitudes toward the police.

The follow-up book, *The Delinquent Way of Life* (West & Farrington, 1977), focused on results obtained in the interviews at age 18, which were fully tape-recorded and transcribed. As always in the CSDD, attrition was low; 389 boys were interviewed out of 410 who were still alive at age 18 (95%). We always made tremendous efforts to secure interviews because of our belief that the most interesting persons in any research on offending tend to be the hardest to locate and the most uncooperative. Surveys in which less than 75% of the target sample is interviewed may produce results that seriously underestimate the true level of criminal behavior. Generally, an increase in the percentage interviewed from 75% to 95% leads to a disproportionate increase in the validity of the results; for example, at age 18, 36% of the one-sixth of the sample who were the most difficult to interview were convicted, compared with only 22% of the majority who were interviewed more easily, a statistically significant difference (West & Farrington, 1977).

The main thrust of the 1977 book was to document the antisocial lifestyles of the convicted boys at age 18. They tended to have unstable job records; to be sexually promiscuous; to spend time hanging about on the street; to get involved in street fights; to take drugs; and to be heavy drinkers, heavy smokers, and heavy gamblers. Generally, we found that multiple risk factors led to multiple social problems, including delinquency (Farrington, 2002). Once again, there was a special chapter on aggression and violence, including violence against the police. In this book, in *Who Becomes Delinquent?* – and in the later book by Zara and Farrington (2016) – we included many case histories to illustrate the statistical conclusions.

A fruitful collaboration with Leonard Berkowitz produced an article comparing individual and group fights at age 18 (Farrington et al., 1982). This article was based on unstructured tape-recorded accounts of physical fights. When the boy fought alone, his opponent was usually alone, he was usually provoked (e.g., the opponent stared at or insulted the boy or his girlfriend), and he usually started the fight. When the boy fought alongside others, he was usually fighting a group; he usually joined in to help a friend or because he was attacked; and the fights were likely to involve weapons, injuries, and police intervention. Fights often occurred when minor incidents escalated because both sides wanted to demonstrate their toughness and masculinity and were unwilling to react to provocation in a conciliatory fashion.

6.6   Ottawa and Washington

Two sabbaticals changed my life. After I finished my stint as Director of the MPhil Course, I spent a year (1978–1979) in Ottawa in the Solicitor General's Department working on the Canadian Young Offenders Act. For this I have Irvin Waller to thank. When I went to Ottawa, I had published very little: a couple of books and about a dozen articles. In my year in Ottawa I completed 15 articles and, for the only time in my life, caught up with all the things that had been hanging around for years. I also wrote a 350-page report on *Juvenile Justice in England and Canada* (Farrington, 1979a) for the Solicitor General, which should have been published as a book but unfortunately was not. However, from then on, I was able to learn from the example of Alan Watson and publish lots and avoid administration like the plague.

One of the papers I finished in Ottawa was a review of longitudinal studies in crime and delinquency that was published in Vol. 1 of *Crime and Justice* (Farrington, 1979b). This was a very important publication, because it brought me to the notice of key American researchers, such as Alfred Blumstein and Albert Reiss, who gave me detailed comments on the first draft that greatly improved the final version. It also brought me into contact with Michael Tonry and Norval Morris, who also proved to be very important in fostering my career. In particular, it massively expanded my knowledge of American longitudinal and criminal career research. Also, during my year in Ottawa, I traveled widely in the United States and visited leading American researchers who had previously visited Cambridge, including Leonard Berkowitz, Gilbert Geis, and James Short.

I soon decided that being on sabbatical leave was the best possible state, and so I applied for another sabbatical in 1981 to be a Visiting Fellow in Washington at the NIJ. While there, I began my collaboration with Patrick Langan (Langan & Farrington, 1983) and further expanded my knowledge of American criminological research and researchers. I reviewed longitudinal research on violence (Farrington, 1982). The NIJ in 1981 was initially rather demoralized by various threats of laying off staff by the new administration, but in my opinion the tenure of James 'Chips' Stewart as Director of NIJ proved to be the golden age of American criminological research.

It was a golden age especially for longitudinal and experimental research, both of which I have always strongly advocated for (see, e.g., Farrington, 2013). While I was at NIJ, I completed a second *Crime and Justice* review of randomized experiments in criminology (Farrington, 1983), which proved almost as influential as the first. The NIJ funded many randomized experiments in the 1980s (e.g., Sherman, 1992). However, the 1980s were mainly memorable to me for the exciting development of longitudinal and criminal career research in the United States.

I found that the great thing about Americans was their optimism that everything was possible. When I advocated randomized experiments in the UK, the reaction was very negative: 'You could never do it'. Instead of thinking about all the problems, the reaction of American researchers was to say, 'Let's go for it'. That is why I was delighted to be involved in so many exciting American research activities in the 1980s.

6.7   Longitudinal and Criminal Career Research in the 1980s

During the 1980s, the most influential American criminologists (at least with the federal government and leading foundations) were Alfred Blumstein, Norval Morris, Lloyd Ohlin, Albert Reiss, James Wilson, and Marvin Wolfgang. Happily, they all advocated longitudinal and criminal career research at this time. I was delighted to be a member of the National Academy of Sciences (NAS) panel on criminal career research (chaired by Alfred Blumstein) in 1983–1986, along with Morris, Reiss, Wilson, Wolfgang, and other luminaries such as Delbert Elliott, Rolf Loeber, and Lee Robins (Blumstein, Cohen, Roth, & Visher, 1986). I really felt that we were developing an exciting new paradigm and that we were pushing back the frontiers of knowledge (although Patrick Langan always chided me that I should say pushing forward the frontiers of knowledge!).

In 1982, the MacArthur Foundation decided that it wanted to advance knowledge about crime and set up a committee chaired by Norval Morris (and containing Lloyd Ohlin and James Wilson). This committee advised the Foundation to mount new longitudinal studies. The Foundation then set up a kind of architectural competition in which 20 researchers were invited to send in designs for a new longitudinal study. I was one of three persons who evaluated the 13 designs submitted. Three designs were chosen as 'winners' to be discussed at a meeting in Chicago in 1983, but unfortunately the Foundation also invited the 'losers' to the meeting, some of whom proceeded to lambaste the 'winners'. The Foundation then decided that, if researchers could not agree among themselves, it would not be funding a new study.

Norval Morris saved the day in 1984 by persuading the Foundation to commission Lloyd Ohlin, James Wilson, and myself to write a book on *Understanding and Controlling Crime* outlining the design of a new study (Farrington, Ohlin, & Wilson, 1986). We advocated a new multiple-cohort longitudinal–experimental study. We proposed that four cohorts should be followed up, from pre-birth to age 6, age 6 to age 12, age 12 to age 18, and age 18 to age 24, with experimental interventions implemented in the middle of each age range. One aim of this accelerated longitudinal design was to build up a picture of development from pre-birth to age 24 in less than 10 years, by linking up comparable cohorts in the same large city.

In 1984–1985, the OJJDP funded a series of 'executive sessions' on juvenile justice and juvenile delinquency organized by Mark Moore and James Wilson (e.g., Wilson & Loury, 1987). It was on the plane home from one of these sessions that James Wilson persuaded Pamela Swain of the OJJDP that they should mount some new longitudinal studies. The OJJDP put out a solicitation in 1986 and selected three new studies for funding, in Denver, Pittsburgh, and Rochester. Unusually, there was an emphasis on comparable data collection and replication. Happily, I became a co-investigator of the PYS, along with Rolf Loeber and

Magda Stouthamer-Loeber. This was a wonderful collaboration for me, as the PYS and the other two studies have really advanced knowledge in numerous ways. And I came to realize that 'Beautiful Pittsburgh' is not an oxymoron!

There have been many studies of violence in the PYS. The book *Violence and Serious Theft* (Loeber, Farrington, Stouthamer-Loeber, & White, 2008) gave a great deal of information about the PYS and reported studies of the prevalence, frequency, risk, and protective factors for violence and serious theft. The book *Young Homicide Offenders and Victims* (Loeber & Farrington, 2011) presented the first prospective longitudinal study of homicide offenders and victims. Other important articles investigated the extent to which racial differences in violence were attributable to racial differences in risk factors and why some age cohorts were more violent than others (Fabio et al., 2006; Farrington, Loeber, & Stouthamer-Loeber, 2003). The comparison of age cohorts showed the influence of large-scale social changes over time. The oldest cohort, whose teenage years coincided with a big increase in societal violence in Pittsburgh and the United States more generally, were much more likely to be serious and violent offenders than the youngest cohort, whose teenage years coincided with a big decrease in violence after the 1993 peak. Magda Stouthamer-Loeber provides more information about findings from the PYS in Chapter 5.

Sad to say, NIJ was rather upset when OJJDP mounted these three studies. There was always rivalry between the two agencies, and NIJ always regarded itself as superior. However, these three high-profile studies – considered the 'jewel in the crown' of OJJDP's research program – threatened this assumption of superiority. Consequently, NIJ decided to collaborate with the MacArthur Foundation (which was now receptive to the idea, after our 1986 book) to mount a bigger and better longitudinal study.

Together, NIJ and the MacArthur Foundation funded the Program on Human Development and Criminal Behavior, led by Michael Tonry, Lloyd Ohlin, and myself, from 1987 to 1989. We set up various working groups to plan a new longitudinal study and had numerous stimulating meetings, culminating in the book *Human Development and Criminal Behavior* (Tonry, Ohlin, & Farrington, 1991). Incidentally, this and many other key books of that time were published in a Springer-Verlag series edited by Alfred Blumstein and myself, and masterminded by a former student of mine, Robert Kidd. This was again a very happy collaboration. The 1991 book proposed a bigger and better multiple-cohort longitudinal survey with seven cohorts beginning prenatally and at ages 3, 6, 9, 12, 15, and 18.

Unfortunately, NIJ and MacArthur reacted to this book not by mounting the project but by suggesting that we should have several more years of planning meetings. At this point, Michael, Lloyd, and myself decided that we were happy to pass the baton to Felton (Tony) Earls and Albert Reiss, who eventually (in the mid-1990s), along with Robert Sampson, mounted the seven-cohort study with over 6,000 participants (Liberman, 2007). I preferred to spend time analyzing the data that had been collected in the CSDD and PYS rather than to spend more time planning a new study.

While the 1980s were an enormously exciting time for me, because I really felt at the cutting edge of incredible new developments, my effort was also enormous. For 3 years between 1987 and 1989, I crossed the Atlantic once a month on average. What with being away for a week and spending another week in preparation, all my British activities were compressed into 2 weeks every month. In 1 month (May 1989) I went back and forth to the United States three times for three successive weekend meetings, and on two of these weekends (in Boston) the hotel had a (false) fire alarm in the middle of the night, which caused us all to stand outside in our nightwear. While observing the likes of Albert Reiss and Lee Robins in pajamas had a certain novelty, I was happy to withdraw from the NIJ–MacArthur initiative in order to have a less frantic life!

6.8   Developments in the 1990s

Unfortunately, my hopes of a less frantic life were not fulfilled, partly because my research became more and more diversified, and partly because of my service to scholarly societies. In 1990, I became President of the British Society of Criminology (BSC) for a 3-year term. I really don't know why I have agreed to be the chair and/or president of so many committees and organizations; these things seemed noble ventures at the time but usually consumed a lot of time that perhaps would have been better spent on research. I agreed to be Chair of the Division of Criminological and Legal Psychology of the British Psychological Society in 1983–1985 because of my messianic zeal to advance the cause of psychological criminology, but in many other cases I am not sure why I agreed to take on these kinds of commitments; maybe I am not very good at saying no to people!

Anyhow, I had what still seems a good idea for my BSC Presidential address in 1990, which was to link up national victim surveys and police, court, and prison data to put numbers and probabilities into the flow diagram from crimes committed to persons imprisoned. The first national British crime victimization survey was for the year 1981, and the third was for 1987, so by 1990 it was possible not only to put numbers in the flow diagram but also to track trends over a reasonable (6-year) period.

Filling in the flow diagram for England and Wales was complicated enough, but I then decided to compare England and the United States in collaboration with Patrick Langan (see, e.g., Langan & Farrington, 1998). This required a huge amount of work to assemble comparable data for the two countries, and I made many trips to Washington. In 1992, we presented the first offense-specific national estimates for the flow of persons from offenses committed to offenders imprisoned (Farrington & Langan, 1992). One of our most important contributions was to include information on co-offending in our calculations, because (as an example) 1 million burglaries should not be directly compared to 50,000 persons convicted for burglary in a year to produce a probability of a burglar being convicted of 5% of burglaries. If, on average, each burglary is committed by two offenders, it is necessary to compare 2 million offender–offense combinations with 50,000 convicted offender–offense combinations to produce a probability of a burglar being convicted of 2.5%, rather than 5%.

I also attended a number of meetings organized by Per-Olof Wikström in Sweden. Per-Olof had great ideas to integrate developmental, eco-logical, and situational theories and approaches. He was much more of a cross-national comparative researcher than I was (he had thought very deeply about all the issues arising), and so he suggested that we should compare the flow diagrams in England, the United States, and Sweden over time. After a lot of work, we compared all three countries between 1981 and 1991 (Farrington, Langan, & Wikström, 1994). We later extended the cross-national comparative study to eight countries between 1980 and 2000: virtually all countries with repeated large-scale national victimization surveys during this time period (Farrington, Langan, & Tonry, 2004). Among other crimes, we studied the violent crimes of homicide, serious assault, rape, and robbery.

In 1989–1992, I was Vice-Chair of the NAS panel on violence (Reiss & Roth, 1993). This produced very good state-of-the-art reviews – espe-cially in the four supplementary volumes – but was not as exciting as the criminal career panel, when we really thought that we were developing a new paradigm. I also enjoyed collaborating with medical and public health researchers like Jonathan Shepherd of Cardiff and Frederick Rivara of Seattle (see, e.g., Rivara & Farrington, 1995; Shepherd & Farrington, 1993), focusing on violence as a public health problem. I think criminologists have a lot to learn from medical and public health researchers, and these collaborations seemed to me to involve real science! I have also enjoyed collaborating with psychiatrists such as Jeremy Coid (e.g., Farrington & Coid, 2003) because of their commitment to hard scientific evidence.

Also, in the 1990s, I became the first (and so far only) President of the ASC based outside North America. I really enjoyed this, and I have very happy memories of the meeting that I presided over in Toronto (and especially of the fabulous Royal Suite at the Royal York Hotel!). Of course, I felt that the ASC was a bit like an ocean liner that could only be turned slightly and slowly. I was happy to keep a very successful society ticking over with few changes during my year in office, although I was very pleased to preside over the creation of a new Division of Corrections and Sentencing (Turner, MacKenzie, & Farrington, 2010).

Also during this period, I was involved in the founding of the European Association of Psychology and Law (EAPL), and became its president in 1997–1999. I gradually had more and more contact with European psychologists, especially in Germany and Spain (see, e.g., Garrido, Farrington, & Welsh, 2006), and became increasingly aware of the high quality of psychological research in other European countries. The formation of the EAPL was intended to bring together previously isolated researchers, and we had a joint meeting with the American Psychology–Law Society in Edinburgh during my term as president. I also spent 5 years on the Scientific Advisory Board of the Netherlands Institute for the Study of Crime and Law Enforcement (NSCR), trying to persuade them to mount a 'crime shuttle' longitudinal study (modeled on the space shuttle!) that could include various sub-studies after it got off the ground.

6.9   Later Results in the CSDD

After I took over as Director of the CSDD in 1982, I sought funding to follow-up the whole sample again, and I managed to get funding from the Home Office in 1984–1987 for a follow-up interview at age 32. At this age, 378 out of 403 men still alive (95%) were interviewed (Farrington, 1989b). In general, success in tracing the men was achieved by persistence and by using a wide variety of methods (Farrington, Gallagher, Morley, St Ledger, & West, 1990). Searching in electoral registers and telephone directories, and visits to a man's presumed address, were the most successful tracing methods for the men who were not particularly elusive. Searches in the Criminal Record Office, National Health Service records, and leads from other men were most useful for the more elusive men. The key factor in obtaining the men's cooperation was probably the pleasantness of the interviewer in the first face-to-face meeting. As at age 18, the interviews enquired about accommodations, relationships, children, employment, illnesses and injuries, parents, smoking, drinking, drug use, physical fights, court appearances, and self-reported offending.

The next funding from the Home Office was obtained in 1993–1994 to search the criminal records of the males and all their relatives (fathers, mothers, brothers, sisters, children, and female partners). These searches demonstrated that offending tends to be concentrated in families. While 40% of Study males were convicted up to age 40 in 1993, this was also true of 28% of their fathers, 13% of their mothers, 43% of their brothers, 12% of their sisters, and 9% of their wives or female partners. The fact that the percentage of brothers convicted was similar to the percentage of Study males convicted suggests that the repeated interviews with the CSDD males had no effect on their likelihood of offending. There were on average 1.5 convicted persons out of 5.5 persons per family (or about 600 convicted persons out of 2,200 searched). While 64% of families contained at least one convicted person, only 6% of families accounted for half of all the convictions of all family members (Farrington, Barnes, & Lambert, 1996).

I have always advocated for within-individual analyses, and one was carried out to investigate the effects of getting married. Convictions of Study males were followed up before and after their marriages, and they were matched with unmarried males on propensity scores (estimating the probability of getting married) and on prior offending. It is often believed that marriage to a good woman is one of the most effective treatments for male offending, and indeed we found that getting married led to a decrease in offending compared with staying single (Theobald & Farrington, 2009). Also, later separation from a wife led to an increase in offending compared with staying married (Theobald & Farrington, 2013).

While a great deal is known about risk factors, there is now a great deal of interest in protective factors. In delinquency prevention, it is a more positive message to try to strengthen protective factors rather than to eliminate risk factors. In recent years, we have made big efforts to study protective factors in the CSDD. A 'protective factor' is defined as a variable that predicts a low probability of offending among a group at risk, while an 'interactive protective' factor is defined as a variable that interacts with a risk factor to nullify its effect. Farrington and Ttofi (2012) discovered that, among boys living in poor housing, the most important protective factors were good maternal discipline, parental interest in education, and low impulsiveness. Later, Farrington, Ttofi, and Piquero (2016) found that high verbal and nonverbal IQ and high school attainment protected against poor child-rearing, high family income protected against a convicted parent, and good parental supervision protected against high dishonesty.

It was always difficult to secure funding for the CSDD, but major funding from the Home Office and the Department of Health was obtained in 1999–2004 by myself in collaboration with Jeremy Coid. This allowed another social interview with the men at age 48, plus a psychiatric interview that included the PCL-SV (a measure of psychopathy). Biological data were also collected on height, weight, waist circumference, pulse rate, blood pressure, respiratory function, and testosterone. The men's female partners were also interviewed (based on advice from Terrie Moffitt). At age 48, 365 of the 394 men who were still alive (93%) were interviewed: a remarkable response rate in a 40-year follow-up study (Farrington et al., 2006).

We have continued to search the criminal records of the Study males and all their biological relatives. For example, in 2004 we searched the Study males up to age 50, in 2011 we searched them up to age 56, and in 2017 we searched them up to age 61. These searches permitted analyses of criminal career duration (e.g., Farrington, 2019c; Kazemian & Farrington, 2018) and life-course-persistent offenders (e.g., Jolliffe, Farrington, Piquero, MacLeod, & Van de Weijer, 2017; Whitten, McGee, Homel, Farrington, & Ttofi, 2019; Zara & Farrington, 2019).

Our most recent interviews were with the generation 3 (G3) children of the Study males (Farrington, Coid, & Murray, 2009). In 2004–2013, attempts were made to interview all biological children of Study males who were aged 18 or older. Children were only targeted if their father had been interviewed, because of the requirement to seek his agreement to interview his child (in order to meet the standards of the South East Region Medical Ethics Committee). In total, 551 out of 653 eligible children were interviewed at the average age of 25 (84%). Therefore, the CSDD is one of the few projects including personal interviews with hundreds of people in three successive generations.

In 2017, the G3 children were searched up to the average age of 34. In recent analyses, Farrington et al. (2015) found that the most important risk factors for G3 convictions tended to be the same as the most important risk factors for generation 2 (G2) convictions (of the original Study males). Auty et al. (2017) and Farrington et al. (2017) investigated the intergenerational transmission of convictions from G2 to G3 and mediating factors. The intergenerational transmission of violence was particularly strong. Farrington et al. (2018) investigated the intergenerational transmission of self-reported offending from G2 to G3 and mediating factors. The most important mediators included poor parental supervision, harsh parental discipline, poor housing, low income, and paternal drug use. Farrington and Crago (2016) documented the concentration of offending in G1–G2 and G2–G3 families.

6.10   Later CSDD Studies of Aggression and Violence

There have been several analyses that focused on childhood risk factors for violence in the CSDD. For example, Farrington (1978) examined risk factors for self-reported violence at age 18 and convictions for violence at ages 10–20. Farrington (1989a) investigated the childhood (ages 8–10), adolescent (ages 12–14), and teenage (ages 16–18) predictors of convictions for violence at ages 10–32 and self-reported violence at age 32.

Farrington (1991) showed that the males who were convicted of violence at ages 10–32 tended to be frequent offenders, averaging seven convictions each. I then compared non-offenders, occasional non-violent offenders (with one or two crimes each), frequent non-violent offenders (with at least three crimes, averaging 6.5 each), and violent offenders on childhood (ages 8–10), adolescent (ages 12–14), teenage (ages 16–18), and adult (age 32) factors. I found that violent offenders and frequent non-violent offenders tended to be quite similar in these factors. Farrington (1978) and Farrington (1991) also demonstrated the continuity of measures of aggression at different ages, beginning with teacher ratings at ages 8–10 and 12–14, and the fact that childhood aggression predicted later violence.

Farrington (2001) then investigated risk factors (at ages 8–10, 12–14, and 16–18) for violence convictions at ages 21–40 and self-reported violence at age 32. Later, Farrington (2012) reviewed childhood risk factors for violence convictions at ages 10–20 and 21–40 and self-reported violence at 18 and 32, as well as childhood risk factors for violence in the PYS. In the latest analyses, Farrington (2018) reported on childhood risk factors for violence convictions of the males at ages 10–21 and 22–56, and similar analyses of childhood risk factors for violence convictions of their sons at ages 10–21. In these analyses, the most important childhood risk factors included family factors such as a convicted parent, harsh parental discipline, poor parental supervision, and a broken family; socio-economic factors such as low family income and large family size; and individual factors such as high daring or risk-taking, high hyperactivity, low intelligence, and low school attainment.

The comparison between self-reports and official records gives some indication of the probability of a violent offender being caught and convicted. Farrington et al. (2013) studied self-reported and official offending in the CSDD from age 10 to age 56. The number of violence convictions increased to a peak at ages 16–20 (43 convictions), but there were still 42 convictions for violence after age 40. Self-reported assaults increased to a peak at ages 15–18 and then decreased. The ratio of self-reported to official assault offenders decreased steadily with age, from 52 at ages 10–14, to 28 at ages 15–18, to 11 at ages 27–32, and 8 at ages 43–48. Farrington et al. (2014) compared criminal career features according to convictions and self-reports, and found that the age of onset was earlier and the duration of criminal careers longer according to self-reports.

There has been a lot of CSDD research on specific topics within the field of aggression and violence. For example, Farrington (1993) studied the continuity of self-reported bullying from ages 14 to 18 to 32 and its relation to violence convictions at ages 10–32. I also investigated childhood, adolescent, teenage, and adult (age 32) predictors and correlates of bullying. Later analyses of bullying were carried out by Farrington and Baldry (2010) – relating bullying to childhood risk factors – and by Farrington and Ttofi (2011) – relating bullying to later life outcomes. Farrington (1994, 2006a) investigated childhood, adolescent, teenage, and adult correlates of football hooliganism at age 18, and Piquero et al. (2015) studied the conviction trajectories of football hooligans. Surprisingly, football hooligans tended to be relatively small. There has also been a great deal of recent research on psychopathy (e.g., Auty, Farrington, & Coid, 2015; Bergstrøm & Farrington, 2018).

Several articles have investigated intimate partner violence at ages 32 and 48. Theobald and Farrington (2012) reported on childhood, adolescent, and teenage predictors, while Theobald et al. (2016b) compared perpetrators of intimate partner violence with violent offenders, finding some differences (in degree more than in kind) between the generally violent males and those who were only violent in the home. These two groups were compared more systematically by Theobald et al. (2016a), especially in regard to psychopathy and life success, while Piquero et al. (2014) investigated ages 8–18 predictors of intimate partner violence at ages 32 and 48 and violence convictions at ages 10–50. Finally, Theobald et al. (2016) studied childhood risk factors for dating violence versus cohabiting violence by the sons and daughters of the CSDD males, finding that more of the daughters than the sons perpetrated at least one act of violence.

There has been quite a lot of CSDD research on particular risk factors that are related to violence. Farrington (1997) found that a low resting heart rate at age 18 was significantly related to violence convictions up to age 40, independently of all other risk factors. Later, Jennings et al.

(2013) showed that a low resting heart rate at age 18 predicted convictions for violence up to age 50. Theobald et al. (2013) investigated mediators between broken homes up to age 14 and violence convictions at ages 10–50, and found that high hyperactivity was an important mediating factor. Reising et al. (2019) studied the relationship between personality disorders and violence. Farrington and Malvaso (2019) reported that harsh parental discipline at age 8 predicted violence convictions of the Study males (G2) at ages 10–21 and 22–56, and physical punishment by the males and their female partners predicted violence convictions of their sons (G3) at ages 10–21. In both generations, harsh discipline/physical punishment was one of the three most important predictors of violence convictions.

The latest analysis of violence convictions up to age 61 (Farrington, 2019b) showed that there were still many convictions for violence at age 40–61 – just as many as at ages 10–20 and 21–39. There was considerable continuity over time in both violence convictions and self-reported violence. It was surprising how strongly early risk factors at age 8–10 predicted violence convictions at age 40–61. The strongest predictors were a convicted father, high daring, harsh parental discipline, low verbal IQ, and high hyperactivity.

6.11   Intervention Research

I have been the co-chair with Rolf Loeber of four study groups: on serious and violent juvenile offenders (Loeber & Farrington, 1998) and child delinquents (Loeber & Farrington, 2001), both funded by OJJDP; on young adult offenders (Loeber & Farrington, 2012b), funded by NIJ; and on protective factors against youth violence (Loeber & Farrington, 2012a), funded by the CDC. These all involved several stimulating meetings over two to three years, as we discussed draft papers and moved toward a final report. We were very concerned to link up fundamental research on development and risk, and protective factors with applied research on prevention and treatment. For example, in the NIJ study group on young adult offenders, we argued that there should be special legal provisions for offenders aged 18–24 because they were similar to juvenile offenders, partly because of societal changes that extended traditionally adolescent patterns of behavior into the 20s (Farrington, Loeber, & Howell, 2012, 2017). I later presented these arguments in a report for Public Safety Canada (Farrington, 2017).

I have been drawn more and more into intervention research in the last 30 years, rather than naturalistic longitudinal follow-ups. I have always been interested in interventions, and our OJJDP and NIJ study group books aimed to be relevant to practitioners and policymakers as well as to scholars, by relating fundamental research on risk and protective factors to applied research on the effectiveness of interventions. Also, I have always advocated developmental or risk-focused prevention (e.g., Farrington, 2000, 2007, 2015; Farrington, Gaffney, Lösel, & Ttofi, 2017; Farrington & Welsh, 2007, 2014), and edited books on crime prevention (e.g., Farrington & Coid, 2003; Welsh & Farrington, 2006, 2012). In risk-focused prevention, knowledge about risk factors is used to select interventions designed to tackle these risk factors.

Inspired by Brandon Welsh, I have carried out a number of cost–benefit analyses of the effectiveness of interventions (see, e.g., Welsh, Farrington, & Sherman, 2001). The argument that $7 is saved for every $1 expended on a program (Schweinhart, Barnes, & Weikart, 1993) seems to be very persuasive with politicians and policymakers, who do not understand other measures of effect size. We showed that the benefits outweighed the costs for many programs (Farrington & Welsh, 2014; Welsh, Farrington, & Gowar, 2015), and that it was preferable to spend money on early intervention rather than on more imprisonment (Welsh & Farrington, 2011).

I have carried out a number of evaluations of the effectiveness of interventions. In particular, I directed a quasi-experimental evaluation of two UK 'boot camps' for young offenders (Farrington et al., 2002). One in the north of England combined military training with cognitive-behavioral skills training programs and a pre-release employment program, while one in the south involved only military training. We found that the northern boot camp was effective in reducing recidivism, but the southern boot camp was not. We concluded that military training was ineffective in reducing recidivism, even though the boys liked the army-style regime. A long-term follow-up of the Northern program (Jolliffe, Farrington, & Howard, 2013) found that the benefit-to-cost ratio (based on the reduced number of convictions) increased from 1.13 after 2 years to 3.93 after 10 years.

I also assisted in evaluating the 'SNAP' (Stop Now and Plan) cognitive-behavioral skills training program for children aged 6–11 who were in trouble with the police in Toronto (Augimeri, Farrington, Koegl, & Day, 2007). A small-scale randomized trial showed that, compared to controls, the treated children decreased on the Delinquency and Aggression scales of the Child Behavior Checklist (CBCL) and also were less likely to have criminal records at follow-up. A later evaluation (Koegl, Farrington, Augimeri, & Day, 2008) concluded that there was a dose-response relationship between treatment intensity (the number of sessions) and the decrease in CBCL scores, and that effects were greater for girls and for older children (ages 10–11), who may have been more cognitively advanced. We estimated that the benefit-to-cost ratio of this program was between 17.3 and 31.8, after scaling up from reduced convictions to reduced self-reported offenses (Farrington & Koegl, 2015).

In 1998, Lawrence Sherman persuaded me to join the crime prevention program at the University of Maryland to help update the very influential Maryland report on the effectiveness of crime reduction methods (Sherman, Farrington, Welsh, & MacKenzie, 2006; Sherman et al., 1997). This was generously funded by Jerry Lee, who is perhaps the greatest benefactor that criminology has ever known. Lawrence Sherman also founded the Academy of Experimental Criminology (AEC) to foster randomized experiments in criminology, and I was President of this from 2001 to 2003; see Farrington et al. (2020) for articles published to celebrate the 20th anniversary of the AEC.

I have been delighted to learn the technology of systematic reviews and meta-analysis in recent years, and I agreed to be the founding chair of the Campbell Collaboration Crime and Justice Group in 2000 (Farrington & Petrosino, 2001; Farrington, Weisburd, & Gill, 2011). The aim of the Group is to carry out systematic reviews of the literature on the effectiveness of criminological interventions, and to make these reviews available to everyone (scholars, policymakers, practitioners, the mass media, and the general public) on the Internet. It is a noble cause that has consumed a huge amount of my time. However, I very much enjoyed chairing the steering committee meetings because the venture was exciting and worthwhile and the participants were very pleasant and stimulating. After 7 years as Chair and then Co-Chair, I stepped down in 2007 but remained on the steering committee until 2017.

I have completed a number of systematic reviews and meta-analyses of the effectiveness of interventions, including family-based programs (Farrington & Welsh, 2003), 'Reasoning and Rehabilitation' (Tong & Farrington, 2008), mentoring (Jolliffe & Farrington, 2008), cognitive-behavioral programs (Zara & Farrington, 2014), self-control programs (Piquero, Jennings, Farrington, Diamond, & Gonzalez, 2016b), parent training programs (Piquero et al., 2016a), and methods of reducing school exclusion (Valdebenito, Eisner, Farrington, Ttofi, & Sutherland, 2019). I also recommended criteria for evaluating methodological quality in evaluation research (Farrington, 2003b). Several Campbell Collaboration reviews are described in the book on *What Works in Crime Prevention and Rehabilitation: Lessons from Systematic Reviews*, edited by Weisburd et al. (2016).

I have also carried out a great deal of research on school bullying and cyberbullying, in collaboration with Maria Ttofi, Anna Baldry, and

Izabela Zych. We completed a systematic review of the effectiveness of school bullying prevention programs, and concluded that they were generally successful and reduced bullying by an average of about 20% (Ttofi & Farrington, 2011; updated by Gaffney, Ttofi, & Farrington, 2019). We also completed a systematic review of the effectiveness of cyberbullying prevention programs, and concluded that they were generally successful and reduced cyberbullying by an average of about 10–15% (Gaffney, Farrington, Espelage, & Ttofi, 2019). The books *Protecting Children against Bullying and Its Consequences* (Zych, Farrington, Llorent, & Ttofi, 2017) and *International Perspectives on Cyberbullying* (Baldry, Blaya, & Farrington, 2018) also provide a great deal of information about effective prevention programs. I have also collaborated in research on bullying in young offender institutions (e.g., Connell, Farrington, & Ireland, 2016; Sekol & Farrington, 2016).

Looking back on my career, I have had the great luxury of being able to pursue my interests, which have been very wide-ranging, in Great Britain and North America. I have carried out research on many different topics, but my main interests have been in developmental criminology and early prevention. I have made big efforts to link up fundamental research on development with applied research on interventions. Along with Tara McGee, I founded the ASC Division of Developmental and Life-Course Criminology, and served as its first chair from 2012 to 2016. I was, of course, very happy to foster research on this topic!

In conclusion, many researchers seem to choose easy topics and easy methods that are guaranteed to produce results within a short time frame. I believe that it is more important to choose the riskier, more challenging scientific methods that I have recommended in order to advance knowledge significantly, such as systematic observation, field experiments, longitudinal studies, randomized experiments on interventions, and the holy grail of the longitudinal–experimental study (Farrington, 2006b). And it is a lot more fun when you are convinced that you are really pushing back (or forward!) the frontiers of knowledge!

Note: This chapter is based on an earlier chapter by Farrington (2014), but it has been extensively revised and updated, with special reference to violence.

References

Augimeri, L. K., Farrington, D. P., Koegl, C. J., & Day, D. M. (2007). The SNAP™ under 12 Outreach Project: Effects of a community based program for children with conduct problems. *Journal of Child and Family Studies*, *16*(6), 799–807.

Auty, K. M., Farrington, D. P., & Coid, J. W. (2015). Intergenerational transmission of psychopathy and mediation via psychosocial risk factors. *The British Journal of Psychiatry*, *206*(1), 26–31.

Auty, K. M., Farrington, D. P., & Coid, J. W. (2017). The intergenerational transmission of criminal offending: Exploring gender-specific mechanisms. *British Journal of Criminology*, *57*(1), 215–237.

Baldry, A. C., Blaya, C., & Farrington, D. P. (Eds.). (2018). *International perspectives on cyberbullying: Prevalence, risk factors and interventions*. London, England: Palgrave Macmillan.

Bergstrøm, H., & Farrington, D. P. (2018). 'The beat of my heart': the relationship between resting heart rate and psychopathy in a prospective longitudinal study. *Journal of Criminal Psychology*, *8*(4), 333–344.

Blumstein, A., Cohen, J., Roth, J. A., & Visher, C. A. (Eds.). (1986). *Criminal careers and 'career criminals'*. Washington, DC: National Academy Press.

Connell, A., Farrington, D. P., & Ireland, J. L. (2016). Characteristics of bullies and victims among incarcerated male young offenders. *Journal of Aggression, Conflict and Peace Research*, *8*(2), 114–123.

Eysenck, H. J. (1953). *Uses and abuses of psychology*. London, England: Penguin.

Eysenck, H. J. (1956). *Sense and nonsense in psychology*. London, England: Penguin.

Fabio, A., Loeber, R., Balasubramani, G. K., Roth, J., Fu, W., & Farrington, D. P. (2006). Why some generations are more violent than others: Assessment of age, period, and cohort effects. *American Journal of Epidemiology*, *164*(2), 151–160.

Farrington, D., & Baldry, A. (2010). Individual risk factors for school bullying. *Journal of Aggression, Conflict and Peace Research*, *2*(1), 4–16.

Farrington, D. P. (1972). Delinquency begins at home. *New Society*, *21*, 495–497.

Farrington, D. P. (1973). Self-reports of deviant behavior: Predictive and stable. *Journal of Criminal Law and Criminology*, *64*, 99–110.

Farrington, D. P. (1978). The family backgrounds of aggressive youths. In L. A. Hersov, M. Bergers, & D. Shaffer (Eds.), *Aggression and antisocial behaviour in childhood and adolescence* (pp. 73–93). Oxford, England: Pergammon.

Farrington, D. P. (1979a). *Juvenile justice in England and Canada*. Ottawa, Toronto, Canada: Report to the Solicitor General of Canada.

Farrington, D. P. (1979b). Longitudinal research on crime and delinquency. In N. Morris & M. Tonry (Eds.), *Crime and justice* (Vol. 1, pp. 289–348). Chicago, IL: University of Chicago Press.

Farrington, D. P. (1982). Longitudinal analyses of criminal violence. In M. E. Wolfgang & N. A. Weiner (Eds.), *Criminal violence* (pp. 171–200). Beverly Hills, CA: Sage.

Farrington, D. P. (1983). Randomized experiments on crime and justice. In M. Tonry & N. Morris (Eds.), *Crime and justice* (Vol. 4, pp. 257–308). Chicago, IL: University of Chicago Press.

Farrington, D. P. (1986). Implications of longitudinal studies for social prevention. *Justice Report*, *3*(2), 6–10.

Farrington, D. P. (1989a). Early predictors of adolescent aggression and adult violence. *Violence and Victims*, *4*, 79–100.

Farrington, D. P. (1989b). Later adult life outcomes of offenders and non-offenders. In M. Brambring, F. Loesel, & H. Skowronek (Eds.), *Children at risk: Assessment, longitudinal research and intervention* (pp. 220–244). Berlin, Germany: De Gruyter.

Farrington, D. P. (1991). Childhood aggression and adult violence: Early precursors and later life outcomes. In D. J. Pepler & K. H. Rubin (Eds.), *The development and treatment of childhood aggression* (pp. 5–29). Hillsdale, NJ: Lawrence Erlbaum.

Farrington, D. P. (1993). Understanding and preventing bullying. In M. Tonry (Ed.), *Crime and justice: A review of research* (Vol. 17, pp. 381–458). Chicago, IL: University of Chicago Press.

Farrington, D. P. (1994). Childhood, adolescent, and adult features of violent males. In L. R. Huesmann (Ed.), *Aggressive behavior: Current perspectives* (pp. 215–240). New York, NY: Plenum Press.

Farrington, D. P. (1995). The development of offending and antisocial behavior from childhood: Key findings from the Cambridge Study in Delinquent Development. *Journal of Child Psychology and Psychiatry, 36,* 929–964.

Farrington, D. P. (1997). The relationship between low resting heart rate and violence. In A. Raine, P. A. Brennan, D. P. Farrington, & S. A. Mednick (Eds.), *Biosocial bases of violence* (pp. 89–105). New York, NY: Plenum.

Farrington, D. P. (2000). Explaining and preventing crime: The globalization of knowledge – The American Society of Criminology 1999 presidential address. *Criminology, 38*(1), 1–24.

Farrington, D. P. (2001). Predicting adult official and self-reported violence. In G.-F. Pinard & L. Pagani (Eds.), *Clinical assessment of dangerousness* (pp. 66–88). Cambridge, England: Cambridge University Press.

Farrington, D. P. (2002). Multiple risk factors for multiple problem violent boys. In R. R. Corrado, R. Roesch, S. D. Hart, & J. K. Gierowski (Eds.), *Multi-problem violent youth: A foundation for comparative research on needs, interventions, and outcomes* (pp. 23–34). Amsterdam, the Netherlands: IOS Press.

Farrington, D. P. (2003a). Key results from the first forty years of the Cambridge study in delinquent development. In T. P. Thornberry & M. D. Krohn (Eds.), *Taking stock of delinquency: An overview of findings from contemporary longitudinal studies* (pp. 137–183). New York, NY: Kluwer Academic/Plenum.

Farrington, D. P. (2003b). Methodological quality standards for evaluation research. *The Annals of the American Academy of Political and Social Science, 587*(1), 49–68.

Farrington, D. P. (2005). The integrated cognitive antisocial potential (ICAP) theory. In D. P. Farrington (Ed.), *Integrated developmental and life-course theories of offending.* New Brunswick, NJ: Transaction.

Farrington, D. P. (2006a). Comparing football hooligans and violent offenders: Childhood, adolescent, teenage and adult features. *Monatsschrift fur Kriminologie und Strafrechtsreform, 89*(1), 193–205.

Farrington, D. P. (2006b). Key longitudinal–experimental studies in criminology. *Journal of Experimental Criminology, 2*(2), 121–141.

Farrington, D. P. (2007). Childhood risk factors and risk-focused prevention. In M. Maguire, R. Morgan, & R. Reiner (Eds.), *The Oxford handbook of criminology* (4th ed., pp. 602–641). New York, NY: Oxford University Press.

Farrington, D. P. (2012). Predictors of violent young offenders. In B. C. Feld & D. M. Bishop (Eds.), *The Oxford handbook of juvenile crime and juvenile justice*. New York, NY: Oxford University Press.

Farrington, D. P. (2013). Longitudinal and experimental research in criminology. In M. Tonry (Ed.), *Crime and justice in America 1975–2025* (pp. 453–527). Chicago, IL: University of Chicago Press.

Farrington, D. P. (2014). Reflections on a life course of developmental criminology. In R. M. Lerner, A. C. Petersen, R. K. Silbereisen, & J. Brooks-Gunn (Eds.), *The developmental science of adolescence: History through autobiography* (pp. 150–166). New York, NY: Psychology Press.

Farrington, D. P. (2015). The developmental evidence base: Prevention. In D. A. Crighton & G. J. Towl (Eds.), *Forensic psychology* (2nd ed., pp. 141–159). Chichester, England: Wiley.

Farrington, D. P. (2017). *Transitions from juvenile delinquency to young adult offending: A review of Canadian and international evidence*. Ottawa, Toronto, Canada: Public Safety Canada (Research Report 2017-R014).

Farrington, D. P. (2018). Origins of violent behavior over the life span. In A. T. Vazsonyi, D. J. Flannery, & M. DeLisi (Eds.), *The Cambridge handbook of violent behavior and aggression* (2nd ed., pp. 3–30). Cambridge, England: Cambridge University Press.

Farrington, D. P. (2019a). The Cambridge Study in Delinquent Development. In D. Eaves, C.D. Webster, Q. Haque, & J. Eaves-Thalken (Eds.), *Risk rules: A practical guide to structured professional judgment and violence prevention* (pp. 225–233). Hove, East Sussex, England: Pavilion.

Farrington, D. P. (2019b). The development of violence from age 8 to 61. *Aggressive Behavior, 45*, 365–376.

Farrington, D. P. (2019c). The duration of criminal careers: How many offenders do not desist up to age 61? *Journal of Developmental and Life-Course Criminology, 5*(1), 4–21.

Farrington, D. P. (2019d). The Integrated Cognitive Antisocial Potential (ICAP) theory: Past, present, and future. *Journal of Developmental and Life-Course Criminology*, 1–16.

Farrington, D. P., Auty, K. M., Coid, J. W., & Turner, R. E. (2013). Self-reported and official offending from age 10 to age 56. *European Journal on Criminal Policy and Research, 19*(2), 135–151.

Farrington, D. P., Barnes, G. C., & Lambert, S. (1996). The concentration of offending in families. *Legal and Criminological Psychology, 1*(1), 47–63.

Farrington, D. P., Berkowitz, L., & West, D. J. (1982). Differences between individual and group fights. *British Journal of Social Psychology, 21*(4), 323–333.

Farrington, D. P., & Coid, J. W. (Eds.). (2003). *Early prevention of adult antisocial behaviour*. Cambridge, England: Cambridge University Press.

Farrington, D. P., Coid, J. W., Harnett, L., Jolliffe, D., Soteriou, N., Turner, R., & West, D. J. (2006). *Criminal careers up to age 50 and life success up to age 48: New findings from the Cambridge Study in Delinquent Development* (Vol. 94). London, England: Home Office (Research Study No. 299).

Farrington, D. P., Coid, J. W., & Murray, J. (2009). Family factors in the intergenerational transmission of offending. *Criminal Behaviour and Mental Health, 19*(2), 109–124.

Farrington, D. P., Coid, J. W., & West, D. J. (2009). The development of offending from age 8 to age 50: Recent results from the Cambridge Study in Delinquent Development. *Monatsschrift fur Kriminologie und Strafrechtsreform*, *92*(2–3), 160–173.

Farrington, D. P., & Crago, R. V. (2016). The concentration of convictions in two generations of families. In A. Kapardis & D. P. Farrington (Eds.), *The psychology of crime, policing and courts* (pp. 7–23). Abingdon, England: Routledge.

Farrington, D. P., Ditchfield, J., Hancock, G., Howard, P., Jolliffe, D., Livingston, M. S., & Painter, K. A. (2002). *Evaluation of two intensive regimes for young offenders*. London, England: Home Office (Research Study No. 239).

Farrington, D. P., Gaffney, H., Lösel, F., & Ttofi, M. M. (2017). Systematic reviews of the effectiveness of developmental prevention programs in reducing delinquency, aggression, and bullying. *Aggression and Violent Behavior*, *33*, 91–106.

Farrington, D. P., Gallagher, B., Morley, L., St Ledger, R. J., & West, D. J. (1990). Minimizing attrition in longitudinal research: Methods of tracing and securing cooperation in a 24-year follow-up study. In D. Magnusson & L. Bergman (Eds.), *Data quality in longitudinal research* (pp. 122–147). Cambridge, England: Cambridge University Press.

Farrington, D. P., Jolliffe, D., Hawkins, J. D., & Catalano, R. F. (2003). Comparing delinquency careers in court records and self-reports. *Criminology*, *41*, 933–958.

Farrington, D. P., Jolliffe, D., & Johnstone, L. (2008). *Assessing violence risk: A framework for practice*. Edinburgh, Scotland: Risk Management Authority Scotland.

Farrington, D. P., & Koegl, C. J. (2015). Monetary benefits and costs of the Stop Now and Plan Program for boys aged 6–11, based on the prevention of later offending. *Journal of Quantitative Criminology*, *31*(2), 263–287.

Farrington, D. P., & Langan, P. A. (1992). Changes in crime and punishment in England and America in the 1980s. *Justice Quarterly*, *9*(1), 5–46.

Farrington, D. P., Langan, P. A., & Tonry, M. (Eds.). (2004). *Cross-national studies in crime and justice*. Washington, DC: U.S. Bureau of Justice Statistics (NCJ 200988).

Farrington, D. P., Langan, P. A., & Wikström, P.-O. (1994). Changes in crime and punishment in America, England and Sweden between the 1980s and the 1990s. *Studies on Crime and Crime Prevention*, *3*, 104–131.

Farrington, D. P., Loeber, R., & Howell, J. C. (2012). Young adult offenders: The need for more effective legislative options and justice processing. *Criminology & Public Policy*, *11*(4), 727–750.

Farrington, D. P., Loeber, R., & Howell, J. C. (2017). Increasing the minimum age for adult court: Is it desirable, and what are the effects? *Criminology and Public Policy*, *16*, 83–92.

Farrington, D. P., Loeber, R., & Stouthamer-Loeber, M. (2003). How can the relationship between race and violence be explained. In D. F. Hawkins (Ed.), *Violent crimes: Assessing race and ethnic differences* (pp. 213–237). Cambridge, England: Cambridge University Press.

Farrington, D. P., Lösel, F., Braga, A. A., Mazerolle, L., Raine, A., Sherman, L. W., & Weisburd, D. (2020). Experimental criminology: Looking back and forward on the 20th anniversary of the Academy of Experimental Criminology. *Journal of Experimental Criminology*, 1–25.

Farrington, D. P., & Malvaso, C. G. (2019). Physical punishment and offending in two successive generations of males. In I. Bryce, Y. Robinson, & W. Petherick (Eds.), *Child abuse and neglect: Forensic issues in evidence, impact and management* (pp. 203–224). London, England: Academic Press.

Farrington, D. P., & McGee, T. R. (2017). The Integrated Cognitive Antisocial Potential (ICAP) theory: Empirical testing. In A. A. J. Blokland & V. R. V. d. Geest (Eds.), *The Routledge international handbook of life-course criminology* (pp. 11–28). London, England: Routledge.

Farrington, D. P., & McGee, T. R. (2019). The Integrated Cognitive Antisocial Potential (ICAP) theory: New empirical tests. In D. P. Farrington, L. Kazemian, & A. R. Piquero (Eds.), *The Oxford handbook of developmental and life-course criminology* (pp. 173–192). New York, NY: Oxford University Press.

Farrington, D. P., Ohlin, L. E., & Wilson, J. Q. (1986). *Understanding and controlling crime: Toward a new research strategy.* New York, NY: Springer-Verlag.

Farrington, D. P., & Petrosino, A. (2001). Campbell Collaboration Crime and Justice Group. *Annals of the American Academy of Political and Social Science*, *578*, 35–49.

Farrington, D. P., Piquero, A. R., & Jennings, W. G. (2013). *Offending from childhood to late middle age: Recent results from the Cambridge Study in Delinquent Development.* New York, NY: Springer Science & Business Media.

Farrington, D. P., & Ttofi, M. M. (2011). Bullying as a predictor of offending, violence and later life outcomes. *Criminal Behaviour and Mental Health*, *21*(2), 90–98.

Farrington, D. P., & Ttofi, M. M. (2012). Protective and promotive factors in the development of offending. In T. Bliesener, A. Beelman, & M. Stemmler (Eds.), *Antisocial behavior and crime: Contributions of developmental and evaluation research to prevention and intervention* (pp. 71–88). Cambridge, MA: Hogrefe.

Farrington, D. P., & Ttofi, M. M. (2018). Developmental and psychological theories of offending. In G. M. Davies & A. R. Beech (Eds.), *Forensic psychology: Crime, justice, law, interventions* (3rd ed., pp. 55–82). Chichester, England: Wiley/British Psychological Society.

Farrington, D. P., Ttofi, M. M., & Crago, R. V. (2017). Intergenerational transmission of convictions for different types of offenses. *Victims & Offenders*, *12*(1), 1–20.

Farrington, D. P., Ttofi, M. M., & Crago, R. V. (2018). Intergenerational transmission of self-reported offending in the Cambridge Study in Delinquent Development. In V. I. Eichelsheim & S. G. A. V. d. Weijer (Eds.), *Intergenerational continuity of criminal and antisocial behaviour: An international overview of studies* (pp. 115–136). Abingdon, England: Routledge.

Farrington, D. P., Ttofi, M. M., Crago, R. V., & Coid, J. W. (2014). Prevalence, frequency, onset, desistance and criminal career duration in self-reports compared with official records. *Criminal Behaviour and Mental Health*, 24(4), 241–253.

Farrington, D. P., Ttofi, M. M., & Piquero, A. R. (2016). Risk, promotive, and protective factors in youth offending: Results from the Cambridge study in delinquent development. *Journal of Criminal Justice*, 45, 63–70.

Farrington, D. P., Weisburd, D. L., & Gill, C. E. (2011). The Campbell Collaboration Crime and Justice Group: A decade of progress. In C. J. Smith, S. X. Zhang, & R. Barberet (Eds.), *Routledge handbook of international criminology* (pp. 53–63). New York, NY: Routledge.

Farrington, D. P., & Welsh, B. C. (2003). Family-based prevention of offending: A meta-analysis. *Australian and New Zealand Journal of Criminology*, 36(2), 127–151.

Farrington, D. P., & Welsh, B. C. (2007). *Saving children from a life of crime: Early risk factors and effective interventions*. New York, NY: Oxford University Press.

Farrington, D. P., & Welsh, B. C. (2014). Saving children from a life of crime: The benefits greatly outweigh the costs! *International Annals of Criminology*, 52(1-2), 67–92.

Farrington, D. P., & West, D. J. (1971). A comparison between early delinquents and young aggressives. *British Journal of Criminology*, 11, 341–358.

Farrington, D. P., & West, D. J. (1981). The Cambridge Study in Delinquent Development. In S. A. Mednick & A. E. Baert (Eds.), *Prospective longitudinal research: An empirical basis for the primary prevention of psychosocial disorders* (pp. 137–145). New York, NY: Oxford University Press.

Farrington, D. P., & West, D. J. (1990). The Cambridge study in delinquent development: A long-term follow-up of 411 London males. In H.-J. Kerner & G. Kaiser (Eds.), *Kriminalitat: Personlichkeit, lebensgeschichte und verhalten [Criminality: personality, behavior and life history]* (pp. 115–138). Berlin, Germany: Springer-Verlag.

Gaffney, H., Farrington, D. P., Espelage, D. L., & Ttofi, M. M. (2019). Are cyberbullying intervention and prevention programs effective? A systematic and meta-analytical review. *Aggression and Violent Behavior*, 45, 134–153.

Gaffney, H., Ttofi, M. M., & Farrington, D. P. (2019). Evaluating the effectiveness of school-bullying prevention programs: An updated meta-analytical review. *Aggression and Violent Behavior*, 45, 111–133.

Garrido, V., Farrington, D. P., & Welsh, B. C. (2006). The importance of an evidence-based approach in the current Spanish policy for crime prevention. *Psicothema*, 18(3), 591–595.

Jennings, W. G., Piquero, A. R., & Farrington, D. P. (2013). Does resting heart rate at age 18 distinguish general and violent offending up to age 50? Findings from the Cambridge Study in Delinquent Development. *Journal of Criminal Justice*, 41(4), 213–219.

Jolliffe, D., & Farrington, D. P. (2008). *The influence of mentoring on reoffending*. Stockholm, Sweden: Swedish National Council for Crime Prevention.

Jolliffe, D., Farrington, D. P., & Howard, P. (2013). How long did it last? A 10-year reconviction follow-up study of high intensity training for young offenders. *Journal of Experimental Criminology*, 9(4), 515–531.

Jolliffe, D., Farrington, D. P., Piquero, A. R., MacLeod, J. F., & Van de Weijer, S. (2017). Prevalence of life-course-persistent, adolescence-limited, and late-onset offenders: A systematic review of prospective longitudinal studies. *Aggression and Violent Behavior, 33,* 4–14.

Kazemian, L., & Farrington, D. P. (2018). Advancing knowledge about residual criminal careers: A follow-up to age 56 from the Cambridge study in delinquent development. *Journal of Criminal Justice, 57,* 1–10.

Koegl, C. J., Farrington, D. P., Augimeri, L. K., & Day, D. M. (2008). Evaluation of a targeted cognitive-behavioral program for children with conduct problems – the SNAP® under 12 outreach project: Service intensity, age and gender effects on short-and long-term outcomes. *Clinical Child Psychology and Psychiatry, 13*(3), 419–434.

Langan, P. A., & Farrington, D. P. (1983). Two-track or one-track justice? Some evidence from an English longitudinal survey. *Journal of Criminal Law and Criminology, 74,* 519–546.

Langan, P. A., & Farrington, D. P. (1998). *Crime and justice in the United States and in England and Wales, 1981–96.* Washington, DC: Bureau of Justice Statistics (NCJ 169284).

Liberman, A. (2007). *Adolescents, neighborhoods, and violence: Recent findings from the Project on Human Development in Chicago Neighborhoods.* Washington, DC: U.S. National Institute of Justice (NCJ 217397).

Loeber, R., & Farrington, D. P. (2011). *Young homicide offenders and victims: Risk factors, prediction, and prevention from childhood.* New York, NY: Springer.

Loeber, R., & Farrington, D. P. (2012a). Advancing knowledge about direct protective factors that may reduce youth violence. *American Journal of Preventive Medicine, 43*(2S1), S24–S27.

Loeber, R., & Farrington, D. P. (Eds.). (1998). *Serious and violent juvenile offenders: Risk factors and successful interventions.* Thousand Oaks, CA: Sage.

Loeber, R., & Farrington, D. P. (Eds.). (2001). *Child delinquents: Development, interventions and service needs.* Thousand Oaks, CA: Sage.

Loeber, R., & Farrington, D. P. (Eds.). (2012b). *From juvenile delinquency to adult crime: Criminal careers, justice policy, and prevention.* New York, NY: Oxford University Press.

Loeber, R., Farrington, D. P., Stouthamer-Loeber, M., & White, H. R. (2008). *Violence and serious theft: Development and prediction from childhood to adulthood.* New York, NY: Routledge.

McGee, T. R., & Farrington, D. P. (2019). Developmental and life-course explanations of offending. *Psychology, Crime & Law, 25*(6), 609–625.

Piquero, A. R., Farrington, D. P., & Blumstein, A. (2007). *Key issues in criminal career research: New analyses of the Cambridge Study in Delinquent Development.* Cambridge, England: Cambridge University Press.

Piquero, A. R., Jennings, W. G., & Farrington, D. P. (2015). The life-course offending trajectories of football hooligans. *European Journal of Criminology, 12*(1), 113–125.

Piquero, A. R., Jennings, W. G., Diamond, B., Farrington, D. P., Tremblay, R. E., Welsh, B. C. & Gonzalez, J. M. R. (2016a). A meta-analysis update on the effects of early family/parent training programs on antisocial behavior and delinquency. *Journal of Experimental Criminology*, 12, 229–248.

Piquero, A. R., Jennings, W. G., Farrington, D. P., Diamond, B., & Gonzalez, J. M. R. (2016b). A meta-analysis update on the effectiveness of early self-control improvement programs to improve self-control and reduce delinquency. *Journal of Experimental Criminology*, 12(2), 249–264.

Piquero, A. R., Theobald, D., & Farrington, D. P. (2014). The overlap between offending trajectories, criminal violence, and intimate partner violence. *International Journal of Offender Therapy and Comparative Criminology*, 58(3), 286–302.

Raine, A., Farrington, D. P., Brennan, P., & Mednick, S. A. (Eds.). (1997). *Biosocial bases of violence*. New York, NY: Plenum.

Raine, A., Reynolds, C., Venables, P. H., Mednick, S. A., & Farrington, D. P. (1998). Fearlessness, stimulation-seeking, and large body size at age 3 years as early predispositions to childhood aggression at age 11 years. *Archives of General Archives*, 55(8), 745–751.

Reising, K., Farrington, D. P., Ttofi, M. M., Piquero, A. R., & Coid, J. W. (2019). Childhood risk factors for personality disorder symptoms related to violence. *Aggression and Violent Behavior*, 49, 101315.

Reiss, A. J., & Roth, J. A. (Eds.). (1993). *Understanding and preventing violence*. Washington, DC: National Academy Press.

Rivara, F. P., & Farrington, D. P. (1995). Prevention of violence: Role of the pediatrician. *Archives of Pediatrics & Adolescent Medicine*, 149(4), 421–429.

Sampson, R. J., & Laub, J. H. (1993). *Crime in the making: Pathways and turning points through life*. Cambridge, MA: Harvard University Press.

Schweinhart, L. L., Barnes, H. V., & Weikart, D. P. (1993). *Significant benefits. The High/Scope Perry School Study through age 27*. Ypsilanti, MI: High/Scope Press.

Sekol, I., & Farrington, D. P. (2016). Personal characteristics of bullying victims in residential care for youth. *Journal of Aggression, Conflict and Peace Research*, 8 (2), 99–113.

Shepherd, J. P., & Farrington, D. P. (1993). Assault as a public health problem: Discussion paper. *Journal of the Royal Society of Medicine*, 86(2), 89–92.

Sherman, L. W. (1992). *Policing domestic violence: Experiments and dilemmas*. New York, NY: Free Press.

Sherman, L. W., Farrington, D. P., Welsh, B. C., & MacKenzie, D. L. (Eds.). (2006). *Evidence-based crime prevention, rev ed.* London, England: Routledge.

Sherman, L. W., Gottfredson, D., MacKenzie, D., Eck, J., Reuter, P., & Bushway, S. (1997). *Preventing crime: What works, what doesn't, what's promising*. Washington, DC: U.S. Office of Justice Programs.

Theobald, D., & Farrington, D. P. (2009). Effects of getting married on offending: Results from a prospective longitudinal survey of males. *European Journal of Criminology*, 6(6), 496–516.

Theobald, D., & Farrington, D. P. (2012). Child and adolescent predictors of male intimate partner violence. *Journal of Child Psychology and Psychiatry*, 53(12), 1242–1249.

Theobald, D., & Farrington, D. P. (2013). The effects of marital breakdown on offending: Results from a prospective longitudinal survey of males. *Psychology,*

Crime & Law, 19(4), 391–408.

Theobald, D., Farrington, D. P., Coid, J. W., & Piquero, A. R. (2016a). Are male perpetrators of intimate partner violence different from convicted violent offenders? Examination of psychopathic traits and life success in males from a community survey. *Journal of Interpersonal Violence, 31*(9), 1687–1718.

Theobald, D., Farrington, D. P., Coid, J. W., & Piquero, A. R. (2016b). A longitudinal analysis of the criminal careers of intimate partner violence offender subtypes: Results from a prospective survey of males. *Violence and Victims, 31*(6), 999–1020.

Theobald, D., Farrington, D. P., & Piquero, A. R. (2013). Childhood broken homes and adult violence: An analysis of moderators and mediators. *Journal of Criminal Justice, 41*(1), 44–52.

Theobald, D., Farrington, D. P., Ttofi, M. M., & Crago, R. V. (2016). Risk factors for dating violence versus cohabiting violence: Results from the third generation of the Cambridge Study in Delinquent Development. *Criminal Behaviour and Mental Health, 26*(4), 229–239.

Tong, L. S. J., & Farrington, D. P. (2008). Effectiveness of 'reasoning and rehabilitation' in reducing reoffending. *Psicothema, 20*(1), 20–28.

Tonry, M., Ohlin, L. E., & Farrington, D. P. (1991). *Human development and criminal behavior: New ways of advancing knowledge.* New York, NY: Springer-Verlag.

Ttofi, M. M., & Farrington, D. P. (2011). Effectiveness of school-based programs to reduce bullying: A systematic and meta-analytic review. *Journal of Experimental Criminology, 7*(1), 27–56.

Turner, S. P., MacKenzie, D. L., & Farrington, D. P. (2010). Celebrating the American Society of Criminology Division on Corrections and Sentencing Tenth Anniversary. *Victims and Offenders, 5*(3), 199–202.

Valdebenito, S., Eisner, M., Farrington, D. P., Ttofi, M. M., & Sutherland, A. (2019). What can we do to reduce disciplinary school exclusion? A systematic review and meta-analysis. *Journal of Experimental Criminology, 15*, 253–287.

Weisburd, D., Farrington, D. P., & Gill, C. (Eds.). (2016). *What works in crime prevention and rehabilitation: Lessons from systematic reviews.* New York, NY: Springer.

Welsh, B. C., & Farrington, D. P. (2011). The benefits and costs of early prevention compared with imprisonment: Toward evidence-based policy. *The Prison Journal, 91*(3S1), 120–137.

Welsh, B. C., & Farrington, D. P. (Eds.). (2006). *Preventing crime: What works for children, offenders, victims and places.* Dordrecht, the Netherlands: Springer.

Welsh, B. C., & Farrington, D. P. (Eds.). (2012). *The Oxford handbook of crime prevention.* New York, NY: Oxford University Press.

Welsh, B. C., Farrington, D. P., & Gowar, B. R. (2015). Benefit-cost analysis of crime prevention programs. In M. Tonry (Ed.), *Crime and justice* (Vol. 44, pp. 447–516).

Welsh, B. C., Farrington, D. P., & Sherman, L. W. (Eds.). (2001). *Costs and benefits of preventing crime.* Boulder, CO: Westview Press.

West, D. J. (1969). *Present conduct and future delinquency.* London, England: Heinemann.

West, D. J. (1982). *Delinquency: Its roots, careers and prospects.* London, England: Heinemann.

West, D. J., & Farrington, D. P. (1973). *Who becomes delinquent?* London, England: Heinemann.

West, D. J., & Farrington, D. P. (1977). *The delinquent way of life.* London, England: Heinemann.

Whitten, T., McGee, T. R., Homel, R., Farrington, D. P., & Ttofi, M. M. (2019). Comparing the criminal careers and childhood risk factors of persistent, chronic, and persistent–chronic offenders. *Australian & New Zealand Journal of Criminology, 52*(2), 151–173.

Wilson, J. Q., & Loury, G. C. (Eds.). (1987). *From children to citizens, Vol. 3: Families, schools, and delinquency prevention.* New York, NY: Springer-Verlag.

Wollheim, R. (1981). *Sigmund Freud.* Cambridge, England: Cambridge University Press.

Zara, G., & Farrington, D. P. (2014). Cognitive-behavioral skills training in preventing offending and reducing recidivism. In E. M. J. Gonzalez & J. L. A. Robles (Eds.), *Criminology and forensic psychology* (pp. 55–102). Charleston, SC: Criminology and Justice.

Zara, G., & Farrington, D. P. (2016). *Criminal recidivism: Explanation, prediction and prevention.* Abingdon, England: Routledge.

Zara, G., & Farrington, D. P. (2019). Unsuccessful life style in middle-aged official and self-reported types of offenders. *Journal of Criminal Justice, 64,* 34–42.

Zych, I., Farrington, D. P., Llorent, V. J., & Ttofi, M. M. (2017). *Protecting children against bullying and its consequences.* New York, NY: Springer.

7 Nurture and Nature
Surviving in the Shadows of War

Menno Reindert Kruk

Menno Reindert Kruk was born on July 12, 1944, in Utrecht (the Netherlands). He became a senior scientist in pharmacology at Leiden University (the Netherlands) in 1975 and received his PhD in 1981 from the University of Leiden for his research on the origins of hypothalamic aggression. He was University Docent and Assistant Professor in the Department of Pharmacology at Leiden University from 1983 until his retirement in 2009. For many years Menno Kruk played an important role in the International Society for Research on Aggression (ISRA). He was the chair of the scientific program from 2004 to 2006 and President of ISRA from 2007 to 2008. He was also Visiting Scientist in the Department of Physics (LION) at Leiden University from 2014 to 2018 and Coordinator of a Hungarian–Dutch cooperation on 'Stress & Aggression Interactions' (1996–2003), which was funded by the Harry Frank Guggenheim Foundation, the Dutch Research Council (NWO), and the Hungarian Scientific Research Fund (OTKA). Menno R. Kruk also coordinated an interdisciplinary multicenter research program funded by the NWO from 1988 to 1995 on 'Neuroanatomy and Temporal Structure of Hypothalamic Responses'.

The main research focus of Menno R. Kruk during his career was the interaction between brain function, hormones, and behavior, with the aim of understanding brain mechanisms during violent behavior. He specifically explored how aggression could be studied using methods from the exact, natural sciences. He used animal models, first, to clarify which hypothalamic neurons mediate attack during electrical stimulation and, second, to register their activity during social conflict in order to improve understanding of 'pathological' processes in aggression. The research methods he used included ethological, pharmacological, endocrine, physiological, and mathematical approaches (Bressers et al., 1995; Haccou et al., 1988; Haller, Halasz, Mikics, & Kruk, 2004; Kruk, 2014; Roeling et al., 1994; Van Erp, Kruk, Semple, & Verbeet, 1993).

Menno R. Kruk developed animal models of functional and pathological aggression and the mathematical tools to describe and analyze the effects of drugs and hormones on behavioral structure and social interactions between animals. In cooperation with József Haller (Budapest University, Hungary), he studied the crucial role of corticosteroid feedback to the brain in the control of aggressive behavior (Haller et al., 2004; Kruk, Halasz, Meelis, & Haller, 2004). With Ewald Naumann and Hartmut Schächinger (University of Trier in Germany) he studied the interactions between the processing of conflict-related stimuli and stress hormones in humans, with support from a grant of the International Research Training Group 'The Psychoendocrinology of Stress' of the German Research Foundation (Bertsch, Böhnke, Kruk, & Naumann, 2009; Bertsch, Böhnke, Kruk, Richter, & Naumann, 2011; Böhnke, Bertsch, Kruk, Richter, & Naumann, 2010).

The research of Menno R. Kruk was funded by several other national and international funding agencies. From the NWO he received a multicenter program subsidy to study hypothalamic behavioral responses. He received funding from the Harry Frank Guggenheim Foundation (New York, United States) to study the behavioral consequences of the hormone responses induced by hypothalamic stimulation. An important Hungarian–Dutch cooperation grant (NWO–OTKA) between 1997 and 2003 enabled him and Jozsef Haller to study the brain mechanism of rapid facilitation of aggression by glucocorticoids. Between 2002 and 2005, the Guggenheim Foundation also funded a cooperative study with Andries Ter Maat from the Free University in Amsterdam (VU) on recording multiple unit activity (MUA) from the 'aggressive area' in the rat hypothalamus.

Menno R. Kruk was President of the Brain and Behavior Study group of the NWO, President of the Netherlands Society for Behavioral Biology (NVG, formerly the Dutch Ethology Study Group of the NWO), Member of the Ethical Committee on Animal Experimentation of Leiden University (1983–2003), and President of the Scientific Advisory Board of Dr. O. Adang's study on Football Hooliganism and Squatters Riots (1984–1988). He was a member of the Book Commissioning Board of the Harry Frank Guggenheim Foundation (HFG) (1995–2001), and a member of the Scientific Advisory Council of the Netherlands Institute of Forensic Psychiatry (NIFP) (2007–2008).

Menno Kruk was twice nominated for the Best Teacher Prize at the University of Leiden. He also received the prize for the best teacher at the Medical Faculty and the prize for organizing the best training course at the Medical Faculty. He organized several large international meetings, such as the second European ISRA Meeting (1983) in Zeist, the Netherlands; the third meeting of the European Behavioral Pharmacology Society (EBPS), and its satellite meeting on

Discrimination of Drugs of Abuse sponsored by the U.S. National Institute for Drug Abuse (NIDA) in Noordwijk, the Netherlands (1992). He organized many national and international multidisciplinary meetings and workshops around the theme of conflict and aggression. Menno Kruk received a large subsidy from the Royal Netherlands Academy of Arts and Sciences (KNAW) for a weeklong meeting in 2009, convening 48 international experts from different disciplines to extensively discuss 'Context, Causes, and Consequences of Conflict'.

7.1   Signposts to Science

On the windowsill in front of my desk, a few seemingly innocent objects sometimes divert my attention from the direct tasks at hand. There is a milk jug in prewar style, its off-white belly cheerfully decorated with red poppies, blue cornflowers, and wheat spikes. It stands close to an old-fashioned low, white porcelain jug once used in hospitals to feed liquid food to patients who had lost command over their hands. A little aside, in strange contrast, stands a postwar- style, straight silver cup with the inscription *Ehrengabe* [gift of honor]. They were given to my parents long before I was born, or in my absence. Yet they define episodes which shaped my life, my choices, and in some ways my modest scientific career. I wasn't really aware of that at the time I was in active research. It became only fully evident while making an illustrated family history for our children and grandchildren, and by recently reading the wartime letters of my parents.

I wasn't a brilliant student. During my high school and bachelor years I used to be just above average. I did my homework, passed my tests and exams, and only became excited enough to earn high marks when there was something challenging, or something outside the regular curriculum, to master. Many adolescent boys are like that. Probably because of that lackluster performance, there was never a prominent teacher or scientist who took me under his wing. That may have been a blessing in disguise. I had to find my own path. However, there were many inspiring persons in my family, at high school, and at university, and several formative events, that nudged me along the road toward the scientific problem that would become my life's vocation: the study of the behavioral neuroscience of aggression.

7.2   Dedication to Education

My parents were born during the First World War. As they grew up, the great economic depression paralyzed the economy while the Nazi party rose to power in Germany. My maternal grandfather, a house carpenter, went bankrupt. The family with six children had to survive on the paltry earnings of my grandmother's work as a modiste and on the income of the oldest daughter. Yet, even by today's standards, they were a modern family. In the summer, they went camping at a farm in homemade tents. They were vegetarian, and, importantly, my grandfather insisted that all children, especially the five girls, finish high school.

My paternal grandfather was a railway employee and did slightly better financially. Yet the family lacked the funds for a university education. Those circumstances shaped their prewar worldview. My parents both took one of the few roads to upward mobility available for them at the time: training at a college of education. But after graduation, while fully qualified, they had to work without any salary as so-called trainees for several years until the start of the Second World War. They had the same duties and responsibilities as regularly paid teachers. It didn't quench their devotion to education and cultural development as a means of fighting inequality and advancing society.

7.3   Strengthening Social Networks

My father was an Anabaptist (or Mennonite), a tolerant denomination in Holland. My mother had embraced theosophy. But they preferred to emphasize similarities rather than differences in their worldviews. Recognizing the devastating effects of alcohol on individuals and society, they joined a youth movement for cultural advancement and outdoor activities that strongly opposed drinking. They tried to mend the same ills that our world still faces. Throughout their lives, my parents remained strongly opposed to drinking. My father became the movement's leader during the war. They thoroughly enjoyed the camping, tracking, nature study, singing, folk dancing, acting, and, most importantly, the emphasis on education. Their prewar idealism and ceremonies may seem rather romantic in hindsight. Romantic or not, their engagement fostered the social network, the friendships, and the mental fortitude that helped them to survive the ordeals that were about to strike the Netherlands. My parents became close friends with 'Appie Lopes', a prominent member of the movement. Abraham Lopes Leão de Laguna was the talented son of a family of nice and unassuming diamond cutters. They were the descendants of Portuguese Jews who had been living peacefully in the Netherlands since the 17th century. My father and Appie made educational radio programs, even during my father's army service on the threshold of war.

7.4   Ostracism, Repression, and Resistance

On May 10, 1940, Nazi Germany invaded the Netherlands. Initially the family passed unharmed through the first hostilities. My parents now had regular jobs in primary schools. But soon afterward, in rapid succession, disaster struck. At the end of May, Appie's older brother, a captain in the Dutch army and a prisoner of war, was summarily executed by the Germans. In October 1940 a drunken German soldier's truck fatally hit my mother's cheerful younger sister of 18. Political organizations were forbidden or forced to join Nazi organizations. Jews were forcefully excluded from the public domain and forced to wear a yellow 'David' star. University teachers and political leaders who protested were arrested or went 'underground'. Anti-Semitic measures escalated. Appie Lopes' letters to my parents testify to the deteriorating life conditions and poor job prospects for Jews. The social network of the movement tried to support Appie and his family, but there was little it could accomplish. In one heart-rending letter, Appie offers the 'eager-to-marry couple' the textile rations of the Lopes family for the winter of 1940–1941. My mother's brother, Wim, joined the underground resistance and was taken prisoner in September 1941. He would spend the rest of the war as a political prisoner marked for execution in extermination camps. In defiance of all adversities, my parents set the date for their marriage on October 3. Appie was to be their best man. In June 1941 Appie was taken by the German political police while he was carrying messages from the leader of a left-wing party that had gone 'underground'. Shortly afterward Appie was murdered in Mauthausen, Austria. Baruch and Frederika Lopes Leão de Laguna, Appie's parents, visited a few weeks after my parents' marriage. They brought the wedding present Appie had already bought for them: the flowery decorated milk jug on my windowsill. It silently tells another story. Baruch and Frederika were murdered in Auschwitz one year later.

7.5   Saving the Survival Network

Youth movements with political aims were forced to join the Dutch equivalent of the German 'Hitlerjugend'. Most refused and went underground. Many of their members joined my father's youth organization. As an explicit anti-alcohol organization, it was easier to avoid the scrutiny of the German authorities. In fact, it was just as left leaning as the forbidden youth organization of the socialist party. It was one of my father's wartime tasks to keep the organization out of sight of the Nazis. Disguised as anti-alcohol meetings, seminars and summer camps were organized to discuss policies for the postwar society. Following the traumatic experiences in their family and circle of close friends, my parents naturally became involved in the underground resistance for so-called illegal activities such as housing messengers carrying anti-German pamphlets with news on Allied advances, false ration cards, or false identity cards for people hiding from the Nazis. Being discovered meant execution or concentration camp for the entire family, but they continued these activities even after my sister was born in November 1942.

7.6   Facing a False Dawn

On June 6, 1944, the Allied Forces landed in Normandy. On July 12, I was born. In the congratulations my parents received, one can see how much everyone expected that I would soon grow up in a peaceful and just world. At the end of August, the Allies had freed Paris and Brussels and advanced toward the German border. Dutch Nazi collaborators fled in great numbers to Germany. Then the British commander Montgomery tried to end the war in one stroke, taking by surprise the bridges over the Meuse and the branches of the Rhine in Holland. Despite heroic efforts, the troops were defeated and had to withdraw. For the rest of the winter a standoff developed in the marshy lowlands between the branches of the lower Rhine. The southern half of the Netherlands was now free. The northern half remained under German occupation (Beevor, 2018).

7.7   Ruthless Revenge and a Survivor's Story

Having seen the jubilant Dutch reception of the Allies in the South and having seen their immense loathing for fleeing Nazi collaborators, the German commanders decided to punish the Dutch by starvation and by rounding up every able-bodied Dutchman for the German war effort. The ruthlessness of the German commanders toward civilians at the time, even their own compatriots, can be judged by the fact that one high officer ordered groups of German prostitutes to 'improve the morale' of his troops. He had them all shot after 14 days, fearing that they would divulge demoralizing soldiers' stories in Germany (Beevor, 2018).

On October 7, 1944, my mother went to the center of Utrecht with my sister, and my father was alone at home with me. When he saw the razzia coming, he quickly buried the 'illegal' papers and pamphlets in the garden and tried to flee by climbing over a high fence, right in front of a waiting soldier. Fleeing was punishable by immediate execution, and he was lined up to be shot. At that very moment my mother came back with my sister, who ran up to him calling, 'Daddy what are you doing?' The German commander heard her. He was a veterinarian who had graduated in the Netherlands and was fluent in Dutch. He couldn't execute a man in front of his daughter and beautiful wife. He told my father to quickly join another line around the corner and told my mother to get him a blanket roll and some clothes. Only the lucky survivors have such narratives.

7.8   A Saved Slit-Trench Letter

In the wartime letters of my parents, I found a barely readable, pencil-written letter. It was composed by the dying light of an oil lamp, late in the evening of Saturday, October 21, 1944. It is written in my father's clear teacher's handwriting. He is crouched in a slit trench under steadily approaching Allied artillery fire. The previous days he and his fellow prisoners were forced to dig slit trenches at gunpoint, ever closer to the Allied lines. They saw the light planes of the English artillery-reconnaissance pop up over the top of the river dikes. The letter describes to my mother the first casualty in his forced-labor group. It tells her not to worry too much, that he will take good care of himself. Yet he is frightened for us and tells her that he will accept all the decisions she will have to make for 'the three of you, after this ...' Then he says he has to end, because the lamp has burned out. That letter was never sent. There was no postal service in a remote slit trench under fire on a Saturday night. Judging by its appearance it was carried for a long time in someone's pocket. My mother found it, and she carefully stored it away. Early next morning, my father was hit by shellfire. It shattered his right hand and seriously injured the other hand and his left leg. He was transferred to a German field hospital behind the lines. His condition rapidly deteriorated because of filthy sanitation and poor medical provision.

7.9   Fever and Friends

An Anabaptist preacher warned the family, and, somehow, my grandmother got my father transferred to the Deaconesses Hospital in Utrecht. Gangrene was raging in his right underarm and left leg. Immediate amputation didn't stop the fever. There were no antibiotics available, so his prospects were grim. While high fevers racked his body, the 'underground' network sent a message to Haaye Veldstra, a family friend and pharmacochemist. Via the same network, Haaye sent some of the first sulphonamide antibiotics secretly synthesized in his lab. They stopped the fever and saved my father's life. He had again been lucky, but it took a long time for him to recover. He had lost command over both hands and, for a while, had to be fed using that low white porcelain medical jug that is now resting on my windowsill. Later Haaye Veldstra would become an important role model for me.

7.10   Surviving Starvation

With my father in hospital, two little children to care for, and no income, my mother moved in with her parents and her unmarried sisters in a nearby village. Due to German orders and general disarray caused by the nearby front, the food situation deteriorated rapidly. The 'Dutch Starvation Winter' had started. That period would become a popular research topic on the lifelong consequences of starvation in surviving children and in children conceived during that period. My mother got 'the three of us' through that period with the help of her sisters and by the preserves Grandfather had made the previous summer. Crucial support also came from their social network in the relatively unaffected rural province of Frisia. A farmer they had befriended sent oats and milk powder via the underground channels of the youth organization. That saved us. Sarah Hrdy had it right: 'it takes a village to raise a child' (Hrdy, 2009).

7.11   Traces of Traumas

In that winter I was still a baby, and I slept in a little basket with our identity and ration cards under the mattress, ready to evacuate. Night after night the Allies bombed an important railway junction half a mile away. For a long time after the war, my mother would jump up shouting, 'the child, the child,' whenever a blast or heavy traffic in the street at night alarmed her. Those traumatic images came back in the last few years of her life. One wonders now if she had some kind of PTSD. There must be millions of similar narratives, told and untold, many much worse than ours. Narratives pieced together from records and memories of family members. Persons who, by sheer luck, resourcefulness, and social connections somehow survived. Dead people tell no stories, and even the lucky survivors are often reluctant to share their memories with the next generation.

I was critically undernourished after the war. Surprisingly, my mother's brother, Wim, returned from the extermination camp Dachau in the spring of 1945. He had been to five other notorious camps. He brought along many tins of Ovaltine for his own recovery, obtained from the Swiss Red Cross, and shared them with my mother. It restored my health. Uncle Wim would become another important role model for me.

7.12   Restoring a Ravaged Country

Seventy-five years after the end of the war, it is hard to have an idea of the social conditions in the Netherlands in the 1940s. Canadian troops had finally liberated the northern half of the country. They were warmly received. But the Germans had ransacked the country and laid waste much of the countryside while fleeing. Polders were inundated. There was a lack of fuel, food, clothing, and housing, and the financial system was in shambles. Supported by the American 'Marshall Plan', it took years to recover. Even more important was the demoralization and disorientation of society. The reconstruction of the country would require social cooperation and a restoration of a sense of community and belonging. Efforts to revive the prewar idealistic youth movement failed. Their prewar meeting points, songs, and ceremonies had been thoroughly contaminated and hijacked by Nazi organizations for their own evil purposes. Moreover, there was the 'jazzy' North American culture to compete with now. Educators had to develop alternative ways to mend society.

7.13   Return to Teaching

My father now had an arm and a leg prosthesis, but he left hospital firmly determined to remain a teacher. He borrowed a blackboard from his old school. Day and night he exercised his remaining, severely damaged left hand and learned to write again. His beautiful right-handed, right-leaning schoolmaster's penmanship was gone. He could write block letters now; that would do in primary school. There were immense problems facing teachers in those first postwar years. Books and other educational materials were scarce, classrooms cold and decrepit. Teachers had to cope with a cohort of children who came with their own wartime experiences. Some hadn't been to school for quite some time. Many children had severe social and educational problems. Teachers had to find ways to restore a sense of belonging and safety before they could start with the regular curriculum. My parents spent much time community singing, playacting, drawing, and storytelling – forms adapted from their youth movement's repertoire. Meanwhile the government had seen fit to send 120,000 young men to fight a hopeless colonial war in Indonesia. Hence there were not enough teachers in the postwar years. The arrival of the postwar 'baby boom' generation at school didn't help. Having 65 or more children in a classroom was not unusual. I sat in one of those outsized classes. Married women could not hold government positions, but my mother, though unpaid, started a 'remedial teaching' program at school for the most affected children. She invented her own new hand-made teaching tools.

7.14   A Happy Childhood in Frisia

I was too young to retain conscious recollections of the war and the first postwar years. I do have good early memories of warm postwar holidays on the farm of the Frisian family that had sent us food during the starvation winter. There was plenty of food directly from the farm now. I very much liked the farmer and his wife. I remember watching barn swallows feeding their young in nests in the hay shed where we slept. I played with Frisian children on the farm, learning to express myself a bit in the beautiful Frisian language. But my family remained strictly vegetarian, and good alternatives for meat and fish were very hard to get in those days. I remained a sickly child till I went to high school and better alternatives became available.

7.15   Reconciliation, Not Revenge

My parents' capacity to overcome the impact of my father's handicaps and the other sequels of war on our family is beyond praise. But even the lucky survivors are often reluctant to share their memories with the next generation. I overheard many bewildering snippets of war stories as a child, but nobody ever told me the entire story in a consistent way. I started reading books on 20th-century history at a young age, trying to make sense of what I heard. I still do that today. Surprisingly, neither my uncle Wim nor my father nurtured any systematic hatred against Germans. When asked, they would say that they were sometimes helped by 'good' Germans during their ordeals and that some of the Dutch had behaved very badly indeed during the war. They doubtless understood that distinguishing and excluding groups of people on imagined general characteristics is one of the most vicious roots of the world's problems. Kipling D. William's book on ostracism (Williams, 2002) helped me to understand the psychosocial mechanisms involved: 'Ostracism is aggression and creates aggression'.

7.16   Gift of Honor

My father could become very angry when someone attributed inherently bad characteristics to Germans or any other national or ethnic group in general. While he was traveling in Germany, people would naturally wonder about the cause of his injury. When asked, he could, off the cuff, give a seminar on its real sources. Not the shell that accidentally hit him, not even the unprovoked German attack on the Netherlands, but rather the vicious ostracism and morally degrading attitude and humiliation that the Nazis had first imposed on the German population and then tried to enforce on the rest of the world. Society should guard against any such extremist political or semi-religious takeover of government. After a war-memorial lecture on that topic in the town of Castrop–Rauxel, he received the silver cup that blinks now on my windowsill. That *Ehrengabe*, the gift of honor, meant much to him: understanding, reconciliation, and inclusiveness. My parents would have approved our cooperation and publishing with children and grandchildren of our former 'enemies' together with those of our allies and liberators. Science did not cause their problems, but the rejection of good science did. They expected that research on social conflict would suggest solutions.

7.17   Nurture Rather Than Nature

My parents' dedication to teaching and cultural advancement was only enhanced by their traumatic war experiences. However, they clearly understood the fundamental question society still had to face in the aftermath of the war. Rejecting the concept of racism was not enough. The question was whether the disastrous violence and hatred that had destroyed society was due to an inherent trait, shared by all of humanity, or caused by a failure of civic education in deprived parts of the population. They were not opposed to biological explanations. After all, the family had experienced how people could act 'instinctively' under stressful conditions. But they had also seen how simplistic biological explanations could be misconstrued for malevolent political purposes. Moreover, there was nothing they could do about the genetics of their pupils, so they took the practical option available to them: teaching. They both continued teaching, coaching, and organizing courses until a few weeks before they died.

7.18   Growing up among Teachers

Virtually every topic raised at home would end in a discussion on what education could, or could not, do about it. That preoccupation got even stronger when my father became Headmaster of a school where my mother became a teacher and my sister and I started classes. As children, we overheard too many adult discussions over learning, problematic children, learning models, and even our own teachers' qualities. I decided never to become a teacher. In the evening my father studied educational sciences and finally earned a summa cum laude Masters in Educational Sciences at the University of Utrecht. My mother got a degree in Dutch linguistics. To escape from the relentless pressure at home on study and moral self-improvement, my sister fled into day-dreaming and drawing, for which she had a great talent. I turned to reading history and walking in the nearby woods and meadows. However, the never-ending emphasis on education at home may have been another blessing in disguise. Later at the university, when called upon to teach, it came easily to me.

7.19   Navigating High School

We moved from Utrecht to Rotterdam, and I started high school. I attended classes, did my homework and tests, and passed exams, but I spent most of my free hours bird watching and studying nature. The Montessori system at high school suited me. It allowed me to study largely at my own discretion. One creative teacher had all high school math and calculus mapped in modules on one single sheet of paper. Top, left, and bottom of the sheet represented arithmetic, geometry, or abstract algebraic entries into math. One was free to enter the study material stepwise, module after module, from any of the three sides of the sheet. There was a test for each module, and one had to pass all the modules' tests to graduate. Math became fun instead of a nightmare. It was a formative experience for me to learn that a complex, initially much-too-difficult problem could be mastered stepwise, from different but converging viewpoints. I used the same approach to teach pharmacology or behavioral neuroscience to students in medicine, pharmacy, biology, psychology, or physical therapy. There is a pathological, an anatomical, a chemical, an evolutionary, a behavioral, or a functional approach to almost every subject. Students loved to help each other find their own approach. Much later, the method was officially introduced as 'the flipped classroom', but it was just a combination of teaching methods I picked up at home and at high school. The students appreciated the autonomy it gave them.

7.20   Observations Outdoors

As a teenager and adolescent, I spent most of my free time in a national youth society for the study of nature (NJN). They organized weekend excursions and outdoor study camps during the holidays. Before the war, that same society had inspired the brothers Niko (the ethologist) and Luuk Tinbergen (the ecologist), as well as my uncle Wim, who was an ardent amateur geologist. Niko Tinbergen was our hero, and we amateurishly emulated his approach. We spent days concealed in a shelter, rowing a boat, or lying behind a dike, watching birds feeding on the muddy shallows or in the estuaries of the big rivers. Noticing the 'natural experiments' among these animals, we understood that animals lived in a rather different sensory world than we did. I read the popular books on animal behavior and bird migration written by the Tinbergen brothers. The idea that 'behavioral mechanisms' could be inherited just like organs and be subject to selection pressures in evolution was captivating. Geology was another pastime. Uncle Wim dated the petrified shark's teeth I found in a glauconite layer between rocks to a minor extinction period in the middle of the Eocene. It made me aware of the enormous depth of the geological time scale involved in evolution. That was another formative moment for me.

7.21   A Primer in Psychopharmacology

After his release from Dachau, Uncle Wim had become a leading pharmacochemist in the Organon Company. Shortly before my graduation from high school, in 1962, he gave me a primer in psychopharmacology: 'Menno, the drugs depressed patients accept unfortunately only help after a delay of several weeks. That is strange, for they enter the central nervous system quickly, and their side effects – blurred vision, dry mouth, and intestinal problems – start immediately. It is a huge problem. The side effects increase their depressive mood and they may become suicidal.' He took a little notebook and showed me: 'These drugs are called tricyclics, since they contain three rings side by side. But they also often have a long tail attached to the middle ring. That tail blocks signals to the eye, mouth, and intestines, and causes those disturbing side effects'. He continued: 'We are now developing drugs where the end of the tail is connected to one of the side rings, creating a tetracyclic structure. That should prevent those nasty side effects on the autonomic nervous system'. This short seminar was an eye opener for me. One apparently could help depressed patients with a synthetic organic molecule, but it would have different effects on different mechanisms in the body. By changing a specific part of that molecule, one could affect those mechanisms differentially, and increase its specificity. One of these molecules became the commercially successful antidepressant mianserin.

It had different side effects, but the delay in therapeutic effects in patients unfortunately persisted.

7.22   Tinbergen and Piaget

Compared with those interesting ideas and my outdoor experiences, the initial biology curriculum at the Leiden University was disappointing. It consisted of lectures all morning, even on Saturday, and practical courses all afternoon and sometimes in the evening. Drawing dissections of plants and animals was the main fare. Other courses required the replication of experiments from the start of the 20th century with instruments dating from the same period or before. Most teachers just scribbled the subject matter on the blackboard. Students took notes in silence. Introductions in physiology, anatomy, ethology, and ecology were given in a chaotic series of classes by an intimidating, sexist professor. With a few exceptions, teachers used old textbooks in German, English, or French with hardly any illustrations. By contrast, Alfred Romer's *The Vertebrate Body* – with color illustrations – (Romer & Parsons, 1962) and Niko Tinbergen's *The Study of Instinct* (Tinbergen, 1951) were wonderful reading. Konrad Lorenz's book *On Aggression* (Lorenz, 1966) rekindled my interest in animal and human conflict. My father was studying Jean Piaget's *La Construction du Réel chez l'Enfant* (Piaget, 1971), a perspective far removed from the 'innate' behavioral concepts of ethology at the time. We had some vivid discussions at home. In fact, we discussed the nurture/nature controversy, and aggression always was a hotly contested part of that debate.

7.23   My Saving Grace

The biology curriculum left hardly any time for fraternities. I wasn't interested anyway. To me hazing was just an efficient method of learning to humiliate others by being humiliated oneself. I saw no point in inside-group formation by ostracism and getting drunk together. But the community of biology students at Leiden had quite a few saving graces. They were a small, socializing, open, and tolerant group, without any formal separation between successive years. Many played a musical instrument, painted, acted, or danced. At night, friends would meet in groups, trying to make sense of lectures and courses by comparing notes. On weekends there were field excursions. The students organized symposia with prominent scientists from abroad. There was a yearly spring festival in the 'hortus botanicus' with music and dance for students and staff.

My own wonderful saving grace in biology is still by my side as I type these words, 57 years later. In my mind's eye I can still see her for the first time, confidently walking into the old University Hall during the introduction ceremony. A stunning, long-legged, blond, blue-eyed beauty. She came in between a group of traditionally dressed girls in dark blue jumpers, checkered 'black-watch' tartan skirts, pumps, and fake pearl necklaces. Martje had made her own cheerful, sunny dress. Viewing her took my breath away. Little could I envision that this multitalented, cheerful, good-natured beauty would be interested in me, but we became a couple within a year and married immediately after receiving our Masters degrees. Martje, the daughter of a math teacher, would introduce me to the world of mathematical modeling of biological processes. On June 16, 1981, she defended her PhD *Foraging Activity of Wood Ants*. One hour later, I defended *Origins of Hypothalamic Aggression in the Rat*. A married couple with two young children earning their PhDs on the same day was a novelty in Leiden.

7.24   Rediscovering Old Connections

Long after we first met, we learned that Martje's parents had been active in the very same 'illegal' Frisian food-supply network that saved our family in the 'starvation winter'. Martje always was my best 'sounding board' or 'sparring partner' on whatever came along in science. She still is. I wouldn't have been able to cope with the competition, rivalry, and setbacks of academic life without her constant practical and mental support. After graduation and raising four healthy children, she earned an MBA in accountancy and financial administration at the University of Rotterdam and worked in industry. In the decade before her retirement, she put the university's Lorentz Center on a firm footing. We both retired in the summer of 2009 by organizing the international, multidisciplinary Lorentz Center Workshop: 'Context, Causes and Consequences of Conflict'.

After our disappointing experience with the biology curriculum, we did a major Masters in the well-organized, biochemistry laboratory of Prof. Dr. Haaye Veldstra. I was totally unaware of the role Veldstra had played in the survival of our family. Veldstra, like my future family-in-law, was not talkative about his wartime exploits. We only found out at my graduation ceremony. Working at Veldstra's lab was a revelation. There were modern instrument rooms with spectrophotometers and ultracentrifuges, and training courses to teach us how to work with those facilities. For the first time in my life, I saw real DNA molecules in a test tube. Moreover, we got interesting assignments and had to report orally and in writing on specific subjects in groups of students. Sometimes I would find a little note on my desk, with a recent reference related to my practical work, left there by Veldstra in the evening. On one of the following days he would ask my opinion on it, and he would not be satisfied with an accurate summary. Rather he wanted to know what I would do next, if I were in the position of the author. I learned that good questions in research are often much more important than established answers. Especially questions on accepted wisdom. My major was on the biochemical activity of the MAO-enzyme in mitochondria and nerve endings in the brain. Veldstra encouraged me to synthesize a chemical compound for our research that was not commercially available, and he urged me to take on an exam on reaction mechanisms actually intended for advanced students in organic chemistry.

7.25   Behavioral Brain Mechanisms

To complete our Masters degrees we returned to biology. I did an unsupervised major in plant physiology and another in sensory physiology. I learned to use signal analysis equipment and to specify and build my own simple electronic tools. After a short period of mandatory military training, I was detached as a biomedical officer to our National Health Institute. For 16 months I assisted in finding antibodies in blood samples of military personnel, while looking for a PhD position that would match my interest in the nervous system and behavior. I wasn't going to return to biochemistry. Grinding up brains to study their constituent enzymes had been interesting but also a rather limited way to study a highly structured signal-processing organ, especially if one was interested in behavior. A friend working at the ethology department in Leiden drew my attention to an interesting opening at the Department of Pharmacology at the Medical Faculty.

Conflict between rodents was a popular tool to detect novel psychoactive drugs in those days. But its predictive, face, and construct validity was poor. It produced a confusing number of different, bewildering behavioral effects. It was clear that one would need an additional approach to understand brain control of behavior. Inspired by an influential publication on brain stimulation in domestic fowl (Von Holst & Von Saint Paul, 1963), a talented ethologist, A. M. (Guus) Van der Poel, at the Department of Pharmacology, had obtained a grant to study the behavioral consequences of brain stimulation in the rat. It would become my PhD project. I was rather ambivalent about it at the start. It was as if we would try to evoke structured images from a television set by short circuiting its electronics. But, if it worked, it would be fascinating. It turned out to be a real challenge.

7.26   The 'Aggression Club'

One stroke of good fortune helped to kick-start my PhD work. In 1971, the ethologist Gerard P. Baerends, the primatologist Jan van Hooff, and the physiologist Leen de Ruiter had persuaded our government to provide a special grant for the study of brain-and-behavior relations. A special section was to be used for an interdisciplinary approach on the origins and functions of aggression. An explicit stipulation was that the grant foster close cooperation between different groups at different institutions. Cooperation was still a living tradition in science in our small country, facilitated as it was by an excellent public transport system. The American competitive model of promoting science was still years in the future, and our collaborative work was a far cry from the individualistic loser–winner notion dominant now. The 'Aggression Club' was formed under the gentle but firm guidance of the behavioral neuroscientist Piet R. Wiepkema. I was fast to join up. It would provide a solid background and a wonderful focus for my PhD project. Moreover, it concerned a problem that had intrigued me since my boyhood. For the next 5 years we would convene every 2 months for a full day in the lab of one of the cooperating groups to openly discuss ideas and findings of the participating PhD students and postdocs. Moreover, the grant allowed us to hire and train a technician, Wout Meelis, whose dedicated, many-sided, reliable, and meticulous skills would remain the technical backbone of all our experiments until the Department of Pharmacology was disbanded 40 years later.

7.27   Interdisciplinary Inspiration

'Aggression Club' meetings were inspiring and formative experiences for all participants. Geert A. van Oortmerssen, an ecology-minded behavioral geneticist, informed us on the role of aggression in the population dynamics of rural wild mice. Van Hooff was fascinated by behavior that stabilizes and conserves the social structure after a conflict. Wiepkema inspired us with his work on cybernetic models of feedback between external and internal factors in feeding behavior. Jan G. Veening tried to reconcile such models with modern neuroanatomical findings. Alexander (Lex) R. Cools shared his reservations on the ethological concept of 'fixed action patterns' in the brain. Lex conceived the brain rather as a 'programming mechanism' open to external and developmental influences. Paul J. A. Timmermans shared his extremely detailed observations on domesticated and wild rats. Young scientists like Bob Bermond, Lex Cools, Jan P. C. de Bruin, Jaap M. Koolhaas, Berend Olivier, Jan Veening, Frans de Waal, and I took advantage of the 'Aggression Club's' formative influence and continued to make our mark in behavioral studies. The 'Aggression Club' created a personal network that would evolve into the Ethology Section of our NWO and finally become the Netherlands Society for Behavioral Biology.

7.28   European Training in France

In 1972, the Training Program for Brain and Behaviour Research of The European Economic Community (EEC) announced grants that allowed young investigators to take courses in different European centers. It was another stroke of good fortune. For 3 months I visited labs in Paris, Bordeaux, and finally Strasbourg, patching up my still fragmentary grasp of neurophysiology. In the lab of J. M. Faure in Bordeaux I learned about the many neuroendocrine feedback loops to the brain. Years later I would follow-up Faure's valuable suggestions. Pierre Karli's group in Strasbourg had already completed a detailed study of the brain mechanisms involved in 'mouse killing', the predatory response of the rat on mice. Pierre Karli had just published a wonderful review of these studies: 'Les Conduites Aggressives' (Karli, 1971). It was all in French, but meanwhile my French had improved. For many years I used it as a roadmap for my studies. In hindsight, the similarities in brain function in intraspecific and interspecific aggression are still striking.

7.29   French Technology and Bibliography

In the lab, Pierre Schmitt taught me to implant chronic electrodes in a rat. The technique was used for mouse killing. Later in Leiden I miniaturized it for the more demanding conditions in fighting between rats. Pierre studied the hedonic properties of hypothalamic stimulation by allowing the animals to press a lever to start hypothalamic stimulation and another lever to stop it. He found that the same stimulation could change from rewarding to aversive, depending on its duration. That was an early hint to the temporal qualities of behavioral responses. When I told Karli that I had a grant for 4 years, he was shocked. He told me: 'For a serious bibliography on aggression, before you even could get started, you will need at least 4 years', implying that I should select another topic. It was another formative moment. I was learning about cultural differences in the scientific approach. But he was right; my grant had just a few, mainly conceptual, references. It was long before we were provided with Internet and PubMed. However, I still struggle to keep up with today's rapid advances in the neuroscience of aggression. I spent most of my remaining time in the Strasbourg library, and during long weekend hikes in the Vosges I pondered how to proceed. During one of those hikes I inadvertently came across the German concentration camp 'Natzweiler', where my uncle Wim had once been incarcerated.

7.30   Getting Started

In France I learned a lot, but I returned to Leiden a little confused. It seemed to me that there were at least three independent versions of the hypothalamus: one involved in specific behavioral responses, another in endocrine regulation and feedback, and yet another in punishment and reward. That couldn't be a coincidence in my view, but the relation between these functions was not clear to me at all. There were only a few studies on the relations. Evidently, part of the answer would have to come from neuroanatomy.

In the pharmacology department I did not have access to an electronic or mechanical workshop. However, I brought sufficient surgical experience from the course in France to assemble a working experimental setup suited for fighting rats. Trainees from a nearby college for electronic engineers helped to build the equipment. Jaap M. Koolhaas had already successfully induced hypothalamic aggression *in a territorial setting* (Koolhaas, 1978). Jaap graciously helped to find a good hypothalamic site to evoke attacks *outside a territory in a new environment*.

In Jaap's territorial setting the aggressive pattern gradually emerged over successive stimulation periods. We used a threshold design, increasing the stimulation strength stepwise until we evoked the complete attack pattern immediately. However, in our setup the stimulation strength required to evoke attacks decreased over subsequent sessions on the following days before stabilizing at about 50% of the intensity required to evoke the first attacks. Stimulation strength would then remain the constant for long periods afterward. That would allow us to optimize stimulation parameters and assess drug and endocrine effects (Kruk, 2014).

7.31   Learned or Innate?

Koolhaas and I had agreed to work with the same rat strain, but the gradual emergence of the response in his study, or the decrease in stimulation strength over the first days in our study, presented a problem directly related to a serious debate over the meaning of hypothalamic responses: Are these responses 'learned by association' with a – supposedly arbitrary – object present during the first stimulation? Or, alternatively, do these responses arise by activating an aversive or rewarding system in the brain? After all, provoking fights by applying inescapable foot shocks to pairs of rats in an enclosure was common practice in those days. In a seminal study Bob and Caroline Blanchard (1977) were showing that this so-called food-shock aggression had little to do with territorial fighting. But perhaps their arguments would not apply to hypothalamic attack. The implication would be that the evoked aggression was not due to the activation of a behaviorally specific network in the brain. Some studies suggested that there was no relation between the site of stimulation and the type of behavioral response evoked. Those studies also stated that the type of response could be changed by lengthy stimulations in the presence of another object, by a sort of 'association learning' (Valenstein, Cox, & Kakolewski, 1970). However, I suspected that terms like 'innate' and 'instinctive' or 'learning', 'association', and 'experience' were often used to conceal ignorance of the underlying brain mechanisms involved.

7.32   How to Identify Aggression-Specific Neurons?

We were quite willing to accept a role for learning or experience in aggression. Aggression wouldn't make sense in a social species without some learning or experience. At the same time, we held on to the idea of behaviorally specific networks in the brain. In our view, the resolution of the nature/nurture controversy in aggression would require a series of steps. First, one had to reject the behavioral 'aspecificity' hypothesis of hypothalamic neural networks and get an idea of their location. At the same time, it was necessary to compare the evoked responses with the corresponding 'spontaneous' behavior. Also, one had to make sure that the same site in the hypothalamus did not depend on an 'association' with the only object presented. We had the tools to get to that point. Next, one should identify the specific neurons involved, measure their activity in different social conflict settings, and study 'loss of function' effects, while temporarily incapacitating those neurons in the same settings. Eventually one should study the effects of experience and development on the activity of that network. It was a tall order, since such recordings had to be done within the rapid time frame of an evolving conflict. We hoped that the technology to do so would soon become available. But we never published those criteria. They seemed too obvious. I only listed them in a late review as a measure of our failure to accomplish what we initially had set out to do (Kruk, 2014). In the final identification of neurons in the mouse hypothalamus that are both 'necessary and sufficient' for aggressive behavior, these criteria were used anew (Kennedy et al., 2014).

7.33   Starting Statistical Neuroanatomy

The histology of the positions of a large series of stimulation sites that had evoked attacks, and sites that had not, should, we believed, have falsified the anatomic 'aspecificity' hypothesis. After all, our stimulation techniques and our electrodes were much more precise than those used in previous studies. But the available brain atlases had insufficient resolution in the hypothalamic area we had aimed at. We made our own stereotaxic atlas of the hypothalamus with slides separated by a distance corresponding with the size of the electrode tips and fed that into a computer mainframe still using old-fashioned Hollerith cards as input. Computer-assisted printing of the localization of the behaviorally characterized electrode tips in the atlas suggested that the place of stimulation did matter. That was a real first at the time. However, it remained difficult to generalize over adjacent slides that sometimes seemed to be at odds.

The anatomical 'aspecificity' hypothesis could be tested statistically, using a nonparametric Bayesian method of discriminant analysis, a method that calculates the probability of a certain outcome in any specific position in a multidimensional space. Our case was simple. It involved the three real stereotaxic dimensions in micrometer, in orthogonal dorso-ventral, medio-lateral, and fronto-caudal directions, and a straightforward outcome: attack or no attack. The program calculated the 'posterior probability' on attack for a regular 3-D grid of 'voxels' in the area explored by our electrodes. The site of stimulation really – significantly – did matter very much. Removing the sites that required the strongest stimulation from our sample population improved the discrimination. Removing sites that evoked only mild attacks from our sample improved it even further. Our computerized atlas allowed us to visualize the analysis from several directions. It revealed a continuous area overlapping with the lateral lobe of the hypothalamic ventromedial nucleus (VMHvl) and the adjacent medial and perifornical hypothalamus. Unfortunately, the area didn't coincide with a classic well-known neural population (Kruk et al., 1983).

Meticulous distribution studies using movable, descending electrodes confirmed our findings (Lammers, Kruk, Meelis, & Van der Poel, 1988a). Those studies also revealed that other hypothalamic areas consistently yielded other different responses in an environment where many different objects were present (Lammers, Kruk, Meelis, & Van der Poel, 1988b). So, a specific hypothalamic behavioral response could not be due to a 'simple' forced 'association' with the only single, arbitrary goal object present.

7.34   The Nature of Hypothalamic Attack

Watching hypothalamic attacks, one inevitably gets the impression that the animal's perception of its social environment changes instantly at the onset of stimulation. Social stimuli suddenly seem to acquire an entirely different meaning. Females attack males and males attack females in settings where such behavior is highly unusual, bypassing the normal, more moderate elements of the aggressive repertoire. Even some inanimate objects are attacked. The similarity between such behavior and the misdirected aggression of infuriated persons under social stress is striking. But it is not a simple motor reflex. The behavioral response is highly directed and finely tuned to the constantly changing behavior of the opponent. Older, often overlooked literature on hypothalamic attack in the cat suggests that the sudden switch to an enraged state is supported by immediate, precise changes in sensory information processing – changes that would allow an instantaneous adaptation to the variable behavior of an adversary (see Kruk, 2014). Such changes in sensory information processing deserve further study.

7.35   Similarities in Several Species

Our results confirmed similar findings in the marmoset, the cat, and the opossum (Lipp & Hunsperger, 1978; Yasukochi, 1960). However, the extremely complicated neuroanatomy of that area made it almost impossible to identify the specific neural population involved in a particular hypothalamic response. We coined the term 'the hypothalamic attack area' (or HAA), but that was rather a term indicating our failure to be more precise. Tracing studies by Tom A. P. Roeling (Roeling et al., 1994) confirmed the intricacy of the neuroanatomy of the area. Our anatomical and recording techniques at the time were clearly insufficient to pick up attack-related neural activity in the HAA in a systematic way. However, our mapping studies may have been stepping stones in the final identification of the neurons critically involved in aggression in mice a quarter of a century later (Lin et al., 2011).

7.36   Thresholds as Tools

In the absence of methods to record specific neural activity in the hypothalamus of a fighting rat, we adopted the attack threshold as a way to assess properties of the activated network in attack. The attack threshold is a measure of the excitability of the activated system. It can be used as a tool to quantify drug, endocrine, or lesion effects. An increased threshold reveals that a substance inhibits the 'aggressive network'. A threshold decrease indicates that it is facilitated. We hoped that such experiments would provide cues on the nature of the neurons directly activated at the electrode tip. It didn't work that way, but it yielded interesting information on brain mechanisms involved in aggression (Kruk, 1991, 2014; Kruk et al., 1998).

Drug experiments revealed differences between hypothalamic and territorial aggression. Hypothalamic attack thresholds appeared insensitive to most drugs that do affect territorial fighting. However, so-called serenics – serotonin agonists, putative drugs once in development at the Duphar company to treat extremely aggressive patients in psychiatry – inhibit hypothalamic attack (Kruk, 1991). However, the serotonergic system projects throughout the entire brain. That did not help us to identify the 'aggressive' neurons in the hypothalamus. However, its insensitivity to other drugs suggests that HAA stimulation only activates the most violent subroutine within the aggressive repertoire of the rat, bypassing all the control mechanisms that normally moderate territorial conflict.

7.37   Controversy over Crime

The neuroscience of aggression research was not a popular subject at the university. The Medical Faculty understandably focused on topics with an immediate clinical impact. Aggression was not seen as a medical problem. That state of affairs became worse after a social scientist from the Ministry of Justice was appointed in Leiden to study the biological basis of criminality. Neither the Law Faculty nor the Medical Faculty would have anything to do with it. The situation became a nationwide public row when it was stated on public TV that criminality could be 'predicted' in youngsters from such notoriously unreliable factors as skin conductance and heart rate, and even more when it was suggested that potential offenders be placed under special surveillance. It was a time when the 'social system' was blamed for psychopathology and criminality. National journals and magazines quickly took positions in the controversy, making any reasonable discussion impossible, and the project was abandoned. The social construct 'criminality' was outside our conceptual framework, and we refrained from joining in a shouting match. For a while the neuroscience of aggression was almost taboo. People often associated it with racial theories.

7.38   Rewards of Teaching

The public controversy made it difficult to find support for our work from the university and the national funding organizations. We had to avert several efforts to disband our group and survived by intensifying our international contacts and by focusing on the quality of our teaching. In contrast to the general sentiment, many students were very interested in our research. Teaching proved a wonderful experience. Watching minds grow is a special privilege. Our most difficult bachelor's course, 'Hormones and the Nervous System', which integrated pathology, neuroanatomy, psychopharmacology, behavior, and molecular biology, became quite popular. The appreciation of the students was a real surprise. Students twice nominated me for the prize for the best university teacher. They also awarded me a prize for the best teacher at the Medical Faculty and another one for organizing the best biomedical course. We taught in English, and exchange students from the Karolinska Institute in Stockholm also followed that course. Afterward, many students joined our group for their Masters research projects. Several students from the University of Edinburg also found us via the ERASMUS student exchange scheme. We considered these student members part of 'our team', future colleagues who would help us to succeed. They often could teach us a few things from their own specific backgrounds. Over the years we probably supervised far more than 100 Masters projects. Sadly, we lost track of many students. They left to go in many different directions. Many accepted positions in other fields. Several trained to become medical specialists. One talented student became a professor in experimental surgery. Only a few continued in conflict research.

7.39   Hormones and Hypothalamic Aggression

Repeated testing invariably facilitates hypothalamic attack over the first few days, and attack thresholds decrease. This facilitation of attack was found consistently in males and females (Kruk et al., 1984) and in different strains of rats. Fighting experience apparently facilitated the network activated via the HAA. Interestingly, the facilitation was limited to the environment where it occurred first. In another social environment – e.g., an established territory – thresholds would be up again and would decrease once more upon repeated testing. That seemed to make sense: In nature, animals should know where to fight and where not. But what was the underlying mechanism?

Interestingly, stimulating the HAA produced a rapid and huge increase in circulating ACTH and corticosterone (Kruk et al., 1998). Stress-induced aggression is a well-known phenomenon, though it is generally attributed to the effects of adrenaline. Could it be that corticosteroid feedback to the brain had a similar role? With Jozsef Haller from the Institute of Experimental Medicine in Budapest and his PhD students Eva Mikics and Joe Halasz, we started to test that idea. We found that corticosteroids do indeed rapidly facilitate hypothalamic attack within the timeframe of one single conflict (Kruk et al., 2004). The rapidity of that feedback was a new and original finding. The classic effects of corticosteroids require protein synthesis via the activation of specific sites at the genome. That takes time. But the effects on hypothalamic attack effects were much too fast and probably nongenomic. We wondered whether corticosteroids would also be involved in the initial facilitation of hypothalamic attack to a novel social challenge. Such ideas triggered a fruitful line of research on the mechanisms of adrenocortical responses in aggression.

7.40 Corticosteroids in Challenging Conflicts

A similarly fast, presumably nongenomic mechanism was found in territorial fighting. Interestingly, this fast mechanism triggered a slower, lasting genomic process that does require protein synthesis (Mikics, Kruk, & Haller, 2004). Paradoxically, total suppression of corticosteroid rhythmicity produces violent 'pathological' attacks. (Haller et al., 2004). That condition seems to mimic the 'allostatic crash', that is, a failure to activate the adrenocortical response as a consequence of repeated traumatic experiences in 'pathological' aggression in humans (Haller, 2018).

Blocking a corticosteroid receptor during the very first test on hypothalamic attack permanently abolishes the usual threshold decreases on subsequent testing. Apparently, a rapid corticosteroid feedback to the brain is necessary for a correct perception of the nature of a conflict in a novel environment. That rapid feedback induces a lasting genomic mechanism that facilitates fighting in subsequent conflicts in the same environment, but not in another environment. It is as if corticosteroids are necessary to initialize a pre-existing aggressive network to meet a specific new social challenge (Kruk, Haller, Meelis, & de Kloet, 2013). That 'initializing hypothesis' predicts that the effects of a corticosteroid response should depend on the place, the social environment, and the previous experience of an individual in that environment. Accordingly, neither the rapid nor the lasting effects of corticosteroids occur in an established colony, i.e., in the absence of a novel social challenge (Mikics, Barsy, & Haller, 2007). Eva now studies the effects of early social deprivation on adult aggression (Miskolczi, Halász, & Mikics, 2019; Tóth, Halász, Mikics, Barsy, & Haller, 2008).

7.41   Stress and Aggression in Humans

Inspired by these ideas, my enthusiastic teaching assistant Maaike M. Kempes did a thesis on the cortisol responses to a social challenge in children with disruptive behavioral disorders (Kempes, De Vries, Matthys, Van Engeland, & Van Hooff, 2008). Currently Maaike manages research in forensic psychiatry. Ewald Naumann at the department of psychobiology at the University of Trier encouraged PhD students Robina Bönke and Katja Bertsch to test some of our ideas in healthy human volunteers. They provoked aggression or exposed volunteers to angry faces and gave them cortisol. They measured their natural cortisol levels, recorded event-related potentials of the brain, and assessed their assertiveness in different combinations. The results supported the idea that adrenocortical feedback to the brain in humans indeed facilitates aggressive behavior by affecting the immediate processing of social signals during a challenge in a gender-dependent way (Bertsch et al., 2009, 2011; Böhnke et al., 2010). Katja continued in Sabine Herpertz's group at the University of Heidelberg, Germany, on the effects of oxytocin on the processing of facial expressions in traumatized borderline females (Bertsch & Herpertz, 2018). Katja was recently appointed Professor in Clinical Psychology at LMU Munich.

7.42   International Interdisciplinary Interest

Gradually the trickle of studies in 'aggressive' brain mechanisms became a stream as more disciplines and professions became interested. That offered opportunities to listen to widely different viewpoints and a chance to try to get a general overview. In 2017 Dr. Kumi Kuroda invited me to give a public lecture on 'Neural Circuits in Aggression' at the Life Science Building 'Bunka Kaika' in Tokyo for an audience of psychiatrists and neuroscientists, and a seminar at the Behavioral Science Institute at Wako on the interaction between corticosteroids and aggression. Dr. Kuroda is an expert on domestic violence and infanticide in humans, as well as a specialist on similar phenomena in rodents and primates

(Esposito et al., 2013). It is heartening to see that students of human social conflict increasingly find ways to test their ideas on the brain mechanisms in animal studies. It is equally satisfying to watch students of animal conflict taking on the challenge of validating their ideas in human social conflict and pathology.

7.43   Facts to Fight Fake

Informing public opinion with established scientific facts on aggression has become more urgent than ever these days. Therefore, an invitation to participate in a series of interdisciplinary meetings by the program officer Karen Colvard of the HFG was a pleasant surprise. The idea was to produce a proposal for a series of books on social conflict that should be comprehensible to the general public. Its board constituted a small group of specialists active in various disciplines: anthropology, biology, sociology, psychology, psychiatry, history, theology, and political science. During a series of long weekends over several years, first principles of disciplines were extensively discussed. These discussions generated many fundamental questions and produced interesting book proposals. One question put by a political scientist to us biologists still sticks in my mind: 'Are you guys really believing in evolution?' It sounded as if 'evolution' – or rather 'survival by natural selection' – is a religion rather than an explanatory theoretical framework that has been tested many times over. We took time to discuss and explain, but the incident clearly revealed the crucial importance of exchange and discussion even between specialists in social conflict. Yet, at interdisciplinary meetings on social conflict, participants tend to go to their own specialist sessions only.

7.44   Convening over Conflict's Causes

At the Lorentz Center, Martje noticed that interdisciplinary meetings between prominent chemists, physicists, astronomers, and mathematicians had been a tradition in the natural sciences in Leiden since the days when Albert Einstein spent his summer sabbaticals as a visiting professor at the Institute of Physics in the 1920s. When our retirement drew nearer, and after organizing more than 400 meetings in 10 years, Martje asked me to organize an interdisciplinary Lorentz Center Workshop on Conflict in 2009. Forty-eight students of social conflict from anthropology, biology, sociology, psychology, educational sciences, psychiatry, genetics, forensic science, and criminology attended. In the course of 1 week a valuable interdisciplinary discussion developed. We recorded and annotated all the discussions for a book, reasoning that the content would anyhow appear in scientific journals. A version of *Discussions on Context Causes and Consequences of Conflict* is available as an e-book (Kruk & Kruk-de Bruin, 2010). Meanwhile, science has moved on, but it may still be interesting to see how the basic themes have changed since then.

7.45   An Exciting Email Exchange

Retirement is mandatory at the age of 65 at Dutch universities. Getting support for research becomes a problem when that date approaches, while administrative and teaching duties increase tremendously. But I took time for an interesting email exchange with a young scientist in California who was trying to induce hypothalamic aggression in mice using electrical stimulation. I had never met Dayu Lin in person. But we had obviously failed to identify the hypothalamic 'aggressive' neurons, and we had reached the end of our technical possibilities in the rat. I suspected that the genetic options available in mice should probably offer new inroads into that question. I made an effort to explain the background of our published experiments, and, probably more valuable, we exchanged results of unpublished pilots on the many unsuccessful deadends we went into. Dayu kept coming up with clever questions, showing an extraordinarily clear scientific mind. However, after a while, to my regret, Dayu mailed that they had finally given up on the project.

7.46   New Tools

Directly after retirement I was invited to speak at the workshop 'Can New Tools Revolutionize Understanding of Hypothalamic Neural Circuits?' in Washington. That was surprising, because my 'tools' had been old-fashioned endocrinology and outdated computer programs. But I was curious and attended, and I met Dayu Lin for the first time. She had not abandoned the project at all but had changed to a much more promising technology. While she enthusiastically showed me her poster, she impressed me with the tremendous potential of optogenetics. A year later I was invited to speak at a meeting on the 'Neurobiology of Aggression and the Social Brain' in Palo Alto, California, convened by Eric Kandel. David Anderson, Dayu's supervisor, showed how this revolutionary optogenetic technology was now rapidly resolving the question that had been on my mind for so long: 'What cells do evoke these hypothalamic attacks?'

7.47   Nurture and Nature in Aggression

It took about 30 years after our first mapping study for David Anderson, Dayu Lin, Annegret Falkner, and Niroa Shah to finally identify a population of estrogen and progesterone receptor-expressing neurons in the lateral lobe of the ventromedial nucleus of the hypothalamus (Anderson, 2016; Falkner, Dollar, Perona, Anderson, & Lin, 2014; Lin et al., 2011; Yang et al., 2013) that are both 'necessary and sufficient' for aggressive behavior in mice (Kennedy et al., 2014). It took optogenetic technology, molecular biology, and advanced signal analysis to get at that point. In my view it is now beyond any doubt that a behaviorally specific network controlling aggression in the brain does exist. The properties of that network can be depicted in a format that would have pleased Niko Tinbergen (Anderson, 2016; Kennedy et al., 2014). Interestingly, that network is controlled by the social environment, the available sensory information, and the history of the contestants (Yang et al., 2017). Moreover, the network is anatomically and functionally modified by social and sexual experience in a gender-dependent way (Hashikawa, Hashikawa, Lischinsky, & Lin, 2018; Remedios et al., 2017). Starting from these VMHvl neurons, several groups are now unraveling the 'aggressive' network and exploring its relations with other responses, such as sexual and grooming behavior, and its role in defensive behavior (Diaz & Lin, 2020; Hong, Kim, & Anderson, 2014). In light of these new findings, the nurture/nature controversy on brain mechanisms in aggression seems to evaporate.

7.48   In Retrospect: Both Sides Now

Looking back over half a century in science, and after causing so much animal suffering, what did we accomplish? We may have contributed to solving a longstanding question, a question that intrigued many scientists before us, as well as my parents and me: aggression and the brain – nurture or nature? It seems to me that both sides have valid points. However, a deeper question remains: Have our findings contributed to making the world a safer place? I am not sure. Or, as Karen Colvard mailed me a couple of months ago: 'We may not have done such a good job at that'.

At my windowsill the flowery milk jug still radiates its hopeful and deceptive innocence. It only needs a little dusting now and then. However, the blinking, silver gift of honor next to it tends to turn black rapidly. It has to be polished every few weeks.

References

Anderson, D. J. (2016). Circuit modules linking internal states and social behaviour in flies and mice. *Nature Reviews Neuroscience, 17*(11), 692–704.

Beevor, A. (2018). *Arnhem: The battle for the bridges, 1944.* London, England: Random House.

Bertsch, K., Böhnke, R., Kruk, M. R., & Naumann, E. (2009). Influence of aggression on information processing in the emotional Stroop task – An event-related potential study. *Frontiers in Behavioral Neuroscience, 3*, 28.

Bertsch, K., Böhnke, R., Kruk, M. R., Richter, S., & Naumann, E. (2011). Exogenous cortisol facilitates responses to social threat under high provocation. *Hormones and Behavior, 59*(4), 428–434.

Bertsch, K., & Herpertz, S. C. (2018). Oxytocin and borderline personality disorder. In R. Hurleman & V. Grinevich (Eds.), *Behavioral pharmacology of neuropeptides: Oxytocin* (pp. 499–514). Stuttgart, Germany: Springer.

Blanchard, R. J., Blanchard, D. C., & Takahashi, L. K. (1977). Reflexive fighting in the albino rat: Aggressive or defensive behavior? *Aggressive Behavior, 3*(2), 145–155.

Böhnke, R., Bertsch, K., Kruk, M. R., Richter, S., & Naumann, E. (2010). Exogenous cortisol enhances aggressive behavior in females, but not in males. *Psychoneuroendocrinology, 35*(7), 1034–1044.

Bressers, W. M. A., Kruk, M. R., Van Erp, A. M. M., Willekens-Bramer, D. C., Haccou, P., & Meelis, E. (1995). Time structure of self-grooming in the rat: Self-facilitation and effects of hypothalamic stimulation and neuropeptides. *Behavioral Neuroscience, 109*(5), 955–964.

Diaz, V., & Lin, D. (2020). Neural circuits for coping with social defeat. *Current Opinion in Neurobiology, 60*, 99–107.

Esposito, G., Yoshida, S., Ohnishi, R., Tsuneoka, Y., del Carmen Rostagno, M., Yokota, S., ... Shimizu, M. (2013). Infant calming responses during maternal carrying in humans and mice. *Current Biology, 23*(9), 739–745.

Falkner, A. L., Dollar, P., Perona, P., Anderson, D. J., & Lin, D. (2014). Decoding ventromedial hypothalamic neural activity during male mouse aggression. *Journal of Neuroscience, 34*(17), 5971–5984.

Haccou, P., Kruk, M. R., Meelis, E., Van Bavel, E. T., Wouterse, K. M., & Meelis, W. (1988). Markov models for social interactions: Analysis of electrical stimulation in the hypothalamic aggression area of rats. *Animal Behaviour, 36*(4), 1145–1163.

Haller, J. (2018). The role of the lateral hypothalamus in violent intraspecific aggression – The glucocorticoid deficit hypothesis. *Frontiers in Systems Neuroscience, 12*, e26.

Haller, J., Halasz, J., Mikics, E., & Kruk, M. R. (2004). Chronic glucocorticoid deficiency-induced abnormal aggression, autonomic hypoarousal, and social deficit in rats. *Journal of Neuroendocrinology, 16*(6), 550–557.

Hashikawa, K., Hashikawa, Y., Lischinsky, J., & Lin, D. (2018). The neural mechanisms of sexually dimorphic aggressive behaviors. *Trends in Genetics, 34*(10), 755–776.

Hong, W., Kim, D.-W., & Anderson, D. J. (2014). Antagonistic control of social versus repetitive self-grooming behaviors by separable amygdala neuronal subsets. *Cell, 158*(6), 1348–1361.

Hrdy, S. B. (2009). *Mothers and others. The evolutionary origins of mutual understanding.* Cambridge, MA: Harvard University Press.

Karli, P. (1971). Les conduites agressives. *La recherche, 18,* 1013–1021.

Kempes, M., De Vries, H., Matthys, W., Van Engeland, H., & Van Hooff, J. (2008). Differences in cortisol response affect the distinction of observed reactive and proactive aggression in children with aggressive behaviour disorders. *Journal of Neural Transmission, 115*(1), 139–147.

Kennedy, A., Asahina, K., Hoopfer, E., Inagaki, H., Jung, Y., Lee, H., ... Anderson, D. J. (2014). Internal states and behavioral decision-making: Toward an integration of emotion and cognition. *Cold Spring Harbor Symposia on Quantitative Biology, 79,* 199–210.

Koolhaas, J. M. (1978). Hypothalamically induced intraspecific aggressive behaviour in the rat. *Experimental Brain Research, 32*(3), 365–375.

Kruk, M. R. (1991). Ethology and pharmacology of hypothalamic aggression in the rat. *Neuroscience & Biobehavioral Reviews, 15*(4), 527–538.

Kruk, M. R. (2014). Hypothalamic attack: A wonderful artifact or a useful perspective on escalation and pathology in aggression? A viewpoint. *Neuroscience of Aggression,* 143–188.

Kruk, M. R., Halasz, J., Meelis, W., & Haller, J. (2004). Fast positive feedback between the adrenocortical stress response and a brain mechanism involved in aggressive behavior. *Behavioral Neuroscience, 118*(5), 1062–1070.

Kruk, M. R., Haller, J., Meelis, W., & de Kloet, E. R. (2013). Mineralocorticoid receptor blockade during a rat's first violent encounter inhibits its subsequent propensity for violence. *Behavioral Neuroscience, 127*(4), 505–514.

Kruk, M. R., & Kruk-de Bruin, M. (2010). *Discussions on context, causes and consequences of conflict.* Leiden, the Netherlands: The Lorentz Center, Leiden University.

Kruk, M. R., Van Der Laan, C. E., Mos, J., Van der Poel, A. M., Meelis, W., & Olivier, B. (1984). Comparison of aggressive behaviour induced by electrical stimulation in the hypothalamus of male and female rats. *Progress in Brain Research, 61,* 303–314.

Kruk, M. R., Van der Poel, A. M., Meelis, W., Hermans, J., Mostert, P. G., Mos, J., & Lohman, A. H. M. (1983). Discriminant analysis of the localization of aggression-inducing electrode placements in the hypothalamus of male rats. *Brain Research, 260*(1), 61–79.

Kruk, M. R., Westphal, K. G. C., Van Erp, A. M. M., van Asperen, J., Cave, B. J., Slater, E., ... Haller, J. (1998). The hypothalamus: Cross-roads of endocrine and behavioural regulation in grooming and aggression. *Neuroscience & Biobehavioral Reviews, 23*(2), 163–177.

Lammers, J. H. C. M., Kruk, M. R., Meelis, W., & Van der Poel, A. M. (1988a). Hypothalamic substrates for brain stimulation-induced attack, teeth-chattering and social grooming in the rat. *Brain Research, 449*(1–2), 311–327.

Lammers, J. H. C. M., Kruk, M. R., Meelis, W., & Van der Poel, A. M. (1988b). Hypothalamic substrates for brain stimulation-induced patterns of locomotion and escape jumps in the rat. *Brain Research, 449*(1–2), 294–310.

Lin, D., Boyle, M. P., Dollar, P., Lee, H., Lein, E. S., Perona, P., & Anderson, D. J. (2011). Functional identification of an aggression locus in the mouse hypothalamus. *Nature, 470*(7333), 221–226.

Lipp, H. P., & Hunsperger, R. W. (1978). Threat, attack and flight elicited by electrical stimulation of the ventromedial hypothalamus of the marmoset monkey Callithrix jacchus. *Brain, Behavior and Evolution, 15*, 260–293.

Lorenz, K. (1966). *On aggression.* New York, NY: Harcourt, Brace, and World.

Mikics, É., Barsy, B., & Haller, J. (2007). The effect of glucocorticoids on aggressiveness in established colonies of rats. *Psychoneuroendocrinology, 32*(2), 160–170.

Mikics, É., Kruk, M. R., & Haller, J. (2004). Genomic and non-genomic effects of glucocorticoids on aggressive behavior in male rats. *Psychoneuroendocrinology, 29*(5), 618–635.

Miskolczi, C., Halász, J., & Mikics, É. (2019). Changes in neuroplasticity following early-life social adversities: The possible role of brain-derived neuro-trophic factor. *Pediatric Research, 85*(2), 225–233.

Piaget, J. (1971). *La construction du réel chez l'enfant.* Paris, France: Delachaux & Niestle.

Remedios, R., Kennedy, A., Zelikowsky, M., Grewe, B. F., Schnitzer, M. J., & Anderson, D. J. (2017). Social behaviour shapes hypothalamic neural ensemble representations of conspecific sex. *Nature, 550*(7676), 388–392.

Roeling, T. A. P., Veening, J. G., Kruk, M. R., Peters, J. P. W., Vermelis, M. E. J., & Nieuwenhuys, R. (1994). Efferent connections of the hypothalamic 'aggression area' in the rat. *Neuroscience, 59*(4), 1001–1024.

Romer, A. S., & Parsons, T. S. (1962). *The vertebrate body.* Philadelphia, PA: Saunders.

Tinbergen, N. (1951). *The study of instinct.* New York, NY: Oxford University Press.

Tóth, M., Halász, J., Mikics, É., Barsy, B., & Haller, J. (2008). Early social deprivation induces disturbed social communication and violent aggression in adulthood. *Behavioral Neuroscience, 122*(4), 849–854.

Valenstein, E. S., Cox, V. C., & Kakolewski, J. W. (1970). Reexamination of the role of the hypothalamus in motivation. *Psychological Review, 77*, 16–31.

Van Erp, A. M. M., Kruk, M. R., Semple, D. M., & Verbeet, D. W. P. (1993). Initiation of self-grooming in resting rats by local PVH infusion of oxytocin but not α-MSH. *Brain Research, 607*(1–2), 108–112.

Von Holst, E., & Von Saint Paul, U. (1963). On the functional organization of drives. *Animal Behaviour, 11*, 1–20.

Williams, K. D. (2002). *Ostracism: The power of silence.* New York, NY: Guilford Press.

Yang, C. F., Chiang, M. C., Gray, D. C., Prabhakaran, M., Alvarado, M., Juntti, S. A., … Shah, N. M. (2013). Sexually dimorphic neurons in the ventromedial hypothalamus govern mating in both sexes and aggression in males. *Cell, 153*(4), 896–909.

Yang, T., Yang, C. F., Chizari, M. D., Maheswaranathan, N., Burke Jr, K. J., Borius, M., ... Ganguli, S. (2017). Social control of hypothalamus-mediated male aggression. *Neuron, 95*(4), 955–970.

Yasukochi, G. (1960). Emotional responses elicited by electrical stimulation of the hypothalamus in cat. *Psychiatry and Clinical Neurosciences, 14*(3), 260–267.

8　From Unruly Child to Political Protester and Promoter of an Ecology-Minded Concept of Development

Rainer K. Silbereisen

Rainer K. Silbereisen was born August 24, 1944, in Freudenstadt, Germany. Until his retirement in 2017, he was Research Professor of Psychology at the Friedrich-Schiller-University of Jena and Director of the Center for Applied Developmental Science (CADS), Germany. He was President of the International Society for the Study of Behavioural Development (ISSBD) and a member of the Board of Governors of the University of Haifa (Israel). Rainer Silbereisen's research was honored when he was elected to the European Academy of Sciences (Academia Europaea, London, England) and the Akademie gemeinnütziger Wissenschaften, Erfurt (Germany).

His research program focused on complex ecology-biology-person interactions. These are often initiated by the individual, with the more-or-less clear aim of resolving age-typical developmental tasks. In his research program, ecology was hypothesized to be a major developmental force. Maladjusted behaviors, such as antisocial behavior during adolescence, were investigated in order to discover their putative constructive role in the development of entrepreneurial behavior during adulthood (e.g., Obschonka, Andersson, Silbereisen, & Sverke, 2013).

Longitudinal studies were conducted on a wide range of topics, such as substance use and delinquency during adolescence, variation in the timing of psychosocial transitions, the impact of social change on adjustment and development, psychological dimensions of entrepreneurship and civic participation, biobehavioral aspects of adolescent development, and acculturation among immigrants. Many of these studies were designed in an explicit cross-national and cross-cultural format. The prevention of maladjustment and scientific advice for policy makers were important dimensions of Rainer Silbereisen's research program.

Studying the effects of globalization and German unification on adjustment in adulthood provided opportunities to investigate how individuals cope with new challenges to their developmental tasks as the result of gross changes in ecological opportunity structures. The major insight gained from these studies was that most youths actively engaged with the challenges, especially if guided by high self-efficacy and internal control. This process led to positive effects on self-esteem and economic success (Körner, Lechner, Pavlova, & Silbereisen, 2015).

Results from the longitudinal studies also showed that, depending on risk factors in the larger societal context, even disengagement may be positive because it provides relief from self-attribution of failures (Tomasik, Silbereisen, Lechner, & Wasilewski, 2013). Comparisons with countries characterized by less generous support systems than those offered in Germany showed that the role of individual agency was less pronounced in Germany. Silbereisen and colleagues found that younger cohorts were more optimistic than older cohorts concerning the challenges of social change (Lechner, Tomasik, & Silbereisen, 2016). In general, individuals higher in the personality attribute of exploration were better equipped to reap the benefits of current social change, but these effects were bounded by the differences in social ecology (Lechner, Obschonka, & Silbereisen, 2017).

The conceptual framework for development-as-action-in-context was used in shedding new light on the effects of migration on adjustment, comparing various diaspora groups and stages of the acculturation process. Concerning delinquency, it became clear that particular risk and protective factors were relevant especially for adolescents at the beginning of acculturation. During the adolescence of migrants, change due to acculturation and age-related change were intertwined (Michel, Titzmann, & Silbereisen, 2012; Titzmann & Silbereisen, 2012). This research with a special comparative longitudinal design compared immigrant and native adolescents' expectations concerning the timing of conventional socially acceptable and oppositional less socially acceptable forms of autonomy. Results revealed that acculturative change was only identified for oppositional forms of autonomy expectations, whereas conventional socially acceptable forms of autonomy changed primarily due to normative ageing. Various trajectories of delinquency and their antecedents in adolescence were identified (Wiesner & Silbereisen, 2003). These results have consequences for group-specific corrective and preventive interventions (Silbereisen, Titzmann, & Shavit, 2014; Titzmann, Raabe, & Silbereisen, 2008; Titzmann & Silbereisen, 2012; Wiesner & Silbereisen, 2003).

Rainer Silbereisen's research was funded by numerous national and international foundations, such as the German National Science Foundation (DFG), the W. T. Grant Foundation, and the Jacobs Foundation, as well as many state and federal governmental funding agencies, and large private companies. He was a member of a research consortium (SFB 580, funded by DFG) on social and political transformations in Germany, and he chaired a research network on acculturation of immigrants funded by the German Federal Ministry of Education and Research, with research sites in Germany and Israel.

His strong commitment to the dissemination of developmental science research to international policy organizations and, in particular, his devotion to the promotion of young scientists around the globe can be seen in the following activities: He was involved in providing research grants to young scholars in Third World and Eastern European countries; he was Co-Director of the Interdisciplinary Graduate School on Human Behaviour in Social and Economic Change (GSBC); he was involved in the International Postdoctoral Fellowship Programme for the Comparative Study of Productive Youth Development (PATHWAYS) and was actively engaged in various mentoring programs for young women scientists. With grants from various foundations (e.g., German Academic Exchange Service, or DAAD) and from international science organizations (e.g., International Council for Science, or ICSU), he established a series of capacity-building programs on psychological research and application for young scientists and professionals, targeting economically challenged countries in Eastern Europe, Central Asia, and the Asia-Pacific region, with a special emphasis on human-made and natural disasters.

He was Editor of the *International Journal of Psychology* as well as the *International Journal of Behavioral Development*. He was Co-Editor of *Developmental Psychopathology* and *European Psychologist*, and Associate Editor of *American Psychologist*. For many years he was Co-Chair of the Review Board for Psychology of the German National Science Foundation.

He served as President of the ISSBD and the International Union of Psychological Science (IUPsyS), the German Psychological Society (DGPs), and the Federation of German Psychological Associations.

For sustained outstanding contribution to the science of psychology, he was elected Fellow of the Association for Psychological Science (APS), the American Psychological Association (APA), and the International Society for the Study of Behavioral Development. He received the Franz-Emanuel-Weinert Award of the DGPs, the Distinguished Scientific Award for the Applications of Behavioral Development Theory and Research of ISSBD, the Lifetime Award of the European Association for Research on Adolescence (EARA), and the Mentoring Award of the DGPs Developmental Division.

8.1 An Upbringing during a Transition from Catastrophe to Prosperity

When I started working on this chapter, we had moved a few weeks earlier to Potsdam, a famous city in former East Germany. It was the conclusion of a circle of movements from Berlin (West), where I spent my early career as Faculty at the Technical University (psychology there was part of British postwar re-education efforts), to Giessen, also in Germany, with a focus on adolescent development, to Pennsylvania State University (PSU) in the United States, with its lifespan orientation, and then back to Germany to the Friedrich-Schiller-University in Jena. The 20 years at Jena represented the climax of my career as a researcher, teacher, and administrator in social and behavioral sciences, from the time of German unification in 1990 to the present day, 30 years later. And now Potsdam, close to Berlin – the irony is that I had an offer from that city and university in the early 1990s, but I turned it down for the University of Jena, with its 450-year history, and, more than a century ago, its reputation as the birthplace of developmental psychology, conceived with a biological and evolutionary understanding. Born in Potsdam, Ernst Haeckel – called 'the German Darwin' – promoted this way of thinking, while British-born psychologist William Thierry Preyer began the empirical study of human development with his *Die Seele des Kindes* [*The Mind of the Child*] (1882).

My decision to go to Jena had a deeply rooted reason – I wanted to live and work in the hotspot of a changing society that was giving people new life prospects. I expected to find opportunities for studying the influence of the changing ecology on the changing individual (and vice versa). This was my mantra from the early Berlin times on, but actually this position has a much longer history. Alexander von Humboldt (1799), the famous explorer and naturalist, wrote, 'My eyes should always be on the harmony of the interaction of the influence of inanimate creation on the living animal and plant world' (pp. 399–401; my translation).

The remainder of this chapter is organized as follows. I will follow my major personal and professional development and describe important topics. The common denominator of my work is focused on a few fundamental aspects of behavior and development, especially developmental tasks and self-esteem, which I investigated under conditions of varying proximal and distal ecologies. The latter are rooted in challenges from transitions between historical periods or transitions between countries. A special emphasis is given to cross-national comparisons as a means of exploring whether the results can be generalized. I draw in part on an earlier chapter (Silbereisen, 2014).

The chapter deals here and there with delinquency of young people, and if and when such delinquency sheds light on more general processes of development in times of social change. I have to confess, however, that this is not my major topic, although I believe, encouraged by the editor, that what I will report has implications for the development and prevention of violent behavior.

I was born in August 1944, with the end of the Second World War in sight, but also at the height of war efforts and related atrocities. My mother lived in the center of Stuttgart with other women in a makeshift shelter in an apartment building sitting at the rim of an elevation over-looking the city center, which was hit by no less than 10 bombing raids, the worst in July, exactly where her apartment was. She and the other women were all shattered by the expectation that 'the bomb' would send the building and its inhabitants down the hill in shambles (the adjacent building was indeed totally destroyed). To give birth, she was evacuated to Freudenstadt in the Black Forest (80 km to the west), a town that was soon also attacked. Finally, she was sent to Neuenbürg in the vicinity of Pforzheim, where in early 1945 a third of the civilian population was killed by the worst bombing raid in Germany. She also experienced occupation by French colonial troops, who had severe disciplinary problems. I am fully aware that all this ultimately was a consequence of German actions and atrocities, but I wanted to tell this story because it may help to explain why I was such a nervous, unruly child (with an often fearful mother), especially in contrast to my brother, who was born in the early 1950s. The newest research on the transgenerational effects of mothers' early life stress on the development of their children, via the switch-off of genes through methylation, might explain what happened during the pregnancy. According to the best-researched case of such effects, the Dutch Famine in 1944–1945 during World War II, the lack of nutrients resulted in epigenetic changes affecting various pathways of the biological stress response system (Tobi et al., 2014; Veenendaal et al., 2013). I should add, though, that hunger was not the problem in my mother's case. The food supply in Germany during the war was good because it was taken from occupied countries like the Netherlands. If there was a prenatal epigenetic effect in my case, it would be from the tremendous psychosocial stress she suffered. At any rate, I was often a disappointment for my parents. Once they consulted a psychiatrist, but his response after a few checks of my reflexes was, 'Good woman, your son is in puberty'.

My father was an engineer and inventor of dual-use technologies during and after the war. Consequently, all occupying forces in Germany were interested in hiring him. To avoid conflict, they decided to let his family and him stay in Germany. The beginning of the Cold War was another argument to maintain friendly relations with German scientists/engineers, especially if they had made a career within big industries. To his dismay, I studied psychology, a field he only accepted as a science when I got a PhD in 1975 from the Technical University in Berlin. He, the engineer, was fully convinced of my success only when I called him in the early 1980s from a psychology conference in Beijing, China, a hotspot of technology transfer by German industries.

My time as a student was another unruly period – I was engaged in left-leaning political activities, not so much as a result of a father–son conflict, as was often the case in my cohort, but due to feelings of 'existential guilt' (as it was called by Martin Hoffman [1976]). The atrocities of the Vietnam War demonstrated to us that we, in the Western world, fared so well while so many others in Asia suffered so badly. All this had consequences for my career. For years, I was blacklisted and was turned down when applying for a professor position in Germany.

When thinking back on those years, I am really thankful to my parents and university teachers who ultimately saw the potential in the protester. I indeed worked hard to develop a philosophy of life that combined broad social responsibility with high individual motivation and achievement. I also learned a lot of soft skills through my activities – how to calm a crowd, how to make a convincing argument, how to lead a group to success.

8.2   First Steps as a Researcher in Berlin during the Cold War

My first scientific undertaking was research on social cognition. Few in Germany had studied this topic at that time. Silbereisen, Heinrich, and Trosiener (1975) found that children's perspective taking was positively associated with an authoritative parental style, but more importantly the profession of the parents was crucial. Those in businesses that required direct interaction with customers were better in perspective taking, and this also seemed to have an influence on their children. The study did not have an important impact, but I gained a postdoctoral position (unusual at that time in Germany) at the Center of Cultural Psychology at the University of Saarbrücken (1975).

However, I preferred to jump on an opportunity that opened up back in Berlin. The city was shaken by a drug epidemic, from experimental party drugs to heroin, with dramatic effects on health (the death rate was high and climbing) and public safety. Nobody was prepared to deal with that, but, as a newly appointed professor of the Technical University (1977), I faced the expectation that we would investigate causes and possible remedies. Substance use among adolescents at that time was seen as antisocial behavior, with almost no reference to development. In contrast, I brought in the tentative notion that drug use and abuse had a biographical history of risk factors and lesser problems, and that in principle its precursors were related to failures in resolving age-typical developmental tasks. Field interviews with young addicts in subway stations and similar hideouts indeed revealed that some experiences had derailed them from normative development, and that, beyond this addiction, their early life looked quite orderly (Projektgruppe Tudrop, 1984). Concepts like protective factors and developmental psychopathology were not yet known in the late 1970s, but I was convinced that only comparative studies of normative and deviant behavior (and often it was both in sequence over adolescence) would shed light on many pathways of development in adolescence. The latter foreshadowed my interest in identifying latent groups in the still-to-come Moffitt (1993) tradition of delinquent trajectories.

With the help of the German Research Council and excellent international scientists I had come into contact with (among others Richard Jessor, Denise Kandel, Eric Labouvie, Urie Bronfenbrenner, Glen Elder), we began the Berlin Youth Longitudinal Study (BYLS) in the 1980s. It was an endeavor carried out by many young researchers in my group, who later became professors (e.g., Peter Noack and Sabine Walper). It was crucial to show that 'problem behaviors' (Jessor's term) play a role in adolescent development but not necessarily always a negative one. We even published a paper with the title 'On the Constructive Role of Substance Use' (Silbereisen & Noack, 1988). Certainly, this was not meant to give drug abuse a whitewash. Rather, we wanted to convey the idea that learning how to use culture-typical psychoactive substances in a responsible way is part of growing up in our Western societies. Abstinence has its own problems, and forming peer groups or initiating romantic friendships often involves opportunities for alcohol consumption and use of other substances.

Within the BYLS we conducted field observations in real-life contexts of young people, like shopping malls, discotheques, or public swimming pools. The main activities of the adolescents were characterized by three elements: watching others, evaluating their behavior by chatting with friends, and trying to mimic what they had seen. Behaving against the rules (usually set by adults) was apparently not so much an indication of under-socialized deviancy as it was a demonstration of one's persona and assets, often targeting the other gender. This is not a unique German behavior, nor is it new – research in the 1930s in the first department store in the country (Leipzig) found that youngsters used the products on display as props to rehearse new roles as adolescents, like shopping and showcasing one's grown-up habits (Muchow & Muchow, 1935). This early work combined development and ecology in the best sense, but, due to ostracism by the Nazis, it took the study half a century to become known and relevant.

Utilizing our longitudinal data, we could further demonstrate that adolescents' behavior in public obviously follows a plan to make new contacts. Once they established a friendship, the same young people retired from the public to the private (Silbereisen, Noack, & von Eye, 1992). Without our knowledge, this research on the developmental potential of contexts was deemed, by Urie Bronfenbrenner and others, as a perfect instance of ecological thinking about human development. We eventually had a conference and published a book on *Development as Action in Context: Problem Behavior and Normal Youth Development* (Silbereisen, Eyferth, & Rudinger, 1986). From then on, I saw this as my identity as a scientist.

I was convinced that ecologies play a crucial role and that they differ within and across societies, but I had not yet followed the obvious conclusion in earnest. We needed comparative data to find out whether what I deemed an important insight could be generalized. I had the good luck to cooperate with Janusz Reykowski of the Polish Academy of Science and his colleague Adam Fraczek to replicate the BYLS in Warsaw. All this happened way before the opening of Eastern European borders and was quite remarkable given the sensitive topic of illicit substance use. The results were a lesson for me. Basically, young Poles did not differ much in their behavior from age-mates in Berlin, except that they reported a later onset and showed lower levels of familiarity with substance use (Silbereisen & Smolenska, 1991). From an ethnocentric view, what appeared as delayed development was a cultural difference, probably based on factors such as religiosity and traditional family values. The role of substance use in growing up, however, did not differ from the Berlin sample.

These results sensitized me to the benefits of comparative research, and we had another opportunity to use this methodology. When the unemployment rate in Germany increased, we worked in the Elder (1974) tradition on the role of economic hardship on adjustment problems of parents and adolescent children, via adjustments of the household economy. The Berlin data showed the same associations as the U.S. data did. However, in Warsaw, the household adjustment had no effect on parents' negative affect (Silbereisen, Walper, & Albrecht, 1990). We interpreted this as due to traditionally close family networks that helped people to overcome hard times. In addition, as data from the East showed, the attribution of the hardship to government failure was relevant (Forkel, Silbereisen, & Wiesner, 2001).

Of course, we had much more information gathered in the BYLS, including data on delinquency. I must admit, however, that I was not much interested in delinquency or tougher deviancy as such, only as far as it enabled us to think about the constraints of adolescent development. Substance use (including hard drug abuse) was the important topic at that time, and because of this pressing problem I had, as a scientist, been brought back to Berlin. Further, substance use showed all the characteristics a lifespan developmentalist was interested in, especially the strong cohort effects and the involvement of ecologies. But let me add a personal remark and a piece of relevant research.

First, delinquency and worse was not beyond my personal experience. I was once arrested and accused of disturbing public order and security (like so many of my generation I had peacefully protested against the Vietnam War, albeit reportedly on the property of the America House) but was later pardoned (this was not good – I should have fought for my innocence). Later. I was denunciated by dear neighbors as a member of terrorist groups, with consequent searches of my home and university office. As a postdoc I had more than one residence; I was male and young, and traveled a lot – all this was enough for the dragnet controls during the 'German Autumn' terrorist attacks at the end of the 1970s (https://en.wikipedia.org/wiki/German_Autumn). I learned a lot about how innocent people can be caught by the law in politically charged times.

Second, in my understanding of human development over time, bad things can turn into good things (and vice versa), except that people often do not have the patience and the prospective longitudinal data needed to investigate this. We had the good luck of getting access to a longitudinal study covering almost 40 years from adolescence to middle adulthood that targeted entrepreneurship. This behavior was of great interest to me because Germany had a surprisingly low share of entrepreneurs, and the mass unemployment in the East (hitting all industries at all levels of qualification) after unification in 1990 (9.7 million employed people were reduced to 6.2 million in 1993; Kowalczuk, 2019) should have been an incentive for entrepreneurship. These data were from Sweden and enabled us (Obschonka et al., 2013) to investigate whether early antisocial rule breaking is indeed prevalent among those who become entrepreneurs, as many anecdotes and police mug shots of famous Silicon Valley entrepreneurs show. After controlling for socio-economic background and intellectual competence, early rule breaking corresponded positively to a subsequent entrepreneurial career, whereas registered crime was rather irrelevant in this regard.

If, with Schumpeter (Cantner, Goethner, & Silbereisen, 2017), one defines an entrepreneur as someone who destroys existing routines and customs, for instance in technology, and comes up with new ideas, this relationship makes sense (our data applied to men, not women). These results probably do not apply in all circumstances and cultures – it requires market and other opportunities for exercising self-efficacy, but unruly times of social change are notorious for that. Research in the former USSR showed, for instance, that such personal dispositions, if combined with free-trade traditions in pre-Soviet times, resulted in much better adjustments to the new circumstances than was prevalent in other former Soviet regions (Titma & Tuma, 2008).

8.3   New Horizons in Giessen Promoted by the Fall of the Berlin Wall and the Unification of Germany

At the University of Giessen, I again had a new group of talented graduate students (among them Bärbel Kracke, Beate Schwarz, and Eva Schmitt-Rodermund, who all hold professor positions now). We had started working on a new wave of a nationwide representative study on adolescence and youth, sponsored by an international company (Shell), when, in 1989, the Berlin Wall suddenly came down. Under the most complicated conditions imaginable, we re-designed the planned study such that it included the newly accessible East Germany, basically with the aim of a systematic comparison of life circumstances and development, thereby renewing my belief in the importance of comparative perspectives. Actually, it was one of those multitopic studies that covered a bit of almost everything, but I was successful in establishing a larger segment addressing various developmental tasks. This enabled us to compare timing and sequence of the tasks in young people's lives. The rationale behind this topic was straightforward. The design enabled us to compare two societies differing in political, economic, and belief systems (socialist versus market economy) that nevertheless shared a long history while they underwent a major transition.

Developmental tasks should reflect such changes – not all, because some are rooted in and shaped by biological processes (like the timing of puberty), whereas others are more or less strongly influenced by societal institutions, such as the timing of first occupational interests, leaving home, and first financial independence, which are triggered by the school and education system, or the housing market. In other words, complex political and cultural factors play a role beyond individual aspirations. Resolving such developmental tasks consequently may have differed due to the ecological differences between the two regions soon after the fall of the Berlin Wall. The timing of occupational interests in the East was heavily influenced by the guiding role of the state, including teachers, who influenced the range of training and job opportunities, whereas, in the West, relevant decisions were more within the realm of parents and offspring. Likewise, housing was in short supply in the East and was regulated by state-provided entitlements, such as the political relevance of one's occupation or family formation, with the side effect that people married and had children at a younger age compared to the West.

Indeed, the timing in East and West differed in the expected direction in regard to institutional tasks. The timing of puberty, however, did not. These results were obviously grist for the mill of our ecology-minded understanding of development, but a crucial question remained, namely, that of stability or change over the evolving political processes of unification. It is important to note that most of the institutional differences waned more or less rapidly after 1990 – the Western school system was taken over by the East, many businesses were privatized and entire industries became obsolete, unemployment in the East reached unprecedented heights, and, of course, individual freedoms (particularly to travel abroad) increased dramatically.

We had the good luck that funds provided by the German Research Council enabled us to repeat the Shell study of 1991 in 1996, 5 years into the unification experience, with a like-designed but independent sample. Thereby dramatic social change could be tapped by a period comparison, assuming that its effect was basically ubiquitous.

A very interesting pattern of results turned up. The earlier differences between East and West began to disappear, dependent on the degree to which social institutions providing the 'social clocks' had changed in the course of unification. The timing of first vocational interests is a case in point. In 1996, first vocational interests in the East were as late as they had been in the West in 1991 and as late as they were in the West in 1996 (there was no change in the West, as none of the relevant institutions had changed), but they were obviously much later than they had been in 1991, when the education system was basically unchanged since the fall of the Wall. Our evidence did not only come from the period comparison as such. As Reitzle and Silbereisen (2000) reported, a much higher share of the young in the East was able to attend college-bound tracks after unification. The habits of parents and youngsters also changed – a pondering of alternatives and longer decision making became a virtue. The essence of a number of other studies with our data clearly demonstrated that the timing of transitions like leaving home was affected in this way (Haase, Silbereisen, & Reitzle, 2008; Juang & Silbereisen, 2001). That contextual disruptions in the political and economic realm observed over a period of just 5 years became the driver of changes in human behavior and development was certainly in part due to the comprehensiveness of the institutional transformations people experienced. For instance, at no time after unification were the destruction of traditional heavy industries in the East and the subsequent reduction of the labor force as severe and widespread as in the mid-1990s (Heimpold, 2010).

Our studies on the effects of the turbulent times soon after unification targeted, of course, other effects than those on developmental timetables, among them delinquency and its antecedents. By and large we did not expect any gross differences between East and West, at least during the last decade of the East German state. This was certainly a gut feeling based on the knowledge that being young was heavily influenced by U.S. Pop culture in both parts of the country. For example, in July 1988, a crowd of 300,000 people attended a Bruce Springsteen concert in East Berlin. The official Free German Youth organization of the East facilitated this to regain contact (and control) over its young generation. A few months earlier the Synth-Rock band Depeche Mode had given a concert. My personal contact with the state-run Youth Institute in Leipzig had informed me that in big cities the young represented a hidden opposition that was disregarded by the politicians, to their disadvantage one should say.

At any rate, when Wiesner and Silbereisen (1998) analyzed data on a 1-year repeated sample of 10- to 13-year-olds from both parts of the country in 1993–1994, our expectation was confirmed. Delinquency items (Lösel, 1975) concerning offence against property, social waywardness, and aggression showed no differences between East and West, with the exception of school truancy, which was lower among former East Germans. This result was once more an instance of the influence of social institutions. In the West, truancy was deemed a developmental problem of students. In the East, however, any disciplinary problem was attributed traditionally to a failure by the teachers. School was seen, beyond the gaining of knowledge, as education for virtues like orderliness, honesty, and punctuality. All that in the West was in the realm of the family. We have no data after the 1990s, but my guess is that such differences will have remained for quite a while (most teachers at that time had been trained following GDR guidelines). Further, we know from timetables related to early behavioral independence (household chores taken over by the kids) that the old standards waned only gradually.

In conclusion, the timing of social development seemed to be especially sensitive to comprehensive changes in the conditions of growing up after German unification. Another instance of such influences was manifested by migration from the former USSR to Germany in the 1980s and the following years, mostly by ethnic Germans who had lived for many generations in Russia and Kazakhstan (their ancestors had moved to Russia as early as the times of emperor Katharina the Great in the 18th century). The opening of the borders for East Germans and across Eastern Europe also brought a large wave of those so-called Aussiedler. For me this group was interesting because they had actually changed country when moving to Germany (which they deemed home in spite of large cultural differences with the majority of German in terms of collectivism), whereas the former East German citizens had not moved (although many had fled to the West anyway), but their entire political, legal, and economic system had changed.

Schmitt-Rodermund and Silbereisen (2009) analyzed developmental timetables of ethnic Germans concerning adolescents' autonomy as reported by the adolescents (aged 10–16 years) and by their parents. Autonomy was assessed as the age at which adolescents were expected to have accomplished tasks like deciding when to come and go without parents' prior permission, having a steady boyfriend or girlfriend, or drinking alcohol other than in the company of parents. Autonomy reflects value orientations – in collectivist settings family connectedness is emphasized, and thus individual autonomy is granted later than in individualistic settings. Data were gathered longitudinally with four assessments at 6-month intervals. We know from our earlier research that on average native adolescents (and their parents) show earlier timing than is common among the migrants studied. Given the strong collectivist value orientation of Aussiedler families, however, we expected no change among the parents over the time observed in Germany. This was indeed the case, especially for families with low conflicts concerning age-typical problem themes (e.g., children's company during leisure). But what about the mutual influence of adolescents and parents on the timetables? Structural equation modeling, conducted separately for families low and high in conflict, revealed that parents with many family conflicts adapted their timetables toward earlier ages, probably as result of adolescents' renegotiation of autonomy expectations. Parents' adaptation of timetables to earlier ages probably brought about relief from ongoing conflicts, perhaps instilled by contacts in school and native peers during leisure.

8.4   Challenges for an Ecology-Minded Developmental Science in Jena

After two years (1992–1994) as Full Professor at PSU I was offered the chance to return to Germany (former East Germany's Jena University) to help in postunification. To make good things even better we had for years an exchange program with PSU, supported by DAAD. This move brought me into a position of not only observing social change and its consequences for human behavior and development but of also taking an active part in shaping the renewal of science and education institutions. My international experiences were very helpful, and I could also count on good friends at PSU like Fred Vondracek, who always had excellent advice.

Bureaucratic examples highlight the overall situation in Germany and the United States at that time. When I was hired as Full Professor at Jena (1994) I had to sign a legal document confirming that I was firmly standing on the ground of the Constitution. This meant that I was a supporter of the democratic order. When I was hired in the United States, all I was asked by the university authorities was which languages I spoke other than English. Things may have changed since then.

To mark the new beginning, I first brought a group of Jena students for a visit to U.S. universities and foundations (including the National Science Foundation [NSF], with its then Deputy Director Anne Petersen, my former Dean at PSU). We organized a big interdisciplinary workshop on unification-related research in Jena, and soon after that I had to take over positions as Department Head, College Dean, and then Senator of the Jena University. It all helped to attract public attention and garner funds for the real scientific endeavors. Against this backdrop, and with a competing job offer by the Jacobs University in Bremen, I was able to found the Center for Applied Developmental Science (CADS) that concentrated on two interdisciplinary investigations. I will turn to both, but I will first provide a glimpse of the conceptual background guiding the research.

8.4.1 Jena Model of Social Change and Human Development

Our earlier research had focused on developmental tasks, basically in the Havighurst (1953) tradition, which indicated that change in the societal situation had an imprint. We also found that inherent experiences were crucial, such as changes in the structure of the educational system. Nonetheless, this was a bit rough, and we still lacked a coherent theoretical rationale that would connect change on the aggregate level with individual change. A new Collaborative Research Center (SFB 580) at Jena funded by the German Research Council on 'Social Development and Post-Socialist Societies – Discontinuity, Tradition, Structural Formation' asked me to join. The mainly sociological framework was a challenge-response model of social change as conceived by Toynbee (1947). Examples of such challenges in former East Germany were the discrepancy between the declared humanistic values of the society and the dire reality of restricted personal freedom. The collective response to that, especially once the grip of the authorities began to crumble in the late 1980s (Laurin, Kay, & Fitzsimons, 2012), varied from open protest to arrangements between old elites and emerging new powers, but, at any rate, it did not happen in any predetermined direction. Rather, it depended on circumstances, a main topic of this research area. From our psychological perspective, the idea was to formulate a structurally equivalent model that would pick up on societal challenges but specify their reflection within an individual's life and especially address how people cope with them, thereby addressing sources and direction of possible individual responses.

Our 'Jena Model of Social Change and Human Development' was our answer to the pending problem of how to connect macro and micro levels (Oishi & Graham, 2010). What follows is the basic structure of the model. The core variable is the 'demands', that is, the experience of recent (often negative and repeated) changes over the past 5 years at the individual level, in domains such as work and family. Given the historic period studied, the demands we were interested in can be traced back to structural changes in the political, legal, and economic system in Germany at the macro level. They were likely to interrupt or disturb the successful resolving of age-typical developmental tasks related to work and family (Silbereisen, Pinquart, & Tomasik, 2010). An example involves the demands entailing growing perceived uncertainties in one's job or concerning one's future planning. As the unemployment rate increased quite dramatically in the early 2000s in both parts of the country (www.indexmundi.com/g/g.aspx?c=gm&v=74), such perceptions have an objective background, but, above and beyond that, they reflect an individual's life circumstances. We controlled for the effects of job promotions and also avoided age-related topics.

The cumulative load of such demands, assessed separately for the two domains, represents the subjective manifestation of societal challenges. According to the Jena Model, they are filtered by a set of conditions, such as geographical region (not all were affected alike and some more than others, especially in the East, due to de-industrialization) or biographical circumstances (single mothers in the East were more than others negatively affected due to job risks and the loss of affordable childcare by a meanwhile defunct former employer who had provided that for free).

8.4.2   *Dealing with Demands of Social Change*

I formed a new group of talented graduate students and already seasoned researchers from East and West of the country (Martin Pinquart, Martin

Tomasik, Martin Obschonka, Peter Titzmann, and Claudia Haase all became professors). Results of our work utilizing large representative samples showed that the load of such demands was indeed higher in the East than in the West of Germany. Supports implicit in stable employment or intact family corresponded also to lower loads (Tomasik & Silbereisen, 2009, 2012; Tomasik, Silbereisen, & Heckhausen, 2010). Understandably, the demand load is not only a reflection of the most recent events under the pressure of social change. It also shows effects of past socialization experiences during adolescence, like (negative) precocious behavioral autonomy (Haase, Tomasik, & Silbereisen, 2008) and (positive) higher competence (Blumenthal, Silbereisen, Pastorelli, & Castellani, 2015).

While the filtering effects influence the level of demands, coping with the demands addresses the process of adaptation. Referring to the concept of developmental self-regulation (Heckhausen, Wrosch, & Schulz, 2010), we distinguished actively engaging and thus attempting to resolve the uncertainties, and disengaging by discounting any harm at all or abandoning an affected developmental task (Tomasik, Silbereisen, & Pinquart, 2010). Most of our analyses were conducted with psychological well-being as a criterion because of its indication of a person's overall quality of life, and thus a negative association with demands was observed. Engagement was preferred over disengagement, engagement had positive effects on well-being, and well-being was highest when control beliefs and coping strategies were matched (Gruemer, Silbereisen, & Heckhausen, 2013). As other evidence for the ecology-minded view on development, the relationship between demands and well-being was moderated by features of the wider context, such as the unemployment rate. If this rate was high (denoting to the individual that their own fate was actually a collective experience), the relationship between (high) demands and well-being even became slightly positive rather than negative on average (Pinquart, Silbereisen, & Körner, 2010). Beyond well-being we also found similar effects of coping with demands on career outcomes like finding a job over the next year among adults (Körner et al., 2015).

Naturally, our approach required checks on applicability to other social and economic contexts. Again we had an opportunity to replicate our findings in Poland. Commonalities were prominent, for example, for the equal level of demand loads, or the distribution of engagement and disengagement when dealing with the demands. Moreover, a group characterized by few negative and many positive demands (e.g., increasing job-related learning tasks) – one may call these winners of social change – was most frequent among people privileged in terms of psychological and social resources, whereas the opposite pattern characterized the least privileged groups (Obschonka, Silbereisen, & Wasilewski, 2012).

Given the differences between the two countries in their welfare model, we expected and found a few differences in how people dealt with the demands. In the Polish sample, the appraisals of demands as challenge or threat did not moderate the response, in contrast to the German sample. We deemed this a consequence of the much lower public support for people in need in Poland. That the demands were about equal in valuation between Poland and Germany, however, should not be misread as a universal feature. A difference in dealing with uncertainties was also found when we compared young people still in education and training between closely matched German and Polish samples. Whereas engagement was alike, disengagement was higher among the young Poles, probably indicating fewer perceived options to withstand the demands (Lechner et al., 2016). In collaborative research with a Chinese research group, we found that uncertainties related to social change were more positively valued than in Germany, especially in big cities (Chen, Bian, Xin, Wang, & Silbereisen, 2010).

Our comparative approach across ecologies was also used in taking a closer look at the role of individual differences in retrieving opportunities sitting in contexts. In most of our research the ecology was indexed by simple measures, such as the time period characterizing challenges of social change. But we also developed a line of research in which the environment was more specifically assessed. A case in point is work by Lechner, Obschonka, and Silbereisen (2017). Here we were interested in the benefits of social change (an often overlooked aspect of changes following unification and globalization more generally). We gathered perceived increase over the last 5 years in lifestyle options (as a manifestation of individualization) and new learning opportunities (reflecting the trend toward lifelong learning). As an indication of differences in resources relevant for the process of coping with demands we assessed the personality attribute exploration. As expected, people in Germany and Poland higher in exploration reported greater perceived lifestyle options and learning opportunities. This effect was moderated, however, by the regional characteristics where people lived. Regions with a higher divorce rate (a proxy for opportunities for individualization on the aggregate level) and regions with higher Internet domain registration rates (a proxy for lifelong learning) revealed a stronger association between exploration and the two aspects of individual benefits. In our interpretation, people higher in the exploration trait are better equipped to reap the benefits of social change offered by the ecology. The role of such individual difference variables is another feature of the Jena Model.

8.4.3   Development and/or Acculturation

Beyond the comprehensive change of basically all major social institutions following unification and its influence on most people's behavior and development in East and West, there was another large group who, at about the same historic time, was confronted with radical change in their lives due to migration. As already mentioned, the largest segment consisted of ethnic German migrants, mostly from Russia and Kazakhstan. It is not well known that Germany is an immigration country – as of 2018, every fourth person living in Germany has a 'migration background', that is, the person or at least one of the parents was not born as German citizens (www.destatis.de/DE/Presse/ Pressemitteilungen/2018/08/PD18_282_12511.html). These and other immigrant groups to Germany moved not least because they saw the country as representing a good adjustment to the new global challenges. In contrast to East Germans after unification, the experience of migration to a different country always includes the necessity of acculturation, that is, a process of change (cultural, social, and psychological) that stems from the interaction and balancing of two cultures. An interesting case in point is adolescents who have to undergo normative age-related development in various issues of life, while they acculturate to the expectations of the receiving society, often referring to the same issues. Gaining a full understanding of the processes means that normative development needs to be differentiated from overlying effects of acculturation pressures.

Using longitudinal data of a newly formed interdisciplinary research consortium I chaired, we compared ethnic German immigrants with other immigrants in Germany and natives, with Jewish Diaspora immigrants to Israel and veteran Israelis. Again we used a comparative approach. The main result was that the lion's share of changes among adolescents can be attributed to normative development rather than to acculturation, but the pace of integration is moderated by the national context (Titzmann, Silbereisen, & Mesch, 2012). Interestingly enough, acculturation among ethnic Germans to the prevailing culture appeared to be smoother than acculturation among Diaspora immigrants to Israel. We attributed this to the formation of ethnic enclaves and economic activities separate from the mainstream in Israel, again representing an ecology-driven process of development.

In an independent study, we again turned to developmental timetables and asked whether ecological transitions, such as from home to kindergarten, had an effect on psychosocial growth, especially among those immigrants who, compared to natives, were disadvantaged due to language problems. The results indeed showed positive effects, but the difference between the groups did not disappear (Silbereisen, Titzmann, Michel, Sagi-Schwartz, & Lavee, 2012). We did not attribute this lack of diminishing differences to deficiencies in the educational program but rather thought that, depending on the cultural niche, different levels of psychosocial functioning may be adaptive. An overview of this interdisciplinary work is provided by Silbereisen et al. (2014).

Our research on immigration and acculturation led me once more to the field of delinquency. According to public perception in Germany, delinquency is higher among immigrants. Our analyses with various datasets revealed differences in adolescent delinquency, although by far not so dramatic as anecdotal evidence suggests. More importantly, however, the predictors of delinquency (e.g., delinquent beliefs and friends, cliques, parental violence, and language problems) are about the same for various groups of immigrants, and explain away differences between the groups (Schmitt-Rodermund & Silbereisen, 2008). At a closer look, however, the predictors seem to vary as a function of the stage in the acculturation process. 'Newcomers' are especially sensitive to parental violence and involvement with delinquent peers (typically of the same ethnicity). This result should have consequences for intervention (Titzmann et al., 2008). In general, I may add, the prediction of delinquency follows general theories of delinquency more than any acculturation specificity. The latter conditions are nevertheless relevant, like acculturation-related hassles or (lacking) school bonding (Titzmann, Silbereisen, & Mesch, 2014).

Inspired by Moffit (1993) we were interested in distinguishing trajectories of delinquency in adolescence, and thereby looked for potential differences between East and West. The sample was 10–13 years at the first of four annual waves, beginning in 1993, representing East and West, and comprising about 700 adolescents at the first wave. Using latent growth mixture modeling (Muthén & Muthén, 2000) with the overall index of annual frequencies of delinquency (Lösel, 1975) as target variable, Wiesner & Silbereisen (2003) could classify high- (14%), medium- (13%), and low-level (20%) offenders and rare offenders (53%). Except for the low-level offenders, who showed a linear growth curve, the other trajectories were best represented by a cubic growth curve. For instance, the high-level group started with the highest level of all, then showed a peak at the second assessment, and finally decreased toward the initial level. Concerning the political region, no differences were found in either of the trajectories. Following our usual interpretation of East–West differences in social behavior as mainly due to the role of social institutions, this would mean that the assessed delinquent behaviors (covering offense against property, social waywardness, and aggression) were not affected overall, at least not in early adolescence. It may also be that entering adolescence after unification (as was the case for this sample) may have washed out differences that existed at earlier times. A single item on school truancy showed a significant difference (lower in the East) (Wiesner & Silbereisen, 1998).

The Wiesner and Silbereisen (2003) study also dealt with the prediction of trajectory membership by a number of well-known risk factors for delinquency: academic self-efficacy, academic achievement, parental empathy, parental monitoring (all low), and high peer tolerance for deviance. Following a suggestion by Labouvie, Pandina, and Johnson (1991), we distinguished between the initial status of these variables at the beginning of adolescence (T1) and the average level across the study period (T4–T1). For instance, higher peer tolerance throughout the 4 years may be a more salient characteristic of the high-level offenders than being high at the entry of adolescence. Using multinomial logistic regression, the rare offenders as reference were compared with each of the other groups. Concerning initial levels of predictors, low parental empathy was related to membership in the medium-level trajectory, and low parental monitoring was associated with the high-level group. Concerning the time-averaged predictors, low parental empathy distinguished all groups from the reference, high peer tolerance of deviance predicted medium- and high-level offenders, low academic achievement predicted low-level offenders, and low parental monitoring was associated with high-level offending. Overall, the four delinquency groups were distinguished better by time-averaged than initial covariates. In other words, higher risks throughout the study period were more salient characteristics than risk at the beginning of early adolescence. This was most consistent for high peer tolerance and low parental empathy. As the example of low parental empathy shows, however, some early risk factors were relevant, although only for one of the trajectories (medium-level offenders), but with time gained in relevance for the distinction of all trajectories.

The existence of different trajectories of problem behavior has consequences for intervention because programs may need to be tailored to the type of growth curve adolescents are on. The concept and evaluation of a universal school-based life-skills program (IPSY) was reported by Weichold and Silbereisen (2014). The aim was to delay and to reduce the regular use and misuse of alcohol in early adolescence. It combined the training of life-skills (like self-awareness, strategies to cope with stress, assertiveness, and communication skills) with substance-specific skills (for instance, how to resist use of substances offered by peers) and knowledge concerning substances (like prevalence rates, psychoactive effects, advertising strategies). The intervention uses role plays and group discussions and is implemented by trained teachers. Due to its nature as a primary prevention program, IPSY starts with Grade 5, before experimentation with alcohol begins at about age 12, followed by booster sessions in Grades 6 and 7.

Spaeth, Weichold, Silbereisen, and Wiesner (2010) reported results of a quasi-experimental prospective intervention/control design with IPSY, covering four assessment waves and a total sample of about 1,500 students. Alcohol use was indexed as the sum of ethanol in grams consumed on a typical drinking occasion, gathered for beer, wine, hard liquor, and mixed drinks. To accommodate the large number of participants who were not drinking at a given time, we used two-part latent growth mixture models, thereby separately analyzing growth curves for use versus non-use and quantity of use. After including several controls (e.g., temperament, social problems, self-worth, and design), two trajectories each were found for prevalence and frequency of use (with very good classification quality): normative use (80% of the sample) and problematic use (20%). The normative use trajectories showed a moderate increase in the likelihood to use alcohol and a flat increase in quantity used. The control group had a stronger linear increase compared to intervention, meaning that IPSY was indeed successful in buffering the increase of alcohol use. The problematic trajectories showed a sharp increase in prevalence and quantity, but there was no difference between intervention and control groups. Based on these results, the question is which elements of IPSY need to be changed for problematic users. It may be that the interactive teaching approach and liberal class climate may be inadequate for a group that has already experienced alcohol and probably shares such typical risk factors as peer use.

The research conducted within the CADS addressed various other topics of great relevance for policies and politics in Germany and beyond, often informed by our conceptual approach. Other examples are innovation and entrepreneurship, a rather underdeveloped part of the German economy (Obschonka, Silbereisen, & Schmitt-Rodermund, 2010); the reflection of societal challenges in aging (Pavlova & Silbereisen, 2016); and civic engagement (Pavlova & Silbereisen, 2017). Beyond the ecological influence we were especially interested in heterogeneity due to personality and other individual differences.

8.5   A Long Way in Support of Science and Application

I mentioned, at the start of this chapter, that many young scholars worked with me, mainly on their own topics and with advantage for their careers. My role often was that of a director and mentor, pulling various strings together for a common product we could be proud of. Through the last 40 years in research, I was involved in activities that helped young scholars around the globe, especially those from less affluent countries, to learn and promote themselves. I did this mainly within the framework of graduate and postgraduate programs, and with the support of science foundations and philanthropies, such as the VolkswagenStiftung, the Jacobs Foundation, the W. T. Grant Foundation, the German Research Council, and the International Union of Psychological Science. That I was the chair of various programs and the president of IUPsyS helped a lot. During my time in such offices I took care to keep my involvement in research, and often collaborated on fronts and topics I could not have expected. A case in point is research on entrepreneurship in China (Zhou, Zhou, Zhang, Obschonka, & Silbereisen, 2019) and a series of workshops on psychological response to disasters, as well as workshops with young developmental scientists (www.youtube.com/watch?v=IFps6mcmb4A&t=631s&index=1&list=PLE3Kq0ws8SD2YaM7K16bG3bBzFozYMVj0) from Africa. I never forgot to tell my mother while she was still around. I am quite sure she liked what I was doing (and the fact that I told her).

My wife, Eva Schmitt-Rodermund, joined me in many of my research endeavors, and my son Julian, during his adolescence, always reminded me that research on adolescence and life as an adolescent can differ quite a lot. When I detected a tattoo on his elbow joint, he disarmed my fatherly disagreement by saying that the tattoo was his birth date in Roman numerals and that it showed that he loves me – wow!

In hindsight, I have investigated quite a range of issues that were not always well connected in others' eyes, I am afraid. One might think that a more focused approach could have had more impact. But it gave me so much pleasure and satisfaction. For instance, the Jena Model of Social Change and Human Development thus far has been used only for the prediction of positive outcomes, like well-being and life satisfaction. We had data on negative outcomes, like alcohol abuse and illness, but it was not in the center of our interest (or I did not find a young scholar who was interested in this topic). As this chapter makes clear, delinquency only played a minor role, although I am sure that the ecology-minded approach could bring new insights in times of social change.

The common denominator of my work has not been a particular theory or a specific scientific topic. From the beginning it was an interest in finding answers to societal problems, with the best methodology (often longitudinal designs, cross-national and cross-cultural comparisons, multi-level modeling, randomized control trials) and adequate mini-theories (the role of coping with demands, for instance). Stressing the role of ecologies increased the relevance of our research for policymakers – after all it is easier to develop policies that change inappropriate social institutions at the aggregate level than to intervene directly at the individual level.

References

Blumenthal, A., Silbereisen, R. K., Pastorelli, C., & Castellani, V. (2015). Academic and social adjustment during adolescence as precursors of work-related uncertainties in early adulthood. *Swiss Journal of Psychology, 74,* 159–168.

Cantner, U., Goethner, M., & Silbereisen, R. K. (2017). Schumpeter's entrepreneur – A rare case. *Journal of Evolutionary Economics, 27*(1), 187–214.

Chen, X., Bian, Y., Xin, T., Wang, L., & Silbereisen, R. K. (2010). Perceived social change and childrearing attitudes in China. *European Psychologist, 15,* 260–270.

Elder, G. H. (1974). *Children of the Great Depression: Social change in life experience.* Chicago, IL: University of Chicago Press.

Forkel, I., Silbereisen, R. K., & Wiesner, M. (2001). Elterliche ökonomische Belastungen und depressive Verstimmung bei Jugendlichen aus den alten und neuen Bundesländern [Parental economic burden and depressive mood among adolescents from the new and old Federal States]. *Zeitschrift für Entwicklungspsychologie und Pädagogische Psychologie, 33*(4), 221–229.

Gruemer, S., Silbereisen, R. K., & Heckhausen, J. (2013). Subjective well-being in times of social change: Congruence of control strategies and perceived control. *International Journal of Psychology, 48*(6), 1246–1259.

Haase, C. M., Silbereisen, R. K., & Reitzle, M. (2008). Adolescents' transitions to behavioral autonomy after German unification. *Journal of Adolescence, 31*(3), 337–353.

Haase, C. M., Tomasik, M. J., & Silbereisen, R. K. (2008). Premature behavioral autonomy: Correlates in late adolescence and young adulthood. *European Psychologist, 13*(4), 255–266.

Havighurst, R. J. (1953). *Human development and education.* New York, NY: Longmans & Green.

Heckhausen, J., Wrosch, C., & Schulz, R. (2010). A motivational theory of life-span development. *Psychological Review, 117*(1), 32–60.

Heimpold, G. (2010). Zwischen Deindustrialisierung und Reindustrialisierung. Die ostdeutsche Industrie–ein Stabilitätsfaktor regionaler Wirtschaftsentwicklung [Between de-industrialization and re-industrialization – a factor of stability in regional economic development]? *Informationen zur Raumentwicklung, 10*(11), 727–732.

Hoffman, M. L. (1976). Empathy, role taking, guilt, and development of altruistic motives. In T. Lickona (Ed.), *Moral development and behavior: Theory, research, and social issues.* New York, NY: Holt, Rinehart, & Winston.

Juang, L. P., & Silbereisen, R. K. (2001). Leaving the parental home for young adults in former East and West Germany: Predictors and consequences in the midst of social change. In J. R. M. Gerris (Ed.), *Dynamics of parenting* (pp. 323–346). Leuven, Germany: Garant Publishers.

Körner, A., Lechner, C. M., Pavlova, M. K., & Silbereisen, R. K. (2015). Goal engagement in coping with occupational uncertainty predicts favorable career-related outcomes. *Journal of Vocational Behavior, 88*, 174–184.

Kowalczuk, I. S. (2019). Das Ende der DDR 1989/90: Von der Revolution über den Mauerfall zur Einheit [The end of the GDR 1989/90: From revolution over the fall of the Wall to unity]. *Aus Politik und Zeitgeschichte, 69*, 35–37.

Labouvie, E. W., Pandina, R. J., & Johnson, V. (1991). Developmental trajectories of substance use in adolescence: Differences and predictors. *International Journal of Behavioral Development, 14*, 305–328.

Laurin, K., Kay, A. C., & Fitzsimons, G. J. (2012). Reactance versus rationalization: Divergent responses to policies that constrain freedom. *Psychological Science, 23*(2), 205–209.

Lechner, C. M., Obschonka, M., & Silbereisen, R. K. (2017). Who reaps the benefits of social change? Exploration and its socioecological boundaries. *Journal of Personality, 85*(2), 257–269.

Lechner, C. M., Tomasik, M. J., & Silbereisen, R. K. (2016). Preparing for uncertain careers: How youth deal with growing occupational uncertainties before the education-to-work transition. *Journal of Vocational Behavior, 95*, 90–101.

Lösel, F. (1975). *Handlungskontrolle und Jugenddelinquenz [Action control and juvenile delinquency]*. Stuttgart, Germany: Enke.

Michel, A., Titzmann, P. F., & Silbereisen, R. K. (2012). Psychological adaptation of adolescent immigrants from the former Soviet Union in Germany: Acculturation versus age-related time trends. *Journal of Cross-Cultural Psychology, 43*(1), 59–76.

Moffitt, T. E. (1993). Adolescence-limited and life-course-persistent antisocial-behavior: A developmental taxonomy. *Psychological Review, 100*(4), 674–701.

Muchow, M., & Muchow, H. H. (1935). *Der Lebensraum des Großstadtkindes [The life-space of the city child]*. Weinheim, Germany: Juventa (Reprint in 1998).

Muthén, B., & Muthén, L. K. (2000). Integrating person-centered and variable-centered analyses: Growth mixture modeling with latent trajectory classes. *Alcoholism: Clinical and Experimental Research, 24*(6), 882–891.

Obschonka, M., Andersson, H., Silbereisen, R. K., & Sverke, M. (2013). Rule-breaking, crime, and entrepreneurship: A replication and extension study with 37-year longitudinal data. *Journal of Vocational Behavior, 83*(3), 386–396.

Obschonka, M., Silbereisen, R. K., & Schmitt-Rodermund, E. (2010). Entrepreneurial intention as developmental outcome. *Journal of Vocational Behavior, 77*, 63–72.

Obschonka, M., Silbereisen, R. K., & Wasilewski, J. (2012). Constellations of new demands concerning careers and jobs: Results from a two-country study on social and economic change. *Journal of Vocational Behavior, 80*, 211–223.

Oishi, S., & Graham, J. (2010). Social ecology: Lost and found in psychological science. *Perspectives on Psychological Science, 5*(4), 356–377.

Pavlova, M. K., & Silbereisen, R. K. (2016). Perceived expectations for active aging, formal productive roles, and psychological adjustment among the young–old. *Research on Aging, 38*, 26–50.

Pavlova, M. K., & Silbereisen, R. K. (2017). Social change and youth civic engagement. In I. Schoon & R. K. Silbereisen (Eds.), *Pathways to adulthood. Educational opportunities, motivation and attainment in times of social change* (pp. 279–298). London, England: UCL IOE Press.

Pinquart, M., Silbereisen, R. K., & Körner, A. (2010). Coping with family demands under difficult economic conditions: Associations with depressive symptoms. *Swiss Journal of Psychology, 69*, 53–63.

Preyer, W. T. (1882). *Die Seele des KIndes. Beobachtungen über die geistige Entwicklung des Menschen in den ersten Lebensjahren [The mind of the child. Observations of the mental development during the first years of life]*. Leipzig, Germany: Grieben.

Projektgruppe Tudrop. (1984). *Heroinabhängigkeit unbetreuter Jugendlicher [Heroin addiction of wayward juveniles]*. Weinheim, Germany: Beltz.

Reitzle, M., & Silbereisen, R. K. (2000). The timing of adolescents' school-to-work transition in the course of social change: The example of German unification. *Swiss Journal of Psychology, 59*(4), 240–255.

Schmitt-Rodermund, E., & Silbereisen, R. K. (2008). The prediction of delinquency among immigrant and non-immigrant youth: Unwrapping the package of culture. *International Journal of Comparative Sociology, 49*, 87–109.

Schmitt-Rodermund, E., & Silbereisen, R. K. (2009). Immigrant parents' age expectations for the development of their adolescent offspring: Transmission effects and changes after immigration. In U. Schönpflug (Ed.), *Cultural transmission: Psychological, developmental, social, and methodological aspects* (pp. 297–313). Cambridge, England: Cambridge University Press.

Silbereisen, R. K. (2014). Development as action in context. In R. M. Lerner, A. C. Petersen, R. K. Silbereisen, & J. Brooks-Gunn (Eds.), *The developmental science of adolescence* (pp. 457–473). New York, NY: Psychology Press.

Silbereisen, R. K., Eyferth, K., & Rudinger, G. (1986). *Development as action in context: Problem behavior and normal youth development*. Heidelberg, Germany: Springer.

Silbereisen, R. K., Heinrich, P., & Trosiener, H.-J. (1975). Untersuchung zur Rollenübernahme: Die Bedeutung von Erziehungsstil, Selbstverantwortlichkeit und sozioökonomischer Struktur [Study on role taking: The role of parental style, self-responsibility, and economic structure]. *Zeitschrift für Sozialpsychologie, 1*, 62–75.

Silbereisen, R. K., & Noack, P. (1988). On the constructive role of problem behavior in adolescence. In N. Bolger, A. Caspi, G. Downey, & M. Moorehouse (Eds.), *Persons in context: Developmental processes* (pp. 152–180). Cambridge, England: Cambridge University Press.

Silbereisen, R. K., Noack, P., & von Eye, A. (1992). Adolescents' development of romantic friendship and change in favorite leisure contexts. *Journal of Adolescent Research, 7*(1), 80–93.

Silbereisen, R. K., Pinquart, M., & Tomasik, M. J. (2010). Demands of social change and psychosocial adjustment: Results from the Jena study. In

R. K. Silbereisen & X. Chen (Eds.), *Social change and human development: Concepts and results* (pp. 125–147). London, England: Sage.

Silbereisen, R. K., & Smolenska, Z. (1991). Überlegungen zu kulturellen Unterschieden der Jugendent-wicklung: Werte und Freizeitverhalten in Warschau und Berlin (West). [Reflections on cultural differences in adolescent development: Values and leisure time activities in Berlin (West) and Warsaw]. In W. Melzer, W. Heitmeyer, L. Liegle, & J. Zinnecker (Eds.), *Osteuropäische Jugend im Wandel. Ergebnisse vergleichender Jugendforschung in der Sowjetunion, Polen, Ungarn und der ehemaligen DDR* (pp. 86–100). Weinheim/München, Germany: Juventa.

Silbereisen, R. K., Titzmann, P. F., Michel, A., Sagi-Schwartz, A., & Lavee, Y. (2012). The role of developmental transitions in psychosocial competence: A comparison of native and immigrant young people in Germany. In A. S. Masten, K. Liebkind, & D. J. Hernandez (Eds.), *Realizing the potential of immigrant youth* (pp. 324–358). New York, NY: Cambridge University Press.

Silbereisen, R. K., Titzmann, P. F., & Shavit, Y. (Eds.). (2014). *The challenges of diaspora migration: Interdisciplinary perspectives on Israel and Germany.* Farnham, England: Ashgate.

Silbereisen, R. K., Walper, S., & Albrecht, H. T. (1990). Family income loss and economic hardship: Antecedents of adolescents' problem behavior. *New Directions for Child and Adolescent Development*, 27–47.

Spaeth, M., Weichold, K., Silbereisen, R. K., & Wiesner, M. (2010). Examining the differential effectiveness of a life skills program (IPSY) on alcohol use trajectories in early adolescence. *Journal of Consulting and Clinical Psychology*, 78, 334–348.

Titma, M., & Tuma, N. B. (2008). Adolescent agency and adult economic success in a transitional society. *International Journal of Psychology*, 42(2), 102–109.

Titzmann, P. F., Raabe, T., & Silbereisen, R. K. (2008). Risk and protective factors for delinquency among male adolescent immigrants at different stages of the acculturation process. *International Journal of Psychology*, 43(1), 19–31.

Titzmann, P. F., & Silbereisen, R. K. (2012). Acculturation or development? Autonomy expectations among ethnic German immigrant adolescents and their native German age-mates. *Child Development*, 83(5), 1640–1654.

Titzmann, P. F., Silbereisen, R. K., & Mesch, G. (2014). Minor delinquency and immigration: A longitudinal study among male adolescents. *Developmental Psychology*, 50, 271–282.

Titzmann, P. F., Silbereisen, R. K., & Mesch, G. S. (2012). Change in friendship homophily: A German Israeli comparison of adolescent immigrants. *Journal of Cross-Cultural Psychology*, 43(3), 410–428.

Tobi, E. W., Goeman, J. J., Monajemi, R., Gu, H., Putter, H., Zhang, Y. Y., … Heimans, B. T. (2014). DNA methylation signatures link prenatal famine exposure to growth and metabolism. *Nature Communications*, 5, 5592.

Tomasik, M. J., & Silbereisen, R. K. (2009). Demands of social change as a function of the political context, institutional filters, and psychosocial resources. *Social Indicators Research*, 94(1), 13–28.

Tomasik, M. J., & Silbereisen, R. K. (2012). Beneficial effects of disengagement from futile struggles with occupational planning: A contextualist-motivational approach. *Developmental Psychology, 48*(6), 1785–1796.

Tomasik, M. J., Silbereisen, R. K., & Heckhausen, J. (2010). Is it adaptive to disengage from demands of social change? Adjustment to developmental barriers in opportunity-deprived regions. *Motivation and Emotion, 34*(4), 384–398.

Tomasik, M. J., Silbereisen, R. K., Lechner, C. M., & Wasilewski, J. (2013). Negotiating demands of social change in young and middle-aged adults from Poland. *International Journal of Stress Management, 20*(3), 222.

Tomasik, M. J., Silbereisen, R. K., & Pinquart, M. (2010). Individuals negotiating demands of social and economic change: A control theoretical approach. *European Psychologist, 15*, 246–259.

Toynbee, A. J. (1947). *A study of history: Abridgement of volumes I – VI by D. C. Somervell.* Oxford, England: Oxford University Press.

Veenendaal, M. V. E., Painter, R. C., de Rooij, S. R., Bossuyt, P. M. M., van der Post, J. A. M., Gluckman, P. D., ... Roseboom, T. J. (2013). Transgenerational effects of prenatal exposure to the 1944–45 Dutch famine. *BJOG: An International Journal of Obstetrics & Gynaecology, 120*(5), 548–554.

von Humboldt, A. (1799). Alexander von Humboldt an den Herausgeber aus Corunna am 5. Jun (i) 1799. *Jahrbücher der Berg- und Hüttenkunde, 4*, 399–401.

Weichold, K., & Silbereisen, R. K. (2014). *Suchtprävention in der Schule: IPSY– Ein Lebenskompetenzenprogramm für die Klassenstufen 5–7 [Prevention of substance use in schools. IPSY – A life-skills program for Grades 5–7].* Göttingen, Germany: Hogrefe Verlag.

Wiesner, M., & Silbereisen, R. K. (1998). Belastungen in frühen Lebensjahren und delinquentes Verhalten bei Frühadoleszenten in Ost und West [Adversities in early life and delinquency of early adolescents in East and West]. In H. Oswald (Ed.), *Sozialisation und Entwicklung in den neuen Bundesländern (2. Beiheft der Zeitschrift für Soziologie der Erziehung und Sozialisation* (pp. 137–153). Weinheim, Germany: Juventa.

Wiesner, M., & Silbereisen, R. K. (2003). Trajectories of delinquent behaviour in adolescence and their covariates: Relations with initial and time-averaged factors. *Journal of Adolescence, 26*(6), 753–771.

Zhou, M., Zhou, Y., Zhang, J., Obschonka, M., & Silbereisen, R. K. (2019). Person–city personality fit and entrepreneurial success: An explorative study in China. *International Journal of Psychology, 54*(2), 155–163.

9   From the Frustration–Aggression Hypothesis to Moral Reasoning and Action

Gian Vittorio Caprara

Gian Vittorio Caprara was born November 1,1944, in Erba, Italy. In 1971 he obtained a degree in psychology from the University of Rome and joined its Faculty of Psychology in 1973. He was promoted to the rank of Professor in 1980 and eventually became Chair of the Department, Coordinator of Graduate Programs, and Dean of the Faculty of Psychology. He was elected Emeritus Professor and Senior Fellow of the School of Advanced Studies after his retirement in 2015. During his career at the University of Rome, he had a temporary teaching appointment at the University of Milano Bicocca in Italy and at three universities in the United States: the University of Michigan, the University of California–Los Angeles, and Stanford University. He was also a fellow at the Netherlands Institute for Advanced Study and a fellow at the Swedish Collegium for Advanced Study. He is a member of the Academia Europaea, and he founded the Interuniversity Center for the Study of Prosocial and Antisocial Motivation.

He has published more than 500 journal articles, book chapters, and books. His publications have focused on three major topics: personality, aggression, and political preferences and participation. He adopted an interactionist and social cognitive approach in which personality is considered a self-regulatory system whose biological potential is largely undefined and whose realizations are mostly conditioned by culture (Caprara, 1996, 2002; Caprara & Cervone, 2000).

Gian Vittorio Caprara initiated the Genzano Longitudinal Study, which followed 472 10-year-old children from elementary school through adolescence. The study focused on the development of aggression and prosocial behavior, personality stability and change, determinants of academic achievement and vocational choices, family and romantic relations, and civic and political behavior. The study investigated how different aspects of personality operate in concert with the aim of clarifying the pathways that lead to maladjusted and risky behaviors. The findings led to the development of a theory that assigns to marginal deviations from normative behaviors a crucial role in the

215

development of maladjusted behavior (Caprara, 1992). The Genzano Longitudinal Study also led to the design of psychosocial interventions aimed at promoting and sustaining healthy developmental transitions in schools (Caprara, Luengo Kanacri, Zuffianò, Gerbino, & Pastorelli, 2015).

Gian Vittorio Caprara and his colleagues studied aggressive and violent behavior with the hypothesis that they are manifestations of an individual's personality, which reflects the knowledge structures and meaning systems shared with others, the capacities to manage affect and interpersonal relations, and the values shared with others. To achieve this aim, they developed new measures of individual differences in irritability, emotional susceptibility, need for reparation, fear of punishment, hostile rumination, tolerance of violence, and moral disengagement. The study was also designed to distinguish between reactive and proactive aggression and to assess the generalizability of the frustration–aggression hypothesis (Caprara, 1986; Caprara et al., 1985; Caprara, Cinanni, & Mazzotti, 1989; Caprara, Manzi, & Perugini, 1992; Caprara, Renzi, Amolini, D'Imperio, & Travaglia, 1984; Caprara, Renzi, et al., 1986).

During his career, Gian Vittorio Caprara was involved in numerous scientific societies. He served as President of the European Association of Personality. He was a member of the Council of the International Society of Research on Aggression, of the Executive Committee of the European Association of Psychological Assessment, and of the Governing Council of the International Society of Political Psychology. He served as Honorary President and Chair of the Scientific Committee of the 14th Congress of Psychology held in Milan in 2015. He was Study Director of the Medical Research Program of the Council of Europe on 'New Trends in the Organization of Mental Health Services at the Primary Care Levels' in 1984, and in 1990 he was the coordinator of the Italian Inter-ministerial Commission for the Study of Psychosocial Risk.

9.1   From childhood to early adulthood

I was born on the first of November 1944 in Erba, a small city close to Milan, where my parents temporarily settled to avoid the massive bombing of the city.

The war ended a few months later, but its memories filled the narratives of my family for a long time. My father was a doctor, a veteran of the unfortunate Italian expedition to Russia. My mother was the eldest of four children, one of whom joined the Fascists and two others the partisans. I loved the stories of courage and learned that family ties can be stronger than ideological divisions.

Mine was a middle-class family, including a strict father and a very warm mother, a child of the war and the twins – a girl and a boy – born right after the war. I grew up and attended public schools in Milan, a foggy and damp city – and an extraordinary milieu full of ideas and ideals fueled by sacrifices and nostalgia – in a time of reconstruction, class confrontations, and profound transformation of the country.

We lived in a comfortable apartment where my father held his medical practice. The apartment, however, was too small to contain the exuberance of three children whose favorite sport was wrestling.

I do not remember when I started to spend time in the street, but certainly it happened when I was still a child, eight or nine years old. In the street I met children from different social conditions, and I learned to fight and to negotiate, to lead, to follow and to retreat, to play cards, and to anticipate troubles. I was intolerant of bullying and cautious in avoiding peers who were indulging in dangerous games.

I remember my mother's tea time with my aunt and my grandmother, the jokes with my brothers and my cousins, the two months of vacations in the mountains and at sea. Memories of a happy childhood under the protection of an extended and close family.

I also remember the fatigue in the faces of the workers lining-up to take the tram to go back home, the houses with outside lavatories on the balustrades, the immigrants from the poorest parts of Italy. Memories of a country re-emerging from the war with all the disparities of the human condition.

After 5 years of elementary schools, and 3 years of junior high school, I entered the Classical Lyceum. I was 14 years old. This was a challenging course of study. It was the only one that gave access to all university courses and to the most prestigious careers. The curriculum included the study of Latin and Greek; of literature, history and philosophy; of mathematics and sciences. The final examination, the so-called *Maturità*, was a long-lasting and recurring nightmare.

The school I attended was the same one my father had attended. It was also a school attended by others who played important roles in the political history of Italy. Among our teachers there were eminent scholars and partisans of opposite political ideals. Ideological struggles were common among students. These included struggles between left and right political orientations, as well as between Catholic and non-religious students. Those were the years of the Cold War and of strong political polarization for and against Russia and the United States. Students played an active role in the various demonstrations in the city. Thus I was initiated into politics.

The courses at the classical lyceum were the last courses I attended regularly. Afterward, I started to travel in the Americas, with the prospect of starting a career in business. Between 1964 and 1965 I crossed the Atlantic twice. First, a freighter brought me to North America, where I spent a winter in Minnesota working as an office boy in a Minneapolis Company. Then I embarked on a supercargo ship that carried cereals from Buenos Aires to Naples. I definitely loved to travel and had experiences that expanded my view of life. I met intriguing people; I learned to adjust and to manage myself in unconventional places.

Back home, having to do my mandatory military service, I applied and was admitted to serve as an officer in the Air Force. I cannot say the extent to which chance, personal inclinations, or will were decisive in my subsequent choices. Political science at the Catholic University of Milan was a choice of convenience to continue my university education, though at a distance.

9.2   Becoming a psychologist

Soon I discovered that I was not made for business. Rather, I enjoyed preparing for my examinations in history, law, economics, sociology, and, finally, psychology, where I ended up discussing my Laurea dissertation *On the Psychological Determinants of Economic Behavior* in 1967, while still fulfilling my military duties.

Holding a degree in political science, I was admitted to the Specialization School in Psychology at the Catholic University of Milan. At the same time, I was hired by IBM Italy to work in the personnel department. This allowed me to have a salary and to start my own family. In 1968 I married Maria Francesca Pazielli, a university companion, and in 1969 we had our first daughter.

Retrospectively, I recognize IBM as an extraordinary apprenticeship in a challenging work environment. Yet, the prospective careers in an organization like IBM were not completely congenial with my aspirations. Thus, in 1971 I took a leave to take a Canada Council Scholarship at the University of Montreal, where I completed my dissertation for my Specialization degree with a review of research on aggression.

In 1973, the promise of an academic career led me to accept a teaching position at the University of Rome as part of the Faculty, which started the first Italian University courses giving a Laurea degree in psychology. Eraldo De Grada introduced me to the new academic environment, and his mentorship exerted a durable influence on my research orientation.

In 1980 I won the national competition to become Full Professor and got my chair at the University of Rome where I remained for the rest of my career. In 1980 I became Director of the Institute of Psychology, then Director of the

Department of Psychology in 1983, Coordinator of the Doctorate Program from 1986 to 2001, and finally Dean of Psychology in 2007.

The university was congenial to my aspirations as it offered a socially prestigious career while satisfying my desire to know, explore, and change. It gave me freedom to choose topics to investigate and to organize my work as I liked. Becoming a full professor at a relatively young age added a sense of independence and confidence that encouraged me to play an active role in academia and helped me to attract a growing number of students.

The years between 1977 and 1982 were those during which Italian universities, and the University of Rome in particular, were particularly engaged in the fight against terrorism. Things returned to normal later, and my career followed the normal path of academia.

My travel abroad became more frequent and led to collaborations with colleagues in other countries. In 1985 I was invited to teach a semester at the University of Michigan in Ann Arbor. Next, I taught at the University of California–Los Angeles (UCLA) and the University of California–Irvine (UCI) in the summers between 1985 and 1989, and then at Stanford in the summer of 1990. The list of colleagues with whom I am indebted for their hospitality, friendship, and wisdom would be too long to include here. Yet, I must mention Donald Brown, who invited me to Ann Arbor, and Andrew Comrey, Mike Goldstein, Neil Malamuth, Raymond Novaco, Bert Raven, Bernie Weiner, and the Feshbachs, who made my stay in Los Angeles as pleasant and productive as possible. In 1990 I was elected President of the European Association of Personality Psychology, where I established a close collaboration with colleagues such as Josè Bermudez from Madrid and Guus Van Heck from Tilburg. In 1996 I was invited by the Netherlands Institute for Advanced Study in the Humanities and Social Science to spend a year at Wassenaar as Golestan Fellow in residence. My experience at the Advanced Center left an important mark on my personal and professional development. A major result of that experience was the book written with Daniel Cervone, *Personality: Determinants, Dynamics and Potentials*. I spent an academic year (2001–2002) and two other semesters in 2013–2014 at the Swedish Collegium for Advanced Study in Uppsala, where I conceived and ultimately completed the book written with Michele Vecchione, *Personalizing Politics and Realizing Democracy*. I view the years spent at the Advanced Center as among the most formidable experiences of my life. They greatly contributed to opening my eyes and my thinking to other disciplines and to the conviction that the vocation and aspirations of psychology can't be fulfilled unless integrated with both the biological and social sciences.

9.3   Research on Personality

Over my entire academic career, personality was the main target of investigation in accordance with my original desire to understand how individuals' and societies' functioning are reciprocally related and to what extent psychological knowledge may contribute to their development.

After an early attraction to psychoanalysis, I turned to interactionism and to social cognitive theory. David Magnusson first, and Albert Bandura later, were very influential in the development of my thinking. I had the privilege of establishing long and warm friendships with both, and our discussions spanned research issues and methods, worldviews and politics.

At the University of Rome I started a program of research to understand how individual differences in personality may help distinguish forms of aggression that, in different degrees, may depend on personal and situational factors.

Being joined by a growing number of brilliant young colleagues was crucial to extending my collaborations with other colleagues around the world and to expanding the scope of my research. Two Fulbright scholarships allowed me to establish durable friendships with people like Albert Pepitone, Seymour and Norma Feshbach, and Len Eron, who had already marked the path of aggression research.

At the International Society for Research on Aggression, I established a close enduring friendship with many other colleagues and, in particular, with Adam Fraczek, who invited me to Poland at the time of the Martial Law and with whom I established an agreement to make regular exchanges of scholars from East and West before the fall of the Iron Curtain.

In 1989 Phil Zimbardo introduced me to Albert Bandura, with whom I had a lasting collaboration. Numerous publications spanning from aggression to prosocial behavior and self-efficacy attest to the importance of this collaboration. Most of these publications derive from the longitudinal study we conducted with Tina Pastorelli in the town of Genzano, near Rome, for over 20 years. This study investigated personality differences that may sustain or prevent aggression and violence from early adolescence to early adulthood. Results led to designing and implementing specific interventions aimed at preventing and reducing aggression while promoting prosocial behavior in schools.

These research activities and collaborations led to the foundation of the Interuniversity Center for the Study of Prosocial and Antisocial Motivation. The aim of the Center was to study aggressive and prosocial behaviors and to promote preventive interventions. It was conceived with two colleagues from the Universities of Florence and Naples, Ada Fonzi and Gustavo Iacono. The Center inaugurated its activities in 1991 and has since then become an important aggregation of competences with broad international connections. Over the years, the founding universities in Rome, Florence, and Naples have been joined by the Catholic University of Milan, with Eugenia Scabini, and then by the Universities of Padova, Catania, Turin, and Aosta. Tina Pastorelli took the helm of the Center after my retirement in 2015.

9.4   The Person in Her/His Sociohistorical Context

Focus on the person in her/his sociohistorical context is the element that has most characterized my research from the very beginning. I was convinced that the task of psychology is to address and to understand the person, even when I did not yet have a clear idea of how the person could be conceptualized. I believed that habits, attitudes, thoughts, and feelings – including what pertains to aggression and violence, and any single manifestation of them – should be addressed as expressions of the person and of her/his relations with the world.

Likewise, I was convinced that what people do, how they think and feel about themselves, how they relate to each other, and ultimately what they may become largely depend on their social–material conditions of life, which may significantly differ across time and social contexts. I cannot say the extent to which these convictions have been influenced by my readings and political inclinations toward various forms of humanist Marxism that were in vogue during my youth. Certainly, I have been strongly influenced by a special reading of psychoanalysis about the conceptualization of the person and by exponents of the Frankfurt school, like Theodor Adorno, Erich Fromm, and Max Horkheimer with regards to the interpretation of history and society.

No less influential were my religious and political inclinations. Although my faith is frail, religion has always been an important quest in my life. I am aware that my private life can't be taken as a model of Catholic virtue, as I remain married to Maria Francesca Pazielli, with whom I had three daughters, and yet have lived for the last 30 years with Laura Borgogni, with whom I had a son. I am still attending church in search of responses to my existential questions.

Likewise, politics has been a topic of great interest. Despite the difficulties of the left, I still believe that their ideals regarding equality, respect, and opportunities for growth are the most congenial to human development, and thus the ones that should guide political action.

It is on these premises that I first engaged in empirical research on aggression, which I viewed as socially relevant and conveniently accessible, and then extended my investigations to self-efficacy, moral disengagement, and prosocial behavior. Over time, I came to conceive personality as a self-regulatory agentic system whose potentials are indefinite and whose boundaries are mostly determined by culture.

Ultimately I came to view aggression and violence as personality's manifestations that largely reflect the knowledge structures and meaning systems that people share with others, their capacities to manage affect and interpersonal relations, and the values they pursue and from whose attainments they draw their self-respect.

This view of personality did not lead me to overlook the important progress made in neurosciences regarding the biological roots of our behavior and achievements. Rather, it led me to appreciate the great plasticity of our biological endowments and to acknowledge the great responsibility of humans in the use they make of their bodies and their brains, thanks to the properties of the human mind. In my view, the mind stays at the core of personality functioning, as a system of structures and processes that emerge from the interaction of the organism with the environment and that significantly impact both of them. The encounter of the organism with the environment establishes the conditions for the emergence of a mental organization that, since its inception, modulates their action and relationships.

While the body, the brain, and the environment all contribute to its functioning, personality summarizes the mental properties that have made possible the development of cultures and that account for the specific achievements that are within the reach of individuals' pursuits in a given context and time.

Even culture is an emerging property of nature that derives from the exchanges of the organism with the environment and that has evolved in concomitance with the emergence and development of mental systems capable of storing knowledge and of benefiting from collective experience to sustain and to extend human control over the environment and life. Culture supplies the meaning systems within which people experience the world and establish the social conditions that lead them to embrace different beliefs and expectations about their being human and about how they should relate to the environment and to each other.

It is due to properties of mind, such as awareness, intentionality, and self-regulation, and to the development and transmission across generations of knowledges and of practices, that humans have extended control over their environments and their lives. And it is the special expression and organization of those properties in given contexts that shape personality as the whole organization of individuals' feelings, thoughts, attitudes, aspirations, and habits.

This leads to viewing personality as a system that largely reflects the opportunities and the constraints of social contexts in which people grow and the knowledge structures that they share with others to make sense of their experience. Yet, personality is not just a vessel of culture and societies. In reality, individual differences in personality attest to degrees of freedom that continuously challenge the regularities of the context and of the times. The development and control that humans have achieved over the environment and over their lives, over the course of time and especially during the last centuries, attest to the extraordinary potentials of biology and culture co-action that enable humans to challenge constantly the limits of their own achievements. In this regard, individual differences and personality play a crucial role as vessels of change and development of the human species. Each individual is a unique source of variation and ultimately of change in the service of evolution as its encounters with the environment establish the conditions needed to express new potentials.

9.5   Bringing a Personological Approach to the Study of Aggression

Aggression was a topic that I addressed in my Specialization's degree dissertation that seemed able to satisfy sufficiently well the conditions I considered to be socially relevant and empirically affordable.

The frustration–aggression hypothesis appeared particularly adequate to assess the validity of a personological approach to address a phenomenon that, like aggression, can be traced to multiple sources, both biological and social, and that may exert multiple functions in the service of protecting one's life and adapting to the social environment.

Bringing a personological approach to the study of aggression led me to question the psychological structures and processes underlying the various phenomena that could be traced to aggression. And then to question the extent to which the various kinds of aggression could be traced to a common basic tendency to react to and interact with the environment, or to distinct psychological components that, in varying degrees, account for behavioral outcomes that can only superficially be viewed as due to the same mechanism across context and time.

Focusing on individual differences like irritability, emotional susceptibility, and hostile rumination, which in varying degrees could be related to the frustration–aggression hypothesis, led me to systematically examine the extent to which personal dispositions like irritability, emotional susceptibility, and hostile rumination could, when confronted with situations such as obstacles, failures, threats, and their interactions, account for aggressive responses under different conditions of awareness and accessibility.

Irritability (i.e., the tendency to react impulsively and aversely at the slightest dissent and provocation) and emotional susceptibility (i.e., the tendency to experience feelings of discomfort, inadequacy, and vulnerability) were intended to highlight how disregulation of basic emotions like anger and sadness may predispose to the use of aggression under disturbing situations (Caprara, Cinanni, et al., 1985). Hostile rumination (i.e., the tendency to experience and nurture ill feelings of retaliation and revenge after being offended) was intended to highlight how ruminative cognitions carrying negative affect prolong, over time, the instigation to aggress that follows a self-threatening stimulation (Caprara, 1986).

Both irritability and emotional susceptibility moderated aggression in experiments where subjects were required to select and deliver a noxious stimulation to an innocent confederate, immediately after the frustrating event, under conditions of limited awareness of the consequences of their choices and limited control over their reactions (Caprara, Renzi, Alcini, D'Imperio, & Travaglia, 1983). No less important, however, were findings showing the different impact of irritability and emotional susceptibility under situations in which the instigation to aggress and the opportunity to aggress occurred in concomitance with enhanced excitation and exposure to aggression-eliciting cues. Enhanced excitation due to physical exercise resulted in higher aggression, mostly in highly emotional subjects who had been previously frustrated. Aggression-eliciting cues, instead, were associated with higher aggression mostly in highly irritable subjects who had been previously frustrated (Caprara et al., 1984; Caprara, Renzi, et al., 1986).

Hostile rumination proved crucial to moderate delayed aggression after a self-threatening experience had been evaluated less positively than one might reasonably have expected. Even a week after receiving the disturbing evaluation, high ruminators targeted their provokers with higher noxious stimulations than low ruminators. This did not happen with highly irritable or highly emotionally susceptible subjects, once hostile rumination was kept under control (Caprara, Coluzzi, Mazzotti, Renzi, & Zelli, 1985).

Irritability and emotional susceptibility amplified the effects that noxious experiences and enhanced excitation may exert over people's behavior and brought to our attention both the role of affect regulation and the contribution of situations in limiting their control. Hostile rumination amplified the effects of self-threat and brought to our attention the role that processes such as attribution, evaluation, and outcome expectation exert in making sense of situations and in determining behavior.

These findings led to an argument for the existence of a general disposition like aggressiveness to account for the various expressions of aggression and to trace the above tendencies to mental structures that reflect different processes and serve different functions, and, finally, to reject the view of aggressive behavior as a unitarian phenomenon. Rather, they corroborated the distinction between a reactive and proactive/ instrumental aggression. Likely, there are forms of aggression that mostly rest upon automatic/impulsive reactions and other forms of aggression that, instead, are intentional and result from planning, forethought, and determination. While the former result from a lack of emotional and cognitive control that limits individual's capacities to resist the instigating power of situations, the latter mostly attest to established agentic capacities to accord actions with purposes, values, and goals.

Most of the earlier studies were conceived with Paolo Renzi, a young colleague, a psychobiologist by training, with extraordinary inventiveness, who later turned his interest toward computers. Among the students who joined our research group in the early 1980s, Tina Pastorelli and Arnaldo Zelli were very active in running experiments, and both have had successful academic careers.

The study of individual differences was crucial to highlight the instigating power of self-threats in comparison to mere failures and the moderating role of feelings and emotions as well as of situational elements capable of enhancing or reducing the available responses. Likewise, it was crucial to examine and assess a whole variety of models regarding the path of relations and influences among the hypothetical mental structures that underlay the various behavioral tendencies.

The capacity to regulate emotional excitation and feelings of anger and despondency proved crucial to mitigate both the aggression-instigating power of failure and self-threat and the accessibility of aggression. At that time it was common, although controversial, to assess aggression using an apparatus like the Buss machine, where subjects were invited to deliver shocks of different intensity to a confederate under previous conditions of frustration or insult, or under neutral conditions. We proved that withholding rewards, other than delivering shocks, was equally effective to assess aggression and hostility, and also less invasive. Subjects under conditions of self-esteem threat selected monetary prizes of minor value to reward the correct responses of the confederates who evaluated them less positively. Furthermore, our studies showed that there were no differences between males and females when they could express their hostility by withholding rewards. Indeed, there were no gender differences in the selected rewards, both when subjects were more generous after being positively evaluated and when subjects were less generous after being evaluated less positively than expected (Caprara, Passerini, Pastorelli, Renzi, & Zelli, 1986). This was a novelty with respect to previous studies where females under conditions of frustration and self-threat were found to deliver shocks of lower intensity than males, whereas they did not differ from males under control situations.

Findings attesting to the power of aggression-eliciting cues in the form of images, objects, or commercials associated with aggression are particularly relevant for the current debate on the risk of easy availability of weapons and on the degree to which mental illness may account for the consequences of easy access to weapons (Caprara et al., 1984; Caprara et al., 1987).

Our findings leave no doubt that certain people are more inclined than others to resort to aggression, both reactive and instrumental. Likewise they do not leave any doubt that the mere availability of weapons is, in itself, a major cause of their use, as their power is in their destructiveness. Mental frailty may contribute to aggression but cannot account for the lethal consequences of free weapons.

Along the same course of reasoning we addressed the role that anticipatory feelings regarding the harmful consequence of ones' actions may play, both to amplify or attenuate the resorting to aggression. To this end, we identified fear of punishment and the need for reparation as two different components of individual differences associated with guilt and remorse that showed a fairly different relation with aggression. While persecutory feelings are associated with enhanced aggression, reparatory feelings attenuate tendencies to turn to aggression (Caprara et al., 1992).

Ultimately we addressed the social attitudes that justify the recourse to violence and the kind of reasons people give to themselves and to others to justify aggressive behaviors. This turned the focus of my investigation to the social sources, meanings and functions of aggression and violence, and to how they get construed and framed in terms of beliefs that make them personally and socially acceptable despite their noxious consequences (Caprara et al., 1989).

The collaboration with Bandura was decisive in my embrace of social cognitive theory and the inclusion of moral disengagement in our research program (Bandura, 1986). This led us to focus on the self-regulatory mechanism and, in particular, on the cognitive strategies that allow people to make use of aggression and violence in the pursuit of their interests and to circumvent remorse and guilt that habitually restrain us from doing harm to others.

As people's self-respect largely depends upon the extent to which they behave in accordance with moral standards that they have endorsed and that commonly imply not harming others, anticipatory guilt and remorse operate as self-reactions that lead people to refuse, blame, and refrain from aggression. Yet, moral standards and self-sanctions do not operate invariantly across situations, as moral judgment does not always turn into congruent moral conduct.

In reality, moral standards can be effective as guides to the extent that they stay at the core of individuals' personal identity and cannot be violated unless people are to jeopardize their own self-respect. Likewise, self-reactions like guilt and remorse can be effective as deterrents to the extent that they are activated as anticipatory sanctions.

A whole variety of self-serving, self-regulatory cognitive mechanisms allow people to elude or mitigate the pressures of moral principles and self-sanctions which can be disengaged from blameful and harmful behaviors by reconstruing the conduct, obscuring and spreading individuals' personal responsibility, misrepresenting, disregarding, minimizing the detrimental consequences of one's actions, and devaluating and blaming the victims of maltreatment.

Bandura pointed to three different points at which cognitive reconstructions allow people to release detrimental behaviors from moral self-sanctions: the conduct, its effects, and the victim. Then, he identified eight mechanisms that, in varying degrees, allow people to divorce the moral values that dictate not harming others from their own actions that violate those values. Moral justification, palliative comparison, and euphemistic labeling allow minimizing, ignoring, and misconstruing the blamable consequences of aggression and violence. Displacement and the sharing of responsibility mitigate the feelings of guilt, remorse, and shame regarding damaging others; dehumanization and attribution of blame allow self-exoneration from any moral concern by downgrading the human dignity and moral status of the victim.

Since the history and theory of moral disengagement have been told several times and recently summarized by Bandura in his latest masterpiece, I do not think that more is needed to attest to its relevance for aggression and violence research and beyond (Bandura, 2016). Rather, it is worth noting that we have been able to reconcile under a common program of research such diverse behavioral and cognitive tendencies as irritability, hostile rumination, and moral disengagement.

With Bandura we developed several scales to assess moral disengagement in adults and children. We came to the conclusion that the eight mechanisms could be treated as expressions of a common dimension despite their manifest diversities (Caprara, Barbaranelli, Vicino, & Bandura, 1996; Caprara, Pastorelli, & Bandura, 1995). Together, we addressed the relations between individual differences in moral disengagement, irritability, and hostile rumination, and showed that, in varying degrees, they were correlated and could all contribute to predict aggression. In an earlier study, path analysis on cross-sectional data supported a model in which moral disengagement fosters harmful behavior by promoting irritability and hostile rumination (Bandura, Barbaranelli, Caprara, & Pastorelli, 1996). A subsequent longitudinal study from adolescence to early adulthood supported a model in which irritability and hostile behavior contributed to each other's development both reciprocally and significantly across time. Furthermore, hostile rumination and moral disengagement mediated the relation between irritability and engagement in aggression and violence as assessed through self-reports and peer evaluation, whereas moral disen-gagement significantly mediated the relation between hostile rumination and engagement in aggression and violence (Caprara et al., 2014).

The implication of these studies for effective interventions aimed at preventing and reducing aggression are noteworthy. The findings, in fact, attested to the usefulness of individual differences to address the mental structures and mechanisms that govern aggressive and violent behavior, and also the usefulness of irritability, hostile rumination, and moral disengagement as dispositions and attitudes that, in varying degrees, reflect how affect and cognition are jointly conducive to aggression and violence.

Irritability, hostile rumination, and moral disengagement all contribute to circumventing individuals' habitual restraints against aggression and violence, albeit through different mechanisms and by exerting different influences at different times. While irritability mostly reflects individuals' inability to resist impulsive aggression, hostile rumination attests to how angry feelings due to self-threatening provocation may turn into desires for retaliation that lead to pursuing aggression as instrumental to restore one's self-esteem and reputation. Taking a developmental perspective, one may guess that some children are more irritable and inclined to respond impulsively to any frustration for a variety of reasons due to their tempera-ment or their environment, and that angry reactions become chronically established under conditions that make them accessible and that reinforce them. Likewise, one may guess that angry reactions foster ruminative thoughts conducive to aggressive behaviors when embedded in systems of social beliefs that make them acceptable as instrumental to affirm or restore ones' self-esteem. Ultimately, moral disengagement operates as a gatekeeper, allowing people to turn negative affect and thoughts into action by supplying the justifications needed to resort to aggression and violence without incurring any painful anticipatory worries.

Yet a common framework to make sense of these relations within a more comprehensive view of personality was still needed.

9.6   Mapping Individual Differences in Aggression within the Personality's Space

I have always believed that personality is more than a collection of behavioral tendencies associated with relatively stable patterns of thoughts and feelings. Yet, I did not doubt that stable patterns of individual differences in affect, cognition, and behavior allow people to recognize and distinguish one individual from another from the early stages of life.

It is likely that people come into the world in some way predisposed, namely equipped, with some kind of potential that enables them to deal with basic tasks of human existence, like making things happen and interacting with others. In this regard, I agree with Bakan (1966) in viewing agency and communion among the basic dimensions of human existence: Humans are agents who tend to extend their influence over the environments in which they live and do so always in relation to others.

Most of the characteristics we habitually take into account to distinguish individuals from one another by using adjectives and nouns and by making reference to hypothetical tendencies, dispositions, or traits can be viewed as manifestations of agency and communion. This does not rule out that other dimensions and predispositions are needed to sustain and promote humans' lives, while it is evident that two dimensions cannot be sufficient to achieve a proper description of a person and to acknowledge what is most distinctive about his or her individuality.

The language people commonly use to speak of themselves and others is a major source to consider when searching for the characteristics and qualities that count most in humans' interactions, namely those that are commonly used to distinguish people from one another and that are most decisive in the choices people make about how to behave with others and about what they should expect from others.

Although thousands of words are commonly used to indicate qualities that make people similar and different from one another, scientists following the psycholexical approach discovered that most descriptors of personality convey similar meanings and can ultimately be traced to a limited number of basic dimensions – the so-called Big Five – that are able to provide a general framework by which to organize major individual differences in personality. Surprisingly, the same dimensions were found by scientists who had long been searching for a comprehensive taxonomy of individual differences in personality using questionnaires and factor analysis.

This convergence of the lexicographic and factor-analytic traditions established the conditions for the great success of the Five-Factor Model as the canonical reference model to describe personality. Despite the notable divergences regarding the nature of factors or dimensions resulting from the factor analysis of descriptors and inventories, extraversion (or energy), agreeableness (or friendliness), conscientiousness, emotional stability (or neuroticism), and openness to experience have been established as the dominant model to map individual differences in personality (Caprara & Cervone, 2000).

The Five-Factor Model also provided the framework we needed in order to examine the semantic space of aggression and to map the various individual differences that have been associated with aggression and violence. In the former case, we examined the words people commonly use to talk of aggression and, in particular, the adjectives people use to judge themselves and others with regards to aggression and violence. In the second case we examined to what extent the above individual differences in aggression could be traced to extraversion, agreeableness, emotional stability, conscientiousness, and openness.

9.7   Both Kinds of Studies Led to Similar Results

The lexical study was conducted with Marco Perugini, who did his doctoral dissertation on the psycholexical approach proving the validity of the Five-Factor Model in the Italian language and subsequently achieved leading positions both in academia and in the European Association of Personality. This study showed that most of the words people use to describe themselves and others with regard to aggression and violence can be traced to two major dimensions: interpersonal orientation and negative affect. One dimension points to the extent to which people's orientation is self- or hetero-centered, and namely more or less attentive to others' needs, while the other dimension concerns the degree of negative affect (Caprara & Perugini, 1992; Caprara, Perugini, & Barbaranelli, 1994).

The factorial study was also conducted with Tina Pastorelli and with Claudio Barbaranelli, who did his dissertation on the children's version of the Big Five questionnaire and later became one of most respected Italian psychometricians (Caprara, Barbaranelli, Pastorelli, & Perugini, 1994).

This study showed that the various measures we developed to assess individual differences in aggression and violence could be traced to the opposite of two main dimensions: hostility (the opposite of agreeableness) and emotional instability (the opposite of emotional stability). Subsequent studies corroborated similar conclusions in adults and children (Caprara, Barbaranelli, et al., 1994).

Similar results were found after including – in addition to irritability, hostile rumination, moral disengagement, and tolerance toward violence – the Trait Anger Scale (Spielberger, Jacobs, Russell, & Crane, 1983) and one of the most commonly used measures like the Aggression Questionnaire (Buss & Perry, 1992). Factor analysis led to the identification of two main factors: positive evaluation of violence and high emotional responsivity, which accounted for about 60% of the variance. Whereas positive evaluation of violence was moderately correlated (negatively) with both agreeableness and emotional stability, high emotional responsivity was only and highly correlated (negatively) with emotional stability. The correlations of both the above factors with extraversion/energy, conscientiousness, and openness were marginal or irrelevant (Caprara, Barbaranelli, & Zimbardo, 1996).

This led us to conclude that current measures of aggression and violence can be traced to two major components: a major affective component that largely overlaps with emotional stability versus emotional instability and a non-irrelevant social cognitive component that mostly correlates with agreeableness versus hostility. The affective component mostly reflects how people manage their emotions, particularly anger. The social cognitive component mostly reflects how people relate with one another as part of the same humanity, carrying the same rights to be respected and protected.

Most of the aggression and violence that we worry about in our daily lives and that is reported by the press reflects a combination of these components. One cannot doubt that disregulated negative affect accounts for most of the violence. Yet, self-serving beliefs and ideologies that legitimize violence and nurture moral disengagement can be no less insidious and lethal.

These findings established the premises of subsequent studies, which aimed to show how the use of individual differences within a comprehensive view of personality might serve to guide interventions aimed at preventing and treating aggression and violence. A first longitudinal study corroborated a conceptual model in which basic traits like emotional stability and agreeableness contribute to aggression and violence through irritability, hostile rumination, and moral disengagement.

The findings pointed to the role played by both emotional stability and agreeableness in countering irritability and hostile rumination, and to the role of defective agreeableness and hostile rumination in fostering moral disengagement, as well as the crucial role of the latter in giving access to aggression and violence (Caprara et al., 2013).

A later study corroborated the validity of the same model (Caprara et al., 2017) on a large group of adolescents referred for externalizing behavior problems, further attesting to the importance of the study of individual differences to examine the interplay of emotion and cognition in the pathways conducive to aggression, and to identify the most effective educational and clinical interventions.

9.8   The Genzano Longitudinal Study

The collaboration with Albert Bandura and Phil Zimbardo was a turning point in my scientific career that revealed extraordinary opportunities of growth for my whole research group in concomitance with frequent and prolonged visits to Stanford between 1990 and 2010.

We met first at a dinner that Phil Zimbardo hosted in his house in San Francisco, with a view to establishing a collaborative agreement between Stanford University and La Sapienza University of Rome under the auspices of the Italian National Council.

The conversation at that dinner set the stage for a long collaboration, which started by conceiving a longitudinal study to be conducted in Genzano di Roma, where we expected to take advantage of collaborations previously established between schools and the town's administration.

Later, an agreement was established between the two universities and further supported by the Fulbright's Italian Commission, while our research benefited over time from the financial support of the Guggenheim, Jacobs, Grant, and Spencer Foundations, in addition to those of La Sapienza University of Rome and of the Italian Ministry of Education.

The longitudinal study started with children aged 8–9 at the elementary school of Genzano, a hill town of 20,000 inhabitants 30 km from Rome. Although officially starting in 1993, it included data that were collected previously in the same schools for other projects. It went on for almost 20 years and harvested data that have still not been fully exploited. At that time my family was living in Genzano, and we benefited from the full support of the mayor and of the school heads. This allowed us to target the entire school population and to follow several cohorts of children from third grade to the end of high school and beyond. First, we collected data every year and then every other year. The participation of teachers and parents was high and continuous, and we reciprocated by providing consultations when needed and delivering special lectures when required. The attrition rate was minimal while children attended elementary school and moderate when the transitions to junior high and senior high schools implied changes of location and courses of study.

Today, most of the children who participated in the study have their own grown-up children.

Tina Pastorelli took care of maintaining excellent relations with the schools and with the town's administration, and supervised the collection of data over the entire project. Claudio Barbaranelli played a major role in making the most skillful use of data. Ultimately, dozens of papers attested to the productivity of our research team and paved the way for the academic careers of our students.

9.9 Marginal Deviations

The theory of marginal deviations is among the most important outcomes of the Genzano Longitudinal Study. The theory points to risk mechanisms leading to various forms of maladjustment, including aggression, as the result of the reciprocal effects of individual differences in personality and social psychological processes of labeling, attribution, and reputation. In this regard my colleagues and I are greatly indebted to both Phil Zimbardo and Ken Dodge, who contributed to ground the theory on solid arguments and research results (Caprara, 1992; Caprara, Dodge, Pastorelli, & Zelli, 2006, 2007; Caprara & Zimbardo, 1996). The theory focuses on how marginal deviations from normative expectations, across a variety of social behaviors, may elicit aversive reactions on the part of peers, teachers, and significant others that contribute to the enhancement of aggression as a response to rejection, and ultimately to an aggressive reputation. This may occur when the disturbing effects of a variety of defective behaviors, often due to lack of proper socialization and adequate self-regulation, become aggregated and amplified over time, fostering avoidant interactions and aggressive attributions, thus fueling a perverse cycle of greater deviations and more negative reactions by others.

The theory posits that many children who come to be characterized as aggressive are simply socially misfit at the beginning. Yet these children may have an aggressive career through a complex sequence of psychological processes that are largely unrecognized or misconstrued by peers and teachers. The aggregated effects of initial behaviors that are only slightly at odds with the norms become amplified and transformed into noxious behaviors through misperceptions, misattributions, and labels that are not conducive to stable dispositions.

While 'aggression' and 'aggressive' are terms used to cover a variety of children's disruptive behaviors, they may have negative consequences when they involve causal attributions that transcend the intentions of children. Once a child is labeled aggressive, rather than just socially inadequate and unskilled, aggression may be the result, rather than the source, of a deviant trajectory.

9.10   Self-Efficacy Beliefs and Prosocial Behavior

The topic that originally led Bandura and me to share our ideas and to conceive a common project of research together was aggression, on the premise that a longitudinal study would allow us to investigate its stability and change, and eventually to illuminate the sources of individual differences that had been previously associated with aggression.

In reality, aggression was destined to take a marginal role in our subsequent research due to the fact that the aggressive behaviors that one can register in the classroom are relatively rare and constitute a very special kind of destructive and violent behavior that threatens our societies. Children who use physical and verbal aggression, such as harming and insulting more frequently than their peers, are often more irritable, more tolerant of violence, more inclined to moral disengagement, and generally less well adjusted. Individual differences associated with aggression are relatively stable, but aggression itself tends to decrease with the advancement of age, after reaching a peak in early adolescence. Likely, social adjustment requires the capacity to manage negative emotions and moods such as anger, grudge holding, fear, jealousy, envy; to refrain from physical and verbal aggression; and to express one's negative affect and feelings through more sociable channels like avoidance, gossip, and criticism. Aggressive children were among the ones more vulnerable to taking deviant pathways, to abandoning school, and to dropping out of our research project.

Without regret I came to the conclusion that much of the aggression and violence that I intended to address was destined to remain out of reach of my research. This was due not to a devaluation of the relevance of earlier studies and of new findings deriving from the longitudinal study, but to a realistic appraisal of what I could and wanted to do. Crimes of violence, terrorism, wars – indeed, most manifestations of human hostility and destructivity – were too far from the experiments I could do and from the populations I could study. Today, I am inclined to believe that clinical and field research can most effectively reveal the mentalities and the contingencies that justify and foster aggression and violence, and ultimately the extent to which their sources can be traced to biology, culture, and experiences of life.

Self-efficacy beliefs came to occupy a central role in our research program, and prosocial behavior appeared a promising topic to investigate in order to sustain education and well-adjustment. Social cognitive theory provided a framework in which self-reflection, intentionality, and self-regulation guide behavior in accordance with personal standards within a context of social relations. Thus, traits, motives, values, and self-beliefs have been viewed as the hypothetical structure of a system – personality – whose development and functioning rest upon the experiences that are made accessible. Individual differences in any of the above structures represent cues to the whole system that one may reconstruct by investigating their relations and changes across situations and over time.

Self-efficacy beliefs exert a key role in orienting behavior and in sustaining motivation. However, one cannot appreciate the power of self-efficacy beliefs without acknowledging the unique faculties that enable human beings to manage their course of life by taking advantage of their and others' experiences while feeling responsible for the outcomes of their actions. One cannot fully appreciate the pervasive impact of self-efficacy beliefs without broadening their conceptualization from specific tasks to domains of functioning, such as emotion regulation and management of interpersonal relations. Feeling capable of managing one's own emotions and interpersonal relations is in fact conditional on self-efficacy beliefs and being successful in most activities (Bandura, Caprara, Barbaranelli, Gerbino, & Pastorelli, 2003; Caprara, 2002).

Deviating from Bandura's orthodox thinking to a certain extent, we addressed individual differences in self-efficacy beliefs and examined their relations with other aspects of personality, such as traits and values, to account for adaptation and achievement across tasks and situations, and to investigate their reciprocal relations.

The study of prosocial behavior, in particular, provided a model of the advantages that may derive from the knowledge of personality by integrating the contributions of different traditions of research like trait theory, Bandura's social cognitive theory (1997), and Shalom Schwartz's theory of values (1992).

First, we showed the relevance of prosocial behavior, as self-reported and rated by others, to predict academic achievement and well-adjustment over several years (Caprara, Barbaranelli, Pastorelli, Bandura, & Zimbardo, 2000). Then, we showed how traits, self-efficacy beliefs, and values – operating in concert – account for most of the variation in prosociality (Caprara, Alessandri, & Eisenberg, 2012).

Mental structures that emerge from the encounter of the organism with the environment and that are mostly shaped by the social environment, traits set the conditions for stable patterns of affect, thought, and action, and earlier development of habit and capacities. Values establish priorities, account for meanings, and dictate the course individuals' behavior should take in order to preserve their self-respect and their social obligations. Self-efficacy beliefs attest to the faculties of mind to learn, to capitalize upon mastery experiences, and to anticipate the outcomes of ones' actions, and are decisive in supplying the motivation to take action, since people, in general, do not address tasks and situations that do not have reasonable chances of success.

Along this line of reasoning we developed an intervention geared to promoting prosocial behaviors that proved valid to foster well-adjustment and to counter aggression and violence (Caprara et al., 2015). All this was made possible thanks to the imagination of a new generation of students, including Guido Alessandri, Maria Grazia Gerbino, Paula Luengo Kanacri, and Antonio Zuffianò – students who soon became colleagues with promising academic careers in Italy and abroad.

I am inclined to believe that the same conceptual model, including traits, values, and self-efficacy beliefs that proved valid to account for prosocial behavior could also prove valid for violence. It is likely that aggressive and violent behaviors, in varying degrees and combinations, are exhibited by people who are predisposed to harming others in the pursuit of their own interests, who are capable of making use of aggression and violence to achieve their goals and to enhance themselves, and do not care much for others' humanity.

In this regard history provides numerous examples of cultures, world-views, and institutions that legitimize and nurture aggression and violence, and have made aggressive individuals very successful.

9.11   Mentors, Peers, and Unfinished Endeavors

Coming to the end of this narrative in which biographical memories interlace with scientific curiosity and ambition, I realize that living long enough has allowed me to stay the course despite my extravagant digressions. There is coherence between the motivations that led me to embrace psychology and the topics that I have addressed, as there is continuity between my earlier and later work. Certainly, chance played a great role in my decisions, as did my encounters.

Yet, the person in society continued to be the object of my interest and the target of my research. My first publication, in 1970, appeared in the proceedings of a conference where I had been invited to give a talk entitled 'Overcoming Psychological Conflicts Which Underlie International Tensions'. My latest book, with Michele Vecchione, was published in 2017 and is entitled *Personalizing Politics and Realizing Democracy*. There is more than a resonance between the ideals that led me to psychology and my subsequent work. Many people I met and the discussions I had with them have exerted a great influence on the development of my thought. I am grateful to many mentors beyond my teachers. In several cases, peers were my mentors. I did research that attracted and addressed topics I believed to be socially relevant and within reach. I cannot regret being an optimist. Being positive has likely been a strength that has become the target of much of my scientific investigation in the last decade (Caprara, Alessandri, & Caprara, 2019). After being a party militant in my youth, I turned to politics with the wisdom of old age, being convinced that democracy, despite its current dysfunctions, is the form of government most congenial to human development and that nothing is more needed for democracy than a theory of the person able to achieve its full realization as the ultimate goal of politics. This occurred in a time of renewed consideration of personality on the part of psychologists and political scientists. Traits and values, in fact, have proved to account for ideology, political preference, and participation much more than any other socioeconomic variable of the past. Traits and values, however, do not seem sufficient to fully account for the conduct of citizens and politicians and, ultimately, for the functioning of democratic institutions. Democracy, in fact, is not just a matter of voicing one's opinions but also of listening to others' views and needs, and basically of recognition and respect for each other's humanity and dignity. Ultimately, it is a moral enterprise that rests upon mutual obligations with regard to the pursuit of the public good in order to grant all individuals a life worth living.

This led me to realize the limits of a theory of personality that does not address ethics and of having paid little attention to morality in my previous work on aggression and violence. In this regard, I am particularly indebted to the discussions that I regularly had with Augusto Blasi after his return to Rome. In addressing values, we largely avoided examining in depth the extent to which the values people prioritize operate as conventional obligations or personal thoughts that they cannot dismiss without jeopardizing their self-respect. Likewise, in addressing moral disengagement, we avoided examining in depth the degree to which the various mechanisms reflect self-serving distortions that accord with conventional systems of beliefs rather than strategies aimed at circumventing internalized moral obligations.

In reality, we underestimated the potential role of morality in extending one's aspirations beyond the care of one's own beloved and the contingencies of one's own course of life to embrace what is good for all humanity. Consequently, we did not pay enough attention to actions that should be taken to sustain moral development and education.

In this regard, I doubt that people are disposed to transcend their personal and in-group's interests in the pursuit of the common good unless they have the conviction that it is fair to do so and unless such a conviction becomes part of their identity. Even in cultures that praise universalistic values and celebrate the virtues of truth, integrity, and honesty, there is a gulf between what people consider morally just and their conduct in everyday life. Indeed, morality is not a matter of intuition but mostly of reasoning and will, since moral agency is a potential of human beings that actualizes to the extent that it is nurtured and practiced. Thus, I doubt that aggression and violence can be properly addressed without addressing in depth the historical and social foundations of the legitimization of harming others and the extent to which individuals' moral development may transcend such a legitimization. Following this reasoning, I realize the limits of my endeavors, but I have no reason to surrender.

References

Bakan, D. (1966). *The duality of human existence: An essay on psychology and religion*. Chicago, IL: Rand McNally.

Bandura, A. (1986). *Social foundations of thought and action: A social cognitive theory*. Englewood Cliffs, NJ: Prentice Hall.

Bandura, A. (1997). *Self-efficacy: The exercise of control*. New York, NY: Freeman.

Bandura, A. (2016). *Moral disengagement: How people do harm and live with themselves*. New York, NY: Worth Publishers Macmillan Learning.

Bandura, A., Barbaranelli, C., Caprara, G. V., & Pastorelli, C. (1996). Mechanisms of moral disengagement in the exercise of moral agency. *Journal of Personality and Social Psychology, 71*(2), 364–374.

Bandura, A., Caprara, G. V., Barbaranelli, C., Gerbino, M., & Pastorelli, C. (2003). Role of affective self-regulatory efficacy in diverse spheres of psychosocial functioning. *Child Development, 74*(3), 769–782.

Buss, A. H., & Perry, M. (1992). The aggression questionnaire. *Journal of Personality and Social Psychology, 63*(3), 452–459.

Caprara, G. V. (1986). Indicators of aggression: The dissipation–rumination scale. *Personality and Individual Differences, 7*(6), 763–769.

Caprara, G. V. (1992). Marginal deviations, aggregate effects, disruption of continuity, and deviation amplifying mechanisms. In P. J. Hettema & I. J. Deary (Eds.), *Foundations of personality* (pp. 227–244). Dordrecht, the Netherlands: Kluwer.

Caprara, G. V. (1996). Structures and processes in personality psychology. *European Psychologist, 1*(1), 14–26.

Caprara, G. V. (2002). Personality psychology: Filling the gap between basic processes and molar functioning. In C. V. Hofsten & L. Backman (Eds.), *Psychology at the turn of the millennium* (Vol. 2, pp. 201–224). Brighton, England: Psychology Press.

Caprara, G. V., Alessandri, G., & Caprara, M. G. (2019). Associations of positive orientation with health and psychosocial adaptation: A review of findings and perspectives. *Asian Journal of Social Psychology*, 22(2), 126–132.

Caprara, G. V., Alessandri, G., & Eisenberg, N. (2012). Prosociality: The contribution of traits, values, and self-efficacy beliefs. *Journal of Personality and Social Psychology*, 102(6), 1289–1303.

Caprara, G. V., Alessandri, G., Tisak, M. S., Paciello, M., Caprara, M. G., Gerbino, M., & Fontaine, R. G. (2013). Individual differences in personality conducive to engagement in aggression and violence. *European Journal of Personality*, 27, 290–303.

Caprara, G. V., Barbaranelli, C., Pastorelli, C., Bandura, A., & Zimbardo, P. G. (2000). Prosocial foundations of children's academic achievement. *Psychological Science*, 11(4), 302–306.

Caprara, G. V., Barbaranelli, C., Pastorelli, C., & Perugini, M. (1994). Individual differences in the study of human aggression. *Aggressive Behavior*, 20(4), 291–303.

Caprara, G. V., Barbaranelli, C., Vicino, S., & Bandura, A. (1996). La misura del disimpegno morale [The assessment of moral disengagement]. *Rassegna di psicologia*, 13, 93–105.

Caprara, G. V., Barbaranelli, C., & Zimbardo, P. G. (1996). Understanding the complexity of human aggression: Affective, cognitive, and social dimensions of individual differences in propensity toward aggression. *European Journal of Personality*, 10(2), 133–155.

Caprara, G. V., & Cervone, D. (2000). *Personality: Determinants, dynamics, and potentials*. Cambridge, England: Cambridge University Press.

Caprara, G. V., Cinanni, V., D'imperio, G., Passerini, S., Renzi, P., & Travaglia, G. (1985). Indicators of impulsive aggression: Present status of research on irritability and emotional susceptibility scales. *Personality and Individual Differences*, 6(6), 665–674.

Caprara, G. V., Cinanni, V., & Mazzotti, E. (1989). Measuring attitudes toward violence. *Personality and Individual Differences*, 10(4), 479–481.

Caprara, G. V., Coluzzi, M., Mazzotti, E., Renzi, P., & Zelli, A. (1985). Effect of insult and dissipation–rumination on delayed aggression and hostility. *Archivio di Psicologia, Neurologia e Psichiatria*, 46, 130–139.

Caprara, G. V., D'Imperio, G., Gentilomo, A., Mammucari, A., Renzi, P., & Travaglia, G. (1987). The intrusive commercial: Influence of aggressive TV commercials on aggression. *European Journal of Social Psychology*, 17, 23–31.

Caprara, G. V., Dodge, K. A., Pastorelli, C., & Zelli, A. (2006). The effects of marginal deviations on behavioral development. *European Psychologist*, 11(2), 79–89.

Caprara, G. V., Dodge, K. A., Pastorelli, C., & Zelli, A. (2007). How marginal deviations sometimes grow into serious aggression. *Child Development Perspectives*, 1(1), 33–39.

Caprara, G. V., Gerbino, M., Perinelli, E., Alessandri, G., Lenti, C., Walder, M., … Nobile, M. (2017). Individual differences in personality associated with aggressive behavior among adolescents referred for externalizing behavior problems. *Journal of Psychopathology and Behavioral Assessment,* *39*(4), 680–692.

Caprara, G. V., Luengo Kanacri, B. P., Zuffianò, A., Gerbino, M., & Pastorelli, C. (2015). Why and how to promote adolescents' prosocial behaviors: Direct, mediated and moderated effects of the CEPIDEA school-based program. *Journal of Youth and Adolescence,* *44*(12), 2211–2229.

Caprara, G. V., Manzi, J., & Perugini, M. (1992). Investigating guilt in relation to emotionality and aggression. *Personality and Individual Differences,* *13*(5), 519–532.

Caprara, G. V., Passerini, S., Pastorelli, C., Renzi, P., & Zelli, A. (1986). Instigating and measuring interpersonal aggression and hostility: A methodological contribution. *Aggressive Behavior,* *12*(4), 237–247.

Caprara, G. V., Pastorelli, C., & Bandura, A. (1995). La misura del disimpegno morale in età evolutiva. *Età evolutiva,* *46*, 18–29.

Caprara, G. V., & Perugini, M. (1992). The semantic space of aggression: Evidence in support of a componential analysis and practical implications. *Ricerche di Psicologia,* *2*, 19–43.

Caprara, G. V., Perugini, M., & Barbaranelli, C. (1994). Studies of individual differences in aggression. In M. Potegal & J. Knutson (Eds.), *The dynamics of aggression. Biological and social processes in dyads and groups.* Hillsdale, NJ: Lawrence Erlbaum.

Caprara, G. V., Renzi, P., Alcini, P., D'Imperio, G., & Travaglia, G. (1983). Instigation to aggress and escalation of aggression examined from a persono-logical perspective: The role of irritability and of emotional susceptibility. *Aggressive Behavior,* *9*(4), 345–351.

Caprara, G. V., Renzi, P., Amolini, P., D'Imperio, G., & Travaglia, G. (1984). The eliciting cue value of aggressive slides reconsidered in a personological perspective: The weapons effect and irritability. *European Journal of Social Psychology,* *14*(3), 313–322.

Caprara, G. V., Renzi, P., D'Augello, D., D'Imperio, G., Rielli, I., & Travaglia, G. (1986). Interpolating physical exercise between instigation to aggress and aggression: The role of irritability and emotional susceptibility. *Aggressive Behavior,* *12*(2), 83–91.

Caprara, G. V., Tisak, M. S., Alessandri, G., Fontaine, R. G., Fida, R., & Paciello, M. (2014). The contribution of moral disengagement in mediating individual tendencies toward aggression and violence. *Developmental Psychology,* *50*, 71–85.

Caprara, G. V., & Zimbardo, P. G. (1996). Aggregation and amplification of marginal deviations in the social construction of personality and maladjust-ment. *European Journal of Personality,* *10*(2), 79–110.

Schwartz, S. H. (1992). Universals in the content and structure of values: Theoretical advances and empirical tests in 20 countries. In M. Zanna (Ed.), *Advances in experimental social psychology* (Vol. 25, pp. 1–65). New York, NY: Academic Press.

Spielberger, C. D., Jacobs, G., Russell, S., & Crane, R. S. (1983). Assessment of anger: The state-trait anger scale. In J. Butcher & C. Spielberger (Eds.), *Advances in personality assessment* (Vol. 2, pp. 161–189). Hillsdale, NJ: Lawrence Erlbaum.

10 A Tortuous Path towards Understanding and Preventing the Development of Chronic Physical Aggression

Richard E. Tremblay

Richard E. Tremblay was born November 23, 1944, in Barrie, Ontario, Canada. He received a PhD in Educational Psychology from the University of London in England in 1976. His first faculty appointment (1976) was at the University of Montreal (Canada), where he is now Emeritus Professor of Pediatrics and Psychology. He is also Emeritus Professor in the School of Public Health at University College Dublin (Ireland). Among his numerous awards, he received the 2017 Stockholm Prize in Criminology, the 2010 John Paul Scott Award for lifetime contributions to research on aggression from the International Society for Research on Aggression (ISRA), and the American Society of Criminology's Sellin-Glueck Award (2005). In addition, he was the first to receive the Joan McCord Prize from the Academy of Experimental Criminology (2004). In 2019 he was named Officer of the Order of Canada, created by Queen Elizabeth II and the highest distinction for a Canadian citizen.

Richard Tremblay participated in the creation of numerous longitudinal and experimental studies to unravel the early development of chronic physical aggression and to identify effective early preventive interventions. He authored and co-authored more than 700 articles that appeared in leading journals of criminology, pediatrics, psychiatry, neuroscience, developmental psychology, epidemiology, psychometrics, and epigenetics, and in leading multidisciplinary scientific journals. He is among the small number of human development researchers who systematically used an integrated bio-psycho-social approach.

'Social learning' of aggression was the dominant hypothesis when Tremblay initiated his first longitudinal and experimental study of children's development in 1984. The aim was to document the social learning hypothesis with annual assessments of 1,037 kindergarten boys from schools in poor areas of Montreal (Canada). One of the most important results (Nagin & Tremblay, 1999), highlighted in *Science*

241

(Holden, 2000), showed that the boys' frequency of physical aggressions from kindergarten to adolescence decreased, rather than increased with age, as would be expected from a social learning perspective. These results led Tremblay to start a population-based longitudinal study of 2,000 children from 5 months of age onward in order to identify the age of onset of physical aggressions and trace their development up to adulthood. Results showed that infants started to physically aggress before the end of the first year of life (Tremblay et al., 1999). Frequency of physical aggressions substantially increased between 8 and 42 months of age (Tremblay et al., 2004), followed by a universal decrease in physical aggression frequency until adulthood (Tremblay & Côté, 2009). In his 2011 best-selling book on the decline of violence over the past centuries, Harvard University professor Steven Pinker (Pinker, 2011) wrote: 'Richard Tremblay ... (has) shown that the most violent stage of life is not adolescence or even young adulthood but the aptly named terrible twos' (p. 483). Tremblay's work clearly showed that the urgent research question asked in the 1960s and 1970s – 'How do children learn to aggress?' – has now been replaced by a new pressing research question, 'How do children learn not to aggress?' (Holden, 2000).

Tremblay's longitudinal study of kindergarten boys from schools in poor areas of Montreal included a randomized clinical trial, thus anticipating the recommendation made by the Justice Study Program Group of the MacArthur Foundation (Farrington, Ohlin, & Wilson, 1986), which concluded: 'We believe that the best method of advancing knowledge about these (and other) key issues is by means of longitudinal-experimental surveys ... The kind of projects proposed here have never before been attempted in the field of criminology' (p. 151–152). The Montreal experimental preventive intervention with physically aggressive kindergarten boys from low socio-economic environments showed, with long-term repeated assessments up to adulthood, significant reductions of substance abuse, school drop-out, juvenile delinquency, and adult criminality (Boisjoli, Vitaro, Lacourse, Barker, & Tremblay, 2007; Castellanos-Ryan, Séguin, Vitaro, Parent, & Tremblay, 2013; Tremblay, Pagani-Kurtz, Mâsse, Vitaro, & Pihl, 1995).

The term 'epigenetics' was used by 19th-century biologists to refer to putative environmental impacts on genetic inheritance, a concept that almost disappeared with the advent of molecular genetics, where the focus was put exclusively on inherited genes. However, epigenetic research exploded over the past two decades because we can now measure gene expression and adverse environmental impacts on the expression of genes. In 2004 Tremblay started working with a cancer epigenetic specialist (Moshe Szyf), after he heard him describe how his team had shown that maternal behavior of rats (licking) had impacts on their offspring's ability to regulate stress through modification of gene expression. In his Joan McCord Award lecture at the American Society of Criminology annual meeting in 2004, Tremblay was the first to describe how epigenetic mechanisms could play a role in the developmental origins of chronic physical aggression (Tremblay, 2005). Ten years later, his pioneering work in criminological epigenetics was featured in the leading science journal *Nature* (Hall, 2014). This work showed that boys and girls on a chronic physical aggression trajectory have a significantly different epigenetic profile from those on a 'normal physical aggression trajectory' (Guillemin et al., 2014; Provençal, Booij, & Tremblay, 2015). It also showed that a pathway from adverse prenatal and postnatal environment to chronic physical aggression might be through epigenetic modifications of brain serotonin synthesis, an important regulator of self-control (Provençal et al., 2015). By showing that chronically aggressive children have atypical DNA expression profiles, his work suggests that prenatal and early postnatal bio-psycho-social interventions are needed to prevent early onset of chronic physical aggression problems that may partly be the consequence of neurodevelopmental problems triggered by adverse environmental impacts on epigenetic mechanisms (Tremblay, Vitaro, & Côté, 2018).

In 2000 Tremblay created the Center of Excellence on Early Childhood Development and the online on Early Childhood Development, which receives more than one million visitors a year. Tremblay received numerous recognitions from national and international societies, besides those mentioned above. They include: the Laufer Prevention Award from the French Academy of Moral and Political Sciences (2008) and the International Research Prize from the Italian Società Libera (2011). He was made Grand Officer of Chile's Gabriella Mistral Order of Merit (2008) by President Michelle Bachelet for his contributions to knowledge on children's early education. He was elected Fellow of the American Society for the Advancement of Science in 2012, Fellow of the Academy of Experimental Criminology in 2002, and Fellow of the Royal Society of Canada in 1997. The awards Tremblay received outside of Canada reflect his extensive international involvement in research, knowledge transfer, and policy. He collaborated in the publication of scientific articles with data from a variety of countries, including Finland, France, Ireland, Italy, the Netherlands, New Zealand, Norway, Russia, the United Kingdom, and the United States. According to Google Scholar, he is among the most frequently cited authors in child development, child psychiatry, criminology, and pediatrics.

10.1   Rivers, Religions, and Revolutions that Divide and Unite (1936–1944)

I was born in the Canadian city of Barrie, on November 23, 1944. The most significant 1939–1945 war event of that day appears to have been the liberation of Alsace and its capital, Strasbourg. Three years later, Strasbourg became the seat of the European Council, and in 1958 the seat of the European Parliament.

The history of Strasbourg is a good example of the history of violent behavior among humans over the past 1,500 years. It is located geographically at the heart of Europe. It sits on the left bank of the Rhine River, which flows 1,233 km from Switzerland to the North Sea, acting as a border for Liechtenstein, Austria, Germany, and France, before running into the Atlantic after having crossed the Netherlands.

Being near the center of this European spinal cord was an advantage for Strasbourg when it came time to choose a city to host the European Parliament. But that advantage has also been a major disadvantage throughout history. The citizens of Strasbourg and Alsace have had to frequently change nationality, language, and religion since 58 B.C. when the Romans controlled Strasbourg (*Argentoratum*). For example, in A.D. 506 Alsace was under the rule of Clovis, the Frank king who created France. In 925 Alsace became German under King Henry 1; in 1648 it became French again under Louis XIV; in 1871 it returned to German rule and again back to France in 1918, with a German occupation from 1940–1944. Physical violence was naturally a major part of these transitions.

In contrast to Strasbourg, the Canadian town of Barrie, my birthplace, was small, and remains largely unknown. However, there are some similarities. Barrie is situated on a trail used by the first humans in North America when they traveled between Lake Ontario and Lake Huron, two of the North American Great Lakes. The area served as a supply depot for British forces during the 1812–1814 North American war between the United States and Britain. The name 'Barrie' was given to the town because the commander of the British forces, in 1812, was Sir Robert Barrie, a famous navy commander who fought against the United States and France, taking numerous prisoners, including Lucien Bonaparte, the brother of Emperor Napoleon Bonaparte (Wikipedia, n.d.).

Although born in Barrie, I never felt that it was my hometown. I simply happened to be born in Barrie because of the war in Europe. As a soldier, my father was stationed at Camp Borden, a military base 31 km from Barrie, and approximately 100 km from Toronto, the largest city in

Canada. Camp Borden was established during the First World War to train soldiers who would be sent to fight in Europe. The Royal Canadian Air Force was created at camp Borden in 1917. Between 1939 and 1945, Camp Borden was the largest Canadian training center for soldiers who had volunteered to fight in Europe (the uncles of Jean Golding who were in the Canadian Air Force were probably trained at Camp Borden, see Chapter 3, page 51).

I consider that my real childhood 'hometown' was 412 km northeast of Barrie: the city of Hull (recently renamed Gatineau), where my father and mother lived before my father became a soldier, and where I was probably conceived. Hull is on the eastern shore of the Ottawa River, which is slightly longer than the Rhine (1,271 km), and faces Canada's capital, Ottawa. The two cities are 'twin cities' separated by the river and linked by bridges. However, Ottawa and Hull are not identical twins! Ottawa is in the province of Ontario, and Hull in the province of Quebec. The Ottawa River, like the Rhine River, separated people who spoke different languages and had different religions: English-speaking Protestants in Ottawa and French-speaking Catholics in Hull.

Both my mother and father were born in the city of Hull. My father (Wilfrid Arthur Tremblay) was born December 7, 1917, while my mother (Hectorine Fournier) was born on January 6, 1920. During his childhood, my father moved with his parents to another border town, Windsor, Ontario, the Canadian city that is separated, by the Detroit River, from the city of Detroit in the United States. My grandfather, a house builder, had taken advantage of the boom created on both sides of the Detroit River by Henry Ford's automobile industry. My father came back to live in Hull at 18 years of age, when he was recruited to play rugby (which was starting to be called 'American football') and baseball, while studying mechanics at the Hull technical school. In 1938 he started to play professional football with the Ottawa Rough Riders. The date on family photos suggests that my father and mother became sweethearts in 1936.

The war started during my father's second year as a professional. His team won the national championship during his third year. Although conscription was voted in 1940, soldiers were sent to Europe only if they volunteered. More than 1.1 million Canadians served in the Canadian Forces (Army, Air Force, and Navy). Approximately 44,000 lost their lives, and 54,000 were wounded. Canadian soldiers specifically played an important role in liberating the Netherlands, while the future Queen, Juliana of the Netherlands, lived in Ottawa and gave birth to her daughter Margriet.

Many professional football players, including my father, were not required to join the army at the start of the war. However, after 1942, the football league had to stop activities because most players had to join the army. My father became Corporal Tremblay and was responsible for the soldiers' physical training before they were sent to fight in Europe.

While my father served at Camp Borden near Barrie, my mother worked for the Federal Government in Ottawa. I was apparently conceived in February 1944 (St. Valentine's Day?!) when my father went to see his sweetheart in Hull, or she went to visit him in Barrie, or they met in Toronto or ... ? My mother was now 24 years old and my father was 26. They decided to get married when my mother discovered she was pregnant. However, they apparently did all they could to hide the fact that I was conceived out of wedlock.

They were living at a time when moral behavior was strictly controlled by the Catholic Church in the Canadian province of Quebec. The marriage took place in Hull, on June 12, 1944. They went to Niagara Falls for their honeymoon and went on to live in Barrie, near the army camp.

I was born on November 23 in the Barrie hospital, but my parents waited until December 23 to announce the birth to their families (by telephone?), explaining that I was born prematurely because my mother had fallen down stairs. They went to Hull at the end of January, and I was baptized on February 4, 1945. My maternal grandparents were my godparents. The official document (the baptism certificate), signed by my parents, my maternal grandparents, and the priest, declared that I was born on December 23, 1944. Baptism certificates recorded in the church archives were, at that time, official birth records used for numerous purposes, including registration at school and obtaining a driver's license or a passport.

At the time of my birth, no one could have predicted the huge cultural revolution that would occur while I was growing up. These important social changes were eventually named the 'quiet revolution'.

Until the late 1950s the Catholic Church dominated everyday life, education, and politics. I remember that, during the summer months, my grandmother would say to my aunts, who were in their 20s, not to go in front of the house if they were wearing shorts in case a parish priest should pass by.

The late 1950s and 1960s saw the decline of the power of the Church in everyday life, in education, and in health services. The Church also lost its political influence. The secular government implemented a welfare state, and there was a strong push for Quebec's independence, which almost led to its separation from Canada between 1976 and 1995.

Being born at the forefront of the baby boom, which fed the quiet revolution in Quebec, I largely benefited from the numerous sociocultural changes that occurred, as well as from the numerous resources that were invested to create the changes in services needed to give adequate educational and health services to the baby boomers. Interestingly, the quiet social revolution was followed by the 'contraceptive pill revolution'. This led the baby boomers to have the lowest reproductive rates in the world, after their grandparents had had some of the highest. Indeed, from 1900 to 2015 the reproduction rate went from 40 to 10 births per 1,000 women (Rocha, 2015).

Because the state eventually took over most of the responsibilities of the Church, civil documents replaced sacred church documents. So, when in 1982 I had to renew my passport to take a sabbatical leave in France, I was required, for the first time, to present an official birth certificate, rather than a baptism certificate. From that official birth certificate, which I obtained from the province of Ontario, I learned my real birth date – I was not the premature baby so often described by my mother's younger sisters as needing careful attention. I don't know how I would have dealt with this secret if my mother had still been alive (she died when I was 12 years old), but on November 23, following my return to Canada from a sabbatical in France, I invited my father for dinner to his club's restaurant and ordered a bottle of Champagne. 'Why the Champagne?', he asked. 'It's my birthday, Dad!' He answered timidly: 'I told your mother that you would eventually find out'.

After I was baptized, my mother did not go back to Barrie, and my father was soon with us again, because Germany unconditionally surrendered 3 months later (May 8, 1945). My parents decided to live with my grandparents for a while. My grandfather was ill, and my father could play the man's role in the house where my mother's four youngest sisters and a brother still lived. I thus spent my early childhood being cared for by six adult women, a weak grandfather, and a very athletic father, who went back to playing professional football.

10.2 From Aspiring Football Player to Physical Education Teacher (1950–1966)

I started elementary school in 1950, and in 1962 I started my BA, specializing in physical education. I was growing up just one step ahead of the first wave of baby boomers. On the radio we heard of the distant Korean War, and, with time, we became very conscious of the Cold War. I remember a morning when I took a bus crossing the Ottawa River to go to school and heard the extremely loud sirens warning of a possible nuclear attack. I was quite certain that it was only an exercise, but I deeply felt that I was living in a very dangerous world.

However, American football and hockey were the center of my life. I started organizing football games with cousins and friends when I was around 10 years old. My success in creating research teams for longitudinal and experimental studies is possibly due, in part, to the long experience I had in getting friends together to play American football, a game where each player has a very specific role and success depends largely on having players who work hard at mastering specific skills and are able to collaborate.

Compared to other team sports, such as soccer, baseball, cricket, basketball, and volleyball, American football is a game that involves serious physical aggression. You need to learn complex skills but also to hit and get hit hard, while maintaining control of your emotions. The fear and anger of being hit, as well as the pleasure of hitting, becomes a way of life. Your bleeding nose, sore knees, and broken ribs are warrior trophies. I realized during my academic career that it probably hurts less to be hit by an opponent when you are running with the football toward his goal line, than when you receive an aggressive anonymous review for a grant proposal or a paper submitted to a scientific journal. During a football game you know who hit you, and you can learn how to run away from that person on the next play or in the next game. To survive in academia, you often need to learn to dodge unknown aggressors!

By the time I was 10 years old, my father was coaching the hockey team in which my younger brother and I learned to excel. My brother eventually became a professional hockey player. Being less talented and more intellectually oriented, I eventually played hockey for the University of Ottawa, where I majored in physical education.

My adolescence was not typical. Adult supervision was minimal because my mother had died and my father traveled a lot. My main goals were to excel in football and hockey while surviving in school. I must also have had some form of leadership skills because I ended up being president and vice president of my class a few times in high school as well as during my undergraduate years. My brother's adolescence was different. Although he was very successful in school when he decided to study, he was peer- and pleasure-oriented. In hindsight, I realize that he probably suffered more from our mother's death because he was younger and more emotionally sensitive. Being a very good hockey player, he was offered a contract from a professional hockey organization and went to live near Toronto. This meant that his peers were similarly talented hockey players who did not invest in high school because they hoped to become professional players. When I compare my brother's life and mine, I am puzzled by the extent to which, having been brought up in the same environment until 15–16 years of age, we had dramatically different trajectories. My brother committed suicide when he was 32.

I believe that I was kept in line by two powerful motivations, my academic interests and my high school sweetheart, whom I married just before my last year in college. Although sports had been the center of my life, I was also strongly attracted to the pleasure of learning, in the sense of getting to the root of things. When I started learning to count in primary school, I took a notebook and started to write the numbers from one onward, with the aim of getting to the end of numbers. I realized that this experience must be common when I read that a famous modern painter, Roman Opalka, had spent the last 46 years of his life doing this on canvas. I was also very much attracted by philosophy, literature, and psychology. By the end of my third year as a major in physical education, it became clear that I had neither the talent nor the desire to become a professional hockey or football player. I could very well see from my father's long and famous football career that lengthy careers in sports ended at best in the early 30s. I also realized that I was not very much attracted by the prospect of becoming a high school physical education teacher.

10.3   First Contacts with Mental Illness and Delinquency (1966–1973)

10.3.1   Mental Illness (1966–1967)

I started my fourth year in physical education when my wife and I came back from our weekend honeymoon. It was time to find the job I would take after my graduation. There were numerous jobs offered on the billboard of the physical education department at the University of Ottawa. One of them especially caught my attention: a newly built psychiatric hospital was looking for a physical education graduate to take responsibility for the patients' recreational program. The reason I was attracted to this offer was serendipitous. During the summer break I had read a novel (*Lilith*) by J. R. Salamanca in which a young male recreational therapist in a mental hospital falls in love with a seductive and bright female patient. I had bought that novel because my wife's nickname happened to be Lilith. Another reason to be attracted by this job offer was that it came with a substantial amount of financial support during that last year at university.

After a visit to the hospital I was offered the job and after graduation moved with my wife to Joliette (a small city northwest of Montreal) in June 1966. There were approximately 2,000 mentally ill patients, and we were four newly graduated physical educators responsible for the organization of their recreational activities. We had half a dozen recreational technicians to implement the recreational program.

I had absolutely no training in recreational therapy. The first thing I did when I arrived at the hospital was to find the library and read up on recreational therapy. It did not take me much time to realize that I had to go back to university to do graduate training in this field if I wanted to do something useful for the patients.

To my surprise the head of the hospital totally agreed and offered to sponsor me for a scholarship from the newly created medical research training fund of the Health Ministry. This was again part of the advantage of being at the forefront of the baby boom and the cultural revolution which invested heavily in higher education.

10.3.2   Juvenile Delinquency (1967–1970)

In September 1967 I started a MSc degree in psychoeducation in the department of psychology at the University of Montreal. This new 3-year program had been specifically designed to train professionals for residential treatment of children and adolescents with behavior problems. The theoretical training was largely based on psychoanalytic ego psychology and Piaget's cognitive development psychology. One of the basic intervention models was taken from Fritz Redl and David Wineman's work in Detroit and published in *The Aggressive Child* (1951) and *Controls from Within* (1952). The lifespan developmental model we were introduced to rested mainly on the work of Erik H. Erickson, and practical training involved work in residential centers for children or adolescents. I had two choices for clinical training: a residential center for young children or a residential treatment center for juvenile delinquents. I chose the latter because adolescence was closer to the work I had done in the psychiatric hospital and would do when I went back to the hospital.

My career as a juvenile delinquency specialist was starting! Having majored in physical education, I eventually became involved in the physical education and sport activities of the residential center. For my MSc degree thesis, I choose to study, through direct observation, how juvenile delinquents, in different phases of their residential treatment, approached the learning of gymnastics. This was a very labor-intensive enterprise, and it started to teach me that you can very easily lose track of where you are going when you dig very deeply into a narrow topic or a technique. But I was learning!

10.3.3 *Living with Murderers (1970–1973)*

After finishing this 3-year MSc degree, funded by the Ministry of Health, I had to work for at least 3 years in a state hospital facility. To keep as close as possible to my new expertise with juvenile delinquents and continue to live in Montreal, I chose to work in a new maximum-security mental hospital where most patients had committed violent crimes. The head of the hospital had decided to experiment with the Therapeutic Community approach (Jones, 1953) to treat psychopaths, drug addicts, schizophrenics, and mentally deficient adults who were now at the end of the line.

The physical environment was spectacularly modern, and the staff was composed mainly of young 1970s idealists who believed that theory, good faith, and hard work would help these unfortunate humans return to a 'normal' life. I learned much about the limits of psychiatry during these 3 years, thanks especially to Henri Ellenberger. He had just published his monumental book on the discovery of the unconscious (Ellenberger, 1970), and he participated in our weekly case studies. I also learned that many of these dangerous patients were humans with whom it was good to talk and play.

One year later (1971), the University of Montreal created the School of Psychoeducation, separate from the Department of Psychology. They wanted to create a scientific discipline focused on the development and treatment of children's behavior problems. Because I was one of the first, and one of the oldest, to receive a MSc in psychoeducation, they offered me a half-time position that could become a full-time tenure-track position if I did a PhD. This was again an opportunity created by being born just ahead of the baby boom. Universities had to expand to educate the baby boomers. I accepted the offer without any hesitation, but I first had to finish my 3-year contract with the hospital. Between September 1971 and June 1973, I worked at the maximum-security psychiatric institute and did team teaching with my former professors at the University of Montreal.

10.4 PhD at the Institute of Education, University of London (1973–1976)

I chose to study at the University of London's Institute of Education because the professor with whom I did team-teaching at the University of Montreal had met the head of the Institute at an international congress and told me that they were doing research on interventions with delinquents. I had considered doing my PhD in the United States and in France, but I did not know of good research on delinquency in France, and I was more attracted to life in Europe than in the United States. I was far from knowing that the Institute of Education would become the best-rated education research institution in the world.

When I arrived at the Institute of Education in September 1973, I was told that the supervisor I had chosen had moved to Leeds University. I was offered the opportunity to follow him, but I chose to stay in London – because I wanted to live in London! Fortunately, they found me another supervisor, Robert G. Andry. He was the director of a training program in forensic psychology and worked as a consultant in prisons in Hong Kong. His PhD research had focused on juvenile delinquency and parental pathology (Andry, 1960). Because of his frequent travel to Hong Kong, I was given a co-supervisor, Daisy Penfold, a statistician who had worked with Cyril Burt (1925) and was close to retirement.

10.4.1 Psychoanalysis and Hans Eysenck

I had decided that I would do my PhD thesis on the impact of residential treatment for juvenile delinquents, more specifically, its impact on the juvenile delinquent's body image. The focus on body image was an attempt to bridge my undergraduate training in physical education and my MSc degree training, which was strongly influenced by psychoanalytical thinking. I was using Seymour Fisher's effort to operationalize Freudian concepts (Fisher & Cleveland, 1968). However, clinical psychology at the University of London was dominated by Hans Eysenck, whom my psychodynamically oriented professors at the University of Montreal referred to as the devil in person. The clash between psychoanalysis and behaviorism, which started early in the 20th century was, from my perspective, very similar to the clash between Catholicism and Protestantism. Having liberated myself from my Catholic education during my adolescence, I was now ready to liberate myself from psychoanalytic theory … without becoming a behaviorist.

I read Eysenck's book *Crime and Personality* (1964) during my first year in London. Although I initially reacted to his ideas with the criticism of my previous professors, I rapidly realized that I understood the logic of his positions much better than I ever did the logic of most of the psychoanalytic ideas I had read over the past 10 years. I had the impression that I was intelligent enough to understand Eysenck's reasoning! An impression I did not have when I read most of the psychoanalysts, especially the French psychoanalysts! This did not prevent me from having friends who were being trained at Anna Freud's Hampstead Clinic (e.g., Jack Novick and Kerry Kelly Novick, two psychoanalysts whose daughter was in a play group with my daughter!). Interestingly, some 20 years later, I was asked by Peter Fonagy to be on the Hampstead Clinic International Advisory Board.

10.4.2   Longitudinal Studies and Developmental Psychology

The second major influence during my PhD was the longitudinal study approach to developmental psychology. Professor Lindley was in charge of the weekly graduate research seminar and introduced us to the importance of the developmental perspective and the use of longitudinal studies. He had been involved in the series of birth cohort longitudinal studies that started in the early 1950s in Belgium, England, France, Sweden, and Switzerland (Sand, 1966; Stattin & Klackenberg-Larsson, 1993).

A few months after I started my PhD, I was given a newspaper clipping of a book review on juvenile delinquency by my upstairs neighbor, a Canadian postdoctoral student in cancer genetics who eventually became President of the Canadian Institutes of Health Research and of the Canadian Institute of Advanced Research (Alan Bernstein). He knew that my thesis was on the treatment of juvenile delinquents and wondered if I had heard of the study described in the book. At that time I was far from realizing that the study I discovered in *Who Becomes Delinquent?* (West & Farrington, 1973) would have such a profound impact on my career. Indeed, my PhD research on the effects of residential treatment for delinquent boys made me realize the importance of understanding the early development of antisocial behavior, and the Cambridge Study in Delinquent Development (Farrington, 2003) was clearly a model.

10.4.3   Statistics for Longitudinal Studies

The third major influence was my co-supervisor, the statistician Daisy Penfold, whom I met with every month in her office at the end of the afternoon, so that we could have a glass of sherry and talk about the challenges of gardening in a cold country like Canada. I attended a few of her lectures on statistics, but her main influence was through her questions during our meetings. They forced me to spend large amounts of time reading up on statistical analyses to find answers to her questions. I knew I had earned my PhD when I presented to her my statistical analyses strategy for longitudinal data based on Wohlwill's (1973) work on developmental stages. She said: 'I have never heard of this type of statistical analyses, but they make sense to me'. My principal supervisor, Robert Andry, was instrumental in forcing me to think about family impact on juvenile delinquency, but more importantly he helped open the doors to the four main residential institutions for juvenile delinquents in the London area.

Eventually the thrust of my PhD was to assess the impact of the residential units' social climate on the changes in behavior of juvenile delinquents over an 8-month period in six residential institutions, four in the London area and two in Canada (Tremblay, 1976). I used the adolescents' and educators' ratings (Moos, 1975) to assess the social climate of the residential units and educators' ratings to assess the adolescents' behavior. The most important impact of the study, besides the experience I gained in doing a 'short' longitudinal study, was in the realm of scientific frauds!

10.4.4 Scientific Frauds

At the end of the study I presented the results to each residential institution and gave each headmaster a copy of the data. A few years later I was alerted by a former staff member of one of the London residential centers that the headmaster had published a book with my data. The book (Mayers, 1980) claimed that an experiment had been done in his residential institution and had shown significant beneficial effects on the behavior of the boys. I eventually wrote an article for the *British Journal of Criminology* showing that my data had been falsified with the intent to show beneficial effects of that residential center. The editor hesitated to publish the article because he was afraid the headmaster would sue the journal. It turned out that David Farrington had recently worked with colleagues from the criminology department at the University of Montreal, and the editor asked him to verify who I was! The article was eventually published (Tremblay, 1984) and, from what I was told, the headmaster was fired, apparently for an accumulation of deceptive behaviors.

A decade later I met Mark Lipsey, who had done meta-analyses of treatment effects for juvenile delinquency. I mentioned the fraud, and he checked and confirmed that Mayer's book was part of his meta-analysis of juvenile delinquency treatment (Lipsey, 1992). He eventually deleted this study from his data bank, but one wonders how many fraudulent datasets have not been discovered.

Having worked for many years in residential settings with deviant adolescents and adults, I could understand why a brazen headmaster would manipulate data to 'save' his institution and become famous. Residential treatment centers for juvenile delinquents and criminals were, at the time, under strong attack (Lipton, Martinson, & Wilks, 1975). From that perspective, we can understand how difficult it must be to work at the rehabilitation of juvenile delinquents if you know that there are no beneficial effects and that there may be iatrogenic effects (Gatti, Tremblay, & Vitaro, 2009; Petitclerc, Gatti, Vitaro, & Tremblay, 2013). This is probably one of the reasons why it is so difficult to convince clinicians to use randomized controlled trials to assess treatment effectiveness. What will they do if the results show there are no positive impacts or if the impacts are negative?

10.5   Assistant Professor at the University of Montreal (1976–1980)

At the end of my PhD (summer of 1976) I went back to the University of Montreal as an assistant professor. I was told that I was expected to eventually replace the head of the department, who had recently and reluctantly accepted the job for one term (4 years). I was also told that taking the responsibility for the undergraduate and graduate programs would give me the experience needed to become director of the department. Naively, I thought that it was normal to do this administrative work, teach, and start a funded research program in a department created 5 years earlier with psychodynamically oriented clinicians who did not particularly appreciate quantitative research. Fortunately, I decided to link my research program to my administrative responsibilities. I created a research team on the training of educators for maladjusted children, including the study of adult–child interactions. The latter enabled me to focus on my growing interest in nonverbal communication and ethology (the study of animal behavior). I created a graduate course on nonverbal communication in human interactions and on the methods of ethology for training professionals working with children with behavior problems. I eventually edited a book (published in Paris in French!) on ethology applied to the study of child development (Tremblay, Provost, & Strayer, 1985). I published that book with two psychologists who were applying the ethological methods to the study of child development. Strayer had been trained as an ethologist studying primate behavior. He encouraged me to study the development of delinquent behavior using an ethological approach.

10.6   The Road from Kindergarten to Juvenile Delinquency (1980–2019+)

10.6.1   Understanding the Development of Aggression

In 1980, the largest school board of Montreal asked me to help them assess the behavior problems of kindergarten children. It did not take me long to realize that this was a wonderful opportunity to start a longitudinal study with a large sample of kindergarten males from low socio-economic areas of Montreal and to study the development of juvenile delinquency. The original aim of the study (Montreal Longitudinal Experimental Study: MLES) was to follow, until adolescence, a large sample of kindergarten boys from low socio-economic neighborhoods in a large North American city to understand which factors explained why some became juvenile delinquents and others did not. I was obviously influenced here by West and Farrington's 1973 book, *Who Becomes Delinquent?*, which my London geneticist neighbor had discovered in a newspaper article! One key difference between my approach and that of the West–Farrington study was that mine would start at an earlier age, since I had access to the teachers of kindergarten children.

The recent creation of a new Canadian federal funding agency on social development helped me realize that our sample was large enough (1,161 boys) to also do a randomized control trial with the boys who were identified by the kindergarten teachers as having serious behavior problems. I met with the head of the agency and he encouraged me to submit a proposal. The plan was to randomly distribute the most aggressive–hyperactive kindergarten boys into experimental and control groups to test the effectiveness of an intensive preventive intervention. The grant proposal I wrote was largely influenced by the paper 'Early Predictors of Male Delinquency', which Rolf Loeber published in *Psychological Bulletin* in 1983 (see Chapter 5; Loeber & Dishion, 1983). Once I obtained the funding, I asked Frank Vitaro to help me with the planning of the intervention program. Frank was a new professor at a small university in Northwest Quebec (Val d'Or). I had met him only once, by accident, at the 1983 Munich meeting of the International Society for the Study of Behavioral Development (ISSBD). Interestingly also, it was at that meeting that I first heard Lea Pulkkinen (see Chapter 4) present the work she was doing on aggression with her longitudinal study from Jyväskylä in Finland. I met Lea again at the 1985 ISSBD meeting in Tours (France), at the 1987 ISSBD meeting in Tokyo (Japan), and at the 1989 ISSBD meeting that she organized in Jyväskylä (Finland). It was only after this later meeting that we decided to compare results from our longitudinal studies (Pulkkinen & Tremblay, 1992). During a visit Lea made to Montreal in the spring of 1991 to work on the paper we were doing together, she mentioned her recent interest in personality factors associated with aggression. This discussion prompted me to read a paper she referred to (Cloninger, 1987), which led to my first paper in the highest impact psychiatry journal at the time and much media coverage (Tremblay, Pihl, Vitaro, & Dobkin, 1994).

From a historical perspective, it is useful to note here that the ISSBD included in the 1980s and 1990s a substantial number of members who studied the development and prevention of aggression (e.g., Bill Hartup, Robert Hinde, Dan Olweus, Lea Pulkinnen, Joan McCord, Grazia Attili, Ken Rubin, Michel Boivin, Frank Vitaro, and two other authors in the present book: Rainer Silbereisen and Gian Vittorio Caprara).

10.6.2 Preventing the Development of Aggression

In 1986 we received funding to start preventive intervention with 7-year-old boys who were rated aggressive and hyperactive by their kindergarten teacher. The intervention included parent training based on the intervention program developed by Gerry Patterson (Patterson, Reid, Jones, & Conger, 1975) and social skills training (Michelson, Sugai, Wood, & Kazdin, 1983). In 1987, Joan McCord and David Farrington convinced me to attend the Life History Meeting that Lee Robins was organizing in St. Louis. Amazingly, 11 years after my PhD, this was the first scientific meeting I attended in the United States!

The enthusiastic support of Joan McCord, David Farrington, Rolf Loeber, David Hawkins, and Lee Robins was extremely encouraging during the early stages of our work. Joan McCord made annual visits to help plan the assessments and work on data analyses. At the Jyväskylä ISSBD meeting that Lea Pulkkinen organized in 1989, we had a symposium on the prevention of antisocial behavior, which led to an edited volume on early prevention of antisocial behavior (McCord & Tremblay, 1992).

David Farrington was clearly convinced that we needed longitudinal–experimental studies such as the one we had started (Farrington, 1992), and he systematically invited me to take part in different committees, including the National Institute of Justice (NIJ)–MacArthur Foundation planning committee for the study that eventually became the Project on Human Development in Chicago Neighborhoods (Sampson, Raudenbush, & Earls, 1997). The 2-year intensive work on this committee, with meetings all over the United States, introduced me to the world of American criminology. I had the pleasure of working with a very large group of American criminologists, including Al Blumstein, Al Reiss, Felton Earls, Lee Robins, Rob Sampson, Denise Kandel, Del Elliott, Joan McCord, Malcolm Klein, David Rowe, David Hawkins, Terry Thornberry, Lloyd Ohlin, Michael Tonry, and James Q. Wilson (Farrington et al., 1990; Tonry, Ohlin, & Farrington, 1991). I believe that David Farrington and I were the only non-American participants.

In 1999, Joan McCord and Kathy Widom invited me to be a member of the U.S. National Research Council and Institute of Medicine Panel on Juvenile Crime (McCord, Widom, & Crowell, 2001). One of the reasons the committee was created was the prediction made by some criminologists that the United States would soon have a wave of 'super-predators'. Fortunately, the prediction did not materialize!

We are still following the 1983–1984 kindergarten boys as they are now in their fourth decade of life. Analyses of the long-term effects of the 2-year intensive intervention with the aggressive–hyperactive kindergarten boys show that the treatment group boys compared to the control group had fewer behavior problems in early adolescence (Tremblay et al., 1995) and fewer problems with substance use and abuse during adolescence (Castellanos-Ryan et al., 2013). More of the boys from the treatment group finished high school (Boisjoli et al., 2007) and fewer of them had a criminal record by 24 years of age (Boisjoli et al., 2007).

10.6.3 Tracing the Developmental Trajectories of Aggression and Other Behavior Problems

Rolf Loeber was the first to collaborate on the analyses of the physical aggression longitudinal data from the MLES. He came to Montreal for a few weeks in 1988 to do the analyses which led to a paper (Loeber, Tremblay, Gagnon, & Charlebois, 1989) that traced the developmental trajectories of physical aggression of the Montreal boys from ages 6 to 9 years. A second series of analyses was published 2 years later (Tremblay et al., 1991).

Two years after the start of the MLES (1984), which was focused on boys from low socio-economic environments in Montreal, we started a longitudinal study with a population-based representative sample of kindergarten children (Quebec Longitudinal Study of Kindergarten Children). One aim was to compare the development of the Montreal boys from low socio-economic areas to a random sample of the population (Broidy et al., 2003; Côté, Tremblay, Nagin, Zoccolillo, & Vitaro, 2002; Fontaine et al., 2008).

The statistical approach to the analysis of the longitudinal data that we had been collecting since 1984 was dramatically changed by an invitation I received from Rolf Loeber in 1995. Al Blumstein, from Carnegie–Mellon University in Pittsburgh, was creating the National Consortium on Violence Research (NCOVR) to obtain funding from the U.S. National Science Foundation (NSF) and the NIJ. My participation in this consortium led to an extremely productive and stimulating collaboration with Daniel Nagin of Carnegie–Mellon University to describe the different developmental trajectories of antisocial behavior. The initial results (Nagin & Tremblay, 1999) clearly showed that the large majority of boys from the poorest inner-city areas of Montreal were using physical aggression less frequently as they grew older. Only a very small group of boys (4%) did not show the declining trend; these were the boys who had the highest level of physical aggression in kindergarten and remained at the highest level until adolescence. When interviewed at ages 15 and 17, they were the boys who reported the highest frequency of physical violence, and they were the ones most frequently found guilty of infractions before 18 years of age. These results showed that there was a serious problem with 'social learning theory' concerning the development of physical aggression from school entry to adulthood. The results clearly showed that the frequency of physical aggressions decreased with increased exposure to aggression from the media and their peers (DHHS, 2001; Tremblay, 2000, 2006). The developmental trajectories also indicated that the increased arrest rates for physical aggression during adolescence were not due to an increased rate of aggression but to a change in the reactions of adults to youth aggression as those youths aged. Because puberty leads to an increase in height, weight, strength, and cognitive skills, it also leads to a dramatic change in the negative consequences of physical aggression. Adults are much more fearful of being aggressed by a 16-year-old than by a 10-year-old. Thus, the police arrest and the judicial system convicts physically violent adolescents who have been physically violent toward others at least since kindergarten. Within the NCOVR collaboration, we replicated these findings using five other longitudinal studies in Canada, New Zealand, and the United States (Broidy et al., 2003).

Results clearly showed that all the boys tended to be at their peak level in frequency of physical aggression at 6 years of age, when they were at the end of their kindergarten year. This observation made me wonder when children start to use physical aggression, if they are at their peak frequency of use in kindergarten.

Having always been focused on juvenile delinquency, like most people interested in violent behavior, it slowly became clear to me that I did not know what we knew on aggression during early childhood. The solution was obviously to review the literature. But it did not take much time to realize that there were very few studies of physical aggression during the preschool years, and essentially no longitudinal studies tracing the development of physical aggression from infancy to adolescence. One of the factors that limited the study of aggression in young children, beside the fact that they have weak limbs, as noted by Saint Augustine (see Chapter 1), was the idea that the physical aggressions of children were not 'true' aggressions, because young children could not intend to aggress (Kagan, 1974).

While looking for research on aggression during early childhood, I remembered that, in the early 1980s, I had assessed the PhD thesis of a French ethologist who had filmed a huge number of social interactions in a daycare center. He had specifically studied the frequency of physical aggressions and prosocial behaviors (Restoin et al., 1985). He reported that the ratio of physically aggressive social interactions to other types of social interactions, substantially increased from 9 to 24 months and then decreased.

10.7   Why Not Start at Birth? (1991–2019+)

I became convinced that Aristotle was wiser than most modern developmental criminologists, psychiatrists, or psychologists when he wrote that an investigation of causes needs to start at the beginning of the phenomena we want to understand. So, following his advice, we finally started to study large cohorts of children from birth, aiming to understand when, how, and why children learn to use physical aggression.

10.7.1   *The National Longitudinal Study of Children and Youth in Canada*

The first occasion we had to start earlier than kindergarten was an invitation I received from the Canadian government in 1991 to help plan a large (20,000 children) accelerated longitudinal study of a random sample of Canadian children from birth to 11 years. Because of the accelerated design, the first data collection in 1994 provided cross-sectional data. We showed that the frequency of biting, kicking and hitting others substantially decreased from age 2 to 11 years (Tremblay et al., 1999). This steady decline with age was confirmed when the longitudinal data was available (Côté, Vaillancourt, LeBlanc, Nagin, & Tremblay, 2006).

10.7.2   *The Quebec Newborn Twin Study*

The next step was to start a birth cohort with twins to assess physical aggressions from infancy to adulthood, while investigating genetic and environmental effects. The study included 667 pairs of twins from the Montreal region and started in 1995 (Boivin et al., 2019). We showed that the frequency of physical aggressions at 20 months was much more strongly determined by genetic factors than it was by the development of language (Dionne, Tremblay, Boivin, Laplante, & Pérusse, 2003). We also showed that genetic factors explained the frequency of physical aggressions, their stability, and their growth rate up to 6 years of age. The contribution of shared environment was found to be modest and to appear at around 4 years of age (Lacourse et al., 2014). We observed similar results between 9 and 12 years when we focused on the Callous–Unemotional (CU) traits (lack of empathy, lack of guilt, and shallow emotions) which characterize adult psychopathy (Henry et al., 2018).

10.7.3   The Quebec Longitudinal Study of Child Development

We eventually established a partnership with an agency of the Quebec government (Health Quebec) to start a large birth cohort with a representative sample of births in 1998 (Quebec Longitudinal Study of Child Development). The first data collection was at 5 months and the second at 17 months. It took all my powers of conviction to get some of my colleagues to accept the inclusion of physical aggression items in the parent rating questionnaires at 17 months. I also managed to include retrospective questions when the parents said their child had been pushing, kicking, and hitting at 17 months. Some colleagues did not want to put in the aggression questions because they were afraid that the questions would shock the parents! Results eventually showed that, from 9 months of age, the frequency of physical aggressions increased substantially up to 42 months, when it started decreasing (Alink et al., 2006; Côté et al., 2006; NICHD, 2004; Tremblay et al., 1999; Tremblay et al., 2004). These results showed that the downward trend started in the preschool years. The same general developmental picture is drawn whether we use data from different periods, different countries, different reporting sources, or different methodologies (e.g., Hay et al., 2011; Ribeiro & Zachrisson, 2019). Frequency of anger outbursts and physical aggressions increases rapidly with motor development, from the end of the first year after birth to approximately the third year, and then the frequency decreases. Thus, children do not learn to use aggression; they learn not to use aggression as their brains develop self-control.

This longitudinal study of a random sample of the population also coincided with the implementation of a state-funded childcare program implemented in the Canadian province of Quebec and enabled us to assess long-term impacts. Children from low socio-economic environments who attended early childcare facilities compared to those who did not were shown to have fewer disruptive behavior problems during adolescence (Orri et al., 2019).

10.7.4   The North Dublin Preventive Experimental Study with Pregnant Women (PFL)

As we approached the new millennium, the Canadian government decided to increase its spending on knowledge transfer for children's services. I received a large grant to create a Center of Excellence on Early Childhood Development and started collaborations with numerous specialists in Canada and around the world, including Jim Heckman (Nobel Prize in Economics, 2000), who became interested in the impact of early childhood development on workforce participation. In 2006 he asked me to help start a preventive experiment with pregnant women in Dublin, Ireland. Following a meeting at University College Dublin (UCD), we both became professors in order to help run the study and create a research center (Doyle, Harmon, Heckman, & Tremblay, 2009).

The PFL prevention program we helped create with Orla Doyle from the economics department at UCD, targeted pregnant women in a relatively poor area of North Dublin. The aim was to improve low levels of school readiness by supporting parents (home visits by a mentor) from pregnancy to the child's school entry at age 5 years. Compared to the control group, the program improved children's cognitive development from 18 months of age onward. Children in the treatment group had better general cognitive functioning, and a large impact was observed at school entry for overall verbal ability and related skills. Significant positive impacts were also observed on externalizing behavior problems for the children with the most severe problems (Côté, Orri, Tremblay, & Doyle, 2018; Doyle, McGlanaghy, O'Farrelly, & Tremblay, 2016).

10.7.5   The Irish Multicentre Evaluation of Sonographic Predictors of Restricted Growth in Twin Study (ESPRiT) (Breathnach et al., 2012)

This ESPRiT study initially assessed the prenatal development and perinatal outcomes of 1,028 twin pregnancies between May 2007 and October 2009. In 2011, I received funding from the Irish Health Research Board to assess the twins' behavior at school entry as well as their epigenetic profiles. A few years later Pol van Lier from the Free University in Amsterdam (the Netherlands) obtained funding from the European Community to assess how school environmental factors may alter the neurobiological basis underlying aggression development. This twin study enabled us to describe children's bio-psycho-social development from pregnancy and to investigate genetic, environmental, and epigenetic effects, with a specific focus on bullying and victimization during elementary school and, eventually, throughout their lives.

10.7.6 The Integrated Research Network in Perinatology of Quebec and Eastern Ontario (IRNPQEO)

In 2010, a group of obstetricians and neonatologists in Canada initiated a neonatal network to start a pregnancy cohort (N = 2,366). There are numerous dimensions to the study, including neurodevelopmental outcomes after assisted reproductive technologies, the impacts of nutrition on health and behavior, as well as the integration of the children when they enter school. The latter study is led by Jean Séguin, who was trained in our previous longitudinal studies.

10.7.7 The Quebec Newborn Monozygotic Twin Study

In our latest twin study, initiated in 2014, the aim is to understand environmental effects on gene expression, especially those that are related to aggressive behavior and other behavior problems. At birth, we selected two different groups of monozygotic twins: in the first group, the twin pairs had a large difference in birth weight. In the second group, the twin pairs had similar birth weight. Because monozygotic twins share the same genes, the differences in birth weight between them must be due to in utero environmental factors. Previous studies have shown that the twin with a substantially lower birth weight is at higher risk of mental health problems during adulthood. The aim of this study is to describe the differences in development between the two types of twin pairs by measuring not only their behavior and mental health but also their DNA methylation and brain development. These studies of identical twins should help us understand environmental mechanisms that have impacts on brain development and on behavior through different mechanisms, including the epigenetic process (Tremblay & Szyf, 2010). The study will complement the epigenetic longitudinal work that has been done with the Avon Longitudinal Study of Parents and Children (ALSPAC) initiated by Jean Golding (see Chapter 3) (Cecil, Walton, Jaffee, et al., 2018; Cecil, Walton, Pingault, et al., 2018).

10.8 Back to the Future …

I have always taken pleasure in looking backward to the history of our planet and the evolution of humans. However, looking backward in time made sense mainly because it helped me think about what I was doing and where I wanted to go. I wrote this chapter and planned this book in the same spirit. I hope that it will help our young colleagues understand where we come from and help them decide where they want to go.

Many of the students I have had the pleasure of working with are now mature researchers at the new frontiers of the developmental sciences. They have initiated collaborations to work on new and ongoing longitudinal and experimental studies. When I did my PhD at the University of London, I could never have imagined that three of my students would eventually become high-performing researchers and academics at my alma mater: Louise Arseneault has been at the Institute of Psychiatry working on British and Australian longitudinal studies for more than 20 years; Ted Barker joined the Institute of Psychiatry more recently and has been working on numerous longitudinal studies, including ALSPAC, the study created by Jean Golding (see Chapter 3, p. XX); and still more recently Jean-Baptiste Pingault joined University College London, where he is also working on numerous longitudinal studies, including ALSPAC (Cecil et al., 2014). Many other former students are continuing to work with the longitudinal and experimental cohorts we created and have started new longitudinal and experimental studies: Linda Booij, René Carbonneau, Sylvana Côté, Ginette Dionne, Marie-Claude Geoffroy, Lisa Girard, Eric Lacourse, Isabelle Ouellet-Morin, Amélie Petitclerc, Nadine Provençal, Jean Séguin, Evelyne Touchette, and Francis Vergunst.

Developmental research on human behavior is becoming more interdisciplinary, more intergenerational, and more international. I envy those who will be studying human development over the next decades. The field will most certainly grow by leaps and bounds. However, I consider myself lucky to have lived at a time when the opposition between the social learning of aggression and the genetics of aggression slowly but surely led to some form of integration of these two essential components. I now feel even luckier to take part in the unforeseen leap to intergenerational environmental effects on gene expression (Cecil, Walton, Jaffee, et al., 2018; Provençal et al., 2012; Tremblay & Szyf, 2010; Wang et al., 2012). There is bound to be a major acceleration of our understanding of bio-psycho-social mechanisms that will lead to more effective preventive interventions (Tremblay et al., 2018).

Carefully analyzing the past 75 years, as I have done to plan this book and write this chapter, made me realize the extent to which my life has been a long series of lucky events: from the mixing of my parent's genes at a time when the worst war ever was raging; to being at the forefront of the 20th-century 'baby boom'; to meeting Lilith when I was turning 17 years old, which led me to work in a psychiatric hospital and have two wonderful children; to being asked to assess immigrant kindergarten children's behavior problems, which led to numerous longitudinal and experimental studies of human development; to having the pleasure of sharing the latter part of my life with a young and dynamic colleague, which led to my having the multiple pleasures of reliving early childhood development with our wonderful son who will in turn have the pleasure of living humanity's exceptional developmental trajectory into the twenty-second century.

I could not have predicted where I would end up from one decade of my life to another. However, when I look backward, I can say that I am making a wonderful voyage on Planet Earth. I hope that my children and my former students will eventually be able to say the same, while helping others to also enjoy the very short time we spend on this planet.

References

Alink, L. R., Mesman, J., van Zeijl, J., Stolk, M. N., Juffer, F., Koot, H. M., ... van Ijzendoorn, M. H. (2006). The early childhood aggression curve: Development of physical aggression in 10- to 50-months-old children. *Child Development*, 77(4), 954–966.

Andry, R. G. (1960). *Delinquency and parental pathology: A study in forensic and clinical psychology*. London, England: Methuen.

Boisjoli, R., Vitaro, F., Lacourse, E., Barker, E. D., & Tremblay, R. E. (2007). Impact and clinical significance of a preventive intervention for disruptive boys: 15-year follow-up. *British Journal of Psychiatry*, 191(5), 415–419. doi:10.1192/bjp.bp.106.030007

Boivin, M., Brendgen, M., Dionne, G., Ouellet-Morin, I., Dubois, L., Pérusse, D., ... Vitaro, F. (2019). The Quebec Newborn Twin Study at 21. *Twin Research and Human Genetics*, 1–7.

Breathnach, F. M., McAuliffe, F. M., Geary, M., Daly, S., Higgins, J. R., Dornan, J., ... Dicker, P. (2012). Optimum timing for planned delivery of uncomplicated monochorionic and dichorionic twin pregnancies. *Obstetrics & Gynecology*, 119(1), 50–59.

Broidy, L. M., Nagin, D. S., Tremblay, R. E., Bates, J. E., Brame, B., Dodge, K. A., ... Vitaro, F. (2003). Developmental trajectories of childhood disruptive behaviors and adolescent delinquency: A six site, cross national study. *Developmental Psychology*, 39(2), 222–245.

Burt, C. L. (1925). *The young delinquent*. London, England: University of London Press.

Castellanos-Ryan, N., Séguin, J. R., Vitaro, F., Parent, S., & Tremblay, R. E. (2013). Impact of a 2-year multimodal intervention for disruptive 6-year-olds on substance use in adolescence: Randomised controlled trial. *British Journal of Psychiatry*, 203(3), 188–195.

Cecil, C. A. M., Lysenko, L. J., Jaffee, S. R., Pingault, J. B., Smith, R. G., Relton, C. L., ... Barker, E. D. (2014). Environmental risk, oxytocin receptor gene

(OXTR) methylation and youth callous–unemotional traits: A 13-year longitudinal study. *Molecular Psychiatry*, *19*(10), 1071–1077.

Cecil, C. A. M., Walton, E., Jaffee, S. R., O'Connor, T., Maughan, B., Relton, C. L., … Ouellet-Morin, I. (2018). Neonatal DNA methylation and early-onset conduct problems: A genome-wide, prospective study. *Development and Psychopathology*, *30*(2), 383–397.

Cecil, C. A. M., Walton, E., Pingault, J. B., Provencal, N., Pappa, I., Vitaro, F., … McCrory, E. J. (2018). DRD4 methylation as a potential biomarker for physical aggression: An epigenome-wide, cross-tissue investigation. *American Journal of Medical Genetics Part B: Neuropsychiatric Genetics*, *177*(8), 746–764.

Cloninger, C. R. (1987). A systematic method for clinical description and classification of personality variants: A proposal. *Archives of General Psychiatry*, *44*, 573–588.

Côté, S. M., Orri, M., Tremblay, R. E., & Doyle, O. (2018). A multicomponent early intervention program and trajectories of behavior, cognition, and health. *Pediatrics*, *141*(5), 1–14 (e20173174).

Côté, S. M., Tremblay, R. E., Nagin, D. S., Zoccolillo, M., & Vitaro, F. (2002). Childhood behavioral profiles leading to adolescent conduct disorder: Risk trajectories for boys and girls. *Journal of the American Academy of Child and Adolescent Psychiatry*, *41*(9), 1086–1094.

Côté, S. M., Vaillancourt, T., LeBlanc, J. C., Nagin, D. S., & Tremblay, R. E. (2006). The development of physical aggression from toddlerhood to pre-adolescence: A nation wide longitudinal study of Canadian children. *Journal of Abnormal Child Psychology*, *34*(1), 71–85.

Dionne, G., Tremblay, R. E., Boivin, M., Laplante, D., & Pérusse, D. (2003). Physical aggression and expressive vocabulary in 19 month-old twins. *Developmental Psychology*, *39*(2), 261–273.

Doyle, O., Harmon, C. P., Heckman, J. J., & Tremblay, R. E. (2009). Investing in early human development: Timing and economic efficiency. *Economics & Human Biology*, *7*(1), 1–6.

Doyle, O., McGlanaghy, E., O'Farrelly, C., & Tremblay, R. E. (2016). Can targeted intervention mitigate early emotional and behavioral problems?: Generating robust evidence within randomized controlled trials. *PLoS One*, *11*(6), 1–25 (e0156397).

Ellenberger, H. F. (1970). *The discovery of the unconscious: The history and evolution of dynamic psychiatry*. New York, NY: Basic Books.

Eysenck, H. J. (1964). *Crime and personality*. London, England: Routledge and Kegan Paul.

Farrington, D. P. (1992). The need for longitudinal experimental research on offending and antisocial behavior. In J. McCord & R. E. Tremblay (Eds.), *Preventing antisocial behavior: Interventions from birth through adolescence* (pp. 353–376). New York, NY: Guilford Press.

Farrington, D. P. (2003). Key results from the first forty years of the Cambridge study in delinquent development. In T. P. Thornberry & M. D. Krohn (Eds.), *Taking stock of delinquency: An overview of findings from contemporary longitudinal studies* (pp. 137–183). New York, NY: Kluwer Academic/Plenum.

Farrington, D. P., Loeber, R., Elliott, D. S., Hawkins, D., Kandel, D. B., Klein, M. W., ... Tremblay, R. E. (1990). Advancing knowledge about the onset of delinquency and crime. In B. B. Lahey & A. E. Kazdin (Eds.), *Advances in Clinical Child Psychology* (Vol. 13, chap. 8, pp. 283–342). New York, NY: Plenum.

Farrington, D. P., Ohlin, L. E., & Wilson, J. Q. (1986). *Understanding and controlling crime: Towards a new research strategy.* New York, NY: Springer-Verlag.

Fisher, S., & Cleveland, S. E. (1968). *Body image and personality* (2nd ed.). Mineola, NY: Dover.

Fontaine, N., Carbonneau, R., Barker, E. D., Vitaro, F., Hébert, M., Côté, S. M., ... Tremblay, R. E. (2008). Girls' hyperactivity and physical aggression during childhood and adjustment problems in early adulthood. *Archives of General Psychiatry, 65*(3), 320–328.

Gatti, U., Tremblay, R. E., & Vitaro, F. (2009). Iatrogenic effect of juvenile justice. *Journal of Child Psychology and Psychiatry, 50*(8), 991–998.

Guillemin, C., Provençal, N., Suderman, M., Côté, S. M., Vitaro, F., Hallett, M., ... Szyf, M. (2014). DNA methylation signature of childhood chronic physical aggression in T cells of both men and women. *PLoS One, 9*(1), 1–16 (e86822). doi:10.1371/journal.pone.0086822

Hall, S. S. (2014). The accidental epigeneticist. *Nature, 505*(7481), 14–17.

Hay, D. F., Mundy, L., Roberts, S., Carta, R., Waters, C. S., Perra, O., ... van Goozen, S. (2011). Known risk factors for violence predict 12-month-old infants' aggressiveness with peers. *Psychological Science, 22*(9), 1205–1211.

Henry, J., Dionne, G., Viding, E., Petitclerc, A., Feng, B., Vitaro, F., ... Boivin, M. (2018). A longitudinal twin study of callous–unemotional traits during childhood. *Journal of Abnormal Psychology, 127*(4), 374–384.

Holden, C. (2000). The violence of the lambs. *Science, 289*, 580–581.

Jones, M. (1953). *The Therapeutic Community: A new treatment method in psychiatry.* Oxford, England: Basic Books.

Kagan, J. (1974). Development and methodological considerations in the study of aggression. In J. de Wit & W. W. Hartup (Eds.), *Determinants and origins of aggressive behavior* (pp. 107–114). The Hague, the Netherlands: Mouton.

Lacourse, E., Boivin, M., Brendgen, M., Petitclerc, A., Girard, A., Vitaro, F., ... Tremblay, R. E. (2014). A longitudinal twin study of physical aggression in early childhood: Evidence for a developmentally dynamic genome. *Psychological Medicine, 44*(12), 2617–2627.

Lipsey, M. W. (1992). Juvenile delinquency treatment: A meta-analytic inquiry into the variability of effects. In T. D. Cook, H. Cooper, D. S. Cordray, H. Hartman, L. V. Hedges, R. J. Light, T. A. Louis, & F. Mosteller (Eds.), *Meta-analysis for explanation* (pp. 83–127). New York, NY: Russell Sage.

Lipton, D., Martinson, R., & Wilks, J. (1975). *The effectiveness of correctional treatment: A survey of treatment evaluation studies.* New York: Praeger.

Loeber, R., & Dishion, T. J. (1983). Early predictors of male delinquency: A review. *Psychological Bulletin, 94*, 68–99.

Loeber, R., Tremblay, R. E., Gagnon, C., & Charlebois, P. (1989). Continuity and desistance in boys' early fighting at school. *Development and Psychopathology, 1*, 39–50.

Mayers, M. O. (1980). *The hard-core delinquent*. Farnborough, Hants, England: Saxon House.

McCord, J., & Tremblay, R. E. (Eds.). (1992). *Preventing antisocial behavior from birth through adolescence: Experimental approaches*. New York, NY: Guilford Press.

McCord, J., Widom, C. S., & Crowell, N. E. (2001). *Juvenile crime, juvenile justice*. Washington, DC: National Academy Press.

Michelson, L., Sugai, D., Wood, R., & Kazdin, A. E. (1983). *Social skills assessment and training with children*. New York, NY: Plenum Press.

Moos, R. H. (1975). *Evaluating correctional and community settings*. London, England: John Wiley & Sons.

Nagin, D., & Tremblay, R. E. (1999). Trajectories of boys' physical aggression, opposition, and hyperactivity on the path to physically violent and nonviolent juvenile delinquency. *Child Development, 70*(5), 1181–1196.

NICHD. (2004). The developmental course of gender differentiation. *Monographs of the Society for Research in Child Development*.

Orri, M., Tremblay, R. E., Japel, C., Boivin, M., Vitaro, F., Losier, T., ... Côté, S. M. (2019). Early childhood child care and disruptive behavior problems during adolescence: A 17-year population-based propensity score study. *Journal of Child Psychology and Psychiatry, 60*(11), 1174–1182.

Patterson, G. R., Reid, J. B., Jones, R. R., & Conger, R. E. (1975). *A social learning approach to family intervention: Vol. 1. Families with aggressive children*. Eugene, OR: Castalia.

Petitclerc, A., Gatti, U., Vitaro, F., & Tremblay, R. E. (2013). Effects of juvenile court exposure on crime in young adulthood. *Journal of Child Psychology and Psychiatry, 54*(3), 291–297.

Pinker, S. (2011). *The better angels of our nature: Why violence has declined*. New York, NY: Viking.

Provençal, N., Booij, L., & Tremblay, R. E. (2015). The developmental origins of chronic physical aggression: Biological pathways triggered by early life adversity. *Journal of Experimental Biology, 218*(1), 123–133. doi:10.1242/jeb.111401

Provençal, N., Suderman, M. J., Guillemin, C., Massart, R., Ruggiero, A., Wang, D., ... Szyf, M. (2012). The signature of maternal rearing in the methylome in rhesus macaque prefrontal cortex and T cells. *Journal of Neuroscience, 32*(44), 15626–15642. doi:10.1523/JNEUROSCI.1470-12.2012

Pulkkinen, L., & Tremblay, R. E. (1992). Patterns of boys' social adjustment in two cultures and at different ages: A longitudinal perspective. *International Journal of Behavioural Development, 15*(4), 527–553.

Redl, F., & Wineman, D. (1951). *The aggressive child: Children who hate*. Glencoe: Free Press.

Redl, F., & Wineman, D. (1952). Controls from within. *AJN The American Journal of Nursing, 52*(10), 1281.

Restoin, A., Montagner, H., Rodriguez, D., Girardot, J. J., L:rent, D., Kontar, F., ... Talpain, B. (1985). Chronologie des comportements de communication et profils de comportement chez le jeune enfant. In R. E. Tremblay, M. A. Provost, & F. F. Strayer (Eds.), *Ethologie et développement de l'enfant* (pp. 93–130). Paris, France: Editions Stock/Laurence Pernoud.

Ribeiro, L. A., & Zachrisson, H. D. (2019). Peer effects on aggressive behavior in Norwegian child care centers. *Child Development, 90*(3), 876–893.

Rocha, R. (Producer). (2015). The evolution of births in Quebec in six charts. *Montreal Gazette*. Retrieved from https://montrealgazette.com/news/local-news/the-evolution-of-births-in-quebec-in-six-charts

Sampson, R. J., Raudenbush, S. W., & Earls, F. (1997). Neighborhood and violent crime: A multilevel study of collective efficacy. *Science, 277*, 918–924.

Sand, E. A. (1966). *Contribution à l'étude du développement de l'enfant. Aspects médico-sociaux et psychologiques.* Bruxelles, Belgique: Éditions de l'Institut de sociologie de l'Université libre de Bruxelles.

Stattin, H., & Klackenberg-Larsson, I. (1993). Early language and intelligence development and their relationship to future criminal behavior. *Journal of Abnormal Psychology, 102*(3), 369–378.

Tonry, M., Ohlin, L. E., & Farrington, D. P. (1991). *Human development and criminal behavior: New ways of advancing knowledge.* New York, NY: Springer-Verlag.

Tremblay, R. E. (1976). *A psycho-educational study of juvenile delinquents during residential treatment.* London, England: University of London.

Tremblay, R. E. (1984). Treatment of hard-core delinquents in residential establishments: The Ardale Case. *British Journal of Criminology, 24*(4), 384–393.

Tremblay, R. E. (2000). The development of aggressive behaviour during childhood: What have we learned in the past century? *International Journal of Behavioral Development, 24*(2), 129–141.

Tremblay, R. E. (2005). Towards an epigenetic approach to experimental criminology: The 2004 Joan McCord Prize Lecture. *Journal of Experimental and Child Psychology, 1*(4), 397–415.

Tremblay, R. E. (2006). Prevention of youth violence: Why not start at the beginning? *Journal of Abnormal Child Psychology, 34*(4), 481–487.

Tremblay, R. E., & Côté, S. M. (2009). Development of sex differences in physical aggression: The maternal link to epigenetic mechanisms [comment]. *Behavioral and Brain Sciences, 32*(3–4), 290–291.

Tremblay, R. E., Japel, C., Pérusse, D., McDuff, P., Boivin, M., Zoccolillo, M., & Montplaisir, J. (1999). The search for the age of 'onset' of physical aggression: Rousseau and Bandura revisited. *Criminal Behavior and Mental Health, 9*(1), 8–23.

Tremblay, R. E., Loeber, R., Gagnon, C., Charlebois, P., Larivée, S., & LeBlanc, M. (1991). Disruptive boys with stable and unstable high fighting behavior patterns during junior elementary school. *Journal of Abnormal Child Psychology, 19*(3), 285–300.

Tremblay, R. E., Nagin, D., Séguin, J. R., Zoccolillo, M., Zelazo, P. D., Boivin, M., ... Japel, C. (2004). Physical aggression during early childhood: Trajectories and predictors. *Pediatrics, 114*(1), e43–e50.

Tremblay, R. E., Pagani-Kurtz, L., Mâsse, L. C., Vitaro, F., & Pihl, R. O. (1995). A bimodal preventive intervention for disruptive kindergarten boys: Its impact through mid-adolescence. *Journal of Consulting and Clinical Psychology, 63*(4), 560–568.

Tremblay, R. E., Pihl, R. O., Vitaro, F., & Dobkin, P. L. (1994). Predicting early-onset of male antisocial-behavior from preschool behavior. *Archives of General Psychiatry, 51*(9), 732–739.

Tremblay, R. E., Provost, M. A., & Strayer, F. F. (Eds.). (1985). *Ethologie et développement de l'enfant*. Paris, France: Stock.

Tremblay, R. E., & Szyf, M. (2010). Developmental origins of chronic physical aggression and epigenetics. *Epigenomics, 2*(4), 495–499.

Tremblay, R. E., Vitaro, F., & Côté, S. M. (2018). Developmental origins of chronic physical aggression: A bio-psycho-social model for the next generation of preventive interventions. *Annual Review of Psychology, 69*, 383–407.

Wang, D., Szyf, M., Benkelfat, C., Provençal, N., Caramaschi, D., Côté, S. M., ... Booij, L. (2012). Peripheral SLC6A4 DNA methylation is associated with in vivo measures of human brain serotonin synthesis and childhood physical aggression. *PLoS One, 7*(6), 1–8 (e39501). doi:10.1371/journal.pone.0039501

West, D. J., & Farrington, D. P. (1973). *Who becomes delinquent?* London, England: Heinemann.

Wikipedia. (n.d.). Robert Barrie. Retrieved November 27, 2019 https://en.wikipedia.org/wiki/Robert_Barrie

Wohlwill, J. F. (1973). *The study of behavioral development*. New York, NY: Academic Press.

11   From Childhood in a Ruined German City to Research on Crime and Violence

Friedrich Lösel

Friedrich Lösel was born in Neuendettelsau (Germany) on July 28, 1945. He received his PhD in 1974 from the Friedrich-Alexander-University Erlangen–Nuremberg (FAU). His first faculty appointment (1975) was in psychology at the FAU. From 1982 to 1987 he was Professor of Psychology at the University of Bielefeld. From 1987 to 2011, he held the Psychology Chair 1 and was Director at the Institute of Psychology of the FAU. He was also Director of the Social Sciences Research Center at Nuremberg from 2002 to 2005 and Director of the Cambridge University Institute of Criminology (UK) from 2005 to 2012. Over 15 years he was the principal investigator at two Advanced Research Centers (SFBs) of the German Research Foundation. He currently holds honorary positions at Cambridge University, Erlangen University, and Berlin Psychological University.

Among numerous prestigious awards, Friedrich Lösel received the Stockholm Prize in Criminology (2006), the Sellin-Glueck Award from the American Society of Criminology (ASC) (2002), and the Joan McCord Award of the Academy of Experimental Criminology (2015). Friedrich Lösel has led more than 30 externally funded research projects on a broad range of topics, for example, on risk and protective factors in the development of crime and delinquency, processes of resilience, developmental prevention, treatment of offenders, football hooliganism, school bullying, psychopathy, prisoners and their families, long-term marital relationships, family education, extremism, and radicalization. Although about half of his 462 publications are in German, his research is internationally well known.

One of his important studies is the Erlangen–Nuremberg Development and Prevention Study (ENDPS). It used a combined prospective longitudinal and experimental design and investigated more than 600 children and their families from kindergarten to adolescence. Whereas most research on developmental pathways focused on youth and adulthood, the ENDPS showed that accumulated individual and social risk factors at preschool age predicted behavior problems in youth, but there was also developmental flexibility (Stemmler & Lösel, 2015; Wallner, Lösel, Stemmler, & Corrado, 2018). The prevention part of the ENDPS implemented a universal training of child social skills, a parent training on positive parenting, and a combination of both. In a controlled evaluation, there were substantial short-term effects and even some long-term promising outcomes after 10 years (Lösel, Stemmler, & Bender, 2013). Based on the encouraging findings, the ENDPS team trained about 2,000 facilitators for a nationwide dissemination of the program (on a nonprofit basis).

At the Bielefeld Advanced Research Center, Friedrich Lösel led the first project on resilience in continental Europe. This project studied youth in residential care institutions who came from seriously deprived and abusing family backgrounds and had a very high risk for developing behavioral problems. In contrast to traditional risk research, this study showed that a subgroup of youngsters coped successfully with their negative childhood experiences and developed rather well. Individual strengths as well as social resources were relevant for this positive development as compared to youngsters with behavior problems (Lösel & Bliesener, 1994).

Friedrich Lösel and his colleagues also carried out an important study on school bullying. It showed that intensive bullying perpetration was not only a school phenomenon but correlated with violence in other contexts and about 10 years later with criminal behavior in adulthood (Bender & Lösel, 2011; Lösel & Bliesener, 2003a). Similarly, his nationwide study on football hooliganism showed that the stereotype of hooliganism as a quasi-chivalric acting out of aggression on weekends was wrong, and hard-core hooligans had similar characteristics to other violent men (Lösel & Bliesener, 2003b). Although Friedrich Lösel's research addressed rather different phenomena of antisocial behavior, different age groups, and different contexts, he mostly found core personality, social, and situational risk and protective factors that were in accordance with various bio-psycho-social theories of crime and violence. This integrative view has also proved valid in a recent project on extremism and radicalization (Lösel, King, Bender, & Jugl, 2018).

Since all studies have specific limitations, Friedrich Lösel was strongly interested in replication and generalization of findings (Lösel, 2018). For this purpose, he carried out systematic reviews and meta-analyses. Early in his career he led an evaluation of social therapy that probably contained the first worldwide meta-analysis on the treatment of adult offenders in custody (Lösel, Köferl, & Weber, 1987). He also conducted frequently cited meta-analyses on the treatment of sexual offenders, one of which received about 1,000 citations (Lösel & Schmucker,

2005). His meta-analyses on social competence training of children (e.g., Lösel & Beelmann, 2003) were also widely cited. He is one of the rare scholars who studied both early prevention and treatment, following his credo that prevention is never too early and never too late (Lösel, 2007).

Friedrich Lösel also initiated the first longitudinal study of prisoners and their families with a whole-family approach, that is, he gathered data from the men, their female partners, and their children (Lösel, Pugh, Markson, Souza, & Lanskey, 2012). This research contributed to increased attention by the British government to the vulnerability of prisoners' families in the Lord Farmer Report. Currently the Cambridge team carries out a long-term follow-up of the families, with a focus on resilience (Lösel et al., 2018).

Where appropriate, Friedrich Lösel aimed to transfer solid research findings into policy and practice. For example, he was Chair of the Psychology Panel of the Violence Commission of the German government, whose comprehensive report contained concrete proposals on prevention, many of which led to policy initiatives and changes. He had numerous other advisory roles, for example, at the Max Planck Institute for Foreign and International Criminal Law; the German Criminological Center; the German Ministry for Family Affairs; and the investigation of sexual abuse in the Catholic Church and other institutions in Germany, Canada, Belgium, the Netherlands, and the United States. Currently, he serves on the Correctional Services Accreditation and Advice Panel of England and Wales, the Programs and Interventions Supervisory Group of the British Ministry of Justice, and the Steering Group of the Campbell Crime and Justice Collaboration, and as Chair of the Division of Developmental and Life- Course Criminology of the ASC. Recently, he was on an expert panel of the German Federal Chancellor where he proposed a new National Center of Crime Prevention, and he is now chairing the steering group for its stepwise development.

Friedrich Lösel has been President of the European Association of Psychology and Law (EAPL), the Criminological Society of the German-Speaking Countries, and the Academy of Experimental Criminology. He also received the Jerry Lee Award of the ASC Division of Experimental Criminology, the Lifetime Achievement Award of the ASC Division of Developmental and Life-Course Criminology, the Lifetime Achievement Award of the EAPL, an honorary Doctorate of Science from Glasgow Caledonian University, two honorary professorships from Chinese universities, the Beccaria Gold Medal of the Criminological Society of the German-Speaking Countries, and the German Psychology Prize.

11.1 Childhood and Youth

I was born on July 28, 1945, and thus conceived in autumn 1944, when my father came home to Nuremberg on a furlough from military service. After several years in Russia he was in Italy and became a prisoner of war of the U.S. Army. One of my uncles died in Russia, and two others became prisoners of the British and French armies and returned home later. During my childhood, my father sometimes met with former comrades. I remember that they rarely talked about gunfire, wounds, and deaths, but more about the cold winter in Russia, the cities and their people, or the comradeship in their company.

I was born in a hospital at Neuendettelsau, a small municipality in Franconia near the village of my mother's family. My parents' house at Nuremberg had been bombed to the ground on January 2, 1945, a few months before the end of the war in May. The beautiful medieval city center was destroyed, 1,800 people died, and about 100,000 became homeless. After the first damage to our house in 1944, my paternal grandfather and my mother provisionally repaired it and still lived there, but for safety reasons my older brother stayed mostly with my mother's family in a rural village. Although I had only 'experienced' the numerous air raids as a fetus, I later reflected on the stress my mother must have felt during her pregnancy with me. My grandfather and mother told me that it was good that our home had a solid cellar so that they survived and could avoid the large anonymous communal shelters.

At this time, nobody reflected on prenatal influences of stress and war-related traumatization of adults. The main aims of my family during and in the first years after the war were survival, rebuilding the home, acquiring food, and collecting wood for heating. Looking back with my later knowledge in clinical and developmental psychology, I feel that my family coped very well and that I did not really suffer as a 'war fetus' and postwar toddler. Perhaps, some of these experiences unconsciously led me to become interested in resilience research.

I grew up in Nuremberg, where I also went to school. After the war, our family lived in a small flat without separate rooms for each child. We had no water toilet, fridge, or TV, and, of course, no car. Before dinners, I walked with our mug to a nearby inn and bought draught beer and a few loose cigarettes for my father and grandfather. Obviously, based on modern standards, our involuntary ecological footprint was 'climate friendly', but nobody complained because other people were in a similar situation. We used the destroyed houses in our neighborhood as playgrounds and did not think about the war and the Nazi cruelties. At age 10, I moved from elementary school to grammar school (the German

'Gymnasium'). At this time, only about 5% of youngsters went to a grammar school, whereas now the rate in Bavaria is about 50% (a huge change at a macro level). My parents and grandfather owned a small grocery and dairy store. Although my father was interested and knowledgeable in history, neither of my parents had any higher education (which was 'normal' in their childhood). However, my parents aimed for a good education for their sons, and my elementary school teacher advised them to register me for higher education. Modern family-oriented prevention programs have overall (moderate) positive effects (Farrington, Gaffney, Lösel, & Ttofi, 2017; Lösel & Bender, 2017), but already my childhood showed me that a family's genuine motivation and values play a key role for child development.

When I was a child, I had to help my grandfather and parents in their shop. In those days, nobody was concerned about children's work in a family business, which was clearly different from the current exploitation of children in Africa. Of course, I sometimes would have preferred playing with my friends; however, I was also a little proud when, at age 10, I had to serve customers or cycle to a wholesaler to pay bills. My parents did not think about the risk of robbery when I had some hundred Deutsche Marks in the wallet. Obviously, there was a recovery of civilization after (or perhaps because of) the times that Kershaw (2016) rightly described in his book *To Hell and Back: Europe 1914–1949*.

As with most schools in Germany at this time, our grammar school was a state school, without fees, and open to qualified children from all social backgrounds. The fathers' professions ranged from unskilled worker to engineer. Our school had only male students, but, after puberty, we enjoyed parties with girls' schools. Diversity was not an issue at this time. Our genuine school building was destroyed so that our classrooms were in another school two miles away. The walk home was welcome, as we could play football in a nearby park. We also played football at the venue where the Nazis had held their rallies. We drank lemonade on the huge tribune where Hitler spoke to his party members and American soldiers blasted the Swastika above his rostrum in 1945. As a child I did not reflect about the history of this place; however, with age I became much interested in Germany's darkest times. Some years ago, local artists and architects asked me to give a lecture from a psychological perspective on what to do with the partially rotten Nazi Rally buildings (Lösel, 2014). It was an irony of fate that these buildings survived the war without damage, whereas the medieval inner city died in a firestorm. Most of my later foreign guests were particularly interested in these Nazi buildings. It shows macro-developmental change that the U.S. Army built their sports fields there and that African American soldiers listened to what the Nazis had called 'nigger music'. In spite of mountains of books on Hitler and the *Third Reich*, it is still difficult to comprehend how the Holocaust and other cruelty could have happened in a civilized country whose (frequently Jewish) scientists and artists were world famous. Although over the centuries civilization seems to have reduced violence (Pinker, 2011), recent wars and civil wars show that mass murders by the followers of Hitler, Stalin, and Mao have had no worldwide lasting cathartic effect. Therefore, research on individual or micro-social origins of violence should not ignore societal and historical contexts.

I graduated from school in 1964 with the qualification for university studies (German *Abitur*, similar to A-levels in Britain). From the five classes in our first year, only two 'survived', and the class size decreased from about 40 in 1955 to 23. Over the years, our classmates developed mutual bonds, and many have met annually up until today, although some of us worked abroad.

11.2   Life after School and University Studies

After school, I was drafted into compulsory military service in the Rhine area. I had no militaristic motivation and saw the 18 months of service partially as a waste of time. However, retrospectively, I also felt that it was an important experience to live close together with young men of all societal, intellectual, and personality backgrounds. It was a challenge when I, a high school graduate, was elected ombudsman of my rank-and-file comrades, of whom many had indigenous jobs as industrial workers, farmers, or salesmen. In retrospective, I think that a short period of societal service of young people in hospitals, homes for the elderly, childcare, or the army can widen the view derived from pursuing narrow academic backgrounds.

In 1966, I began studying psychology at Erlangen. During my school years, I had never thought about this discipline. However, psychology seemed to be a compromise between my good grades in German language and the sound science education in my school. It was surprising that three of the 23 graduates in our class chose psychology at a time when psychology (founded in Germany by Wilhelm Wundt in 1879) was still in its infancy. We later reflected about our atypical choice. Perhaps an older teacher who taught literature and history in a psychologically sensible manner may have had some influence; and our mathematical education did not scare us away despite the rumors about statistics in psychology. Would I ever have become a scholar of psychology and social sciences if I had not attended this school? I do not know, but my later research showed me that *individual* developments are not as clear as group-based pathways suggest.

I studied at the University of Erlangen–Nuremberg, founded in 1743. My alma mater had a comprehensive spectrum of disciplines and was the first traditional German university that established a Technical Faculty (whose many patents recently led to the second rank in innovation among European universities). When I started, the university had about 9,000 students. Its current enrollment of 38,000 students shows the huge changes over time that have had an impact on academic life. I had no advice on how to plan an academic career, for example, studying abroad at universities with famous professors. Now students know more about these issues and think more strategically. Financial issues were also relevant for me, and I benefited from a stipend. I met my future wife in our first semester, and we had a child when we were undergraduates. Accordingly, studying abroad was not on the top of our list of plans.

We both agreed that we could cope with this – in scientific terminology – 'critical life event'. It was not too difficult because university life gave us freedom. Without thinking about a 'modern partnership', each of us cared for the boy when the partner was at the university. I learned how to change nappies, and I was the only father together with 25 mothers on an excursion for kindergarten children. Our son seems not to have suffered from his (at this time) unconventional upbringing; he later became a physicist and international entrepreneur with patents in laser surgery. As students, we benefited from my parents' support, as they let to us a small flat in their house. Perhaps these experiences triggered some of my later interest in social support as a protective factor (Bender & Lösel, 1997; Lösel & Bliesener, 1990). During semester breaks, I earned some money in consumer research, construction firms, and furniture transport. In consumer research, I investigated the images of packages and brand names for coffee, jam, children's food, and so on. In one study, I asked experienced whiskey drinkers to taste the content of different bottles. Their ratings were different, and many did not detect that a cheap German whiskey was in all the bottles. Such practical experiences gave 'flesh to the bones' of my university seminars on consumer psychology. I could also relate other practical experiences to my studies. For example, in one of my construction duties I had to clean the steel sheets used for fixing concrete. This was a particularly bad job because one had to erase the concrete with a steel brush and then put dirty oil on the plate. The regular workers avoided this duty, and I did not like it either. Although the metal scratching was not at all music, I got some satisfaction when I improved my technique and could clean more steel plates per day (without payment for output). At the university,

I learned how this personal experience fit McClelland's theory of achievement motivation and Atkinson's theory on a realistic increase of levels of aspiration.

Although I studied in provincial Franconia, our Institute of Psychology had some international flair. We had lecturers from various countries, and the main person was Walter Toman who held the Chair Psychology 1. Toman was an assistant professor at Vienna but had moved to Harvard (where Gordon Allport was an international leader in psychology). After a professorship at Brandeis University, Toman returned to Europe. At Erlangen, he taught a broad range of topics with a specific interest in clinical psychology. Toman founded no academic 'school' as some other chairs in Germany did, but he was a model of combining clinical, quantitative, and experimental thinking. He published on family constellations (Toman, 1961) and his quantitative developmental theory of motivation (Toman, 1959). I was also influenced by other academic teachers, for example, Hans Werbik (who worked on action theory and violence); Joachim Franke (a pioneer in environmental psychology); and Wilhelm Kamlah and Paul Lorenzen, who founded the 'Erlangen School' on logical propaedeutic and philosophy of science.

11.3   Research Assistant and Doctorate

After I graduated in 1971, Toman offered me a position as Research Assistant in an Advanced Research Center ('Sonderforschungsbereich', or SFB) of the German Research Foundation (DFG) at Nuremberg. These SFBs were and still are highly competitive and prestigious, and, as it was my first job offer, I happily accepted.

11.3.1   First Research on Juvenile Delinquency

The research center comprised about 10 projects on the topic of 'Socialization and Communication'. Our project was on juvenile delinquency, and thus I entered into an area that remained one of my research topics over many years. Perhaps my career would have been different without this job offer. Looking back, I think that young scholars should not make too detailed plans for the future but grasp an opportunity if they have good gut feelings about it. Our project benefited from the research of Glueck and Glueck (1968) at Harvard and the Cambridge Study in Delinquent Development (West & Farrington, 1973), which both became landmarks of longitudinal research. We assessed the development of juvenile delinquents in prisons and halfway houses and compared them with youngsters in the community. Our specific focus was on family processes and social risk factors in development (Lösel, Dillig, Wüstendörfer, & Linz, 1974). We also published on methodological issues of self-reported versus official crime, imputation of missing data, and hypotheses of the labeling approach (Lösel, 1978). In 1973, I got a lecturer post in Erlangen but continued my research at the SFB in Nuremberg.

Unfortunately, most of my early publications were in German and not read in the Anglo-American world. An exception was Hans Eysenck, who emigrated from Germany in 1934. He even wrote a recommendation of a book I edited on criminal psychology and cited one of our studies over decades as a German proof of his three-dimensional personality theory (although we found that not extraversion in general but the subfactor of impulsivity was relevant for delinquency). At this time, researchers may have assumed that their articles in German journals would be read in other countries (as was the case when German physics was internationally pre-eminent in the early 20th century). I remember that I was happy when a prestigious peer-reviewed German journal accepted two of my papers without revision. In psychology, we read the articles from North America and Britain, but this was a one-way exchange. Overall, half of my nearly 460 publications were internationally buried in the language waste bin. In the 1990s the DFG promoted English publications to increase international visibility. I welcomed this development, although it often causes double work because one has to write German articles as well in order to reach practitioners. In criminal law, most scholars still publish in German, knowing that the German juridical system is highly regarded and different from the Anglo-American system.

11.3.2 Doctoral Dissertation

The limited international impact of German publications became particularly obvious to me much later. I got my Dr. phil. (German PhD) in 1974. My dissertation was on *Handlungskontrolle und Delinquenz [Action Control and Delinquency]*, and I completed exams in psychology, educational science, and psychiatry. My dissertation aimed for an integration of personality theories of delinquency. I published a slightly revised version as a German book (Lösel, 1975) with a modified title ('juvenile delinquency' instead of 'delinquency') because I felt that my research was mainly relevant for young offenders. My theory was similar to what Gottfredson and Hirschi (1990) published in their book on self-control as a general theory of crime. I had ambivalent feelings when I read it. I was proud that two eminent American scholars had similar thoughts to the ones I had had in 1974, but I was somewhat disappointed that, perhaps due to language barriers, they did not cite my work.

In my theory, delinquent acts are the result of a decision to offend, that is, to violate a norm of criminal law. According to action theories, decisions depend on an estimation of the subjective value and probability of reaching a specific goal situation. I conceived decisions not as a dichotomy at one time, but as a chain reaction with transitions that contain both incentives and obstacles. The core of my theory was self-control, defined as the individual's capability to analyze short- and long-term consequences of his or her own behavior and act accordingly. I integrated various theoretical constructs, for example, deferred gratification, cognitive impulsivity, and time perspective. I also assumed that characteristics of self-control are interrelated, develop through bio-social interactions, are *relatively* stable over time, and are related to cognitive competences.

In my empirical study, I used self-reports, teacher ratings, and direct behavioral measures. As expected, delinquency and measures of low self-control correlated significantly, particularly when assessed by question-naire scales. The behavioral measures correlated less with delinquency and with each other. I concluded that self-control is an important origin for some forms of delinquency, but it is a heterogeneous construct with several facets. Data from our later studies pointed in the same direction (Beelmann, Bliesener, & Lösel, 2000; Lösel, 1980; Lösel & Bliesener, 2003a). International authors also questioned the concept of self-control as a *general* theory of crime (see Lösel, 2017).

In Germany, doctoral candidates are not students in the Anglo-American sense, but can have academic positions with lecturing duties. This ensured my family income. My supervisor, Walter Toman, was liberal and trusted in me. I met him in the context of our research center, but for my PhD I only came three times to his office: first when I submitted my proposal, then for a progress report after a year, and finally when I handed over my dissertation. Looking back, I think that it helped me that I had developed a sense of self-reliance and autonomy in childhood. During my academic career, I supervised about 40 PhD candidates, and when appropriate I avoided too rigorous monitoring. However, supervision needs to be flexible because PhD students and topics are very different.

11.4   University Lectureships and First Professorship

In 1975, I got the position of University Lecturer (Assistant Professor) at Erlangen. Parallel to this job my colleagues and I carried out another project in the Advanced Study Center at Nuremberg. Our team aimed to 'translate' our research on crime to the practice of rehabilitation. We carried out representative surveys on attitudes and role problems of prison officers in Bavaria and developed a structured cognitive-behavioral program for training them in psychological competences (Blickhan, Braune, Klapprott, Linz, & Lösel, 1978). In a randomized controlled trial we found positive effects, and a later study of these data (Lösel & Wittmann, 1989) showed me the importance of what is de facto going on in control groups (Farrington et al., 2019).

In 1978, I moved to a tenured senior lectureship for developmental psychology and methodology at the University of Bamberg. As with most university lecturers in Germany, I had only a fixed-term contract at Erlangen and aimed for more security for our family. In the same year, I got the degree of Dr. phil. habil. ('Habilitation'), the necessary qualification (but no guarantee) for a professorship. I gave my Habilitation lecture on behavioral genetics and crime. Although this was a controversial topic due to Germany's Nazi history, the lecture went well. A little later, I got the offer of a professorship from a prestigious university in Baden–Württemberg, but Bavaria also offered me a professorship. After a difficult decision, I returned from Bamberg to Erlangen.

11.5 My Work at Bielefeld University

In 1982, I became Professor of Psychology at the University of Bielefeld (North Rhine–Westphalia), which had a strong reputation in the social sciences. At Bielefeld, I again enjoyed interdisciplinary cooperation. We successfully applied for an SFB of the DFG on 'Prevention and Intervention in Childhood and Adolescence'. Various books give an overview on our work (Brambring, Lösel, & Skowronek, 1989; Hurrelmann, Kaufmann, & Lösel, 1987; Hurrelmann & Lösel, 1990).

11.5.1 Research on Resilience

My own project was on resilience in high-risk children, the first study on this topic on the European continent. In my previous research on risk factors, I saw many individuals with similar risk patterns compared to those who became delinquent, but they showed no behavior problems. Therefore, we wanted to investigate 'the other side of the coin', that is, protective processes in development. Hereby, we benefited from the work of Emmy Werner, Norman Garmezy, Michael Rutter, Ann Masten, and other pioneers of resilience research. Through a stepwise case-oriented assessment, we selected youngsters who were in institutional care due to serious neglect and abuse in their family backgrounds. We compared two groups that we recruited from more than 50 institutions: one showed a rather positive development in spite of accumulated risks, whereas another group at the same risk level exhibited serious behavioral problems (Bender, Bliesener, & Lösel, 1996; Lösel & Bliesener, 1994). We followed the youngsters from early to later adolescence and found various buffering protective factors. Stable resilient youngsters had a more flexible temperament, less impulsivity, a more realistic future orientation, a better relation to school, a more active coping style, fewer feelings of helplessness, satisfactory social support, positive relationships with their educators, less contact with their (often problematic) father, and warmth and acceptance as well as supervision in the care homes. Social protective factors seemed to be more relevant than personal resources, which spoke against resilience as only an individual trait. There were also two subgroups whose outcome behavior changed over time, that is, from resilience to deviance or vice versa. These groups were smaller and differed in fewer significant factors that predicted positive versus negative change. However, social support, educational climate, and more active versus passive coping behavior were relevant for change.

In the 1980s–1990s, resilience and protective factors became important topics. In comparison to prior risk-oriented research, people liked the more encouraging message. Similarly, positive psychology became popular. Recently I experienced a revival of media interest in resilience and assume that feelings of insecurity in a fast-changing world led to reflections on how to strengthen the family in difficult times. As we carried out research on both risk factors/deficits and protective factors/strengths we did not adhere to the controversies on pathogenetic versus salutogenetic perspectives. Both need to be brought together in order to explain more outcome variance and to consider the basic developmental principles of equifinality and multifinality. Risk and protective factors are not simply the other side of the coin but require differentiated research strategies on interaction and buffering effects (Lösel & Bender, 2003; Lösel & Farrington, 2012). Depending on the context of other variables and type of outcome, a specific variable can even have a risk as well as a protective effect (Bender & Lösel, 1997).

11.5.2 Research on Offender Treatment

At Bielefeld we also carried out a comprehensive meta-evaluation on correctional treatment (Lösel & Köferl, 1989; Lösel et al., 1987). To our knowledge, our book contained the first meta-analysis on the treatment of serious adult offenders. At about the same time, Lipsey (1992) published a much more comprehensive meta-analysis on the treatment of juvenile offenders. Both studies found significant mean treatment effects in contrast to the widespread slogan of 'nothing works' that was due to misinterpretations of the review of Lipton et al. (1975). Together with the work of international researchers, our study contributed to the move from 'nothing works' to 'what works' in Germany and elsewhere.

Developmental prevention and offender treatment seem to be rather separate topics. Researchers and practitioners mainly work on one but not the other issue. However, a closer look at both fields shows basic similarities in (mainly cognitive-behavioral) programs and research findings (Lösel, 2007). Early prevention rarely reaches most children at risk, even the best programs have only moderate effects, and there are no clear effect size differences between age groups (Beelmann & Lösel, 2019). For these and other reasons, I proposed a more integrated science of developmental intervention instead of too much segmentation. Tertiary prevention or treatment of offenders often covers long periods of follow-up, and, as prisoners' families are particularly vulnerable (Lanskey, Lösel, Markson, & Souza, 2019), a positive influence on delinquent parents can have a primary preventive effect on their offspring (see below).

11.6   Back at the University of Erlangen–Nuremberg

In 1987, I returned to the University of Erlangen–Nuremberg and took over the Chair Psychology 1 (in succession of Walter Toman). During the first years, I also traveled regularly to Bielefeld to complete my research projects there. At Erlangen, I had to cope with much administration as Head of the Department and later Faculty Dean and Member of the Senate. In teaching, I was responsible for clinical psychology and psychotherapy, psychological assessment, methodology (i.e., evaluation), and psychology and law. I had to give the main lectures on these disciplines and rarely could hold a seminar on my special research topics. However, trying to be up-to-date in a broad range of fields helped me connect knowledge instead of following a too-narrow 'silo approach'. In research, I started new projects, for example, the following:

11.6.1   Study on School Bullying

Funded by the German Federal Police Office, we carried out a study of more than 1,100 students on violence at school. We showed strong relations between bullying perpetration and delinquent or violent behavior in other contexts (Lösel & Bliesener, 2003a). Most characteristics of 'hard core' bullies were similar to youth violence in general. For example, their families showed lower income, more aggression and neglect, inconsistent parenting, alcohol misuse, and other problems. On the individual level, bullies were more impulsive, lower in attentiveness, more aggressive in their cognitions, worse in school achievement, more truant, more affiliated with delinquent peers, and more interested in low-structured leisure activities and violence consumption in the media. An unfavorable school climate also played a role. The typical victims were vulnerable, as they showed social isolation, internalizing problems, an unfavorable family climate, and low social support at school. By comparing subgroups at high risk, we also found similar protective factors and mechanisms compared to those of our previous resilience study.

After 2 years, we carried out a follow-up of a subsample that included prototypical bullying perpetrators, victims, and other (non-deviant) students. We used questionnaires, teacher ratings, standardized tests and behavioral observations. The latter contained experimental situations for triads of youngsters who had not known each other before (i.e., had no established bully–victim relation). The bullies were even more aggressive and intimidating in the laboratory context, but perceived more hostile intentions in the other boys, reported fewer non-aggressive cognitive schemata, evaluated aggression more positively, had lower heart rates, and were more dominant. Our results confirmed theories of social information processing (SIP) on aggressive behavior (Dodge & Pettit, 2003). Whereas most studies addressed SIP as a cause of aggression, we also showed that aggression-prone schemata correlated with prior experiences of aggression in the family, at school, in peer groups, and in the media (Lösel, Bliesener, & Bender, 2007).

11.6.2 *Violent Children in Youth Welfare*

In a case-oriented project on seriously violent children in youth care (funded by the Oak Foundation) we aimed to validate our previous findings on the accumulation of bio-psycho-social risk factors for anti-social development (see also Hawkins et al., 1998). We used prototypical case vignettes of youngsters who had developed serious violence and were very difficult to care for (Bender & Lösel, 2006). We sent these vignettes to a national sample of practitioners who worked in family- and childcare services and asked them to report similar cases. The findings showed the difficulties to be encountered in helping these youngsters, who were both very aggressive and had been victimized in their own childhood. The youngsters had experienced between zero and eight different placements (e.g., foster care, child psychiatry, halfway houses, or intensive treatment abroad). Their problematic characteristics included family violence, neglect, deprived neighborhoods, school problems, ADHS, delinquent peers, substance misuse, neurological impairment, and so forth. This person-oriented study clearly supported our findings in variable-oriented studies.

Based on our various research projects, Lösel and Bender (2003) generated a model of main risk and potentially protective domains in antisocial development.

Of course, this is not a causal model with a strict sequence. Each box of domains contains various variables, and there may be feedback processes between them (the reason we avoided arrows). Protective effects in some domains can interrupt an undesirable chain reaction. Both risk and protective mechanisms function according to a dose-response relationship (Lösel & Farrington, 2012). Practitioners felt that the model is useful for targeted multimodal prevention.

11.6.3 Survey and Evaluation of Family-Oriented Prevention Programs

Early prevention became a policy topic in Germany in the 1990s (delayed in comparison to North America). The Ministry of Family Affairs asked us to carry out a survey and evaluation on family-oriented prevention programs. In a nationwide representative survey, we gathered data from more than 2,000 institutions that delivered nearly 200,000 offers per annum and reached about two million families with young children (Lösel, Schmucker, Plankensteiner, & Weiss, 2006). Although we could describe details of what was going on in this field, the results on evaluation were sobering. There were only some systematic evaluations on parenting programs and prenatal courses, but none on other frequently used measures of prevention. We also carried out a meta-analysis of the controlled studies and found significant effects on parenting and child behavior. In a more recent meta-analysis we updated this moderately positive finding (Weiss, Schmucker, & Lösel, 2015). However, as is true worldwide, the follow-ups of most studies are too short (Farrington et al., 2017).

11.6.4 The Erlangen–Nuremberg Development and Prevention Study

Due to the unsatisfactory state of evaluation of developmental prevention, we carried out the Erlangen–Nuremberg Development and Prevention Study. This was a big project funded by the German Federal Ministry of Family Affairs, the Red Cross, and various federal states

(Lösel, Schmucker, et al., 2006; Lösel et al., 2013). Our project combined a prospective longitudinal and experimental design as recommended by Farrington, et al. (1986). Hereby we benefited from the work of leading developmental researchers, in particular from David Farrington, Rolf Loeber, and Richard Tremblay. Our project contained various studies. The main sample consisted of 675 kindergarten children in the area of Erlangen and Nuremberg. The first waves took place annually, the others after longer intervals. Retention rates varied between 87% and 99%. Parts of our sample participated in a universal child social skills training, a parent training on positive parenting, or a combination of both (EFFEKT program: Promoting Development in Families: Parent and Child Training). In the assignment to the treatment and control groups, we used a group-based randomization with additional matching.

The program showed desirable effects on externalizing behavior problems after 2–3 months, 2–3 years, and 4–5 years (Lösel & Stemmler, 2012b). After about 10 years, there were still some significant outcomes, that is, on boys' self-reported property offending (Lösel et al., 2013). We also found desirable effects in shorter evaluations of adapted program versions in samples from deprived migrant backgrounds (Runkel, Lösel, Stemmler, & Jaursch, 2017) and families with emotional problems (Bühler, Kötter, Jaursch, & Lösel, 2011). Overall, the project showed promising effects, although findings varied across different follow-up periods, outcome measures, and subprograms. Most promising was the combination of parent and child training.

On request by the funding ministry, we implemented a universal and not a risk-based program. Although the effects of universal programs are typically lower than in indicated prevention (Beelmann & Lösel, 2019 ; Lösel & Beelmann, 2003; Lösel & Bender, 2017), they can reduce problems in subgroups who are most at risk (Coid, 2003; Lösel, Beelmann, Stemmler, & Jaursch, 2006). Even small preventive effects can save costs for the society (Cohen & Piquero, 2009). As our program had no negative effects, we disseminated it nationwide on a nonprofit basis. We trained nearly 2,000 facilitators who were satisfied with the program, but an evaluation of the large-scale implementation is desirable because effects in routine practice are smaller than in demonstration projects.

The findings of our evaluation were in accordance with integrative reviews of meta-analyses on developmental prevention of crime and violence (Farrington et al., 2017; Lösel, 2012a). However, the effect sizes vary substantially and even between identical or similar programs. Therefore, I dealt with the issue of replication in my 2015 Joan McCord Award Lecture (Lösel, 2018). Colleagues endorsed my view and addressed various topics of replication (Farrington et al., 2019). Most experts agree that one cannot generally say that this or that program of developmental prevention 'works', but we need to focus more on the specific circumstances of moderators of outcome effects.

Beyond the prevention part of our project, we carried out numerous developmental analyses on specific issues. For example, Stemmler and Lösel (2015) found five developmental trajectories of externalizing problems from preschool to youth age that were similar to the many studies on delinquency of older groups. The small 'high-chronic' group differed in individual and social characteristics from the 'low-chronics' and other groups. An aggregation of risk factors had high predictive validity with odds ratios up to 10 (Wallner et al., 2018). We also carried out individual-oriented analyses of developmental types and found somewhat different patterns for boys and girls (Lösel & Stemmler, 2012a, 2012b). In a study on the controversial issue of working mothers and external care of toddlers there was no negative effect on the children's behavior from preschool to youth age (Jaursch & Lösel, 2011). A study on the relation between pregnancy and birth complications and child behavior problems revealed only a very small detrimental effect for those children who grew up in low SES family backgrounds (Koglin & Lösel, 2014).

11.6.5   Football Hooliganism

Perhaps triggered by my interest in football, we carried out a project on the dark side of this sport, that is, on hooligan violence. In a nationwide study (funded by the German Federal Ministry of the Interior) we surveyed 'hard-core' hooligans, and experts from the police, criminal justice system, social work, and fan support (Lösel & Bliesener, 2003b; Lösel, Bliesener, Fischer, & Pabst, 2001). In contrast to widespread stereotypes, the hooligans were mostly interested in football, had been recruited in close networks, did not adhere to a code of fairness in their fights, exhibited other forms of offending, and showed the same personality, family, school, peer group, and employment risk factors that we found in other studies of violence. Ringleaders had more psycho-pathic characteristics, were more intelligent, and had less problematic biographical backgrounds. The local 'hooligan scenes' and prevention measures varied widely between the cities of the German football league.

11.6.6   Risk and Protective Factors in Long-Term Marriages

We aimed to compare our research on 'at risk' families with more 'normal' families. Funded by the German Ministry for Family Affairs, we studied couples who were in a long-lasting marriage (M = 27 years). In a sample of 222 individuals, we used intensive interviews and questionnaires (Lösel & Bender, 2005). Although assessed separately, the partners' marital satisfaction correlated strongly. The experience of stressors over time showed a U-shaped curve. It was enhanced in the first 7 years of the partnership (e.g., due to births of children and problems with the wider family), was low in the middle periods, and increased again in the last phase (e.g., due to health problem and care for parents). We compared two subsamples of couples who had both experienced a high level of stressors and strains but reported low versus high marital quality. Similar to our other studies on resilience we found buffering protective factors that differed between both groups (good sense of coherence, social support, secure attachment, social competence, and flexible adaptation when pursued goals were no longer reachable). We generated a developmental model of family resilience that we used later in a study on prisoners' families (see below).

11.7   My Work at Cambridge

In 2015, I became Director of the Institute of Criminology (IoC) at Cambridge University, England. Although I closely cooperated with criminological research institutions in Germany, I never intended to become a professor of criminology. Psychology is a larger discipline, and much of my research and teaching addressed psychological topics. Furthermore, German criminology was and is located in Law Faculties that only appoint professors with a law degree (a structural problem of German criminology). The offer from Cambridge was attractive because the IoC is a world leader in its field, with a strong empirical orientation. Leading an institute in a different academic culture was a challenge, but I benefited from advice and support from David Farrington, Tony Bottoms, Per-Olof Wikström, and my predecessor Michael Tonry. After long struggles with the German pension system, I could move to Cambridge on unpaid leave from Bavaria. At Erlangen, I still led research projects and had to prepare a big conference that I had promised to organize long before. These duties required frequent commuting between both countries and regular work on weekends. Without the support of Doris Bender and others, I would not have been able to cope with these challenges in the first year after my move to England.

At Cambridge, I could quickly settle in. Regular administrative meetings in the Institute, Law Faculty, and School of Humanities and Social Sciences (SHSS) were time consuming but happened in a cooperative climate. My most important challenge was the university's plan to merge

various institutes in the SHSS. I spent nearly a whole sabbatical networking and providing facts against a merger. The Law Faculty also supported us, and so we were the only institute that could preserve its
independence. Parallel to my German research I started various projects
in Britain, including the following:

11.7.1   Strengthening Transnational Approaches to Reducing Reoffending (STARR)

Funded by the European Commission I led a study within an
international consortium on the treatment of offenders. Our
Cambridge project undertook surveys and systematic reviews on the
treatment of young offenders, substance-misusing offenders, and domestic violence perpetrators (Lösel, Koehler, Hamilton, Humphreys, &
Akoensi, 2011). We showed that only very few of the 27 European
countries had any controlled evaluations on our topics. Studies on the
treatment of young offenders revealed mean positive effects on recidivism. We also showed promising effects of substitution programs for
substance misusing offenders, but methodologically weak effects for
treatment of domestic violence perpetrators.

11.7.2   Risk and Protective Factors in Prisoners' Families

Funded by the UK Big Lottery Fund and in cooperation with the
Ormiston Children and Family Trust we carried out a prospective longitudinal study on incarcerated fathers and their families. Prisoners' families are particularly vulnerable to undesirable developments between
children and parents. We assessed prisoners and their families during
the sentence and again 6 months after release (Lösel et al., 2012). To our
knowledge, this was the first project in Europe with a 'whole family
approach', that is, gathering data from the father, the female partner,
and their children. We found that resettlement after release was more
successful when families had more contact and better communication
during the imprisonment (Markson, Lösel, Souza, & Lanskey, 2015),
even when we controlled for the prior family relationship. We also
showed that the women had a more realistic view of the men's difficulties
after release (Souza, Lösel, Markson, & Lanskey, 2015), and various
characteristics of family interaction had a positive effect on the children's
development (Lanskey, Lösel, Markson, & Souza, 2016).

Recently we got a grant from the UK Economic and Social Research
Council for a follow-up of these families. This study has its focus on
processes of resilience, and covers 7 years of the families' development.

We also worked on conceptual articles on the rapidly increasing research on prisoners' families (Lanskey et al., 2019) and analyzed data of the U.S. Fragile Families and Child Wellbeing Project (Markson, Lamb, & Lösel, 2016). As large longitudinal projects often contain only a few items on specific constructs, the effects were lower than in our in-depth investigation of a smaller sample.

11.8   Recent Research in Germany

As at Cambridge, Erlangen–Nuremberg has mandatory retirement. However, due to my externally funded research I hold a position as Honorary Fellow of Psychology. My current projects address the following topics:

11.8.1   *Protective Factors against Extremism and Radicalization*

This topic is currently highly relevant. Whereas most studies on the various forms of extremism and radicalization dealt with risk factors, we carried out a project on protective factors (funded by the European Commission). In systematic quantitative and qualitative reviews, we showed that in spite of thousands of publications, sound research on protective factors is very rare. We also revealed various protective factors (Lösel, Bender, Jugl, & King, 2019; Lösel et al., 2018). Most of them were similar compared with those related to general violence among young people (Lösel & Farrington, 2012). For example, self-control, employment, positive parenting behavior, school achievement, bonds to school, non-deviant peers, illness/depression, basic adherence to law, and acceptance of police legitimacy seemed to have a protective function in early phases of radicalization. Similar factors had a 'pull' effect in processes of de-radicalization and disengagement, but 'push' factors like disillusionment and negative experiences in the radical group played an important role. Based on these correlational findings, we recently started a project on the evaluation of prevention programs against radicalization in development (funded by the German Federal Ministry of the Interior).

11.8.2   *Treatment of Sexual Offenders*

In contrast to public stereotypes, sexual re-offending rates are much lower than in other fields of violence. However, every case is one too many. Although meta-analyses have shown mean positive effects of treatment (Schmucker & Lösel, 2017), there is still controversy about treatment in prisons (Lösel & Schmucker, 2017). A recent study of the British Ministry of Justice (Mews, Di Bella, & Purver, 2017) even revealed some negative effects that became notorious in the mass media. As I was involved in prepublication reviews of this study, I concurrently led a project on sex offender treatment in prisons (funded by the Bavarian Ministry of Justice). In a first phase, we compared different matching procedures and found not only desirable effects on general and serious reoffending, but also some differences between both methods in sexual re-offending (Lösel, Link, et al., 2019). Currently we are expanding our sample and preparing differentiated analyses that take the seriousness of offences and differences between institutions into account.

11.9   Practical Work, Functions, Honors and Awards

As described above, I carried out basic, applied, and translational research. I always felt that researchers should give something back to societies that are funding their projects and paying their salaries. Often reports on practically relevant research disappear in the drawers of policymakers, but I also experienced that we can have an impact if we catch the moment (see my interview in the Oral History Project of the European Society of Criminology: www.youtube.com/watch?v= DUBOY2akUTk). As G. A. Miller (1969) stipulated in his famous APA address, I aimed to give parts of my research away. For example, as a not very religious Protestant, I worked with the International Catholic Child Bureau on the application of the concept of resilience in projects in Africa and South America. I also gave numerous lectures to practitioners and policymakers, provided expert evidence for courts and prisons, and trained practitioners in the German Department for Migration and Asylum Seekers. I also served on many policy-relevant committees. For some of these, see the abstract, for others my website at Cambridge: www.crim.cam.ac.uk/People/professor-friedrich-losel.

I received more than a dozen international honors and awards (see the abstract and my website). I was also recognized by appointment to many editorial boards and several offers of professorships that I had to decline. Obviously, with age the probability of getting an honor increases. As a boy who grew up in the ruins of Nuremberg and later as a young German researcher, I never thought about such possibilities. Perhaps they did not happen 100% by chance, but they were not predictable.

11.10   Conclusions

This is my first article that triggered a retrospective assessment of my academic career and some personal parts of my life. In my review of nearly 50 years of research, I focused on a selection of projects. Most of these studies originated from my genuine interest, but occasionally there was an urgent need for funding to extend contracts of good research assistants. Sometimes I would have welcomed more time for working on a specific topic. This was the case for the origins of psychopathy (Lösel & Schmucker, 2004), biological risk factors (Bender & Lösel, 2015), and the recent 'crime drop' (Lösel, Bender, Sünkel, & Stemmler, 2016). In modern times we researchers have to cope with the 'needs and speeds' at universities, where grants only fund fieldwork.

I was always interested in delinquency and violence among young people, family and personality issues in risk research, protective factors and processes of resilience that buffer the impact of risks, early developmental prevention, offender treatment, sound program evaluation, and relations between these different areas. It was fascinating to study the similarities of personality, social, and situational origins of phenomena that looked rather different at first glance. However, I was also skeptical about theories that pretended to explain very different phenomena and bio-psycho-social influences. Most criminological theories are not really falsified (Bernard, 1990), and we need more theoretical competition, integration, and differentiation (Farrington et al., 2020; Lösel, 2018). My conclusion on research methods is similar. I used a range of different designs. Although I liked the strengths of randomized experiments, I had to strive for the best design under given circumstances and was skeptical regarding sweeping controversies about the one and only 'gold standard' (see also Farrington et al., 2020).

I can only speculate about whether some of my childhood experiences may have contributed to the topics and methods of my research. I learned in childhood and youth about mastering difficulties, particularly within a secure family and school context. In my view, bonding and mutual trust were highly important for coping with problems in postwar Germany. Within a supportive social context, human beings can adapt flexibly but also be firm when necessary. I had excellent and humane schooling and academic teachers from whom I learned for my own development. A solid and broad education in sciences and the arts, sound academic training in empirical methods, and some philosophy of science helped me to address different topics and draw some perhaps generalizable conclusions.

I benefited a lot from support by leading international scholars, although I could only mention a few in this article. They and other colleagues contributed to a volume that Bliesener, Beelmann, and Stemmler (2012) prepared without my knowledge when I officially retired at Erlangen. I was always skeptical about the heterogeneous

Festschrifts that are popular in law. However, my three younger colleagues produced a homogeneous book about developmental and intervention research on antisocial behavior. I am grateful to all contributors for their excellent papers. Last, but not least, I wish to thank the many younger colleagues whose engagement enabled me to carry out my empirical projects in the past and – if I stay healthy – may perhaps complement them in the future. As the late Rolf Loeber printed on the T-shirts he gave some colleagues and friends: 'There is no cure for curiosity'.

References

Beelmann, A., Bliesener, T., & Lösel, F. (2000). Dimensions of impulsivity and their relation to antisocial behavior in male adolescents. In A. Czerederecka, T. Jaskiewicz-Obydzinska, & C. J. Krakow (Eds.), *Forensic psychology and law* (pp. 49–57). Cracow, Poland: Forensic Research.
Beelmann, A., & Lösel, F. (2019). A comprehensive meta-analysis of randomized evaluations of the effect of child social skills training on antisocial development. *(under review)*.
Bender, D., Bliesener, T., & Lösel, F. (1996). Deviance or resilience? A longitudinal study of adolescents in residential care. In G. Davies, S. Lloyd-Bostock, M. McMurran, & C. Wilson (Eds.), *Psychology, law, and criminal justice* (pp. 409–423). Berlin, Germany: de Gruyter.
Bender, D., & Lösel, F. (1997). Protective and risk effects of peer relations and social support on antisocial behaviour in adolescents from multi-problem milieus. *Journal of Adolescence, 20*(6), 661–678.
Bender, D., & Lösel, F. (2006). Working with violent children in German youth services: Results of a survey. In A. Hagell & R. J. Dent (Eds.), *Children who commit acts of serious interpersonal violence: Messages for practice* (pp. 167–185). London, England: Jessica Kingsley.
Bender, D., & Lösel, F. (2011). Bullying at school as a predictor of delinquency, violence and other anti-social behaviour in adulthood. *Criminal Behaviour and Mental Health, 21*(2), 99–106.
Bender, D., & Lösel, F. (2015). *Resting and stress-induced heart rate and antisocial behavior in youth: A study on moderator effects and longitudinal relations.* Paper presented at the Conference of the European Society of Criminology, Porto, Portugal.
Bernard, T. (1990). Twenty years of testing theories: What have we learned and why? *Journal of Research in Crime and Delinquency, 27*(4), 325–347.
Blickhan, C., Braune, P., Klapprott, J., Linz, P., & Lösel, F. (1978). *Psychologische Fortbildung für den Strafvollzug [Psychological training of prison staff].* Stuttgart, Germany: Enke Verlag.
Bliesener, T., Beelmann, A., & Stemmler, M. (Eds.). (2012). *Antisocial behavior and crime: Contributions of developmental and evaluation research to prevention and intervention.* Cambridge, MA: Hogrefe.

Brambring, M., Lösel, F., & Skowronek, H. (Eds.). (1989). *Children at risk: Assessment, longitudinal research and intervention*. Berlin, Germany: De Gruyter.

Bühler, A., Kötter, C., Jaursch, S., & Lösel, F. (2011). Prevention of familial transmission of depression: EFFEKT-E, a selective program for emotionally burdened families. *Journal of Public Health, 19*(4), 321–327.

Cohen, M. A., & Piquero, A. R. (2009). New evidence on the monetary value of saving a high risk youth. *Journal of Quantitative Criminology, 25*, 25–49.

Coid, J. W. (2003). Formulating strategies for the primary prevention of adult antisocial behaviour: 'High risk' or 'population' strategies? In D. P. Farrington & J. W. Coid (Eds.), *Early prevention of adult antisocial behaviour*. Cambridge, England: Cambridge University Press.

Dodge, K. A., & Pettit, G. S. (2003). A biopsychosocial model of the development of chronic conduct problems in adolescence. *Developmental Psychology, 39*(2), 349–371.

Farrington, D. P., Gaffney, H., Lösel, F., & Ttofi, M. M. (2017). Systematic reviews of the effectiveness of developmental prevention programs in reducing delinquency, aggression, and bullying. *Aggression and Violent Behavior, 33*, 91–106.

Farrington, D. P., Lösel, F., Boruch, R. F., Gottfredson, D. C., Mazerolle, L., Sherman, L. W., & Weisburd, D. (2019). Advancing knowledge about replication in criminology. *Journal of Experimental Criminology, 15*(3), 373–396.

Farrington, D. P., Lösel, F., Braga, A. A., Mazerolle, L., Raine, A., Sherman, L. W., & Weisburd, D. (2020). Experimental criminology: Looking back and forward on the 20th anniversary of the Academy of Experimental Criminology. *Journal of Experimental Criminology*, 1–25.

Farrington, D. P., Ohlin, L. E., & Wilson, J. Q. (1986). *Understanding and controlling crime: Toward a new research strategy*. New York, NY: Springer-Verlag.

Glueck, S., & Glueck, E. (1968). *Unraveling juvenile delinquency* (4th ed.). Cambridge, MA: Harvard University Press.

Gottfredson, M. R., & Hirschi, T. (1990). *A general theory of crime*. Stanford, CA: Stanford University Press.

Hawkins, J. D., Herrenkohl, T., Farrington, D. P., Brewer, D., Catalano, R. F., & Harachi, T. W. (1998). A review of predictors of youth violence. In R. Loeber & D. P. Farrington (Eds.), *Serious and violent juvenile offenders: Risk factors and successful interventions*. Thousand Oaks, CA: Sage.

Hurrelmann, K., Kaufmann, F.-X., & Lösel, F. (Eds.). (1987). *Social intervention: Potential and constraints*. Berlin, Germany: de Gruyter.

Hurrelmann, K., & Lösel, F. (Eds.). (1990). *Health hazards in adolescence*. Berlin, Germany: de Gruyter.

Jaursch, S., & Lösel, F. (2011). Mütterliche Berufstätigkeit und kindliches Sozialverhalten: A longitudinal study [Maternal employment and children's social behavior]. *Kindheit und Entwicklung, 20*, 164–172.

Kershaw, I. (2016). *To hell and back: Europe 1914–1949*. London, England: Penguin.

Koglin, U., & Lösel, F. (2014). Pregnancy and birth complications and externalizing behavioral problems in preschoolers. *Monatsschrift für Kriminologie und Strafrechtsreform/Journal of Criminology and Penal Reform, 97*, 451–461.

Lanskey, C., Lösel, F., Markson, L., & Souza, K. A. (2016). Children's contact with their imprisoned fathers and the father–child relationship following release: An interactional perspective. *Families, Relationships and Societies*, 5, 43–58.

Lanskey, C., Lösel, F., Markson, L., & Souza, K. A. (2019). Prisoners' families' research: Developments, debates and directions. In M. Hutton & D. Moran (Eds.), *The Palgrave handbook of prison and the family* (pp. 15–40). Abingdon, England: Palgrave McMillan.

Lipsey, M. W. (1992). The effect of treatment on juvenile delinquents: Results from meta-analysis. In F. Lösel, D. Bender, & T. Bliesener (Eds.), *Psychology and law: International perspectives* (pp. 131–143). Berlin, Germany: de Gruyter.

Lipton, D. S., Martinson, R., & Wilks, J. (1975). *The effectiveness of correctional treatment: A survey of treatment evaluation studies.* New York, NY: Praeger.

Lösel, F. (1975). *Handlungskontrolle und Jugenddelinquenz: Persönlichkeitspsychologische Erklärungsansätze delinquenten Verhaltens - Theoretische Integration und empirische Prüfung [Self- control and juvenile delinquency: Integration of personality theories on delinquency and an empirical test].* Stuttgart, Germany: Enke Verlag.

Lösel, F. (1978). Über elementare Konzepte sozialer Devianz und ihre Beziehungen. Ein Beitrag zur Explikation und ein empirischer Prüfversuch [Elementary models of social deviance and their relation: An explication and an empirical test]. *Zeitschrift für Sozialpsychologie*, 9, 2–18.

Lösel, F. (1980). On the differentiation of cognitive reflection–impulsivity. *Perceptual and Motor Skills*, 60, 1311–1324.

Lösel, F. (2007). It's never too early and never too late: Towards an integrated science of developmental intervention in criminology. *Criminologist*, 35(2), 1–8.

Lösel, F. (2012a). Entwicklungsbezogene Prävention von Gewalt und Kriminalität: Ansätze und Wirkungen [Developmental prevention of violence and crime: Approaches and effects]. *Forensische Psychiatrie, Psychologie und Kriminologie*, 6, 71–84.

Lösel, F. (2014). Was tun mit dem Reichsparteitagsgelände? Bemerkungen aus psychologischer Sicht. [What to do with the Nazi Rally Area? Remarks from a psychological perspective]. In BauLust (Ed.), *Positionen 2014: Zum Umgang mit dem Reichsparteitagsgelände und der Zeppelintribüne [Reflections on what to do with the Zeppelin Tribune and the Nazi Rally Area]* (pp. 8–15). Nuremberg, Germany: BauLust Initiative for Architecture and Community.

Lösel, F. (2017). Self-control as a theory of crime: A brief stocktaking after 27/42 years. In C. Bijlefeld & P. v. d. Laan (Eds.), *Liber amoricum for Gerben Bruinsma* (pp. 232–238). The Hague, the Netherlands: Boom.

Lösel, F. (2018). Evidence comes by replication, but needs differentiation: The reproducibility issue in science and its relevance for criminology. *Journal of Experimental Criminology*, 14(3), 257–278.

Lösel, F., & Beelmann, A. (2003). Effects of child skills training in preventing antisocial behavior: A systematic review of randomized evaluations. *The Annals of the American Academy of Political and Social Science*, 587, 84–109.

Lösel, F., Beelmann, A., Stemmler, M., & Jaursch, S. (2006). Prävention von problemen des sozialverhaltens im vorschulalter: Evaluation des Eltern- und

Kindertrainings EFFEKT. [Prevention of conduct problems in preschool age: Evaluation of the parent- and child-oriented program EFFEKT]. *Zeitschrift für Klinische Psychologie und Psychotherapie, 35*(2), 127–139.

Lösel, F., & Bender, D. (2003). Protective factors and resilience. In D. P. Farrington & J. Coid (Eds.), *Early prevention of adult antisocial behaviour* (pp. 130–204). Cambridge, England: Cambridge University Press.

Lösel, F., & Bender, D. (2005). *Protektive Faktoren der Ehequalität and Ehestabilität [Protective factors of marital quality and stability].* Research report. Berlin, Germany: German Federal Ministry for Family Affairs, Senior Citizens, Women and Youth.

Lösel, F., & Bender, D. (2017). Parenting and family-oriented programmes for preventing child behaviour problems. What the evidence tells us. *Journal of Family Research, 11*, 217–239.

Lösel, F., Bender, D., Jugl, I., & King, S. (2019). Resilience against political and religious extremism, radicalization, and related violence: A systematic review of studies on protective factors. In D. Weisburd, E. Savona, B. Hasisi, & F. Calderoni (Eds.), *Understanding recruitment to organized crime and terrorism: Social, psychological and economic drivers.* New York, NY: Springer.

Lösel, F., Bender, D., Sünkel, Z., & Stemmler, M. (2016). Self-reported juvenile delinquency in three surveys over 38 years: A German study on the crime drop. In A. Kapardis & D. P. Farrington (Eds.), *The psychology of crime, policing and courts* (pp. 24–43). Milton Park, England: Routledge.

Lösel, F., & Bliesener, T. (1994). Some high-risk adolescents do not develop conduct problems: A study of protective factors. *Journal of Behavioral Development, 17*(4), 753–777.

Lösel, F., & Bliesener, T. (1990). Resilience in adolescence: A study on the generalizability of protective factors. *Health Hazards in Adolescence*, 299–320.

Lösel, F., & Bliesener, T. (2003a). *Aggression und Delinquenz unter Jugendlichen: Untersuchungen von kognitiven und sozialen Bedingungen [Aggression and delinquency in adolescence: Studies on cognitive and social origins].* Neuwied, Germany: Luchterhand.

Lösel, F., & Bliesener, T. (2003b). Hooligan violence: A study on its prevalence, origins, and prevention. In F. Dünkel & K. Drenkhahn (Eds.), *Youth violence: New patterns and local responses* (pp. 245–265). Mönchengladbach, Germany: Forum Verlag.

Lösel, F., Bliesener, T., & Bender, D. (2007). Social information processing, experiences of aggression in social contexts, and aggressive behavior in adolescents. *Criminal Justice and Behavior, 34*(3), 330–347.

Lösel, F., Bliesener, T., Fischer, T., & Pabst, M. (2001). *Hooliganismus in Deutschland: Ursachen, Entwicklung, Prävention und Intervention [Football hooliganism in Germany: Origins, development, prevention, and intervention].* Berlin, Germany: German Federal Ministry of the Interior.

Lösel, F., Dillig, P., Wüstendörfer, W., & Linz, P. (1974). Über Zusammenhänge zwischen Merkmalen der sozialen Umwelt und der Kriminalitätsbelastung jugendlicher Straftäter [Relations between characteristics of the social environment and juvenile delinquency]. *Monatsschrift fur Kriminologie und Strafrechtsreform, 57*, 198–213.

Lösel, F., & Farrington, D. (2012). Direct protective and buffering protective factors in the development of youth violence. *American Journal of Preventive Medicine*, *43*(2), S8–S23.

Lösel, F., King, S., Bender, D., & Jugl, I. (2018). Protective factors against extremism and violent radicalization: A systematic review of research. *International Journal of Developmental Science*, *12*, 89–102.

Lösel, F., & Köferl, P. (1989). Evaluation research on correctional treatment in West Germany: A meta-analysis. In H. Wegener, F. Lösel, & J. Haisch (Eds.), *Criminal behavior and the justice system: Psychological perspectives* (pp. 334–355). New York, NY: Springer.

Lösel, F., Köferl, P., & Weber, F. (1987). *Meta-Evaluation der Sozialtherapie [Meta-evaluation of social-therapeutic prisons]*. Stuttgart, Germany: Enke.

Lösel, F., Link, E., Schmucker, M., Bender, D., Breuer, M., Carl, L., ... Lauchs, L. (2019). On the effectiveness of sexual offender treatment in prisons: A comparison of two different evaluation designs in routine practice (Online). *Sexual Abuse*.

Lösel, F., Pugh, G., Markson, L., Souza, K. A., & Lanskey, C. (2012). *Risk and protective factors in the resettlement of imprisoned fathers with their families*. Norwich, England: Ormiston Children and Families Trust.

Lösel, F., & Schmucker, M. (2004). Psychopathy, risk taking, and attention: A differentiated test of the somatic marker hypothesis. *Journal of Abnormal Psychology*, *113*(4), 522–529.

Lösel, F., & Schmucker, M. (2005). The effectiveness of treatment for sexual offenders: A comprehensive meta-analysis. *Journal of Experimental Criminology*, *1*(1), 117–146.

Lösel, F., & Schmucker, M. (2017). Treatment of sexual offenders: Concepts and empirical evaluations. In T. Sanders (Ed.), *The Oxford handbook on sex offences and sex offenders* (pp. 392–414). New York, NY: Oxford University Press.

Lösel, F., Schmucker, M., Plankensteiner, B., & Weiss, M. (2006). *Bestandsaufnahme und Evaluation der Elternbildung [Survey and evaluation of parent education in Germany]*. Berlin, Germany: Federal Ministry for Family Affairs, Senior Citizens, Women and Youth.

Lösel, F., & Stemmler, M. (2012a). Continuity and patterns of externalizing and internalizing behavior problems in girls: A variable-and person-oriented study from preschool to youth age. *Psychological Test and Assessment Modeling*, *54*(3), 307–319.

Lösel, F., & Stemmler, M. (2012b). Preventing child behavior problems in the Erlangen–Nuremberg Development and Prevention Study: Results from pre-school to secondary school age. *International Journal of Conflict and Violence*, *6*(2), 214–224.

Lösel, F., Stemmler, M., & Bender, D. (2013). Long-term evaluation of a bimodal universal prevention program: Effects on antisocial development from kindergarten to adolescence. *Journal of Experimental Criminology*, *9*(4), 429–449.

Lösel, F., & Wittmann, W. (1989). The relationship of treatment integrity and intensity to outcome criteria. *New Directions for Program Evaluation*, *42*, 97–108.

Lösel, F. A., Koehler, J. A., Hamilton, L., Humphreys, D. K., & Akoensi, T. D. (2011). *Strengthening transnational approaches to reducing reoffending: Final report*. London, England: UK Ministry of Justice and European Commission.

Markson, L., Lamb, M. E., & Lösel, F. (2016). The impact of contextual family risks on prisoners' children's behavioural outcomes and the potential protective role of family functioning moderators. *European Journal of Developmental Psychology*, *13*(3), 325–340.

Markson, L., Lösel, F., Souza, K. A., & Lanskey, C. (2015). Male prisoners' family relationships and resilience in resettlement. *Criminology and Criminal Justice*, *15*(4), 423–441.

Mews, A., Di Bella, L., & Purver, M. (2017). *Impact evaluation of the prison-based Core Sex Offender Treatment Programme (Ministry of Justice Analytical Series)*. London, England.

Miller, G. A. (1969). Psychology as a means of promoting human welfare. *American Psychologist*, *24*(12), 1063–1075.

Pinker, S. (2011). *The better angels of our nature: Why violence has declined*. New York, NY: Viking.

Runkel, D., Lösel, F., Stemmler, M., & Jaursch, S. (2017). *Preventing social behavior problems in children from deprived migrant families: Evaluation of a child and parent training in Europe. Research Report*. Erlangen, Germany: Department of Psychology, University of Erlangen–Nuremberg.

Schmucker, M., & Lösel, F. (2017). Sexual offender treatment for reducing recidivism among convicted sex offenders: A systematic review and meta-analysis. *Campbell Systematic Reviews*, *13*(1), 1–75.

Souza, K. A., Lösel, F., Markson, L., & Lanskey, C. (2015). Pre-release expectations and post-release experiences of prisoners and their (ex-) partners. *Legal and Criminological Psychology*, *20*(2), 306–323.

Stemmler, M., & Lösel, F. (2015). Developmental pathways of externalizing behavior from preschool age to adolescence: An application of general growth mixture modeling. In M. Stemmler, A. V. Eye, & W. Wiedermann (Eds.), *Dependent data in social sciences research: Forms, issues, and methods of analysis* (pp. 91–106). New York, NY: Springer.

Toman, W. (1959). A general formula for the quantitative treatment of human motivation. *Journal of Abnormal and Social Psychology*, *58*, 91–99.

Toman, W. (1961). *Family constellation: Theory and practice of a psychological game*. New York, NY: Springer.

Wallner, S., Lösel, F., Stemmler, M., & Corrado, R. (2018). The validity of the Cracow Instrument in the prediction of antisocial development in preschool children: A five-year longitudinal community-based study. *International Journal of Forensic Mental Health*, *17*(2), 181–194.

Weiss, M., Schmucker, M., & Lösel, F. (2015). Meta-Analyse zur Wirkung familienbezogener Präventionsmaßnahmen in Deutschland [Meta-analysis on the effects of family-oriented prevention programs in Germany]. *Zeitschrift für Klinische Psychologie und Pychotherapie*, *44*, 27–44.

West, D. J., & Farrington, D. P. (1973). *Who becomes delinquent?* London, England: Heinemann.

12   The Last War Baby
A Life of Studying Antisocial Behavior in Context

Benjamin B. Lahey

Benjamin B. Lahey was born on December 4, 1945, in Daytona Beach, Florida (United States). He received his PhD in psychology from the University of Tennessee (United States) in 1970 and a faculty appointment the same year at Florida Technological University (FTU). He is the Irving B. Harris Professor of Psychiatry at the University of Chicago (United States), where he became Chief of Psychology in the Department of Psychiatry in 1994. He was President of the International Society for Research in Child and Adolescent Psychopathology and the Society of Clinical Child and Adolescent Psychology. Among many prestigious awards and recognitions, he received the National Academy of Neuropsychology research prize for his work on attention-deficit/hyperactivity disorder (ADHD), and he received a distinguished research contributions award from the Society for Clinical Child and Adolescent Psychology.

Through the first decade of his career at the University of Georgia, Benjamin Lahey conducted research on the effectiveness of behavior therapy with children placed in classes for learning disabilities. Although behavior therapy treatment outcomes with children met with great initial success in academic circles, it became clear to Lahey that treatment needed to be reapplied multiple times to have long-term effectiveness. This research experience led to an interest in the attention deficits and hyperactivity that he observed in many children with learning disabilities. He also discovered the importance of a developmental perspective on psychopathology when he met Rolf Loeber, Magda Stouthamer-Loeber (see Chapter 5), and David Farrington (see Chapter 6).

In the early 1990s he moved to the University of Miami at the encouragement of Herb Quay, and he directed the American Psychiatric Association's field trials on disruptive behavior disorders in children. The aim of the field trials was to create an empirical basis for considering possible changes to the psychiatric nomenclature in the upcoming *DSM-IV*. He had also moved to the University of Miami in 1990 at the encouragement of Herb Quay. With the help of Brooks Applegate's statistical knowhow, and with the contributions of many other investigators, he was able to use the field trial data to carefully evaluate every potential symptom for each mental disorder and recommend the symptoms with the greatest psychometric utility (Frick et al., 1994; Lahey et al., 1994). Having these data led to his being invited to become a member of the *DSM-IV* child disorders work group, which he describes as 'the most intense period of swimming with the sharks of my career. I saw astonishingly boorish behavior and watched formidable scientists brought tears in those work group meetings'.

During the same period, Benjamin Lahey was awarded a grant from the National Institute of Mental Health (NIMH) to conduct a multisite study to develop methods for epidemiologic research in which lay interviewers conducted computer-assisted scripted diagnostic interviews of children and their parents in their homes: The Methods for the Epidemiology of Child and Adolescent Mental Disorders Study (MECA) established that reliable and valid assessments of psychological problems could be conducted in large samples (Lahey et al., 1996). Data from the MECA Study led to over 100 published papers by many scholars and helped give birth to child psychiatric epidemiology. This led to his present position at the University of Chicago in the epidemiology division of the Department of Public Health Sciences.

With his colleague Bill Pelham, he initiated a longitudinal study that helped to document the long-term problems encountered by young children who met criteria for attention-deficit/hyperactivity disorder. He focused on the subset of children with hyperactivity and conduct problems, and, with Rolf and Magda Loeber, investigated the adolescent outcomes of that group.

With Rolf Loeber he also created the Developmental Trends Study of clinic-referred prepubertal boys, some of whom had serious problems of hyperactivity, some with serious conduct problems, some with both kinds of problems, and some with anxiety and other problems. The study eventually followed the boys into early adulthood and confirmed that the presence of conduct problems was a stronger predictor of antisocial personality disorder than hyperactivity problems (Lahey, Loeber, Burke, & Applegate, 2005a).

Intrigued by the correlations among the behavioral dimensions of his previous studies, he studied a large representative sample of twins with the biostatistician Paul Rathouz. They found that more than half of the genetic variance in each dimension of psychological problems was shared with other dimensions, rather than being dimension-specific. The results from these studies led him and his colleagues to propose a hierarchical causal model of psychological problems (Lahey, Krueger, Rathouz, Waldman, & Zald, 2017) in which the hypothesized general factor of psychopathology plays a central role. The key idea is that the causes and mechanisms of each dimension of psychological problems cannot be studied and understood separately; they are far too intertwined.

During his career Benjamin Lahey had numerous international collaborations as President of the International Society for Research in Child and Adolescent Psychopathology, including a visiting fellowship at the Norwegian Academy of Sciences and Letters. Professor Lahey says that he is not retiring because he enjoys running statistical models, writing, teaching, and … playing bluegrass guitar while singing off-key.

The theme of this book is the influence on our lives of growing up as part the cohort of war babies. I will address that issue as best as I can, but I must say that the process of writing this chapter has greatly strengthened my belief in the importance of *turning points* in development (Pickles & Rutter, 1991). Independent of the general experience of growing up as a war baby, I now believe that a number of events have shaped my life and career to an extent that I had not appreciated until I wrote this chapter. Autobiography is not science, as one cannot address counterfactuals in autobiography, but it is food for thought. Consistent with the views of Arnold Sameroff, I suspect that these life-changing events occurred partly because of my own characteristics and actions, but only partly (Sameroff, 2009). They were unexpected events and quite surprising to me as they unfolded. Nonetheless, as Sameroff suggested, I am sure that my personal characteristics interacted with the events in shaping my life and career.

12.1   Childhood after the War

To tell my story as a war baby in the context of World War II, it is necessary to begin with my parents, the ones who actually lived through and fought in the war. My father became ensnared by the technology of this era at an early age. Long before the war, he left high school because he had mastered the first technology of wireless communication among people at a distance – radio. As a teenager, he parlayed his skills in Morse code and building and operating radios into well-paid jobs on cargo ships sailing to South America. Radio allowed ships to monitor the weather and stay in touch with shore in real time for the first time, so his skills were in high demand.

My father gave up seafaring when he married my mother, at least for a time. My mother had grown up in St. Petersburg, Florida, and she was my father's typing teacher at Bixby Business School there. He had taken a trip off to bring his father south for the winter because my grandfather was not faring well after the death of his wife. He studied typing to pass the time. My parents soon married, had one son, and were living peacefully in St. Petersburg when the Japanese attacked Pearl Harbor in 1941. Because my father was married and was at the older end of the draftable age range, he might have avoided military service. Nonetheless, out of patriotism that was tempered by my mother's wish to keep him out of harm's way, he volunteered for the Coast Guard. The Navy immediately commandeered him, however, and made him the radio officer on a destroyer escort. The USS *Howard D. Crow* crossed the North Atlantic many times, guarding troop and supply ships from submarines. My father's ship saw some combat action, but the real danger for him came from the brutal storms of the North Pacific. Late in the war, he was tossed into the corner of a desk during a storm and injured badly enough to be reassigned to shore duty. His last assignment was taking down the communications among enemy ships in Morse code from the west coast of Florida. It was the kind of mental challenge that he loved, typing out messages in real time, letter by letter, in a language that he didn't speak. This assignment also meant that my mother could join him in New Smyrna, Florida. Given my birth date, I reckon I was conceived on the east Florida coast two months before the German surrender. Thus, I am one of the very last war babies.

I was born during the last month of 1945 and grew up in a booming and carefree America. In my family, I heard about the war years only through occasional statements by my parents and hushed conversations about a family friend who had been blinded by the Japanese in Bataan. When I asked my father about his experiences in the war, he either gave short answers or went off on tangents that I did not fully understand. I suspected, even then, that his tangents were augmented by his Irish blarney.

I grew up in the prosperous postwar era. World War II was a vivid part of my youth, but only through comic books, movies, and the fantasy of play. We saw all manner of war hero movies, including the *Legend of Audie Murphy*, and most of our comic books depicted heroic victories over German and Japanese soldiers. Because of my father's role in the war, I watched every episode of *Victory at Sea* on television, complete with a heroic classical music score and a running narrative by Walter Cronkite. Although the war was over, the enemy was still portrayed in the media in outrageously negative propaganda style.

Army–Navy surplus stores were a big thing then, through which the government sold the military supplies they no longer needed. My father equipped my brothers and me with full army regalia at one of those stores. I had a green fatigue shirt, a web belt with a canteen, an actual army helmet, and, to top it off, a rifle that had been modified so that it could not shoot. I played 'army' endlessly, shooting and killing my neighbors and siblings, but they somehow always missed me when they returned my fire. I was a happy child and believed in the goodness of the United States and had a deep distrust of both Germans and the Japanese. Those attitudes only left me as I met people from those countries who defied my wartime stereotypes, but it may be no accident that I have never visited either country even though I have traveled widely.

I grew up in St. Petersburg without a care during my childhood. Before adolescence, I rode my bicycle throughout the city without a second thought. I lived on the swampy south side, and my friends and I swam in swamps with lazy alligators, and we never spoke of ambitions for the future. We made it to the local beach as often as possible, as if sunburns were cool. It was a very Florida childhood.

Writing this chapter has led me to consider the role that World War II played in my gravitating to research on antisocial behavior in children and adolescents. It is interesting to me to muse about why I chose conduct disorder and the problems that are correlated with it for my focus. There's no way to be sure, of course, but I did play 'war' almost every day as a child, and I read countless comic books in which the villains were the bloodthirsty German and Japanese aggressors. So, perhaps I study antisocial behavior partly because of my fascination with the antisocial acts of soldiers, even if I learned about the violence of war in a highly sanitized form that was suitable for children.

My personal experiences with aggression probably played a bigger role, however. My father made a decent living in the merchant marine and was at sea during most of my childhood. This left the care of the three boys to my wonderful mother. That was mostly good, but my older brother was 7 years older and he made his younger brothers his slaves. If we refused his requests, he clobbered us often enough that we fetched him water and snacks when he wanted them. That situation was generally tolerable until the occasional times when my father was home on leave. He and my older brother were nitro and glycerine, and my otherwise decent dad lost his temper with my older brother a couple of memorable times in truly terrifying ways.

Still, I was a generally well-adjusted boy who gave as good as he got in the occasional physical scuffles among elementary school boys. It was when I left my comfortable parochial school and entered a public junior high that I was introduced to the world of aggressive conduct disorder. Not only did I get my own personal bully at South Side Junior High, but he was 2 years older than me, and twice as tough, and, as if that was not enough, he had an equally antisocial twin! And the two twins were never without a red-headed poster child for callous–unemotional traits who was as mean as he was big! Those were terribly unhappy days for me, but if research is partly 'me search,' I owe a lot to those three lads. I will let you decide if it is a coincidence that my largest study was based on a sample of twins.

A last thought about the war. If we believe that childhood is the parent of adulthood, it is actually shocking that I became the person I am. I have come to view the U.S. military in a very different way as an adult. The frequent uses by the United States of our military forces to advance our economic interests in oil-rich regions of the world has taught me a deep distrust of the military. I am not a pacifist, as I still believe that defensive wars are ethical under some circumstances, but, over the years from my childhood through my adulthood, I have come to view most military actions by most countries as murder. Except under rare circumstances, I see no difference between one group of persons killing another group of persons for profit under the name of gang warfare or military campaigns by governments. There is no excuse for solving disputes and enriching one group through violence in either case, and the violence kills innocent bystanders in both cases.

12.2   Undergraduate and Graduate Studies

My undergraduate years were spent at Eckerd College and Davidson College. As I had in high school, I underachieved through the first 2 years of college. Things changed dramatically, however, when I took abnormal psychology and physiological psychology during my junior year. I literally fell in love with those topics, and I have never wanted to be anything but a psychologist since. I had fabulous teachers at Davidson College, and I learned a great deal about psychology. They intentionally exposed us to every topic and every viewpoint, but I was only open to psychologists who argued with data rather than words. I loved the work of Skinner, Tolman, Spence, and the other behaviorists. They were scientists who made Freud and Rogers look like little more than clever poets to me. The behaviorists gave me something to sink my intellectual teeth into. I was not easily convinced by what I was told in college, and I fell into academia and research very naturally. It suits me to doubt what others say, but I particularly value the dispassionate way in which differences of opinion are resolved with data using the rules of science. I became an academic out of self-motivated passion for science, and I constantly marvel that I am paid for having fun teaching and doing research.

My college grades improved when I found psychology, but with my low overall grade-point average, I was lucky to get into two graduate schools.

I chose the University of Tennessee because Bill Verplanck had just moved there from Harvard University to become the department chair. I had read a book that he co-authored in which he advocated the approach of B. F. Skinner but criticized Skinner for lapsing into theoretical speculation too often. I was sold – a professor who thought Skinner was not rigorous enough was just up my alley! When I was a first-year graduate student, Verplanck had me read two papers that profoundly influenced my thinking. The first was a tongue-in-cheek paper that used the logic of aerodynamic principles to demonstrate that bumblebees cannot fly. The other was the *Logic of Modern Physics*, published in 1927 by Nobel laureate Percy Bridgman. Bridgman introduced the concept of operational definitions into science to explain the concept of relativity in physics, but Verplanck made it clear that operational definitions, rather than theoretical arguments, were the foundation of every science. These two works still define my data first, theory second approach to science.

As a graduate student, I met B. F. Skinner because he was a personal friend of Bill Verplanck. I even had dinner with Skinner a couple of times, engaging in less than memorable dinnertime conversations with him. Far more importantly, I fell into the Skinnerian applied behavior analysis movement through the influence of a wonderful young professor at the University of Tennessee, Bob Wahler. With his tutelage and warm support, I became a researcher on the use of behavior therapy with children. This was a truly exciting time, as behavior therapy was new and it offered a way to use data to solve human ills. In addition, it effectively pushed back against the psychodynamic approach that dominated clinical psychology at that time. We behaviorists were convinced that we could solve all of the problems of humankind. In my first research studies, I developed and tested methods that effectively helped children with academic learning deficits such as mirror writing (Lahey, Busemeyer, Ohara, & Beggs, 1977) and problems in reading comprehension (Lahey, McNees, & Brown, 1973) using simple principles of operant learning. Because academia allows us to follow our intellectual noses, however, I moved into studies of the subset of children with learning problems who exhibit problems of inattention, hyperactivity, and impulsivity. I later focused on the subset of children with attention problems who had conduct problems on the assumption that their adult outcomes were most likely to be poor.

12.3 My Early Academic Years and the Columbia University Turning Point

I received my PhD in 1970 and immediately returned to Florida to teach at what was then called Florida Technological University (FTU), now the University of Central Florida. Florida Technological University was originally slated to be Florida's version of Georgia Tech, but its mission was radically changed shortly after I arrived during one of Florida's worst periods of anti-intellectualism. During my second year on the faculty, we were called into a meeting by the dean. He said that our teaching loads were being doubled and that, although we could continue to conduct research, the more we published the more our commitment to teaching would be questioned. I decided that FTU was not for me and took a position at the University of South Carolina without sufficiently considering how great the differences were in the Deep South at that time. My job there was great, but a family came to our door shortly after we moved in to say that a black family had moved onto our block. I will never forget the look on our neighbors' faces when we naively said, 'That's great; their kids can play with our kids!' That helped us decide to move to the University of Georgia where the climate was a bit more liberal.

I continued to conduct research on the effectiveness of behavior therapy with children through the first decade of my career at the University of Georgia. Behavior therapy with children met with great initial success in academic circles, but it became clear to me that it needed to be reapplied multiple times to have long-term effectiveness. Although I am still a very strong believer in evidence-based behavior therapy methods, I felt then that the field of behavior therapy needed 'engineers' who could work out the best ways of exporting behavior therapies that worked in university clinics to community settings. That continues to be an enormously important and challenging field today. I think I might have helped more human beings had I continued to work on better ways to implement behavior therapies by polishing the engineering, but I personally leaned toward more basic science. I thought I might be able to serve children in need better in the long run by looking for the next scientific breakthrough that would improve the effectiveness and durability of behavior change therapies. To accomplish that, I decided that I needed to understand the *causes* of each kind of psychological problem before I could think effectively about better methods of prevention or treatment. That quickly led me to the realization that I could not discover the etiology of problem X without being able to describe, classify, and measure X. I decided to focus on the taxonomy of the 'disruptive behavior disorders' of conduct disorder and oppositional defiant disorder. It soon became obvious to me that these problems change dramatically over the course of development, so I decided that I needed to adopt a life-history approach.

In the late 1980s, I met Herbert Quay, who was one of the pioneers in research on the taxonomy of child psychological problems. His views strongly influenced mine, and we became friends during several conversations about those ideas. Our friendship was helped, I am sure, by the fact that we learned that we had gone to the same high school in Florida and that his family knew my family. Herb asked me in 1982 to be a member of the editorial board of the *Journal of Abnormal Child Psychology*, of which he was the founding editor. At an editorial board meeting a few years later, I enthusiastically supported his suggestion that the members of that editorial board found the International Society for Research on Child and Adolescent Psychopathology. He was the founding president of the society, and I served as its president in 1994. The journal and the society formed my intellectual home base for many years.

In those early years, I did research for the sheer fun of it, taking great pride in seeing papers appear in print. I still miss the smell of a new issue of a journal on paper and the joy of seeing a paper on which I was an author in print. In my youthful enthusiasm for research, I had not seriously considered that other researchers would read my papers, and it certainly had not occurred to me that they would find serious fault with them. It is astonishing to recall my naiveté! Most of my first published papers were really quite weak and were conducted without grant support. These studies were based on small samples and used limited methods of measurements. One of those papers caught the eye of a child psychiatrist trained in England, however, who thought too much was made of the importance of hyperactivity by Americans. He had read my paper, which seemed to show that hyperactivity added nothing to the prediction of impaired school and social functioning above and beyond conduct problems. To my great embarrassment as I look back on it today, it was based on 100 parochial children, none of whom likely had impairing behavior problems of either sort. Nonetheless, I used those data to question the validity of the newly defined *DSM-III* diagnostic category of ADHD (Lahey, Green, & Forehand, 1980). A major turning point in my career came as the result of a kind invitation by David Shaffer. He had just moved to the United States and invited me to give grand rounds in child psychiatry at Columbia University, based on that paper, in front of many of the psychiatrists and psychologists who had written *DSM-III*. They politely listened, and then, with equal politeness, pointed out how utterly weak and inconclusive my study was. I could only agree with each of their obviously valid points in a barely audible voice. Then, consistent with what I came to understand was her truly generous nature, Rachel Gittelman Klein invited me to dinner at her home to discuss my work with her and her husband, Donald Klein. I was too embarrassed to go. Instead, I sat in my hotel room and decided that I either had to stop conducting research or do it in a way that was strong enough to withstand the kind of appropriate scrutiny that it would receive from other scientists. This is the essential scrutiny-by-peers process that defines science. I learned an important lesson in New York that I hope improved the quality of my research somewhat.

12.4   Rolf and Magda Loeber

The second and most fortunate turning point in my career was meeting Rolf and Magda Loeber. They helped me enormously to turn my emerging ideas about what I wanted to learn about antisocial behavior into studies that could address those issues. Meeting them was a genuine turning point in my life. Rolf and Magda were trained in behavior therapy like me, and they had just completed postdoctoral work with Gerald Patterson at the influential Oregon Social Learning Center. Like me, they were interested in conduct problems in children, but they understood the immense importance of longitudinal research far better than I and were much more savvy about what it takes to secure grants.

Rolf and I met at a behavior therapy meeting in the early 1980s. We each gave papers in a symposium that asserted, based on very little evidence at that time, that the prevailing theory of childhood hyperactivity as the precursor to later adult antisocial personality disorder was incorrect. We hypothesized that childhood conduct problems were far more important than hyperactivity in predicting poor adult outcomes in a symposium. I remember that we said essentially the same thing in our talks, and we each thought that the other must be pretty smart to see the wisdom of our ideas! And we just instantly liked one another. We had lunch after the symposium in a restaurant that used white paper tablecloths and provided small boxes of crayons so that children could doodle until the food arrived. Rolf and I wrote the specific aims of our first grant proposal on the paper tablecloth in red crayon! Somehow that medium perfectly fit our youthful optimism and energy. Based on Rolf's good ideas and knowledge of how to put together a proposal, we got the grant. It funded the Developmental Trends Study, which became a longitudinal study of clinic-referred prepubertal boys, some of them with serious problems of hyperactivity, some with serious conduct problems, some with both kinds of problems, and some with anxiety and other problems. The study eventually followed the boys into early adulthood and confirmed our suspicion that the presence of conduct problems was a stronger predictor of antisocial personality disorder than hyperactivity (Lahey, Loeber, et al., 2005a). Based on larger studies, I later came to believe that both hyperactivity and conduct problems during childhood predict antisocial outcomes to varying degrees, but I think the general conclusion of our study has stood the test of time. Over the years during which this longitudinal study played out, Rolf, Magda, and I had many truly enjoyable conversations about developmental psychology, conduct problems, art prints, and Irish history, all over the most marvelous Dutch coffee and lovely meals. Somehow, Rolf and I also realized that we were both mad about Giorgio Armani ties, and we regularly rested from our work by shopping for the next wonderful tie. I hardly wear ties anymore, but my Armanis still hang in my closet where they remind me of Rolf and are taken out for the occasional suit-and-tie occasion.

I learned the importance of a developmental perspective on psycho-pathology from Rolf and Magda, and from David Farrington, to whom they introduced me. In the beginning, the Loebers and I thought in terms of early childhood precursors to later childhood conduct problems. In particular, we wrote several papers about oppositional–defiant behavior as a precursor to childhood conduct disorder (Loeber, Burke, Lahey, Winters, & Zera, 2000). I am happy to have this occasion to acknowledge the important contribution of Richard Tremblay to our thinking on this topic. His groundbreaking longitudinal studies began at a much earlier age than our studies, and he showed us that age-appropriate versions of antisocial behaviors – kicking, hitting, taking, and the like – were present in early childhood at the same time as early oppositional behavior (Tremblay et al., 1999). His data changed how we thought about the early development of antisocial behavior. In time, Rolf and I both felt the need for larger and more representative samples, and each of us was successful in conducting new developmental studies. We mostly conducted our new studies independently, but with frequent joint papers and conversations.

It is impossible for me to think of my research and forays into theory from this point on without mentioning other colleagues who made it possible. I quickly learned that I could not master all of the skills needed to answer the questions that I wanted to tackle. Many people, including many students and fellows, allowed me to do much more than I was capable of by myself. My collaborators extended my scientific reach and protected me from making mistakes based on what I didn't know I didn't know. Brooks Applegate, Paul Rathouz, Carol Van Hulle, and Irwin Waldman, particularly, made inestimably valuable statistical and meth-odological contributions.

12.5   Turning Points in the 1990s

Around 1990, the American Psychiatric Association won grant support from NIMH to conduct research to create an empirical basis for considering possible changes to the psychiatric nomenclature in the upcoming *DSM-IV*. Rolf Loeber was asked to direct the field trials to collect data relevant to disruptive behavior disorders in children. He turned down the opportunity and suggested me. I eagerly accepted the role. I knew I would be doing a great deal of time-consuming work collecting data for the psychiatrists who ran the *DSM-IV* show, but I thought that having access to the data would give me a chance to express my views on what they meant.

I moved to the University of Miami in 1990 at the encouragement of Herb Quay, where I met my now long-term friend and collaborator Brooks Applegate. With his statistical help, and with the contributions of many other investigators, we were able to use field trial data to carefully evaluate every potential symptom for each mental disorder and recommend the symptoms with the greatest psychometric utility (Frick et al., 1994; Lahey et al., 1994). Having these data led to my being invited to be a member of the *DSM-IV* child disorders work group. It was the most intense period of swimming with the sharks of my career. I saw astonishingly boorish behavior and watched formidable scientists brought tears in those work group meetings, but this time I went into the shark tank with strong data on my side.

I left the University of Miami in 1994 and took my current position at the University of Chicago when I married Kate Keenan. My work on *DSM-IV* led to my second longitudinal study at that time. The optimal diagnostic criteria for ADHD identified in cross-sectional data on 4–17-year-olds from the *DSM-IV* field trials indicated that some children with high levels of hyperactivity–impulsivity, but not high levels of inattention, displayed impairment in their daily functioning. This led to the adoption of the predominantly hyperactive–impulsive subtype of ADHD in *DSM-IV*. I supported this decision in the *DSM-IV* meetings, but with serious reservations because most of the children in the field trials sample who met criteria for this new subtype were 4–6 years of age. The data were clear in supporting the new subtype, but they were only cross-sectional data gathered at a single point in time. One possibility that we could not evaluate with these data was that children who met criteria for the predominantly hyperactive–impulsive subtype would come to exhibit more inattention symptoms as their attentional capacities were challenged when they entered elementary school. If that were the case, the *DSM-IV* criteria would be useful in facilitating the early identification of children with ADHD. On the other hand, the reason that there were almost no children in the *DSM-IV* field trials sample who met criteria for the predominantly hyperactive–impulsive subtype above the age of 6 years could be because their problems resolved quickly as they matured! If that were the case, the revised *DSM-IV* criteria would have psychiatrized normal childhood exuberance and exposed the children to unnecessary treatments and labeling.

You can imagine the pressure I felt to determine if the *DSM-IV* process in which I played a role had resulted in helping or harming young children. Bill Pelham and I quickly submitted a grant proposal on this question to NIMH that essentially wrote itself. The need for longitudinal research on the new subtype of ADHD was so clear that the proposal received the best priority score of my career. That longitudinal study lasted for 16 years, and the findings strongly suggested that the diagnosis of ADHD was valid for preschool children (Lahey et al., 2016). Preschoolers who met criteria for the predominantly hyperactive–impulsive subtype mostly went on to meet criteria for the combined type of ADHD when they reached elementary school (Lahey, Pelham, et al., 2004). Furthermore, this longitudinal study showed that very few of the preschoolers who met criteria for any of the subtypes of ADHD were entirely free of symptoms and functional impairment by the close of adolescence (Lee, Lahey, Owens, & Hinshaw, 2008). Indeed, we were horrified to see that the preschool children who met criteria for ADHD were at markedly increased risk for suicide attempts in childhood and adolescence (Chronis-Tuscano et al., 2010). Interestingly, this study also showed that the subtype classifications were too unstable over time to take seriously as enduring subtypes (Lahey, Pelham, Loney, Lee, & Willcutt, 2005). Children were quite consistent in continuing to meet criteria for ADHD, but their classification into the three subtypes changed frequently from year to year. This led to the change in *DSM-5* from defining subtypes of ADHD to defining the 'current presentation' of the ADHD symptoms.

Also in the 1990s, NIMH solicited proposals to conduct a multisite study to develop methods for epidemiologic research in which lay interviewers conducted computer-assisted scripted diagnostic interviews of children and their parents in their homes. Because I played a small role in the development of such an interview, I received one of the grants. The MECA Study established that reliable and valid assessments of psychological problems could be conducted in large representative samples (Lahey et al., 1996). Data from the MECA Study led to over 100 published papers by many scholars and helped give birth to child psychiatric epidemiology. My current position at the University of Chicago is in the epidemiology division of the Department of Public Health Sciences in large part because of what I learned about conducting research in population-based samples during the MECA Study.

12.6   My (Twisting) Turn to the Dimensional Assessment of Psychological Problems

My seeming reward for participating in MECA was that I was in a good position to apply for a large grant to conduct a national epidemiologic study of psychological problems in children and adolescents when NIMH called for proposals. I was awarded a breathtaking $10 million dollars in the 1990s to conduct the study. Four other teams also were awarded grants to conduct local area studies of mental health services use. We spent 3 years preparing to launch the study and were weeks away from launching data collection when the director of NIMH was fired for a seemingly racist remark in a speech and was replaced by a director who had no understanding of, or appreciation for, epidemiology. The new director wanted to make psychiatry a molecular science. He looked at the large sum of money devoted to epidemiology in his portfolio and decided to cancel all of it to create funds for molecular psychiatry. That was the most disappointing and anger-filled moment in my scientific career. It was a mistake for the epidemiology of psychological problems in children on a monumental scale that has never been corrected and a personal loss for me.

Still, it turns out that rotten events like the cancellation of a grant can become adaptive turning points. In my case, the new director did not know that he could not take back all of the already awarded grant funds that we were bankrolling for the national epidemiologic study. I was able to use a considerable amount of this funding for a new purpose. I was given an unexpected gift in the process that I did not appreciate at the time. I was allowed to use the funds to create a new instrument that measured psychological problems in dimensional rather than diagnostic terms, which I called the Child and Adolescent Psychopathology Scale (CAPS). I honestly was not enthusiastic about developing this new measure at the time, but I quickly realized that the leftover funds from the cancelled study had opened a door for me. I developed a new measure that asked one question about each symptom and had the informant rate each symptom on a Likert-like scale in terms of how characteristic it was of the child and how serious it was for the child. Unlike a structured interview designed to yield categorical diagnoses of mental disorders, I was able to present the items in randomized order, so that factor analyses of the items to generate dimensions would not yield factors based on, say, all of the items about depression being asked in a row. I was even able to control for order effects by counterbalancing the order in which different participants were asked the questions. We knew from the MECA Study that informants endorse fewer and fewer problems in themselves or their children as the interview progresses, but we had not been able to control order effects within the modules of diagnostic interviews that asked questions about symptoms in fixed order.

Because we were not chasing categorical diagnoses, the new instrument abandoned the common practice in diagnostic interviews of having informants answer a few leading questions about each diagnosis and then skipping the remaining questions if the person could not meet criteria for the diagnosis. For example, persons who denied dysphoria, anhedonia, and irritability were not asked about the remaining symptoms of major depression, such as sleep problems, weight loss, and suicidal behavior in structured diagnostic interviews. Skip patterns make sense if we only care about diagnoses because this reduces administration times, but it makes it impossible to study the underlying dimensions of psychological problems because not all symptoms are queried.

My consolation prize from the cancelled study actually felt like a prize when I realized how valuable this dimensional scale could be. I could conduct empirical studies of the dimensions that underlie the full range of problems that define the mental disorder diagnoses most often given to children and adolescents. Previous studies of parent and teacher rating scales had revealed the dimensional structure of many psychological problems, of course, but those scales did not address all of the problems that create distress and impairment for children and adolescents. When I conducted factor analysis of the items measured by the new instrument, I had a wonderful aha moment. My work on the *DSM-IV* field trials had convinced me that psychological problems are inherently dimensional in nature, but because clinicians must make the dichotomous decision to treat or not to treat, it did not seem wrong to me to use data to try to establish the best point for dichotomizing the dimensions in diagnoses. But I realized for the first time that we had never actually studied the dimensions of psychological problems because of the skip patterns in diagnostic interviews. This realization should have come to me much earlier since child and adolescent psychologists had been using dimensional measures as long as there has been a field, in part because there were essentially no diagnostic categories for children until *DSM-III*.

12.7   A Hierarchical Causal Taxonomy of Psychological Problems

I used the CAPS to measure psychological problems dimensionally in a population-based study of some 1,800 children and adolescents (Lahey, Applegate, et al., 2004) and received a new grant to use the same instrument in a study of a representative sample of 2,000 pairs of twins – the Tennessee Twins Study (Lahey, Rathouz, et al., 2008). In both studies, I was struck by how highly correlated with one another the individual child and adolescent psychological problems proved to be when measured with the CAPS. These correlations yielded first-order factors that were similar to, but a bit different from, what one would expect based on *DSM-IV* mental disorders. Furthermore, factor analysis of the first-order dimensions based on the CAPS yielded second-order factors that looked remarkably similar to the internalizing and externalizing factors that Tom Achenbach had identified many years before (Achenbach, 1966; Achenbach, Conners, Quay, Verhulst, & Howell, 1989; Achenbach & Edelbrock, 1978). Notably, although the correlations among dimensions within the internalizing and externalizing domains were high, many of the correlations between dimensions *across* those domains were almost as high (Lahey, Applegate, et al., 2004; Lahey, Rathouz, et al., 2008). Another way of saying the same thing is that, like Achenbach's internalizing and externalizing factors, the corresponding second-order internalizing and externalizing factors in the CAPS data were correlated at about r = .50. I have been mightily puzzled by that correlation since I first saw it 50 years ago in Achenbach's data! The fact that the internalizing and externalizing factors are not inversely correlated clearly means that the second-order factors are not referring to fundamentally opposite forms of psychological problems – acting in versus acting out. My replication of Tom Achenbach's correlation between the internalizing and externalizing domains made me wonder what the positive correlation did represent. I could think of only two explanations: Either the correlation is a spurious reflection of common method variance—a tendency to rate one's child high or low on every item without regard to the problem to which it referred—or all of the problems are correlated because they are influenced to a considerable extent by the *same set of nonspecific causal influences*.

My colleagues and I tested the hypothesis that the ubiquitous correlations among first-order dimensions reflect highly nonspecific shared causal influences in 2011 using data gathered using the CAPs in the Tennessee Twin Study. Twin analyses led by Paul Rathouz showed that the additive genetic influences on each dimension were *mostly not specific to each dimension*. Rather, genetic influences were robustly pleiotropic, meaning that they were shared by every dimension of psychological problems (Lahey, Van Hulle, Singh, Waldman, & Rathouz, 2011). This broad sharing of genetic influences operates at two levels. First, the twin analyses revealed that there are strong genetic factors that nonspecifically influence every dimension of psychological problems.

That is, some genetic variants increase or decrease the likelihood that a person will exhibit some kind of psychological problem but do not determine which psychological problems will be exhibited. These shared genetic influences are strong enough to cause every first-order dimension of psychological problems to be positively correlated. In addition, we found evidence of two other orthogonal sets of genetic factors that influence only the first-order dimensions in the externalizing domain, and only the first-order dimensions in the internalizing domain. The influence of these additional pleiotropic genetic factors were nonspecific *within* the externalizing domain (e.g., they nonspecifically influenced conduct problems, inattention, and hyperactivity–impulsivity) and *within* the internalizing domains (e.g., they nonspecifically influenced fears, worries, and depression), but neither of these orthogonal sets of pleiotropic genetic factors influenced first-order dimensions in the *other* domain. Finally, less than half of the genetic influences were specific to each first-order domain. Some, but *not most*, genetic influences are specific to a particular dimension of psychological problems.

These findings from the Tennessee Twins Study suggested a radical departure from our implicit expectation that each first-order dimension of psychological problems has its own distinct etiology. This unfounded expectation has long justified the case-control approach to genetic studies in which each study compares groups of persons who do and do not meet criteria for a particular diagnosis to discover the genetic variants related to that disorder. Setting aside the glaring problems of case-control studies in general, this is the wrong strategy because only a minority of genetic influences are dimension-specific. In contrast, the analyses of data from the Tennessee Twin Study analyses showed that environmental influences that are specific to each person are mostly dimension-specific. This suggests that the role of such experiences is to help differentiate the various dimensions of psychological problems. The exception seems to be that child abuse may be an environmental factor that contributes nonspecifically to risk for all forms of psychological problems (Caspi et al., 2014).

In 2011, we first suggested that these findings from twin analyses indicate that there may be a *general factor of psychopathology* that reflects the most nonspecific causal influences. We extended the general factor hypothesis to adults the next year (Lahey et al., 2012) and formally hypothesized a hierarchical causal taxonomy of the dimensions of psychological problems across the lifespan after 5 years of reviewing of the data (Lahey et al., 2017). Fortunately, Avshalom Caspi, Terrie Moffitt, and their colleagues have replicated the general factor in their data set and dubbed it the p factor (Caspi et al., 2014).

12.8   Lumping and Splitting

During the early phases of my career, I was an ardent scientific splitter. A key example was our testing the hypothesis that the subset of children with problems of hyperactivity who also exhibited conduct problems was at greater risk for adult antisocial behavior than children with only hyperactivity (Lahey, Loeber, Burke, & Applegate, 2005b). We split a large group into two smaller groups to improve predictions regarding each group. I similarly found that only the parents of the subset of children with hyperactivity and conduct problems had high rates of antisocial personality (Frick et al., 1992), whereas the parents of other children with hyperactivity did not. Rolf Loeber and I also found evidence that among children who met diagnostic criteria for conduct disorder, those with the most nonaggressive conduct problems were at the greatest risk of meeting criteria for antisocial personality disorder as adults (Lahey, Loeber, et al., 2005b). Splitting in each case improved our understanding. Today, I now see the absolute necessity of both lumping and splitting. We need to think in 'lumpy' ways because *some etiologic factors influence all psychological problems* and others influence all of the externalizing or all of the internalizing dimensions, but also we need to split the first-order dimensions to identify their dimension-specific genetic and environmental influences.

12.9   Which Brings Us Back to Conduct Problems

I have followed my scientific nose where it took me during my career, with my trajectory often being deflected in new directions by unforeseen events. As a result, I *think* I am beginning to see the big picture: We need to *understand every first-order dimension of psychological problems in relation to every other dimension*. I have not forgotten the dimension of conduct problems, but as my co-authors and I said in 2012, we need to understand conduct problems in the context of the full, hypothesized causal hierarchy (Lahey & Waldman, 2012). Some of the etiologic factors that we want to identify for conduct problems will likely be specific to conduct problems, especially environmental factors not shared with other siblings. On the other hand, many of the etiologic factors for conduct problems will prove to be shared with other externalizing dimensions, and other causal risk factors will be shared with every dimension of psychological problems. In my opinion, we will learn more about conduct problems if we understand them as inextricably linked to every form of psychological problems. Conduct problems are not bad behavior; they are manifestations of the complex etiologic network that connects all forms of psychological problems.

If I may speak out of chronological order, Rolf Loeber and our colleagues noticed in the Developmental Trends Study that conduct problems were not constant in each year of the longitudinal study, but fluctuated up and down irregularly. Strikingly, we saw that other dimensions of psychological problems waxed and waned in concert with the conduct problems, including dimensions that are not part of the externalizing domain. As conduct problems rose and fell over the years in these boys, their symptoms of depression rose and fell along with them (Lahey, Loeber, Burke, Rathouz, & McBurnett, 2002). This shocked us at the time, but it makes perfect sense if we assume that some of the mechanisms that are common to all forms of psychological problems, including conduct problems, fluctuate over time. In our paper, we speculated that this might be state-like variations in a tendency to experience negative emotions, which might be common to all forms of psychological problems.

12.10   Quasi-Experimental Designs and Causal Inference

Along the way of my scientific career, I had the very good fortune to meet Brian D'Onofrio. He played a central role in a set of quasi-experimental analyses of data from the Children of the National Longitudinal Survey of Youth. With funding from the National Institute of Child Health and Human Development, we compared full siblings who had different prenatal environmental exposures to draw stronger causal inferences about their possible etiologic roles (Lahey & D'Onofrio, 2010). If some reasonable assumptions are met, sibling comparisons can automatically and completely rule out all systematic familial confounds of prenatal exposures and distinguish what are likely to be true causal risk pathways. For example, Brian showed that the siblings whose mother smoked during pregnancy had significantly lower birth weights than other siblings in the same family when the mother did not smoke during their pregnancies. This suggests a causal effect of smoking during pregnancy on birth weight. In contrast, the sibling comparisons did not indicate that smoking during pregnancy increased risk for conduct problems in the offspring (D'Onofrio et al., 2008; D'Onofrio, Van Hulle, Goodnight, Rathouz, & Lahey, 2012). It is likely that previous studies in which one child per family was studied incorrectly suggested that it was a causal risk factor for offspring conduct problems because families in which the mother smokes during pregnancy tend to be different in ways that are related to risk for conduct problems in the offspring. In contrast, sibling comparisons in the same study indicated that younger maternal age probably does have a causal effect that increases risk for conduct problems in the offspring. Brian has gone on to apply a number of quasi-experimental methods with great benefit in other samples, but, unfortunately, I have not had the bandwidth to go with him on these new studies. Such quasi-experimental approaches are enormously important to efforts to identify environmental risk factors for conduct problems.

12.11   Developmental Propensity Model of Antisocial Behavior

Although I fully accept the findings of Richard Tremblay that conduct problems emerge so early in life that we do not need to focus on developmental precursors, I still believe that some dispositional constructs can help us understand the complexity and heterogeneity of conduct problems. In 1999, my colleagues and I first offered the developmental propensity model of antisocial behavior (Lahey & Waldman, 2003; Lahey, Waldman, & McBurnett, 1999). We hypothesized that three broad socio-emotional dispositions are both associated with conduct problems in childhood and predict later adult antisocial personality disorder: high negative emotionality, high daring (sensation seeking), and low prosociality (the inverse part of Paul Frick's construct of callous–unemotional traits). We developed a measure of these dispositional constructs that was free of items that were synonyms or antonyms of any dimension of psychological problems to allow uncontaminated tests of the hypothesis (Lahey, Applegate, et al., 2008; Lahey, Rathouz, Applegate, Tackett, & Waldman, 2010). We found that all three dimensions were robustly associated with, and shared the same genetic variance with, conduct problems in analyses of the Tennessee Twin Study data (Waldman et al., 2011). In addition, the three dispositions predict the symptoms of antisocial personality disorder 12 years later in adulthood in the same sample (Lahey et al., 2018). This makes me think that the socio-emotional processes associated with each disposition are all intimately related to conduct problems. Furthermore, because these dispositions each account for independent variables in the prediction of conduct problems, conduct problems may be *heterogeneous* in these ways. Some antisocial individuals may exhibit deviant levels in any one of these dispositions, or, of course, may be deviant in any combination of the dispositions. That suggests that conduct problems could be a set of maladaptive behaviors that can reflect a wide range of different socio-emotional dispositions, causes, and mechanisms.

It is important that the disposition of negative emotionality is both cross-sectionally and prospectively associated with the general factor of psychological problems in the Tennessee Twins Study at both phenotypic and genetic levels (Class et al., 2019; Tackett et al., 2013). This supports our earlier musings that conduct problems and other forms of psychological problems may all reflect, in part, a tendency to experience negative emotions.

12.12   My Students

I love the academic life. Until this point in this chapter, I have mostly mentioned the joyful pursuit of potentially important knowledge. I have equally loved the role of the teacher, however, whether as a lecturer in formal classes or in one-on-one mentoring of advanced students. I have had the very good fortune of teaching scores of bright graduate students. Most of them are clinical psychologists today who have devoted themselves to helping families with psychological problems, but more than a few are now among the leaders of the current generation of scholars. I am hesitant to name names, as I am famous for my bad memory and I do not want to leave anyone out. To mention just a few graduate students, however, Caryn Carlson, Alan Delamater, Paul Frick, Keith McBurnett, John Piacentini, LaVome Robinson, and Libby Schaughency are enjoying genuinely significant academic careers in spite of my being their major professor. I have also worked with some truly wonderful postdoctoral fellows and research interns. Again, to mention only a few who are enjoying stellar academic careers, I was very lucky to work with Andrea Chronis-Toscano, Quetzal Class, Rachel Gordon, Terry Miller, Cynthia Hartung, Steve Lee, Frank Treiber, and Erik Willcutt. Each one has been a genuinely valued collaborator and a joy to know.

12.13   My Recommendations

Each of the authors of chapters in this book has been asked to make recommendations to future generations of students and scientists on the best ways to use research to advance the field. I don't feel particularly qualified to do that, but I'll say what comes to mind. Always remember that what you are doing is, first and foremost, important to the lives of other human beings. We have to pay attention to grants and publications, but contributing to the betterment of the human condition is the ultimate goal of an academic career. You will do that if you let the joys of teaching and research pull you along; take advantage of even the most agonizing turning points, as they bend your work in better directions; surround yourself with your intellectual superiors; mind your causal inferences; and don't buy any logical arguments without hard evidence to back them up, especially about bumblebees.

References

Achenbach, T. M. (1966). Classification of children's psychiatric symptoms: A factor analytic study. *Psychological Monographs*, *80*, 1–37.

Achenbach, T. M., Conners, C. K., Quay, H. C., Verhulst, F. C., & Howell, C. T. (1989). Replication of empirically derived syndromes as a basis for taxonomy of child and adolescent psychopathology. *Journal of Abnormal Child Psychology*, *17*, 299–323.

Achenbach, T. M., & Edelbrock, C. S. (1978). Classification of child psychopathology: Review and analysis of empirical efforts. *Psychological Bulletin*, *85*, 1275–1301.

Caspi, A., Houts, R. M., Belsky, D. W., Goldman-Mellor, S. J., Harrington, H., Israel, S., ... Moffitt, T. E. (2014). The p factor: One general psychopathology factor in the structure of psychiatric disorders? *Clinical Psychological Science*, *2*, 119–137.

Chronis-Tuscano, A., Molina, B. S. G., Pelham, W. E., Applegate, B., Dahlke, A., Overmyer, M., & Lahey, B. B. (2010). Very early predictors of adolescent depression and suicide attempts in children with attention-deficit/hyperactivity disorder. *Archives of General Psychiatry*, *67*, 1044–1051.

Class, Q. A., Rathouz, P. J., Van Hulle, C. A., Applegate, B., Waldman, I. D., Zald, D. H., & Lahey, B. B. (2019). Socioemotional dispositions of children and adolescents predict general and specific second-order factors of psychopathology in early adulthood across informants: A 12-year prospective study. *Journal of Abnormal Psychology*, *128*, 574–584.

D'Onofrio, B. M., Van Hulle, C. A., Goodnight, J. A., Rathouz, P. J., & Lahey, B. B. (2012). Is maternal smoking during pregnancy a causal environmental risk factor for adolescent antisocial behavior? Testing etiological theories and assumptions. *Psychological Medicine*, *42*(7), 1535–1545. doi:10.1017/s0033291711002443

D'Onofrio, B. M., Van Hulle, C. A., Waldman, I. D., Rodgers, J. L., Harden, K. P., Rathouz, P. J., & Lahey, B. B. (2008). Smoking during pregnancy and offspring externalizing problems: An exploration of genetic and environmental confounds. *Development and Psychopathology*, *20*, 139–164.

Frick, P. J., Lahey, B. B., Applegate, B., Kerdyck, L., Ollendick, T., Hynd, G. W., ... Waldman, I. (1994). DSM-IV field trials for the disruptive behavior disorders: Symptom utility estimates. *Journal of the American Academy of Child and Adolescent Psychiatry*, *33*, 529–539.

Frick, P. J., Lahey, B. B., Loeber, R., Stouthamer-Loeber, M., Christ, M. A. G., & Hanson, K. (1992). Familial risk factors to oppositional defiant disorder and conduct disorder: Parental psychopathology and maternal parenting. *Journal of Consulting and Clinical Psychology*, *60*, 49–55. doi:10.1037/0022-006x.60.1.49

Lahey, B. B., Applegate, B., Barkley, R. A., Garfinkel, B., McBurnett, K., Kerdyk, L., ... Shaffer, D. (1994). DSM-IV field trials for oppositional defiant disorder and conduct disorder in children and adolescents. *American Journal of Psychiatry*, *151*, 1163–1171.

Lahey, B. B., Applegate, B., Chronis, A. M., Jones, H. A., Williams, S. H., Loney, J., & Waldman, I. D. (2008). Psychometric characteristics of a measure of emotional dispositions developed to test a developmental propensity model of conduct disorder. *Journal of Clinical Child and Adolescent Psychology, 37*, 794–807.

Lahey, B. B., Applegate, B., Hakes, J. K., Zald, D. H., Hariri, A. R., & Rathouz, P. J. (2012). Is there a general factor of prevalent psychopathology during adulthood? *Journal of Abnormal Psychology, 121*(4), 971–977.

Lahey, B. B., Applegate, B., Waldman, I. D., Loft, J. D., Hankin, B. L., & Rick, J. (2004). The structure of child and adolescent psychopathology: Generating new hypotheses. *Journal of Abnormal Psychology, 113*, 358–385.

Lahey, B. B., Busemeyer, M. K., Ohara, C., & Beggs, V. E. (1977). Treatment of severe perceptual-motors disorders in children diagnosed as learning disabled. *Behavior Modification, 1*(1), 123–140. doi:10.1177/014544557711008

Lahey, B. B., Class, Q. A., Zald, D. H., Rathouz, P. J., Applegate, B., & Waldman, I. D. (2018). Prospective test of the developmental propensity model of antisocial behavior: From childhood and adolescence into early adulthood. *Journal of Child Psychology and Psychiatry, 59*, 676–683.

Lahey, B. B., & D'Onofrio, B. M. (2010). All in the family: Comparing siblings to test causal hypotheses regarding environmental influences on behavior. *Current Directions in Psychological Science, 19*, 319–323.

Lahey, B. B., Flagg, E. W., Bird, H. R., SchwabStone, M. E., Canino, G., Dulcan, M. K., … Regier, D. A. (1996). The NIMH Methods for the Epidemiology of Child and Adolescent Mental Disorders (MECA) Study: Background and methodology. *Journal of the American Academy of Child and Adolescent Psychiatry, 35*, 855–864.

Lahey, B. B., Green, K. D., & Forehand, R. (1980). On the independence of ratings of hyperactivity, conduct problems, and attention deficits in children – A multiple-regression analysis. *Journal of Consulting and Clinical Psychology, 48*(5), 566–574. doi:10.1037/0022-006x.48.5.566

Lahey, B. B., Krueger, R. F., Rathouz, P. J., Waldman, I. D., & Zald, D. H. (2017). A hierarchical causal taxonomy of psychopathology across the life span. *Psychological Bulletin, 143*(2), 142–186.

Lahey, B. B., Lee, S. S., Sibley, M. H., Applegate, B., Molina, B. S. G., & Pelham, W. E. (2016). Predictors of adolescent outcomes among 4–6 year old children with attention-deficit/hyperactivity disorder. *Journal of Abnormal Psychology, 125*, 168–181.

Lahey, B. B., Loeber, R., Burke, J., Rathouz, P. J., & McBurnett, K. (2002). Waxing and waning in concert: Dynamic comorbidity of conduct disorder with other disruptive and emotional problems over 17 years among clinic-referred boys. *Journal of Abnormal Psychology, 111*, 556–567.

Lahey, B. B., Loeber, R., Burke, J. D., & Applegate, B. (2005a). Predicting future antisocial personality disorder in males from a clinical assessment in childhood. *Journal of Consulting and Clinical Psychology, 73*(3), 389–399.

Lahey, B. B., Loeber, R., Burke, J. D., & Applegate, B. (2005b). Predicting future antisocial personality disorder in males from a clinical assessment in childhood. *Journal of Consulting and Clinical Psychology, 73*, 389–399.

Lahey, B. B., McNees, M. P., & Brown, C. C. (1973). Modification of deficits in reading comprehension. *Journal of Applied Behavior Analysis, 6*(3), 475–480. doi:10.1901/jaba.1973.6-475

Lahey, B. B., Pelham, W. E., Loney, J., Kipp, H., Ehrhardt, A., Lee, S. S., ... Massetti, G. (2004). Three-year predictive validity of DSM-IV attention deficit/hyperactivity disorder in children diagnosed at 4-6 years of age. *American Journal of Psychiatry*, *161*, 2014–2020.

Lahey, B. B., Pelham, W. E., Loney, J., Lee, S. S., & Willcutt, E. (2005). Instability of the DSM-IV subtypes of ADHD from preschool through elementary school. *Archives of General Psychiatry*, *62*, 896–902.

Lahey, B. B., Rathouz, P. J., Applegate, B., Tackett, J. L., & Waldman, I. D. (2010). Psychometrics of a self-report version of the child and adolescent dispositions scale. *Journal of Clinical Child and Adolescent Psychology*, *39*, 351–361.

Lahey, B. B., Rathouz, P. J., Applegate, B., Van Hulle, C., Garriock, H. A., Urbano, R. C., ... Waldman, I. D. (2008). Testing structural models of DSM-IV symptoms of common forms of child and adolescent psychopathology. *Journal of Abnormal Child Psychology*, *36*, 187–206.

Lahey, B. B., Van Hulle, C. A., Singh, A. L., Waldman, I. D., & Rathouz, P. J. (2011). Higher-order genetic and environmental structure of prevalent forms of child and adolescent psychopathology. *Archives of General Psychiatry*, *68*, 181–189.

Lahey, B. B., & Waldman, I. D. (2003). A developmental propensity model of the origins of conduct problems during childhood and adolescence. In B. B. Lahey, T. E. Moffitt, & A. Caspi (Eds.), *Causes of conduct disorder and juvenile delinquency* (pp. 76–117). New York, NY: Guilford Press.

Lahey, B. B., & Waldman, I. D. (2012). Annual research review: Phenotypic and causal structure of conduct disorder in the broader context of prevalent forms of psychopathology. *Journal of Child Psychology and Psychiatry*, *53*, 536–557.

Lahey, B. B., Waldman, I. D., & McBurnett, K. (1999). Annotation: The development of antisocial behavior: An integrative causal model. *Journal of Child Psychology and Psychiatry*, *40*, 669–682.

Lee, S. S., Lahey, B. B., Owens, E. B., & Hinshaw, S. P. (2008). Few preschool boys and girls with ADHD are well-adjusted during adolescence. *Journal of Abnormal Child Psychology*, *36*, 373–383.

Loeber, R., Burke, J. D., Lahey, B. B., Winters, A., & Zera, M. (2000). Oppositional defiant and conduct disorder: A review of the past 10 years, part I. *Journal of the American Academy of Child and Adolescent Psychiatry*, *39*(12), 1468–1484.

Pickles, A., & Rutter, M. (1991). Statistical and conceptual models of 'turning points' in developmental processes. In D. Magnusson, L. R. Bergman, G. Rudinger, & B. Torestand (Eds.), *Problems and methods in longitudinal research: Stability and change* (pp. 133–165). Cambridge, England: Cambridge University Press.

Sameroff, A. J. E. (Ed.) (2009). *The transactional model of development: How children and contexts shape each other*. Washington, DC: American Psychological Association.

Tackett, J. L., Lahey, B. B., Van Hulle, C. A., Waldman, I. D., Krueger, R. F., & Rathouz, P. J. (2013). Common genetic influences on negative emotionality and a general psychopathology factor in childhood and adolescence. *Journal of Abnormal Psychology*, *122*, 1142–1153.

Tremblay, R. E., Japel, C., Perusse, D., Mcduff, P., Boivin, M., Zoccolillo, M., & Montplaisir, J. (1999). The search for the age of 'onset' of physical aggression: Rousseau and Bandura revisited. *Criminal Behaviour and Mental Health*, *9*, 8–23.

Waldman, I. D., Tackett, J. L., Van Hulle, C. A., Applegate, B., Pardini, D., Frick, P. J., & Lahey, B. B. (2011). Child and adolescent conduct disorder substantially shares genetic influences with three socioemotional dispositions. *Journal of Abnormal Psychology*, *120*, 57–70. doi:10.1037/a0021351

13 Comments on the Autobiographies of the World War II Babies by Younger Peers

Daniel S. Nagin, Dale F. Hay, Manuel Eisner, Brandon C. Welsh, Sylvana M. Côté, and Isabelle Ouellet-Morin

13.1 THE GOOD FORTUNE OF WORLD WAR II BABIES

Daniel S. Nagin

Born November 29, 1948, in Philadelphia, United States

Teresa and H. John Heinz III University Professor of Public Policy and Statistics at Carnegie–Mellon University's Heinz College

I am a little more than 3 years out from being a World War II baby myself. Richard Tremblay asked me to reminisce about three of my seniors whom I know well – Jane Costello, David Farrington, and Friedrich Lösel. All have made major contributions to the study of human development, which their essays do a much better job of summarizing than I can. Instead I will comment on how fortunate all of us, including myself, have been to come of age in the 1960s, only 15 years out from the end of World War II.

In some ways our circumstances could not be more different. I grew up in an upper-middle-class home in Pittsburgh, Pennsylvania, in a country that had not been ravaged by World War II. Indeed, the United States emerged from World War II as the wealthiest and most powerful nation in the world by a long shot, a fact that probably explains the social and economic forces behind British women like Jane Costello having spent a good share of their adult lives in the USA. Jane and fellow Briton David Farrington came of age in war-ravaged Britain. For both, the continuation of rationing for nearly a decade after the conclusion of the war remains a vivid memory. Jane and David, however, came from very different backgrounds. Both of Jane's parents, like mine, were well educated, which is probably the origin of her 'posh' accent for which she was ridiculed in grade school. By contrast, David comes from more humble economic roots. His family was working class, and his parents were not well educated. David, who is one of criminology's most articulate spokespersons, reports that upon his matriculation at Cambridge he had an accent that marked his humble origins in class-conscious

England. He also reports that in the ensuing years that accent has softened. Friedrich Lösel grew up on the losing side of the war – in Germany. He describes a world in his youth of bombed-out houses and meager circumstances. What united the four of us, however, were generally happy childhoods in stable families, even though our social and economic circumstances were so different.

Why then do I say we were fortunate to have come of age before World War II was a distant memory? For one, we have all benefited mightily from the prosperity that followed from European countries finally setting aside the warring imperial rivalries that had ravaged the European continent for centuries and the entire world for the first half of the 20th century. Peace set the stage for Germany to become a rich and powerful nation that leads rather than wars with its former rivals. It also made it possible for World War II German baby Friedrich Lösel to become Director of the Cambridge Institute of Criminology in 2005 – in 1945 who would have thought that possible?

The prosperity of the postwar years, which was immediate in the case of the United States but came more slowly to Britain and Germany, provided the economic capacity to fund our research. It was also an era in which scientific leadership created political support for funding basic research, and, as David Farrington describes, empirical research in the social sciences was supported in ways that theretofore it hadn't been.

Another important characteristic that all four of us have in common is having grown up in stable homes with parents who valued education. As I already indicated, Jane's and my parents were well educated whereas David's and Friedrich's were not. The point, however, is not the level of our parents' education but their commitment to the education of their children. Perhaps coincidentally, the enduring importance of parenting is a major theme in all of our research.

How should future generations of investigators of human development follow in our tracks? It is already standard practice that newly initiated longitudinal studies be genetically informative. That should continue because gene–environment interactions are so complex that the riddle of their interaction will take many decades to crack. In my view, cracking the riddle will require a better understanding of how gene–environment interactions affect decision making processes, particularly as they involve risky decision making in emotion-laden circumstances. I thus recommend that the assessments of participants in longitudinal studies include placing them in emotionally charged circumstances, perhaps using virtual reality, and then eliciting their perceptions of the risks and rewards of alternative courses of action in those circumstances. For example, using virtual reality technology, young adult males might be placed in a bar where they come into conflict with another male patron who requires them either to walk away or fight. They could then be asked about the risks, rewards, and costs of fighting or walking away. A good deal of this type of research has already been done in criminology and psychology. To my knowledge, however, it has never been done where respondents were participants in a genetically informative longitudinal study. Relating their responses to their developmental history and genetics should be a future priority.

We are also in the midst of a revolution in analytics involving advances in artificial intelligence and machine learning (ML). Machine learning methods, in particular, may hold great promise for the analysis of longitudinal datasets, especially for those with genetic information, and can be powerful tools for identifying heretofore-undetected relationships among variables in complex datasets. Specifically, the forte of ML methods is developing predictive models relating an outcome of interest, say violence, with other variables in the dataset, which in ML parlance are called 'features'. Using conventional regression models for this purpose requires the researcher to select predictor variables to include in the model. The researcher must also specify the functional form of the relationship between the outcome and the selected predictor variables. In contrast, ML methods are designed to search for the best set of predictor variables, a.k.a. features, and the optimal functional form of their relationship to the outcome of interest. In complex datasets, such as those collected in longitudinal studies, ML methods can 'bring a lot to the table' in their analysis. I, thus, recommend greater use of ML methods by the next generation of researchers, which will, of course, require their training in ML methods.

In closing, I wish I could be confident that future generations of scholars will be as fortunate as the four of us have been. At least in the United States, there is a pulling back from support for both education and basic research. Concerning education, David, Jane, and Friedrich each describe the critical importance of the educational opportunities afforded them in their childhood, even in the impoverished circumstances of Britain and Germany during their youth. Given the vastly greater resources of the present day, governments should be doubling down on present levels of investments in education and research, not cutting back.

The four of us have also been the beneficiaries of not only peaceful but also genuinely friendly and cooperative relations among European and North American countries. The withdrawal of Great Britain from the European Union, trade frictions, the rising tide of hostility to immigrants, and xenophobic nationalism are troubling signs that postwar international cooperation is fraying.

I hope that I am wrong about the future because I wish our same good fortune to future generations of scientists.

13.2   TALKING ABOUT THEIR GENERATION

Dale F. Hay

Born April 9, 1950, in Bridgeport, Connecticut, United States
Professor Emerita
Centre for Human Developmental Science
Cardiff University, England

Introduction

In this book, an impressive array of developmental scientists cast their eyes on their own pathways through time, the life journeys they made in the midst of global events that, as is usual for children and adults alike, were mainly out of their control. In this commentary I focus on the stories told by four distinguished scholars from Finland, Britain, Canada, and the United States, respectively. Did their early experiences set them on a trajectory to scientific curiosity and intellectual acumen? Did their interest in the life course stem from their own experiences in childhood, youth, and adulthood? Is it possible to discern any general developmental patterns from the minutiae of individual lives? In this commentary, I will reflect on general lessons that can be learned from these rich pieces of life writing and then consider how their work has set the agenda for the generations of scholars that follow.

Life Lessons

These four scholars have all identified important developmental trends and predictors of developmental outcomes, and they have all acknowledged the importance of biological predispositions as well as social experiences. It is perhaps not surprising that, when they turn their lenses on their own lives, they reflect on the many sources of change and continuity that they have explored in their research on large longitudinal cohorts. At the same time, they tell idiosyncratic stories set in specific times and places. As a commentator who happens to be both a developmental scientist and a novelist, I shall now draw attention to several sources of influence stemming from their wartime childhoods that might have had a significant impact on their academic choices and their scientific work.

Their Parents' and Grandparents' Lives

The four children who tell their life stories in these chapters, of course, had parents whose own lives were disrupted and endangered by the war. Most of their parents had themselves been war babies – born during or soon after the Great War – and grew up during the politically and economically turbulent 1930s. Stress and trauma impinged on three generations. For example, economic necessity led Lea Pulkinnen's grandparents to move their family across Finland in 1922, traveling in a freight train and, for the last stage of the journey, pulling a sledge through the snow. Jean Golding's father left his school in Cornwall at the (then legal) age of 14, needing to support his family after his own father's several bankruptcies and eventual death.

Beyond the global impact of the Depression and wartime, these scholars also draw attention to the clash of cultures that arise even in small towns and villages. Richard Tremblay describes two cities on opposite sides of the Ottawa River – French-speaking, Roman Catholic Hull in Quebec across from Ottawa and the English-speaking and largely Protestant capital of Canada. Jean Golding in turn describes the religious schisms within two strands of Protestantism in the Cornish town of Hayle (population 4,000): the strict Wesleyan Methodists of the Coppertown neighborhood where her father lived and the somewhat less strict Anglicans of the Foundry neighborhood, where her Canadian mother had come to visit relatives. In recent years, longitudinal researchers have not focused much on the impact of religious belief on children's development, but for those children born during the Second World War, these religious and cultural differences may have impacted on their own view of childhood, aggression, and socialization.

It is also clear from these memoirs that when children are born into a particular family, they are embedded within a maze of stories, legends, secrets, and lies. For example, Lea Pulkkinen tells the story of how her grandparents drew lots with her grandfather's siblings to determine who would stay on the family land and who would have to move; she writes that their religious belief helped them accept this random chance as a righteous call to action. Richard Tremblay describes how he found out that his parents had lied about his birth date and how he eventually told his father that he knew the truth. As developmental scientists, we pay less attention to these complex aspects of a family's history than do qualitative family researchers and writers of fiction. Yet an individual child's pathway to aggression and delinquency or, alternatively, his or her ambition for education and a meaningful life may have roots in the complex culture of family life, where some stories are told, while others are withheld.

The Correlates of Wartime

Lea Pulkkinen, who has been a member of the international peace movement, is at pains to distinguish war from aggression, stating that 'a war is an institution in itself' (Chapter 4, p. XX) which needs to be understood on many different levels. These life stories draw attention to the different ways that war is experienced, by those who serve in the military, those who suffer as civilian casualties, and those who quite literally keep the home fires burning while others are away fighting in the war. Because these four writers were born in different places and different years of the war, their early experiences during the war differ.

Jean Golding draws attention to the war-related stressors that impinged on her family before and after her own birth. These included her mother's isolation from her family in Canada, since travel across the Atlantic was impossible; her father's dangerous nighttime work guarding large tanks of gas; and the death, imprisonment, and long-term trauma of her mother's brothers who fought in the war. During the war, Jean herself experienced severe illness and hospitalization, which at that time meant she was isolated, and her parents were unable to stay with her. Food restrictions also had an adverse effect on nutrition for all the families in her community.

At the same time, the war babies observed some models of community and prosocial behavior in the face of adversity. Lea Pulkkinen remembers family members pulling together on the estate owned by her grandparents, taking in refugees from the province of Karelia. She paints a happy picture of some aspects of her country childhood: 'I have vivid memories of how to make potato flour, syrup, soap, sausages, fruit and berry conserves, how to milk a cow by hand and feed the animals, and how to grow linen and sheer sheep and spin thread from the linen and the wool for clothes making' (Chapter 4, p. XX). Yet her father came home damaged from his wartime experiences; her mother told her that he was not the same man she had married. The legacy of his war led to problem drinking and an early death on the day he was to visit Lea and see her newborn baby. These memories remind us that wars do not end when peace documents are signed.

The younger war babies had fathers who served in the war as well. Richard Tremblay's father, who had been a professional football player, was stationed at Camp Borden in Ontario, where he trained other soldiers; Richard notes that it is likely Jean Golding's uncles also received their training for the Canadian Air Force at Camp Borden, which reminds us of the international connections in what was truly a worldwide war.

Ben Lahey's father, who before the war had been a radio operator on cargo ships, volunteered for the Coast Guard, but because of his Morse code skills was seconded to the Navy and made several dangerous voyages across the North Atlantic. However, by the time Ben was born, his father had been injured and had been sent back to Florida. Ben writes evocatively of the way in which the children who grew up in the postwar years reenacted their fathers' wartime experiences by 'playing army'. As a slightly younger baby boomer, I can testify that the boys and girls in Connecticut similarly reenacted World War II, throwing invisible grenades and rolling down the hilly front lawns in our neighborhood. (I had thought this was an almost universal experience for my cohort, but, sadly, my southern friends have told me they were still playing Yanks versus Rebels.) These stories from childhood remind us that one of the legacies of war on children is the hold it has on the imaginations of those who were too young to fight. It also highlights the important differences between 'play fighting' and serious aggression in childhood.

Risk, Protection, and Resilience

It is perhaps not surprising that these four eminent scholars pursued their educations, despite serious setbacks along the way. Their stories remind us about risk and protective factors in childhood and adolescence. Furthermore, they testify to one of the most important concepts in longitudinal research, *resilience.* Lea Pulkkinen tells us how her life was affected by her father's problematic drinking and the impact it had on her mother. Jean Golding's educational choices were affected by the fact that she contracted polio when she was 13 years old, shortly after she had made a difficult transition to a new secondary school. The legacy of polio meant that she had to focus on mathematics, rather than pursue zoology, which would have required more active fieldwork. Yet she reflects on how this apparent setback may have helped her with her life's work:

I was an observer. The various hospital admissions had been in public hospitals where I was surrounded by people from all walks of life (nurses, cleaners, and doctors from around the world, as well as other patients) with different beliefs and attitudes. I realize now that this enabled me to have an understanding of the various attitudes and habits of all members of the population that I later studied in the longitudinal survey that I designed. (Chapter 3, p. XX)

Experiences in childhood and adolescence have contributed to these scholars' interest in aggression and psychological problems more generally. Richard Tremblay's mother died when he was young, and his father was often traveling away; Richard notes that he focused on football and hockey but also became the president of his high school class. He talks movingly about how his younger brother was badly affected by their mother's death and consequently had a more difficult adolescence. Ben Lahey remembers his own experiences with an aggressive sibling and bullying peers, especially after transferring from a small, supportive school to the more hostile environment of a larger junior high. All of these experiences no doubt contributed to these scholars' many insights into the complex dynamics of aggression and its relation to other behavioral and emotional problems; the study of the factors that promote aggression may itself be seen as a sign of resilience.

All of these writers testify to their own intellectual curiosity and their pursuit of education. As Richard Tremblay comments, 'Although sports had been the center of my life, I was also strongly attracted to the pleasure of learning, in the sense of getting to the root of things' (Chapter 10, p. 249), an intellectual trait that is clearly manifested in his determination to explore the developmental origins of aggression. Nonetheless, these talented scholars also reflect on structural factors that impacted negatively on their educations and subsequent careers. Both Lea Pulkkinen and Jean Golding comment upon the obstacles they faced as women applying for academic positions. Ben Lahey speaks of the spirit of anti-intellectualism of some academic institutions in the 1970s and the racism that was voiced in communities where he worked. The fact that all four scholars have contributed so positively to the study of aggression and, more generally, lives through time, testifies to their own resilience. As Lea writes, 'In the dimension of emotion regulation, children's constructive behavior including active coping with a problem, positive thinking, and consideration of others, leads to the resilient style of life and successful adulthood' (Chapter 4, p. XX). The four chapters exemplify those features of both personal and intellectual resilience.

The Legacy of These Four Programs of Research

The work produced by four scholars (and the others whose work is represented in this book) has significantly contributed to the study of human development, both in terms of methodological advances, the creation of important longitudinal cohorts, contribution to developmental theory, and identification of pathways to prevention and intervention. Jean Golding's efforts in longitudinal research, in particular the creation of the important two-generational Avon Longitudinal Study of Parents and Children (ALSPAC), has made an extraordinary contribution to our understanding of health and human development. Lea Pulkkinen has drawn attention to the interplay between biological processes underlying aggression and its social context, in particular the contrast between reactive and proactive aggression, which has implications for different types of prevention and rehabilitation strategies. Richard Tremblay's longitudinal studies have mapped out the developmental course of aggression over time and the biological, cognitive, and social factors that contribute to its manifestation at different ages, from infancy to adulthood. His search for evidence of epigenetic factors that influence aggression plots a course to take the field beyond the never-ending nature–nurture debate. Ben Lahey's conceptual analysis of the underlying phenomena that contribute to disparate medical diagnoses is both a theoretical advance and sets the course for more effective approaches to children's behavioral problems. Taken together, the 'war babies' represented in this book have redefined the study of aggression in the last two decades.

Priorities for the Next Half-Century of Research

The work described in this book has effectively mapped out the developmental course of aggression and the risk and protective factors that influence how aggressive children are and what forms their aggression takes, and has also helped identify early markers of problematic levels of violence. Can this nonetheless translate into effective prevention strategies? That may depend not just on national- and community-level resources but also on resolution of theoretical debates about the developmental origins of aggression. For example, in the introduction to this volume, Richard Tremblay has drawn attention to centuries of thought about the early origins and apparent universality of infants' aggression. At the same time, an equally strong case is being made by evolutionary, social, and developmental psychologists for the early origins and apparent universality of infants' empathy and helpfulness. If both things are true, how do infants balance their aggressive and prosocial impulses? Do the existing longitudinal datasets provide enough information about both domains of behavior to address that question? My own research in a longitudinal study of moderate size suggests that these two types of behavior are positively related to begin with, being two ways to interact nonverbally with other human beings, and only gradually disaggregate over the first years of life. At the same time, individual differences in both domains are marked. In the next half-century, it would be helpful to examine the factors that foster or work against prosocial solutions to social conflict, from infancy through to adulthood.

It is noteworthy that two of these four scholars, Lea Pulkkinen and Ben Lahey, have written that they feel strongly about the need to work for peace. In the next 50 years, will it be possible for the psychologists who study aggression and altruism to cast a wider net and collaborate with other biological and social scientists who study group conflict and, at the extreme, war and the kind of reconciliation and future thinking that leads to peace? That would be an appropriate legacy of the war babies' longitudinal analyses. It would require an expansion of the education and training of aggression researchers, integrating bioscientists with social scientists, moral philosophers, and policymakers. It would also require the level of intellectual curiosity, personal resilience, and scientific ambition that is so exemplified by the life stories of the scholars represented in this book.

13.3   GOING GLOBAL – LEARNING FROM THE WAR BABIES ON HOW TO ATTEMPT A GLOBAL BIRTH COHORT STUDY

Manuel Eisner

Born May 7, 1959, in Strasbourg, France
Professor of Comparative and Developmental Criminology
Deputy Director of the University of Cambridge's Institute of Criminology,
Great Britain

I was born in 1959, roughly 20 years after the first war baby in this volume. But even so, World War II probably played a role in shaping my interests in violence research. As I learned during adolescence, my father's family had fled Germany in 1933. My mother's family, in contrast, had lived in Düsseldorf throughout the war. She survived the Holocaust as a so-called half-Jew. Yet on the rare occasions she talked about her experiences, she described, amongst others, how she had said good-bye, at the age of 15, to her two aunts as they were deported to the concentration camps and her fear of neighbors when she was queuing for bread. Of course, there was nothing predictable in my becoming a violence researcher, but it may not have been entirely random either.

The cohort of researchers represented in this volume has made extraordinary contributions to helping us better understand the causes and the prevention of violence through a developmental lens. So what new studies are worth doing to advance our understanding of the development and the prevention of violence? And how can these new studies benefit from the experiences and knowledge accumulated in the work of the war babies?

Going Global

David Farrington recommends that researchers should choose to conduct difficult studies that push back the boundaries of knowledge. This is particularly true for longitudinal studies. They require a huge amount of work and many years of persistence until they generate new knowledge. To make them worthwhile, they therefore need to be designed to answer multiple questions from different angles, including questions nobody imagined when the study was begun.

In line with ideas developed by Rainer Silbereisen and Jean Golding, my own answer is that we sorely lack comparative analyses of children growing up in different societies across the world. I am therefore working, together with an interdisciplinary group of colleagues, to launch a global birth cohort study of 12,000 children born in 2021. The project, called 'Evidence for Better Lives Study' (EBLS), will focus on eight middle-income cities across world, namely Valenzuela (Philippines), Hue (Vietnam), Ragama (Sri Lanka), Tarlai (Pakistan), Khayelitsha (South Africa), Koforidua (Ghana), Cluj (Romania), and Kingston (Jamaica). If successful, it will track the lives of 1,500 children in each city. And it will follow the insight, expressed throughout this volume, that research on violence and the consequences of exposure to violence must be firmly rooted in a broader understanding of the development of psychosocial well-being.

Evidence for Better Lives will start at the beginning. We will conduct a first data collection in the third trimester of the pregnancy of the mothers, followed by data collection at 6 and 15 months after birth. The plan is to continue assessments in early and middle childhood and eventually into adolescence and early adulthood. It will follow children in more varied cultures and different socio-economic situations than any prior cohort study. Moreover, the challenges these children will meet and the opportunities they will have in the 21st century will be dramatically different from those of the cohorts from Pittsburgh, Montreal, London, Bristol, or Genzano.

We completed a pilot study (Evidence for Better Lives Consortium, 2019), which involved recruiting and interviewing 150 pregnant women in each study site, collecting biological samples, and recontacting participants 3 months after birth. The results suggest that conducting eight parallel birth cohort studies is feasible if every stage is planned meticulously and a large amount of time is devoted to coordination and quality control.

Solve the Singapore–Jamaica Problem

One of the big questions I would like EBLS to shed light on is informed by my background as a historian and sociologist of violence. I have come to call it the 'Singapore–Jamaica Problem': Singapore currently has a homicide rate of 0.3 per 100,000, while Jamaica has a homicide rate of 50 per 100,000. The two societies thus currently differ in levels of lethal violence by a factor of 1:150. Why?

Answers by macro-level sociologists tend to emphasize factors like different developments of the political system, economic wealth, or drug markets. However, within a bio-psycho-social framework, we would like to understand what developmental processes – at the individual, family, and community levels – generate such large differences in society-wide levels of violence. This includes such simple questions as: At what age do society-wide differences in aggressive behavior and symptoms of poor psychosocial well-being emerge? And what are the causally relevant mechanisms that bring about big population-wide differences? Is it poor parenting, poverty and deprivation, lack of access to services, cultural beliefs that support resilience, or ease of access to guns and drugs?

In my view, a comparative long-term birth cohort study that comprises children in all major regions of the world would contribute important answers to some of these questions. The chapters in this volume suggest that this requires overcoming considerable logistical and financial challenges but that it also may lead to exciting methodological innovations that will more fully capture the variability of human experience.

Integrate Moral Development

Another priority for the next decades is to advance our understanding of the link between aggression and moral development. Among the authors of this volume, Gian Vittorio Caprara is the only researcher whose work largely revolves around the link between moral development and aggression. The limited interest by the others is understandable from a historical perspective. World War II and the Holocaust had been moral catastrophes. Also, the 1960s, 1970s, and 1980s were periods of widespread critique of old-fashioned moral rigidities. Several authors talk about breaking free from the narrow moral controls that still dominated their adolescence and early adulthood.

However, it is becoming clear that children already have an understanding of fairness, retribution, and altruistic helping in the first years of life; that these skills are an essential basis to human cooperation; and that they likely unfold ontogenetically as the result of an interaction between culturally specific contexts and universal species-wide maturational processes (Bloom, 2013; Tomasello, 2016). In other words, moral development guides children's cooperation with collaborative partners, their enforcement of social norms, and their response to conflicts of interests.

In my view, a global birth cohort study would be an opportunity to advance our understanding of the transactional links between moral development and aggression in different societies from the first years onward. For example, it would be useful to better understand whether, and at what age, behaviors related to reciprocity and fairness start to differ between societies, and whether such differences might be related to epigenetic changes resulting from chronic exposure to violence and adversity.

Address the Frames per Life Problem

Films take 24 frames per second. This is the frame rate at which visual stimuli become coded, in the brain of the viewer, as a natural movement over time. Yet most developmental studies represented in this volume take less than one frame per year. In the Pittsburgh Youth Study, Rolf and Magda Loeber collected data every 6 months for some years. However, they realized that this was a good way to drive participants, interviewers, and researchers to despair.

Yet, the issue of how frequently longitudinal studies need to make assessments to understand human development remains pressing. There is a yawning gap between the frame rate of seconds at which we analyze neurocognitive processes involved in aggressive responses (see Chapter 7) and the frame rate of years commonly used in longitudinal studies. What happens at time intervals of minutes, hours, days, weeks, and months? And how can processes at such shorter time intervals be integrated into what we have learned about the slower dynamics that have been captured so well in existing studies?

To address these issues, we need to innovate in several ways: One approach made possible by mobile phones is to integrate an experience-sampling element into a longitudinal study (Borah, Murray, Eisner, & Jugl, 2018). These data provide new insight into the relationship between state and trait, and between the short-term dynamics of situational triggers and the much slower change in personality characteristics. Also, it would be desirable to integrate experiments that measure children's short-term neurocognitive responses to standardized situations into the EBLS study. This will require, amongst others, methodological innovation and careful piloting in order to make sure that such measures adequately capture cross-cultural differences and can be administered in low-resource settings.

Engage in the Global Violence Prevention Agenda

Over the past 30 years, violence prevention has become a major global field of policy and research (Krug, Mercy, Dahlberg, & Zwi, 2002). Its salience is highlighted in the Sustainable Development Goals (SDGs) adopted by the United Nations in 2015. Several SDGs put the reduction of violence and access to justice at the heart of sustainable development. Moreover, reducing violence is intertwined with SDGs related to good health and well-being for all, gender equality, inclusive and equitable education, reduced inequalities, and sustainable and safe cities and communities.

The work by the contributors to this volume has laid the basis for effective violence prevention in families, in schools, and in communities internationally. In my view, the next generation of studies has to be coordinated with the agenda of the SDGs. In particular, we must understand better how and when evidence-based practices and policies are adopted in real-life settings in different cultures and political systems. We should not neglect experimental–longitudinal studies. But we should equally design observational studies so that they can advance our understanding of the implementation, scaling, and institutionalization of practices to prevent behavioral and mental health problems (Fishbein, Ridenour, Stahl, & Sussman, 2016).

In EBLS we focus on medium-sized cities as the study units because we believe that municipalities are important agents of change. As part of the pilot study, we have therefore conducted, in each participating city, a needs and resources assessment relating to violence prevention, based on interviews with local experts and stakeholders (Evidence for Better Lives Consortium, 2019). Results show that the eight cities differ in their gaps and priorities. In the future, we hope that research findings on the development of 'their' children will help each city to become a 'pathfinder city' that develops a comprehensive strategy to optimally support child development, through collaboration among local and regional authorities and possibly supported by international organizations.

Conclusion: The Biggest Challenge

The contributors to this volume are the giants in the field. Not least, they show what an extraordinary achievement it is to launch and maintain a longitudinal study over years and decades, remaining open to new ideas and promoting early career scholars while applying for grants and keeping attrition under control. Hence, I believe that the biggest challenge for a global birth cohort study like EBLS is to figure out how to make a major long-term collaborative project work over many years, with teams from different academic and cultural backgrounds. Surely a lot can be learned from publications on research management. The contributions to this book suggest that patience, commitment, creativity, and generosity are among the qualities that can help.

References

Bloom, P. (2013). *Just babies: The origins of good and evil*. New York, NY: Broadway Books.

Borah, T. J., Murray, A. L., Eisner, M., & Jugl, I. (2018). Developing and validating an experience sampling measure of aggression: The Aggression-ES Scale. *Journal of Interpersonal Violence*, 0886260518812068.

Evidence for Better Lives Consortium. (2019). *Addressing violence against children: Mapping the needs and resources in eight cities across the world*. Cambridge, England: Institute of Criminology.

Fishbein, D. H., Ridenour, T. A., Stahl, M., & Sussman, S. (2016). The full translational spectrum of prevention science: Facilitating the transfer of knowledge to practices and policies that prevent behavioral health problems. *Translational Behavioral Medicine*, 6(1), 5–16.

Krug, E. G., Mercy, J. A., Dahlberg, L. L., & Zwi, A. B. (2002). The world report on violence and health. *The Lancet*, *360*(9339), 1083–1088.

Tomasello, M. (2016). *A natural history of human morality*. Cambridge, MA: Harvard University Press.

13.4   'LIFE'S WEALTH IS TO DO': REFLECTIONS ON DEVELOPMENTAL AND PREVENTION SCIENCE PIONEERS IN UNDERSTANDING AND PREVENTING VIOLENCE

Brandon C. Welsh

Born January 4, 1969, Vancouver, British Columbia, Canada

Professor, School of Criminology and Criminal Justice

Northeastern University, Boston, United States

Introduction

The quote that serves as the main title of this chapter captures a rather important outlook on life, something that is characteristic of each of the five scientists examined in this chapter—and more than likely, I suspect, of all of the scientists in this book. However, this quote is incomplete. The full quote, by the famous British poet Siegfried Sassoon (1945, p. 154), does even more justice to the five scientists and their lifework; it reads: 'Life's wealth is to do; its loss – to dream and wait'. It is safe to say that there was not much, if any, dreaming and waiting going on among these five scientists! This is best exemplified through their individual pioneering research as well as prolific writing in the cause of advancing knowledge on the development and prevention of violence. By any measure, their respective bodies of work have made major gains in pushing the field forward and have made lasting contributions to society.

I have elected to write about five scientists who are the subject of four chapters in this volume: David Farrington; Rolf and Magda Loeber; Friedrich Lösel; and Richard Tremblay. I have done so because of their singular contributions to understanding and preventing violence, as well as the fact that each has influenced—with some continuing to influence—my own academic career in the prevention of antisocial behavior and violent offending.

A few personal remarks on these five scientists seem warranted. David Farrington provided the inspiration for me to attend Cambridge University and chaired my PhD dissertation, and together we have written several books and scores of scientific articles. With Rolf and Magda Loeber, I collaborated on a study drawing on the youngest sample of the Pittsburgh Youth Study and (with Rolf) wrote a Festschrift for David Farrington on his (supposed!) retirement. Alongside Friedrich Lösel, I have had the honor to serve as a member of the Campbell Collaboration's Crime and Justice Coordinating Group. With Richard Tremblay, I have written several scientific articles, including a biography of Joan McCord's contributions to criminology. In no small measure, I hold each responsible for helping prepare me for a new chapter in my career: continuing the life-work of Joan McCord, by directing and carrying out a new program of research on the Cambridge–Somerville Youth Study (see, e.g., Welsh, Dill, & Zane, 2019; Welsh, Zane, Zimmerman, & Yohros, 2019; Zane, Welsh, & Zimmerman, 2019). The phrase 'standing on the shoulders of giants' seems quite fitting.

In the pages that follow, I offer my views on how these five scientists – pioneers in developmental and prevention science – have made a difference in understanding and preventing violence (with a heavy emphasis on the latter), as well as the importance this holds for the future of violence prevention. I begin with some key lessons that I have learned from their life and career trajectories.

Lessons Learned from Life and Career Trajectories

I have been fortunate to come in contact with these and other world-class developmental and prevention scientists from an early stage in my academic training and career. This has allowed me to experience firsthand some of the events these five scientists describe in their chapters. But it is the lessons learned from their life and career trajectories that stand the test of time, and several lessons are especially notable. One is the intellectual curiosity that guided from an early stage each of the scientists. As noted by Tremblay, 'I was also strongly attracted to the pleasure of learning, in the sense of getting to the root of things' (Chapter 10, p. XX). Closely related is the quest for knowledge – pushing the boundaries of science and answering pressing social questions. This too began at an early stage for these scientists and did not wane with age or experience.

A second lesson, which has already been noted in the introductory remarks, is the spirit of getting on with the work; the doing that is central to being productive. Farrington captures this best with his trademark saying, 'Let's go for it' (Chapter 6, p. XX). Sometimes this means taking a risk or forging a new path where no one else has wandered; sometimes it may even mean accepting the prospect of failure, what Firestein (2015) argues is at the core of advancing science.

Of more practical value is the lesson that has to do with attention to detail in the conduct of experimental and longitudinal research. More specifically, this calls for meticulous record keeping and doggedness in tracing participants over sometimes lengthy periods of time. As noted by the Loebers, 'A study is only as good as the participation rate and the quality of the data' (Chapter 5, p. XX).

Perspectives on Research Legacies for Research Needed in the Next Half-Century

Readers of the chapters by these five scientists will marvel at how each of them has managed to initiate, direct, and sustain—for several decades in some cases—a number of the field's landmark prospective longitudinal and longitudinal–experimental studies. These include Farrington's Cambridge Study in Delinquent Development (CSDD); the Loebers' Pittsburgh Youth Study (PYS) and Pittsburgh Girls Study; Lösel's Erlangen–Nuremberg Development and Prevention Study (ENDPS); and Tremblay's Montreal Longitudinal–Experimental Study (MLES) and Preparing for Life Study.

Readers' interest will be even more heightened with the studies' contributions to science and public policy. It is, in my opinion, these landmark studies and how they will continue to be utilized that point to the research that is needed in the next half-century. For example, through the CSDD, Farrington has been at the forefront of advocating for and demonstrating the importance of linking up fundamental research on development and risk and protective factors for criminal offending (the focus of his study) with applied research on the prevention of crime and violence. Better known as risk-focused prevention, research in this area will be in even greater demand in the years to come. Following from Tremblay's research in the area of epigenetics, there will also be a need for expanded research on 'prenatal and early postnatal bio-psycho-social interventions' designed to 'prevent early onset of chronic physical aggression problems' (Chapter 10, p. XX). This work will take on added importance as we learn more about the intergenerational transmission of the effects of violence prevention programs (see Bailey, Hill, Epstein, Steeger, & Hawkins, 2018).

Priorities for Future Research

Building on the research legacies of these five scientists, this section sketches out some personal views on what should be key priorities for research on violence over the next half-century. One priority is a need to begin to shift from research on the development of violence to research on the prevention of violence. By no means is this suggesting that we have learned everything there is to know about the development of violence. Rather, it is an acknowledgment of the impressive body of knowledge on the development of violence that has been produced so far—thanks in part to these five scientists—and a real sense of urgency to (1) translate this knowledge into preventive action and (2) provide greater understanding about evidence-based violence prevention programs and local- and state-level violence prevention networks that are using research evidence.

Also important to this shift in priorities is the recognition of the growing body of high-quality scientific evidence on the effectiveness of childhood and adolescent violence prevention programs and from which evidence-based conclusions can be drawn. This was a central argument advanced more than a decade ago by one of these scientists in the book, *Saving Children from a Life of Crime* (Farrington & Welsh, 2007). It seems reasonable that 80–85% of spending on violence research should be allocated to projects with direct impact on the prevention of violence.

Closely related to this focus on research on violence prevention is the need for greater understanding of scaling up evidence-based programs for wider dissemination and achieving population-level impacts. Both of these issues are at the heart of evidence-based policymaking for preventing violence (Dodge & Mandel, 2012). Research is needed on the underlying processes and interactions of the key factors (e.g., implementation context, heterogeneity in target populations and service providers, fidelity to the model) that contribute to attenuation of effects as preventive interventions move from efficacy trials, to effectiveness trials, to large-scale delivery systems. Research is also needed to improve our knowledge on how the full potential of evidence-based programs can be realized by producing effects that are beneficial as well as sustainable for large segments of society.

Training the Next Generation of Scientists

At a time of increasing public skepticism toward scientific facts and an all-out attack on some areas of science in the United States and in other countries (Oreskes, 2019; Plumer & Davenport, 2019), it is more important than ever that we renew our commitment to train the next generation of scientists in the conduct of basic and applied research on the development and prevention of violence. This should begin with championing support – in an unequivocal way – for what David Olds (2009) calls 'disciplined passion'. In the context of program evaluation, for example, it is by no means the case that a program developer cannot also serve as program evaluator. There is nothing here that even raises a hint of any potential bias or conflict of interest. The reason for this has everything to do with the scientific training received by the investigator. This is the discipline – the scientific integrity – that is exercised in the conduct of research. In addition to establishing their commitment to using the highest standards of scientific inquiry, it also gives investigators the ability to follow their interests – their passions – in pursuit of advancing knowledge and improving public policy.

Conclusion

Criminologists sometimes speculate about where we would be as a discipline and even as a society if one brilliant scientist or another had decided to pursue a different career path, thereby sweeping away all of their important contributions to understanding and preventing violence. This is to say nothing of what would have become of the scores of young scientists whom they trained and the many who continue to collaborate with them. It is not a pleasant thought. Thankfully, we can take great comfort in the fact that each of these five developmental and prevention scientists committed themselves to a life of discovery in this field. We are richer for their pioneering works; we are better scientists for their leadership.

References

Bailey, J. A., Hill, K. G., Epstein, M., Steeger, C., & Hawkins, J. D. (2018). Seattle Social Development Project – The Intergenerational Project (SSDP–TIP). In V. I. Eichelsheim & S. G. A. v. d. Weijer (Eds.), *Intergenerational continuity of criminal and antisocial behaviour* (pp. 186–213). London, England: Routledge.

Dodge, K. A., & Mandel, A. D. (2012). Building evidence for evidence-based policy making. *Criminology & Public Policy*, *11*(3), 525–534.

Farrington, D. P., & Welsh, B. C. (2007). *Saving children from a life of crime: Early risk factors and effective interventions*. New York, NY: Oxford University Press.

Firestein, S. (2015). *Failure: Why science is so successful*. New York, NY: Oxford University Press.

Olds, D. (2009). In support of disciplined passion. *Journal of Experimental Criminology*, *5*(2), 201–214.

Oreskes, N. (2019). *Why trust science?* Princeton, NJ: Princeton University Press.

Plumer, B., & Davenport, C. (2019). *Trump eroding role of science in government*. New York Times, pp. A1, A16–A17.

Sassoon, S. (1945). *Siegfried's journey 1916–1920*. London, England: Faber and Faber.

Welsh, B. C., Dill, N. E., & Zane, S. N. (2019). The first delinquency prevention experiment: A socio-historical review of the origins of the Cambridge–Somerville Youth Study's research design. *Journal of Experimental Criminology*, *15*(3), 441–451.

Welsh, B. C., Zane, S. N., Zimmerman, G. M., & Yohros, A. (2019). Association of a crime prevention program for boys with mortality 72 years after the intervention: Follow-up of a randomized clinical trial. *JAMA Netw Open*, *2*(3), e190782.

Zane, S. N., Welsh, B. C., & Zimmerman, G. M. (2019). Criminal offending and mortality over the full life-course: A 70-year follow-up of the Cambridge–Somerville Youth Study. *Journal of Quantitative Criminology*, *35*(4), 691–713.

13.5   SEIZING OPPORTUNITIES AND OVERCOMING DIFFICULTIES: HOW THREE WOMEN BECAME TRAILBLAZERS IN DEVELOPMENTAL SCIENCE

Sylvana M. Côté
Born April 4, 1972 in Chicoutimi, Quebec, Canada
Professor of Public Health
Director, Research Unit on Children's Psycho-Social Maladjustment (GRIP)
Université de Montréal

Lessons Learned from Career Trajectories

Personal Life

Jean Golding, Jane Costello, and Magda Stouthamer-Loeber were born in Europe during the Second World War. Their personal and professional trajectories have important similarities. They were exposed to similar aspects of the war, notably the sound of the war planes overhead and the rationing of food during and for several years after the war. Interestingly, all three report that their childhood was happy, despite being at the center of the worst war ever. Jean, Jane, and Magda were under 6 years of age during the war and appear to have been sheltered from the worries that their parents must have experienced.

From a psychological perspective, this raises an interesting question about resilience. Adverse childhood experiences are measured in most longitudinal studies, including those launched by Jean, Jane, and Magda. Events such as parental stress, lack of food, and restricted access to many resources would be coded in most longitudinal studies as important adverse childhood experiences. The number of these childhood adverse experiences is typically correlated with poor developmental outcomes. However, the war experiences were normative, in the sense that entire communities were exposed to the same stressors. In that sense, war stressors may have strengthened family and community links and created resilience instead of risk. The war stressors were not interpreted as stressful by the young Jean, Jane, and Magda. What mattered to them as children was, not surprisingly, their immediate family environment. This is in line with the notion that interpersonal adverse experiences (e.g., abuse, neglect by parents) are often shown to be most detrimental. Jean, Jane, and Magda refer to their parents as loving and caring – undoubtedly important protective factors.

In terms of methodological implications for studying the associations between early childhood adverse experiences and future outcomes, these anecdotes are a reminder that it is the deviation from the norm that represents risk, and that interpersonal stressors are an important focus of scientific attention. It also suggests that the accuracy of the assessment of adverse childhood experiences may be reinforced by questions related to the interpretation of the stressors. The perception of adversity may be more strongly correlated with future outcomes than the adverse event itself. This also speaks to the importance of personality factors in facing life's challenges and taking up opportunities. Jean, Jane, and Magda clearly have strong personalities as well as a pragmatic and optimistic outlook on life, and solid foundations for success in life, despite the challenges they faced.

Professional Life

It is striking that these three women were not on a direct pathway to become exceptional developmental scientists. In fact, the end point – becoming a lifespan epidemiologist or a life-course criminologist – did not even exist when they were students. We are still struggling to define the professional identity of those who make a living using a mix of mathematics, statistics, psychology, epidemiology, and experimental science to study human development using a population-based approach. How could their career path be straightforward, when the destination was unknown? This is a lesson for those who are searching for a direction in life and who worry about making a wrong turn. A desire to contribute to science, perseverance, and a capacity to plug away in the face of challenges are probably more important than having a clear view of the destination.

Jean, Jane, and Magda studied at a time when the ratio of women to men in universities was 1:10. Would their professional trajectories have been different if they had studied medicine, psychology, or epidemiology today, when the sex ratios are reversed (in the range of 3–5 women for one man)? The three of them report having made some academic choices that were not in line with the competencies that they would eventually need for doing developmental research. But none of them view this as a waste of time. In Jean Golding's words her 'career has been a series of chance occurrences' (Chapter 3, p. XX).

Magda's account of her career with her husband, Rolf Loeber, summarizes well the notion that their professional life was not planned: 'for the longest time Rolf and I did not have a life plan. However, once you start a longitudinal study, commitment and structure is required ... for most of us the curiosity of "what is next" takes over. It is like a good book that you cannot put down, and the eventual termination of a project may be painful' (Chapter 5, p. XX).

The perception of chances is subjective. Jean, Jane, and Magda faced, by todays' standard, a high number of challenges: they were minorities, as few women were pursuing graduate studies, and they were trailblazers. They had fewer opportunities compared to women who want to follow a similar career path today. At the same time, the competition was less fierce. They were pioneers, and this may have conferred some advantages. They were also leaders, as is evidenced by the fact that they could secure financial and human resources to create innovative longitudinal studies.

The Legacy of Their Research

The legacy of Jean, Jane, and Magda can be seen at two main levels. The first, if we take a long-term perspective, is historic. Their studies provide detailed accounts of the normative and atypical developmental trajectories of four large cohorts of individuals born at the end of the 20th century in two Anglo-Saxon countries – England and the United States. In 100, 300, and 500 years, the data will be available to those who will want to understand the life of human beings living between the end of the 20th and start of the 21st centuries. Data will be available to understand the average exposure to risks and protective factors, and the evolution of adaptive and maladaptive psychosocial and health factors. Imagine what we could learn about the evolution of humans' living conditions and health if we had such data on 15,000 people born in 1520, 1720, and 1920. This illustrates the putative value of conducting large international studies at set intervals to characterize human development in specific places and times.

The second legacy concerns the advancement of contemporary science. Each cohort has a cutting-edge component that makes it particularly relevant for the study of a multitude of phenomena that are important yet difficult to study.

Jean Golding initiated the ALSPAC study, designed to assess 14,500 pregnant women, their environment, and their child's development (Golding, Pembrey, & Jones, 2001). It is, to this day, a highly innovative and unique study because of its sample size, its inception during pregnancy, and its unique biobank, including blood samples collected at birth and during childhood for state-of-the-art genetic and epigenetic studies. In the sense that ALSPAC is one of the rare developmental studies to have put in place data sharing procedures, allowing researchers from all over the world to easily use the data, it is a model for data sharing.

Jane Costello initiated the Great Smoky Mountains Study (GSMS). We owe to her the refinement of the evaluation of psychopathology in youth using structured interviews based on standard diagnostic criteria. This is a major contribution to the evaluation of psychiatric disorders and to our capacity to track the development of psychiatric problems across time and populations. In addition, the GSMS compared the development of American Indian and non-Indian participants in response to a natural experiment due to a newly opened casino on the reserve. They found no effect of additional revenue on behavior problems for children of the well-off members of the American Indian community, but marked effects on children from poor families (Costello, Compton, Keeler, & Angold, 2003). This groundbreaking work has important implications for social policy aiming to reduce social inequalities, suggesting that targeting the most vulnerable in a population may yield the largest benefits.

The Pittsburgh studies led by Magda and Rolf Loeber are unique in identifying the etiology of homicides in males and of antisocial behaviors in females. They recruited 4,000 participants to specifically allow the study of this rare and traumatic criminal behavior. Using these unique cohorts, Magda and Rolf Loeber had a major impact on the science of violent behavior development. With their cohort studies and their seminal literature reviews, they pioneered the articulation and expansion of developmental and life-course criminology.

Data generated by Jean Golding, Jane Costello, and Magda Loeber have been and will be used by several generations of researchers to improve knowledge of the risk and protective factors involved in human development. Given the breadth and the richness of the data collected, researchers from multiple disciplines have been involved in the design, financing, and use of the data. They created a goldmine for present and future generations of scientists.

Priorities for the Next Half-Century of Research on the Prevention of Violence

Over the past 50 years, Jean, Jane, and Magda substantially contributed to the accumulation of knowledge on early risk factors for mental health problems and antisocial behaviors. The priority for the next half-century should be to test the extent to which reducing the identified risk factors has preventive or therapeutic effects. For instance, what is the impact of reducing family conflict, peer victimization, poor parenting practices, or child abuse and neglect on one's developmental trajectory?

Intervention research is crucial for three reasons. First, this research yields knowledge on the efficacy of approaches aiming to relieve personal suffering and social burden. In itself, this is a sufficient reason, if we assume that science should ultimately serve to improve human living conditions. Second, astronomical human and financial resources are devoted to treating children and families who suffer from mental health problems or to victims of antisocial behavior. Every day, many putatively therapeutic or preventive actions are conducted by professionals. But we do not know whether these actions have positive or negative consequences because we do not measure the impact of these interventions. We cannot consistently, and in all contexts, measure the impact of our actions. However, compared to the medical sciences, where a practice or an intervention (surgical or pharmacological) needs to be rigorously tested before it is widely recommended, social science professionals have a long way to go. We are much less systematic and demanding about obtaining proofs of the efficacy of an intervention before we use it. This is potentially a serious mistake, and it certainly undermines our capacity to make significant progress toward identifying effective interventions.

Third, intervention research provides information on the putative causal role of a risk factor. Take the example of the well-documented association between coercive parenting and disruptive behaviors.

Coercive parenting may be correlated with children's disruptive behaviors, but the relation may not be causal. Parents may use coercive parenting practices because they themselves have antisocial behavior problems. The fact that both children and parents share the same antisocial behavioral phenotype may be attributable to environmental causes (e.g., stressful and deprived environment) or to common genes. However, if improving parenting practices, within the context of a randomized controlled trial, significantly reduces the disruptive behaviors among children in the intervention group (compared to control), we then have evidence that poor parenting causes disruptive behaviors.

There are three main challenges to testing the efficacy of specific interventions and improving our knowledge of causality. First, mental health problems, including antisocial behaviors, are highly complex and multidetermined phenomena. When one sets out to do an intervention, multiple causal factors are targeted. That challenge can partly be resolved via careful assessment of putative mediators of the intervention. For instance, if an intervention aims at improving parenting practices and academic support in school, an assessment of parenting and of school performance would provide information concerning the route through which the intervention has an impact. In an even stronger design, children would be randomized to (1) a parenting intervention, (2) an academic support intervention, (3) both interventions, and (4) services as usual.

The second problem is supposedly an ethical one. Children who need services should obtain them. This is why the areas of prevention and health promotion are particularly suited for intervention research: We can study a high-risk population who would not, if it were not for the research, receive an intervention. A partnership between public health services and researchers can maximize resources to preventive intervention and assess impacts. The third problem is the lack of faith in science or, worse, the fear that evaluation will lead to uncovering fatal flaws in the professional practices that are in place. This is an important and often unrecognized area of resistance among professionals. I suggest that it is up to scientists to build trusting relationships with professionals conducting interventions, and it is also up to the governing agencies to instill a culture where professionals can see the benefits of the evaluation process.

Over the next century, longitudinal studies should have large enough samples to include preventive randomized control experiments targeting risk factors for mental health problems and antisocial behaviors. The nesting of an experimental study within a large population-based sample provides a robust design for testing epidemiological and therapeutic research questions. Ideally, the possibility that the intervention has an impact on biological markers of health should be tested. In addition, reliance on administrative data is necessary for two reasons. First, administrative data typically insures wide or total population coverage. Given that the most vulnerable populations are those less likely to participate in research, this design maximizes the chances of assessing those most likely to benefit from treatment. Second, the number of invitations to participate in research or surveys has reached such a high level that we can hardly expect good response rates over many decades.

Jean, Jane, and Magda did what no one else had done at the time they started. Their plans seemed unrealistic at many points during the journey. So, if the above plan sounds unrealistic, it may be a good sign.

The Changes Needed in Training the Next Generation of Researchers on the Development and Prevention of Violent Behavior

Jean, Jane, and Magda were relatively late starters, if we consider what they ended up doing during their career: longitudinal research on human development. Yet it seems as if the prior training they received was useful, even though it was not aimed at developing skills to do longitudinal epidemiology research.

Thus, what could be improved, if the developmental paths to a scientific career are highly heterogeneous and unplanned? I propose that the general scientific education of the population needs to be improved, rather than the specific training given at the graduate level. Specifically, general scientific training needs to be reinforced so that children are exposed to scientific principles and methods. This exposure would help them choose to specialize in one type of scientific training or another. It appears particularly important that scientific training of the highest quality in the social sciences be offered to children and adolescents. Training in the pure sciences (chemistry, physics, and engineering) appears to be much more advanced than scientific training in the social sciences. Yet, if we want to develop the minds of young children to be competent in understanding human behavior and statistics at the school level, we have a long way to go.

There is, at the population level, a high prevalence of thinking non-scientifically when it comes to human behavior. Consider the large number of people who believe that their astrological sign determines part of their lives and who consequently read their horoscope to anticipate the future. Consider also the number of people who buy homeopathic products or other placebo-like products for which there is no scientific evidence of their efficacy. Humans need to believe in ideas, whether they are grounded in science or not. This way of thinking is certainly, to some extent, adaptive. However, in some cases, it does not – and it certainly should not – apply to most decisions that people make about their behavior and their health.

Ideologies are rampant in the social sciences and often lead to sterile debate. Consider the difficulty in accepting the genetic underpinning of psychiatric conditions. Fortunately, things are improving but only very slowly. Most people, even those with high levels of education, and those studying psychology at the graduate level, are surprised by the notion that mental illnesses have strong genetic underpinnings. People accept that children physically look like their parents, but they do not imagine that parents and children also look alike in terms of brain anatomy and brain functioning.

This lack of consciousness about basic science in the understanding of human behavior prevents us from attracting candidates who are interested in fundamental science and social sciences. A better integration of fundamental sciences (chemistry, mathematics, neuroscience) and social sciences during the primary and secondary school years may widen the pool of brilliant people who want to study human development from a multidisciplinary perspective. I believe that this would increase our chances of having more Jean Goldings, Jane Costellos, and Magda Stouthamer-Loebers attracted to the scientific study of human development.

References

Costello, E. J., Compton, S. N., Keeler, G., & Angold, A. (2003). Relationships between poverty and psychopathology: A natural experiment. *Journal of the American Medical Association, 290*(15), 2023–2029.

Golding, J., Pembrey, M., & Jones, R. (2001). ALSPAC – The Avon Longitudinal Study of Parents and Children. I. Study methodology. *Paediatric and Perinatal Epidemiology, 15*(1), 74–87.

13.6   HOW INDIVIDUAL STRENGTHS AND OPPORTUNITIES SHAPED THE CAREERS OF THREE SCIENTISTS AND, INCIDENTALLY, THE BIRTH OF A RESEARCH FIELD

Isabelle Ouellet-Morin

Born July 22, 1977, Québec City, Canada

Canada Research Chair on the Developmental Origins of Vulnerabilities and Resilience

School of Criminology

Université de Montréal, Canada

Introduction

It is not every day that young scientists are invited to share their thoughts about the life trajectories and careers of eminent researchers. From the time I was a graduate student, and now through the lenses of an independent researcher, the work led by Jean Golding, David P. Farrington, and Benjamin B. Lahey has always been part of the theoretical, empirical, and even – dare I say – cultural influences at the root of contemporary research on the development and prevention of violence. Their influences have shaped the scientific environment in which the field continues to evolve. The diversity of the methodologies they used, as well as the countless publications they authored, pushed 'forward' the frontiers of knowledge by defining key risk and protective factors involved in the onset of violence and by attempting to elucidate the mechanisms by which these factors are expressed, from conception to senescence.

This chapter is an opportunity to look back at the colossal work they have accomplished and attempt to distill lessons from their trajectories. This exercise is also an opportunity to look forward and see where the field is heading. The perspective shared in this chapter obviously depends on the standpoint of the writer.

Beyond the Individual Trajectories ...

The careers of these eminent scientists cannot be reduced to a single profile. Each of them faced personal and professional challenges, starting with being 'wartime babies' in different settings. However, they all had the opportunity to start their careers at a time of history characterized by an unprecedented interest in identifying the risk and protective factors associated with violence and antisocial behavior. As elegantly summarized by Richard Tremblay in the introduction, their work was probably under the partial influence of philosophical debates instigated centuries ago about the human origins of aggression and violence. In retrospect, the research questions they delineated and the projects they conducted marked a renewed interest in these questions, now firmly grounded in a scientific approach whereby alternative explanations are carefully investigated and the idea of causation examined with the outmost caution.

Readers of this book are probably well accustomed to the challenges faced by researchers when trying to estimate the magnitude of the impact an environmental factor has on developmental trajectories. The influence of social selection processes cannot be overlooked. Thus, while their lives' narratives depict their unicity, they also show qualities that may have contributed to bringing about their career opportunities.

My attention was particularly drawn to certain qualities that, I believe, still promote success in science today. First and foremost, I was struck by the relentless and ferocious curiosity they manifested, from the time they were students. The breadth of interests explored in their training included mathematics, chemistry, astronomy, experimental psychology, and behaviorism, before they invested in psychology, pediatric research, developmental psychopathology, developmental criminology, and epidemiology. Their personal accounts of their careers also illuminate the joy and intrinsic motivation in the pursuit of knowledge and its impacts on society. Enthusiasm was also expressed about instigating new projects with a plethora of colleagues, of whom many became friends. I guess that this circles back to the joy of research, whereby sharing their passion with similarly motivated colleagues fueled more collaborative research. This likely helped them take the unbeaten path and instigate research projects of gigantic proportions in terms of financial and logistical commitments. All in all, it is fascinating to consider retrospectively how these individual characteristics and career opportunities (combined with a lot of work!) influenced their career trajectories.

From Potential to Actualization

Golding, Farrington, and Lahey made indisputable contributions to research on the development and prevention of violence. I tried to identify the contributions that appear to have had the most influence in defining the core of this field of research. First, these scientists – and perhaps more prominently David Farrington – argued that, in order to better understand violence and antisocial behaviors, one needs to describe individual differences to capture the factors underlying their stability and changes over time. Describing only what makes individuals different at one point in time is insufficient. This crucial argument called for the use of a wide range of longitudinal study designs within which violent behavior – and a wide range of risk, promotive, protective, and vulnerability factors – ought to be prospectively measured. Yet, it is not the methodology that defines the research field, as that is merely a tool.

Second, these researchers argued that a lifelong perspective was required. This standpoint drastically contrasted with the disproportionate attention devoted to adolescence and early adulthood at the time, namely because of the high prevalence rates of crime. For instance, Jean Golding argued and applied in the now well-known ALSPAC study, the relevance of examining environmental factors occurring early in life, starting during the prenatal period, to understand the onset of socio-emotional and cognitive deficits that may persist over time and increase the risk for antisocial behavior later on. Furthermore, as shown by David Farrington in his recent work (Farrington, 2019), events occurring later in life deserve more attention in order for us to understand the processes of deceleration and de-escalation. Third, a contribution more apparent in the work published by Benjamin Lahey is the value of 'lumping and splitting'. When carefully investigated according to clinically and scientifically sound hypotheses, splitting may help to uncover distinct etiologies and long-term prognoses among children with distinct profiles of externalized behavioral problems (e.g., hyperactivity with/without conduct problems [Lahey, Loeber, Burke, & Applegate, 2005]). Conversely, the presence of typologies should not be assumed, considering that many risk factors, such as child maltreatment, exert nonspecific causal influences across the externalizing domains. This indirectly emphasizes the inherent dimensional nature of these behaviors and profiles. A last legacy that drew my attention was their inclusion of multiple levels of analyses to study developmental trajectories of violence and antisocial behavior, from genetic to cultural sources of influences. Notwithstanding the ethical and logistical challenges of collecting biological samples to measure differences in DNA or sexual hormones, for instance, they persuaded their peers to integrate biological assessments in longitudinal studies. In the aftermath of the old nature versus nurture debate, these scientists make one crucial argument: the etiology of violence and antisocial behaviors is based on complex and dynamic interactions between biological, psychological, and social sources of influences.

Priorities for the Next Half-Century

The adoption of a multilevel and transactional perspective to investigate the trajectories of violence and antisocial behaviors, from conception to senescence, is now widely accepted. In my view, future research will likely continue to follow these conceptual guidelines. While there is a great deal of knowledge about risk and protective factors (see David Farrington, Chapter 6), much work remains to be done to clarify the mechanisms involved. For example, do these factors cumulate additively or nonadditively over time? Are these influences sequential or mediated, or do they involve transactional bidirectional effects? These are simple questions but represent nonetheless considerable challenges to study in an integrated manner, across biological, psychological, and social levels of analysis (Sameroff, 2010). From all the lines of research deserving our attention in the next half-century, I was invited to pay closer attention to research priorities involving genetic sources of influence. The limited scope of this chapter precludes an extensive review. A few lines of enquiry are nevertheless offered, as they exemplify how the work of these scientists will live on in future research.

Recent findings emerging from twin studies have shown that a stronger contribution of genetic factors is noted in youth with early onset and more persisting and severe antisocial behaviors, as well as for those with psychopathic traits (Gard, Dotterer, & Hyde, 2019; Moffitt, 2018). This echoes the potential benefit of adopting the splitting approach argued by Benjamin Lahey. Anchored in a within-individual perspective, a growing body of research shows that genetic factors account for stability and changes in externalizing behaviors (Lacourse et al., 2014; Porsch et al., 2016). This calls for a more careful examination of the extent to which genetic innovation (i.e., new genetic influences) explains behavioral changes over time. At the molecular level, individual variations present within the dopamine and serotonergic candidate genes, including the frequently studied polymorphisms 5HTTLPR and MAOA-UVNTR, have been associated with violence and antisocial behaviors (Ficks & Waldman, 2014). More work is now required to look past these single variants within (Langevin et al., 2019) and beyond these candidate genes, and consider environments, good and bad, that may modify their expression. Furthermore, the consideration of single nucleotide polymorphisms (SNPs) present across the genome, for which the cumulated weighted influence on phenotypes such as violence and antisocial behavior can be indexed in so-called genome-wide polygenic risk scores, will also contribute to keep the field busy for some time (Pappa et al., 2016). To this end, the developmentally sensitive nature of these phenotypes needs to be considered. In addition to empirically driven risk scores, biologically informed polygenic risk scores could target genes that are part of biological systems hypothesized to be involved in violence and antisocial behavior (Elam, Clifford, Shaw, Wilson, & Lemery-Chalfant, 2019). Research in the next decade will also further investigate whether chemical changes in the DNA, in particular the addition or removal of methyl groups (DNA methylation), independently or jointly, explain how the environment influences behavioral trajectories (Boyce & Kobor, 2015). While the investigation of the role played by epigenetics in violence is still in its infancy (Provençal et al., 2014), studies should investigate these processes developmentally.

How Will Training the Next Generation of Researchers Help to Tackle These Complex Questions?

Clearly, we are still at an exciting time to study the development and prevention of violent behavior. To successfully address future challenges, we will need to acquire extensive knowledge on normative socioemotional development before understanding pathological development. Furthermore, to achieve this goal we require a multidisciplinary approach, which necessitates sustained efforts to navigate across the different disciplines' vocabulary and paradigms. Specifically, students in psychology, criminology, and related disciplines should be exposed much more to genetics and neurophysiology, while students in biology should be exposed to more psychosocial developmental research. Finally, considering the exponentially growing information collected to explain violence and antisocial behavior – including genome- and epigenome-wide data, as well as real-time assessments – adequate training in data science, bioinformatics, and ML will become essential. What is certain is that the next generation of researchers will have much to discover, with the overarching objective being the successful bio-psycho-social development of future generations ... and we are doing it!!

References

Boyce, W. T., & Kobor, M. S. (2015). Development and the epigenome: The 'synapse' of gene-environment interplay. *Developmental Science, 18*(1), 1–23. doi:10.1111/desc.12282

Elam, K. K., Clifford, S., Shaw, D. S., Wilson, M. N., & Lemery-Chalfant, K. (2019). Gene set enrichment analysis to create polygenic scores: A developmental examination of aggression. *Translational Psychiatry, 9*(1), 212. doi:10.1038/s41398-019-0513-7

Farrington, D. P. (2019). The development of violence from age 8 to 61. *Aggressive Behavior, 45*, 365–376.

Ficks, C. A., & Waldman, I. D. (2014). Candidate genes for aggression and antisocial behavior: A meta-analysis of association studies of the 5HTTLPR and MAOA-uVNTR. *Behavior Genetics, 44*(5), 427–444. doi:10.1007/s10519-014-9661-y

Gard, A. M., Dotterer, H. L., & Hyde, L. W. (2019). Genetic influences on antisocial behavior: Recent advances and future directions. *Current Opinion in Psychology, 27*, 46–55. doi:10.1016/j.copsyc.2018.07.013

Lacourse, E., Boivin, M., Brendgen, M., Petitclerc, A., Girard, A., Vitaro, F., ... Tremblay, R. E. (2014). A longitudinal twin study of physical aggression during early childhood: Evidence for a developmentally dynamic genome. *Psychological Medicine, 44*(12), 2617–2627. doi:10.1017/S0033291713003218

Lahey, B. B., Loeber, R., Burke, J. D., & Applegate, B. (2005). Predicting future antisocial personality disorder in males from a clinical assessment in childhood. *Journal of Consulting and Clinical Psychology, 73*, 389–399.

Langevin, S., Mascheretti, S., Cote, S. M., Vitaro, F., Boivin, M., Turecki, G., ... Ouellet-Morin, I. (2019). Cumulative risk and protection effect of serotonergic genes on male antisocial behaviour: Results from a prospective cohort assessed in adolescence and early adulthood. *British Journal of Psychiatry, 214*(3), 137–145. doi:10.1192/bjp.2018.251

Moffitt, T. E. (2018). Male antisocial behaviour in adolescence and beyond. *Nature Human Behavior, 2*, 177–186.

Pappa, I., St Pourcain, B., Benke, K., Cavadino, A., Hakulinen, C., Nivard, M. G., ... Tiemeier, H. (2016). A genome-wide approach to children's aggressive behavior: The EAGLE consortium. *American Journal of Medical Genetics Part B Neuropsychiatric Genetics, 171*(5), 562–572. doi:10.1002/ajmg.b.32333

Porsch, R. M., Middeldorp, C. M., Cherny, S. S., Krapohl, E., van Beijsterveldt, C. E., Loukola, A., ... Bartels, M. (2016). Longitudinal heritability of childhood aggression. *American Journal of Medical Genetics Part B Neuropsychiatric Genetics, 171*(5), 697–707. doi:10.1002/ajmg.b.32420

Provençal, N., Suderman, M. J., Guillemin, C., Wang, D., Vitaro, F., Côté, S. M., ... Szyf, M. (2014). Association of childhood chronic physical aggression with a DNA methylation signature in adult human T cells. *PLoS One, 9*, e89839.

Sameroff, A. (2010). A unified theory of development: A dialectic integration of nature and nurture. *Child Development, 81*(1), 6–22.

Index

For EU product safety concerns, contact us at Calle de José Abascal, 56–1°,
28003 Madrid, Spain or eugpsr@cambridge.org.

www.ingramcontent.com/pod-product-compliance
Ingram Content Group UK Ltd.
Pitfield, Milton Keynes, MK11 3LW, UK
UKHW030643250425
457871UK00017B/170